Japanese-English
Model Work Rules – Third Edition

Michihiro Mori
Hiroaki Matsui / Aya Kijima / Takeo Tsukamoto
Nishimura & Asahi Labor Law Practice Group

和文・英文対照 モデル就業規則 第3版

森 倫洋 [編集代表]
松井博昭・木島 彩・塚本健夫 [編]
西村あさひ法律事務所労働法グループ [著]

中央経済社

第3版 はしがき

　第2版の刊行から早くも5年近くが経過した。

　今般「働き方改革」関連の法改正があったところ，第2版以降にされた労働者派遣法・育児介護休業法の改正なども反映して，新たに第3版を出版させていただくこととなった。

　構成は，第2版のものを維持しつつ，労働者派遣法に関する説明を加え，また，法改正にとどまらず，ガイドラインの改定やＬＧＢＴ問題に関する近年の対応状況なども反映している。

　改訂作業は，弊職の統括，木島彩，松井博昭，塚本健夫の3名の取り纏めのもと，中川佳宣，大村慧，益田美佳，松本周，杉浦起大，東條桜子，江口響子，大日方史野が担当した。

　企業活動のグローバル化が進み，外国人雇用が一層増える中で，本書が企業の人事・法務関係者の皆様方のお役に立てば望外の喜びである。

　最後に，本書の刊行にあたっては，中央経済社の露本敦氏に多大なご尽力を頂いたことに，改めて深く感謝の意を表したい。

2018年12月

　　　　　　　　　　　　　　　　編著者を代表して
　　　　　　　　　　　　　　　　西村あさひ法律事務所　パートナー

　　　　　　　　　　　　　　　　弁護士　森　倫洋

Preface to the Third Edition

Time flies. Five years have passed since the second edition of Japanese-English Model Work Rules was published.

Recently there have been significant changes in labor laws relating to "Work Style Reform". We reflect such changes in the third edition, as well as amendments to the Worker Dispatch Act and to the Act on Childcare Leave, Caregiver Leave, and Other Measures for the Welfare of Workers Caring for Children or Other Family Members.

The composition of the third edition is basically the same as that of the second edition, but we have added a basic explanation on the Worker Dispatch Act. Moreover, we did not only reflect the revision of the law, we also made revisions to respond to new guidelines regarding labor related matters, and the current work situation, such as the treatment of LGBT people.

Aya Kijima, Hiroaki Matsui and Takeo Tsukamoto lead the revision under my supervision, and Yoshinobu Nakagawa, Satoshi Omura, Mika Masuda, Itaru Matsumoto, Yukihiro Sugiura, Sakurako Tojo, Kyoko Eguchi and Fumiya Obinata assisted with the revision work.

As globalization of corporate activities progresses and employment of foreigners in Japan is increasing, we hope this book will help legal or HR personnel who are in charge of such employment activities.

Finally, I would like to express my sincere appreciation for the great efforts of Mr. Atsushi Tsuyumoto of CHUOKEIZAI-SHA, INC. in the publication of this book.

December 2018

On behalf of the authors and editors,

Michihiro Mori, partner and attorney-at-law
Nishimura & Asahi Law Office

第2版 はしがき

　本書の初版の刊行から2年が経過した。この間，有期労働契約について，「雇止め法理」の法定化，通算契約期間が5年を超える場合の無期労働契約への転換申込権の付与，不合理な労働条件の禁止を定める労働契約法改正や，継続雇用制度の対象者を限定できる仕組みを廃止し，公的年金支給開始年齢の引上げに応じて希望者全員に65歳までの継続雇用を確保することなどを内容とする高年齢者雇用安定法の改正がなされるなど，重要な労働法制の改正があった。

　今回の改訂では，これらの改正や近時の実務的動向を踏まえて，①解説及びモデル就業規則・附属規程に補筆・修正を加え，定年後再雇用規程を追加するとともに，よりユーザーのニーズに応えられるよう，新たに，②有期労働契約や継続雇用制度による嘱託社員雇用契約，解雇通知・解雇理由証明書，退職合意書などの書式を加え，更に，③FAQ（Frequently Asked Questions）の部を設けて，内容の充実を図った。

　改訂作業に当たっては，大幅にメンバーを増員し，①解説及び就業規則（本則部分）については，高山陽太郎※，木野博徳，松井博昭，金子正紀，村田智美，黒田はるひ，②附属規程及び書式については，木島彩（旧姓：青木（初版時））※，由良知也，大石真帆，塚本健夫，③FAQについては，下向智子※，鈴木正靖，中村崇志，料屋恵美の各弁護士が担当し，改めて全体の記載を見直した（※印は各パートのとりまとめ役）。また，翻訳については，初版に続いて，池田崇ニューヨーク州弁護士の助力を得た。

　多くの弁護士による共同作業を経て，本書が初版にも増して，読者の皆様方の実務のお役に立つものとなっていれば望外の喜びである。

本書の刊行にあたっては，初版に続き，中央経済社の和田豊氏に多大なご尽力を頂いた。ここに心から謝意を表したい。

2014年1月

編著者を代表して
西村あさひ法律事務所　パートナー

弁護士　**森　倫洋**

Preface to the Second Edition

Two years have passed since the publication of the first edition of this book. During that time, important amendments have been made to labor laws such as i) amendments of the Employment Agreement Act that stipulate the Doctrine of Non-Renewal of a Fixed Term Employment Agreement, grant an option to request a conversion to non-fixed term employment if the cumulative period of several fixed term agreements exceeds five years, and prohibit imposing unreasonably different employment conditions, and ii) amendments to the Law Concerning Stabilization of Employment of Older Persons which abolish the framework for the selection of persons who can be hired continuously after retirement age, and require employers to secure continuous employment for any persons who wish to work until the age of 65, corresponding to a rise in the age at which an individual can begin receiving public pensions.

In light of these amendments and recent practical trends, this revised version aims to enhance the contents by: (i) revising/amending the Commentary and Model Work Rules/Supplementary Provisions, and adding a sample Regulation for re-employment after retirement to meet better the readers' needs; (ii) adding new standard form documents such as a fixed term employment agreement, a shokutaku worker employment agreement for re-employed retirees pursuant to the continuous employment system, a dismissal notice, a certificate for reasons for dismissal, and a termination agreement; and (3) further creating a FAQ (Frequently Asked Questions) section.

We have significantly increased the number of co-authors to assist us with the revisions. The following attorneys were responsible for the respective sessions, as well as providing reviews of the book in its entirety: (i) in the Commentary and Model

Work Rules (the rules portion) portions, Yotaro Takayama*, Hironori Kino, Hiroaki Matsui, Masanori Kaneko, Tomomi Murata, and Haruhi Kuroda; (ii) in the Supplementary Provisions and form documents portions, Aya Kijima* (nee Aoki in the first edition), Tomoya Yura, Maho Oishi, and Takeo Tsukamoto; and (iii) in the FAQ portion, Tomoko Shimomukai*, Masayasu Suzuki, Takashi Nakamura and Megumi Ryoya (* indicates attorneys who were coordinators for the respective portions). In addition, we also received a great deal of support and advice from Mr. Takashi Ikeda, attorney-at-law in the State of New York, both here as well as in the first edition.

Thanks to the collaborative efforts of the many attorneys involved in this project, we hope that this second edition will prove to be more useful to our readers than the previous edition.

Finally, in addition to his support with the first edition, we would like to express our heartfelt thanks to Mr. Yutaka Wada of CHUOKEIZAI-SHA, INC. for his continuing dedication to the publishing of this book.

January 2014

On behalf of the authors and editors,

Michihiro Mori, partner and attorney-at-law
Nishimura & Asahi Law Office

はしがき

　企業活動のグローバル化が進む中，外資系企業だけでなく，日本企業の中でも英語を社内公用語とする企業が出てきている。他方で，労使関係については，各国の文化的背景，雇用情勢などの社会的背景や歴史的沿革などから，それぞれの国で異なる規制がされており，それに適合した制度を導入しなければならないことはいうまでもない。ことに，日本の労働法規制においては，裁判例や通達の果たす役割も大きく，外資系企業からすると認識・理解しづらい規制も多いと思われる。

　筆者らは，これまで多くの外資系企業に対して，労務問題に関して英語でのアドバイスを行い，就業規則・諸規程類の策定・改定・レビュー等を行ってきたが，就業規則の英訳の中には，正しく規制内容が理解されていないために，そもそも意味内容が変わってしまっていたり，（辞書的に同じような単語でも）英語では法的な意味の異なる語に置き換えられているものがしばしば見受けられる。

　本書は，こうした経験から，筆者らの属する西村あさひ法律事務所の労働法グループにおいて蓄積した和英就業規則や日本の労働法制の基本的説明に関する英文メモを素材にして，改めてスタンダードな就業規則を法的に誤りのない和英文で提供できるようとりまとめるとともに，日本の労働法制を理解・説明する上で最低限必要な基本的事項を簡潔に解説したものである。

　本書は，和英の解説編，就業規則本則及び附属規程・書式の３部構成になっており，本書の特徴的な点は，以下のとおりである。

　まず，第１に，本書は，労働法に通じた弁護士が自らとりまとめた就業規則

を基に外国法弁護士と共同して翻訳を行い，ネイティブによる英文のチェックを受けて作成している点である。

第2に，就業規則の規定の意味を理解するために必要な事項について，①制度理解のための基本的な事項は解説編において説明し，②各規定の理解に必要な事項はさらにそれぞれ該当の規定において補注を加える形で説明している。

第3に，過去の経験から特に問題になりそうな規定については，ディスカッションを重ね，必ずしも一般に流通している就業規則・諸規程類の規定ぶりにとらわれず，見直しを図っている点である。

本書が英語を用いる企業の関係者の皆様，さらには，必ずしも日常的に英語を用いなくても，外国人を採用している企業の関係者の皆様方のお役に立てば望外の喜びである。

最後に，本書の執筆・翻訳にあたっては，西村あさひ法律事務所のForeign AttorneyであるChung L. Andrew氏のほか，森脇夕子氏，曽根千晶氏，山田瑠璃子氏，広川倫太郎氏をはじめとする多くの方々の助力・アドバイスを受けた。また，本書の刊行にあたっては，中央経済社の和田豊氏に多大なご尽力を頂いた。ここに改めて深く感謝の意を表したい。

2012年1月

編著者を代表して
西村あさひ法律事務所　パートナー
弁護士　森　倫洋

Preface

Amidst ongoing globalization of corporate activities, not only foreign companies, but also Japanese companies increasingly tend to use English as their internal official language. Meanwhile, labor-management issues are regulated differently in each country, reflecting their respective cultural backgrounds, social backgrounds, employment situations, and historical development. Accordingly, each company is required to employ a system that complies with regulatory requirements in each country. In particular, in the framework of Japanese employment and labor laws and regulations, court precedents and official notices play important roles, leaving foreign companies often having difficulties in understanding and coping with such laws and regulations.

The authors of this book have vast experience in providing advice in English on Japanese employment and labor issues to numerous foreign companies, as well as preparing, revising, and reviewing their work rules and other internal regulations. In doing so, we have often found that an English translation of the work rules does not accurately reflect the original intent of the rules, generally as a result of a misunderstanding of the details of the regulations or incorrect translations due to certain Japanese words being translated into English using a synonym that has a different legal meaning.

Based on the above-mentioned experience, the Employment and Labor Law Group of Nishimura & Asahi, to which the authors belong, collected many extracts from work rules in Japanese, with their corresponding English translations, and memos explaining Japanese employment and labor legislation in English. Using these materials, we organized this book in such a way as to provide a source for standard work rules that are legally correct in both Japanese and English. We also provide brief commentaries on basic matters that are essential to understand and that help to explain Japanese employment and labor legislation.

This book comprises three parts: (1) commentary in both Japanese and English, (2) the main text of the work rules, and (3) supplementary regulations and forms. The characteristics of this book are as follows.

First, those attorneys who have expertise in employment and labor laws prepared a draft work rules, translated them into English in collaboration with foreign attorneys, and had the English translation proofread by native English-speaking editors.

Second, regarding matters required to understand the meaning of each provision of the work rules, we (i) explained basic issues in the commentary section to understand the Japanese labor-management system, and (ii) added supplementary notes to the relevant provisions for better understanding of each provision.

Third, we discussed provisions likely to be problematic, drawing on our experience, and we revised the work rules accordingly and not necessarily adhering to any prevailing work rules and related regulations.

We would be delighted if this book serves well those working at companies at which English is typically used, as well as at companies that do not use English on a daily basis but have foreign employees.

Finally, yet importantly, when authoring and translating this book, we received great support and advice from Mr. Andrew L. Chung, a foreign attorney of Nishimura & Asahi, and many N&A staff members, including Ms. Yuko Moriwaki, Ms. Chiaki Sone, Ms. Ruriko Yamada, and Mr. Rintaro Hirokawa, among others. In addition, Mr. Yutaka Wada of CHUOKEIZAI-SHA, INC. greatly contributed towards publishing this book. We would like to express our great appreciation for their dedicated support.

January 2012

On behalf of the authors and editors,

Michihiro Mori, partner and attorney-at-law
Nishimura & Asahi Law Office

目　　次

第1部　解　説

第1章　日本の労働法に関する概説 ── 2

1. 労働条件規制構造 …………………………………… 2
    1-1　法令（強行法規）／2
    1-2　判例法理／4
    1-3　労働協約／4
    1-4　就業規則／6
    1-5　労働契約／6
2. 就業規則の作成・変更手続 ………………………… 8
    2-1　就業規則の作成／8
        2-1-1　就業規則の意義／8
        2-1-2　就業規則の作成手続／8
    2-2　就業規則の変更手続／12
3. 労働条件の（不利益な）変更
   （特に就業規則の不利益変更の法理）…………… 14
    3-1　就業規則の効力・就業規則の不利益変更の法理／14
    3-2　就業規則の不利益変更の法理の成文化／16
4. 労働時間 …………………………………………… 18
    4-1　労働時間とは／18
    4-2　労働時間・休日労働規制／18

Contents

Part I COMMENTARY

Chapter I.
Overview of Japanese Employment and Labor Law —— 3

1. Regulatory Structure of Employment Conditions ············ 3
   - 1-1 Compulsory Laws／3
   - 1-2 Doctrines Based on Court Precedents／5
   - 1-3 Collective Labor Agreements／5
   - 1-4 Work Rules／7
   - 1-5 Employment Agreement／7
2. Procedures for Providing and Changing Work Rules ············ 9
   - 2-1 Providing Work Rules／9
     - 2-1-1 Work Rules-Defined／9
     - 2-1-2 Procedures for Providing Work Rules／9
   - 2-2 Procedures for Changing Work Rules／13
3. (Disadvantageous) Changes to Employment Conditions
   (in particular, the Doctrine of Disadvantageous Change of Work Rules) ······15
   - 3-1 Effect of Work Rules and the Doctrine of Disadvantageous Change of Work Rules／15
   - 3-2 Codification of the Doctrine of Disadvantageous Change of Work Rules／17
4. Working Hours ···19
   - 4-1 Definition of Working Hours／19
   - 4-2 Regulations on Working Hours and Work on Holidays／19

  4-3 労働時間の管理／22
5．賃金 …………………………………………………………………24
 5-1 総論／24
 5-2 不合理な待遇の相違の禁止／26
6．労働契約の終了 ………………………………………………28
 6-1 解雇以外の労働契約の終了事由／28
  6-1-1 合意解約／28
  6-1-2 辞　　職／30
  6-1-3 期間の満了（有期労働契約）／30
  6-1-4 定　　年／32
 6-2 解雇による労働契約の終了／32
  6-2-1 解　　雇／32
  6-2-2 解雇権濫用法理／34
  6-2-3 有期労働契約における解雇／42

7．有期労働契約に関する労働契約法上の特則 …………42
 7-1 有期労働契約の無期労働契約への転換／42
 7-2 雇止め制限の法理／44
 7-3 期間の定めがあることによる不合理な労働条件の禁止／46

8．競業避止義務・秘密保持義務 ………………………………48
 8-1 競業避止義務／48
  8-1-1 在職中の競業避止義務／48
  8-1-2 労働関係の終了後の競業避止義務／48
 8-2 秘密保持義務／50

4-3　Administration of Working Hours／23
5. Wages ……………………………………………………………………25
　　　5-1　General Introduction／25
　　　5-2　Prohibition on Unreasonably Different Treatment／27
6. Termination of Employment Agreements ……………………………29
　　　6-1　Events of Termination of Employment Agreements except Dismissal／29
　　　　　　6-1-1　Termination Based on Agreement／29
　　　　　　6-1-2　Resignation／31
　　　　　　6-1-3　Expiration of the Term of a Fixed Term Employment Agreement／31
　　　　　　6-1-4　Retirement Age／33
　　　6-2　Termination of Employment Agreement due to Dismissals／33
　　　　　　6-2-1　Dismissal／33
　　　　　　6-2-2　Doctrine of an Abuse of the Right to Dismiss Employees／35
　　　　　　6-2-3　Dismissal of Employees Hired under Fixed Term Employment Agreements／43
7. Special Provisions on Fixed Term Employment Agreement in the Employment Agreement Act …………………………………………43
　　　7-1　Conversion of a Fixed Term Employment Agreement to a Non-Fixed Term Employment Agreement／43
　　　7-2　Doctrine of Restriction of Non-Renewal on a Fixed Term Employment Agreement／45
　　　7-3　Prohibition on Imposing Unreasonably Different Employment Conditions due to the Fixed Term／47
8. Non-Competition Obligations and Confidentiality Obligations ……49
　　　8-1　Non-Competition Obligations／49
　　　　　　8-1-1　Non-Competition Obligations During Employment／49
　　　　　　8-1-2　Non-Competition Obligations after the Termination of an Employment Relationship／49

8-2-1　在職中の秘密保持義務／50
　　　8-2-2　労働関係の終了後の秘密保持義務／52
　　　8-2-3　不正競争防止法／54
9．労働者派遣 ……………………………………………………54
　　9-1　労働者派遣の意義／54
　　9-2　派遣可能期間の制限／56
　　9-3　労働契約申込みみなし制度／60

第2章　就業規則の記載事項　――――――――62

　1-1　絶対的必要記載事項／62
　　　1-1-1　労働時間・休日等／62
　　　1-1-2　賃　　金／64
　　　1-1-3　退　　職／64
　1-2　相対的必要記載事項／66
　　　1-2-1　退職手当／66
　　　1-2-2　臨時の賃金等／66
　　　1-2-3　食費，作業用品その他の負担／66
　　　1-2-4　安全及び衛生／66
　　　1-2-5　職業訓練／68
　　　1-2-6　災害補償及び業務外の傷病扶助／68
　　　1-2-7　表彰及び制裁／68
　　　1-2-8　そ の 他／68
　1-3　任意的記載事項／70

    8-2 Confidentiality Obligations／51
        8-2-1 Confidentiality Obligations During Employment／51
        8-2-2 Confidentiality Obligations after the Termination of an Employment Relationship／53
        8-2-3 Unfair Competition Prevention Act／55
9. Worker Dispatching ·········55
    9-1 Meaning of Worker Dispatching／55
    9-2 Restrictions on the Length of Time for Dispatch Arrangements／57
    9-3 Policy for Constructive Offer of Employment／61

Chapter II. Work Rules Matters —————63

    1-1 Required Matters／63
        1-1-1 Working Hours, Holidays and the Like／63
        1-1-2 Wages／65
        1-1-3 Retirement／65
    1-2 Conditionally Required Matters／67
        1-2-1 Retirement Allowance／67
        1-2-2 Extraordinary Wages, etc.／67
        1-2-3 Obligations Imposed on Employees to Bear Expenses pertaining to Food or Operating Equipment／67
        1-2-4 Safety and Health／67
        1-2-5 Vocational Training／69
        1-2-6 Compensation for Accidents During the Course of Employment and Support for Injury or Illness Outside of Work／69
        1-2-7 Commendations and / or Sanctions／69
        1-2-8 Others／69
    1-3 Voluntary Matters／71

第2部　就業規則（本則）

第1章　総　　則 ──────── 74

　　第1条（目　的）／74
　　第2条（就業規則の遵守義務）／74
　　第3条（社員の定義）／74
　　第4条（適用範囲）／74
　　第5条（労働条件の変更）／78

第2章　人　　事 ──────── 78

第1節　採　　用 ……………… 78
　　◆労働条件の明示／78
　　◆採用内定／80
　　◆募集・採用に当たっての差別禁止等／80
　　第6条（採用時の提出書類）／82
　　第7条（社員の個人情報等の取扱い）／84
　　第8条（試用期間）／86

第2節　人事異動及び出向 …………… 90
　　第9条（人事異動）／90
　　第10条（出　向）／92
　　第11条（業務の引継ぎ）／94
　　第12条（降　格）／94

第3節　休職及び復職 ……………… 96
　　第13条（休職事由）／96
　　第14条（休職期間）／100
　　第15条（休職期間中の賃金）／102
　　第16条（復　職）／102
　　第17条（勤続年数）／106

Part II WORK RULES

Chapter I. General —————————————————75

   Article 1.　(Purpose)／75
   Article 2.　(Obligation to Observe the Work Rules)／75
   Article 3.　(Definition of Employee)／75
   Article 4.　(Scope of Application)／75
   Article 5.　(Change in Employment Conditions)／79

Chapter II. Personnel Affairs ——————————79

   Section 1. Employment ···79
       ◆ Clear Statement of the Employment Conditions／79
       ◆ Hiring Decision／81
       ◆ Prohibition Against Discrimination During the Offering of Employment and Recruitment／81
      Article 6.　(Documents to be Submitted upon Employment)／83
      Article 7.　(Handling of Employees' Personal Information, Etc.)／85
      Article 8.　(Probation Period)／87
   Section 2. Intercompany Transfer and Secondment ···········91
      Article 9.　(Intercompany Transfer)／91
      Article 10.　(Secondment)／93
      Article 11.　(Transition of Duties)／95
      Article 12.　(Demotion)／95
   Section 3. Leave of Absence and Resumption of Duties ············97
      Article 13.　(Reasons for Leave of Absence)／97
      Article 14.　(Leave of Absence Period)／101
      Article 15.　(Wages during the Leave of Absence Period)／103
      Article 16.　(Resumption of Duties)／103

第4節　定年，退職及び解雇 —————————— 106

第18条　（退職事由）／106
第19条　（自己都合退職の手続）／108
第20条　（定年退職）／112
第21条　（普通解雇）／114
第22条　（解雇制限）／118
第23条　（業務引継ぎ）／118
第24条　（社員の会社に対する義務）／120

第3章　勤　　務 —————————————— 122

第1節　労働時間，休憩及び休日 ————————— 122

第25条　（労働時間）／122
　　　◆勤務間インターバル／126
第26条　（休　　日）／128
第27条　（代　　休）／130
　　　◆1か月単位の変形労働時間制／134
　　　◆1年単位の変形労働時間制／136
　　　◆フレックスタイム制／138
　　　◆専門業務型裁量労働制／140
　　　◆企画業務型裁量労働制／144
　　　◆高度プロフェッショナル制度／148

第2節　事業場外労働及び出張 ————————— 152

第28条　（事業場外労働及び出張）／152

第3節　時間外労働及び休日労働 ———————— 156

第29条　（時間外労働，休日労働及び深夜労働）／156
第30条　（非常時及び災害時の例外）／158

Article 17. (Years of Service)／107
Section 4.　Retirement Age, Resignation and Dismissal ············ 107
Article 18. (Reasons for Retirement)／107
Article 19. (Procedure of Voluntary Retirement)／109
Article 20. (Retirement due to Retirement Age)／113
Article 21. (Ordinary Dismissal)／115
Article 22. (Restrictions on Dismissal)／119
Article 23. (Transition of Duties)／119
Article 24. (Employee's Obligations to the Company)／121

Chapter III.　Performance of Duties ─────── 123

Section 1.　Working Hours, Breaks and Holidays ····················· 123
Article 25. (Working Hours)／123
　◆ Interval Between Working Days／127
Article 26. (Holidays)／129
Article 27. (Compensatory Holidays)／131
　◆ Modified Monthly Working Hours／135
　◆ Modified Annual Working Hours／137
　◆ Flexible Working Hours／139
　◆ Discretionary Working System for Expert Employees／141
　◆ Discretionary Working System for Planning Employees／145
　◆ Advanced Professionals System／149
Section 2.　Work Outside of the Workplace and Business Trips ··· 153
Article 28. (Work Outside of the Workplace and Business Trips)／153
Section 3.　Overtime Work and Work on Holidays ···················· 157
Article 29. (Overtime Work, Work on Holidays and Late Hour Work)／157
Article 30. (Exceptions for Emergencies and Disasters)／159

第4節 遅刻，早退，欠勤 …………………………………………… 158
 第31条（出　　勤）／158
 第32条（遅刻，早退及び私用外出）／158
 第33条（欠　　勤）／160
 第34条（公民権の行使）／160

第5節 適用除外 …………………………………………………… 162
 第35条（適用除外）／162

第4章　休　　暇 ──────────────────────── 166

 第36条（年次有給休暇）／166
 第37条（疾病休暇）／176
 第38条（特別有給休暇）／176
 第39条（代替休暇）／180

第5章　母性健康管理の措置 ──────────────── 184

 第40条（労働時間の取扱い）／184
 第41条（妊娠中の通院等）／184
 第42条（通勤緩和の措置）／186
 第43条（休憩の措置）／188
 第44条（産前・産後休業）／188
 第45条（妊娠中及び産後の症状等に対応する措置）／190
 第46条（育児時間）／192
 第47条（生理休暇）／192
 第48条（措置中の待遇）／192

Section 4. Late Arrival, Early Departure and Absence 159
 Article 31. (Attendance)／159
 Article 32. (Late Arrival, Early Departure and Leaving for Personal Matters)／159
 Article 33. (Absence)／161
 Article 34. (Exercise of Civil Rights)／161
Section 5. Exception 163
 Article 35. (Exception)／163

Chapter IV. Leave ——————————————— 167

 Article 36. (Annual Paid Leave)／167
 Article 37. (Sick Leave)／177
 Article 38. (Special Paid Leave)／177
 Article 39. (Substitute Leave)／181

Chapter V. Maternal Healthcare ——————— 185

 Article 40. (Working Hours in view of Protection)／185
 Article 41. (Hospital Visit During Pregnancy)／185
 Article 42. (Commuting Relief)／187
 Article 43. (Permission of Breaks)／189
 Article 44. (Pre- and Post-Childbirth Leave)／189
 Article 45. (Care for Symptoms of Pregnant and After-Childbirth Employees)／191
 Article 46. (Childcare Break)／193
 Article 47. (Menstruation Leave)／193
 Article 48. (Treatment during Maternal Health Care)／193

第6章　育児休業及び介護休業等 ────── 192

　　第49条　（育児休業及び介護休業等）／192

第7章　賃金，退職金 ────── 194

　　第50条　（賃金の構成）／194
　　第51条　（賃金の支払）／196
　　第52条　（非常時払）／200
　　第53条　（欠　　勤）／200
　　第54条　（年 俸 制）／200
　　第55条　（年俸額の決め方）／202
　　第56条　（年俸の配分）／204
　　第57条　（給与年度内の昇進）／208
　　第58条　（時間外労働割増賃金）／208
　　第59条　（所定休日労働割増賃金）／212
　　第60条　（法定休日労働割増賃金）／214
　　第61条　（深夜労働割増賃金）／214
　　第62条　（割増賃金手当の計算方法）／216
　　第63条　（通勤手当）／216
　　第64条　（退 職 金）／216

第8章　服務規律 ────── 218

　　第65条　（服務の原則）／218
　　第66条　（一般禁止行為）／218
　　第67条　（副業・兼業）／220
　　第68条　（就業禁止）／224
　　第69条　（電子端末の利用）／226

Chapter VI.
Child Care Leave and Nursing Care Leave —— 193

    Article 49. (Child Care Leave and Nursing Care Leave)／193

Chapter VII.
Wages and Retirement Allowance —————— 195

    Article 50. (Structure of Wages)／195
    Article 51. (Payment of Wages)／197
    Article 52. (Payment upon Emergency)／201
    Article 53. (Absence)／201
    Article 54. (Annual Wage System)／201
    Article 55. (Method for Determining the Amount of Annual Wages)／203
    Article 56. (Allocation of Annual Wage)／205
    Article 57. (Promotion and Demotion within the Wage Year)／209
    Article 58. (Extra Wages for Overtime Work)／209
    Article 59. (Extra Wages for Work on Designated Holidays)／213
    Article 60. (Extra Wages for Work on Statutory Holidays)／215
    Article 61. (Extra Wages for Late Hour Work)／215
    Article 62. (Method of Calculation of Extra Wage Allowance)／217
    Article 63. (Commuting Allowance)／217
    Article 64. (Retirement Allowance)／217

Chapter VIII. Work Discipline ————————— 219

    Article 65. (Observance of Discipline)／219
    Article 66. (Generally Prohibited Acts)／219
    Article 67. (Secondary Occupation/Side Occupation)／221
    Article 68. (Work Suspension)／225
    Article 69. (Use of Electronic Devices)／227

第70条　（所持品検査及び会社が貸与した物品の喪失）／226

第9章　職務発明 —————————————————— 228

　　　第71条　（知的財産権の帰属）／228

第10章　社員福利厚生及び訓練 ————————————— 230

　　　第72条　（福利厚生）／230
　　　第73条　（訓　　練）／230

第11章　表　　彰 ——————————————————— 230

　　　第74条　（表彰の基準）／232
　　　第75条　（表彰の方法）／232

第12章　懲　　戒 ——————————————————— 234

　　　第76条　（懲戒の種類）／236
　　　第77条　（譴責，減給，出勤停止及び降格の事由）／240
　　　第78条　（諭旨解雇及び懲戒解雇の事由）／244
　　　第79条　（損害賠償）／246

第13章　安全及び衛生 ————————————————— 248

　　第1節　安　　全 ……………………………………………… 248
　　　第80条　（安全の確保）／248
　　　第81条　（安全の心得）／248

Article 70. (Inspection of Belongings and Loss of Articles Lent by the Company)／227

Chapter IX. Employee Inventions ——————— 229

Article 71. (Attribution of Intellectual Property Rights)／229

Chapter X.
Employees Welfare Benefits and Training —— 231

Article 72. (Welfare Benefits)／231
Article 73. (Training)／231

Chapter XI. Commendation ———————————— 231

Article 74. (Commendation Criteria)／233
Article 75. (Commendation Methods)／233

Chapter XII. Disciplinary Action————————— 235

Article 76. (Types of Disciplinary Action)／237
Article 77. (Grounds for Reprimand, Pay Cut, Suspension, and Demotion)／241
Article 78. (Grounds for Counseled Dismissal and Disciplinary Dismissal)／245
Article 79. (Compensation for Damage)／247

Chapter XIII. Safety and Sanitation ——————— 249

Section 1. Safety ·· 249
Article 80. (Ensuring Safety)／249
Article 81. (Safety Readiness)／249

第2節　衛　　生 …… 248

　　第82条　（衛生の確保）／248
　　第83条　（衛生担当者）／250
　　第84条　（衛生のための遵守事項）／250
　　第85条　（健康診断）／250
　　第86条　（ストレスチェック）／254
　　第87条　（健康管理上の個人情報の取扱い）／256
　　第88条　（応急処置）／258
　　第89条　（病者の就業禁止）／258
　　第90条　（法定感染症発生時の措置）／258
　　第91条　（安全・衛生教育）／260

第14章　災害補償 ── 262

　　第92条　（災害補償）／262
　　第93条　（療養義務）／264
　　第94条　（通勤災害）／264

第15章　附　　則 ── 264

　　第95条　（施行日）／264

Section 2.　Sanitation ·· 249
 Article 82.　(Sanitation)／249
 Article 83.　(Person in Charge of Sanitation)／251
 Article 84.　(Matters to be Observed for Sanitation)／251
 Article 85.　(Medical Examination)／251
 Article 86.　(Stress Check)／255
 Article 87.　(Handling of Personal Information for Health Management Purposes)／257
 Article 88.　(Emergency Measures)／259
 Article 89.　(Compulsory Leave for Sick Persons)／259
 Article 90.　(Measures in the Event of the Occurrence of Infectious Diseases)／259
 Article 91.　(Safety and Health Training)／261

Chapter XIV.　Accident Compensation ——— 263

 Article 92.　(Accident Compensation)／263
 Article 93.　(Obligation to Undergo Medical Treatment)／265
 Article 94.　(Commuting-Related Accidents)／265

Chapter XV.　Supplementary Provisions ——— 265

 Article 95.　(Date of Enforcement)／265

第3部　附属規程・書式

育児・介護休業規程 ································ 268

ハラスメント防止規程 ······························ 322

定年後再雇用規程 ································· 334

労働条件通知書 ··································· 348

契約社員雇用契約書 ······························· 354

嘱託社員雇用契約書 ······························· 366

誓約書（入社時） ································· 376

秘密保持誓約書 ··································· 380

誓約書（退社時） ································· 390

解雇通知書 ······································· 398

懲戒解雇通知書 ··································· 400

Part III SUPPLEMENTARY REGULATIONS / FORMS

Regulations for Child Care / Nursing Care Leave ····· 269

Regulations on the Prevention of Harassment ·········· 323

Regulations for Re-employment after Retirement ····· 335

Notification of Employment Conditions ···················· 351

Contract Employee Employment Agreement ··········· 355

SHOKUTAKU Worker Employment Agreement ······· 367

Pledge Letter(Upon Joining the Company) ················ 377

Confidentiality Pledge Letter ····································· 381

Pledge Letter(Upon Retirement/Resignation from the Company) ·· 391

Dismissal Notice ··· 399

Disciplinary Dismissal Notice ··································· 401

解雇理由証明書 ……………………………… 402

退職合意書1 …………………………………… 404

退職合意書2 …………………………………… 410

三六協定 ………………………………………… 420

第4部　FAQ

　＜就業規則の作成・変更手続＞ ……………… 430
　＜採用＞ ………………………………………… 432
　＜競業避止義務＞ ……………………………… 436
　＜労働者派遣＞ ………………………………… 436
　＜出向＞ ………………………………………… 438
　＜労働時間＞ …………………………………… 440
　＜有給休暇＞ …………………………………… 448
　＜賃金＞ ………………………………………… 450
　＜服務規律＞ …………………………………… 452
　＜労働契約の終了＞ …………………………… 454
　＜その他＞ ……………………………………… 458
　＜民法改正＞ …………………………………… 464

Certificate for Reasons for Dismissal ·········· 403

Termination Agreement 1 ············· 405

Termination Agreement 2 ············· 411

Labor-Management Agreement regarding Overtime Work and Work on Holidays ·········· 424

Part IV FAQ

<Procedures for Providing and Changing Work Rules> ·········· 431
<Recruitment> ·········· 433
<Non-Competition Obligation> ·········· 437
<Worker Dispatching> ·········· 437
<Secondment> ·········· 439
<Working Hours> ·········· 441
<Paid Leave> ·········· 449
<Wages> ·········· 451
<Work Discipline> ·········· 453
<Termination of an Employment Agreement> ·········· 455
<Others> ·········· 459
<Amendment to the Civil Code> ·········· 465

第1部
解 説

Part I
COMMENTARY

第1章

日本の労働法に関する概説

1. 労働条件規制構造

　個別の労働条件は，使用者と労働者とが対等な立場で交渉し，合意した労働契約によって定められるのが原則です。しかし，歴史的経緯から明らかなとおり，労働契約の交渉において使用者は労働者よりも優越した立場にあることが多く，このような交渉力の違いから，一般的に労働者に不利な労働条件が合意されがちです。

　そこで，労働者を保護するために，労働条件は，法令（強行法規），判例法理，労働協約，就業規則等によって規律されています。

　それらの効力関係は，法令（強行法規）＞判例法理＞労働協約＞就業規則＞労働契約（合意）となっています。

1-1　法令（強行法規）

　労働条件の基準を強行的に規律する法令の中で，もっとも重要な法令は労働基準法であり，労働関係の基本原則や労働条件の最低基準を設定しています。その他の重要な法令（強行法規）としては，労働契約法，最低賃金法，労働安

Chapter I.

Overview of Japanese Employment and Labor Law

1. Regulatory Structure of Employment Conditions

Employment conditions in Japan are, in principle, determined in accordance with negotiated employment agreements between an employer and its employees at arms' length. Historically, however, because employers tended to have more bargaining power than their employees during negotiations, the agreed employment conditions were generally more unfavorable for employees.

Therefore, in order to protect employees, compulsory laws, doctrines based on court precedents, collective labor agreements, and work rules have been established or put in place to regulate employment conditions.

The following is the order of binding authority of such tools from strongest to weakest: (i) compulsory laws, (ii) doctrines based on court precedents, (iii) collective labor agreements, (iv) work rules and (v) employment agreements.

1-1 Compulsory Laws

The Labor Standards Act is the most important compulsory law and it establishes the primary principles relating to the employment relationship and sets minimum standards for employment conditions. Other important compulsory laws are the Employment

全衛生法，労働者災害補償保険法，育児休業，介護休業等育児又は家族介護を行う労働者の福祉に関する法律（育児介護休業法），雇用の分野における男女の均等な機会及び待遇の確保等に関する法律（男女雇用機会均等法）等があります。

1-2 判例法理

判例法理は，法令ではありませんが，労働関係において労働者保護のための強行規範として機能する場面があります。このような判例法理として，例えば，就業規則の不利益変更の法理（3参照），解雇権濫用法理（6-2-2参照），整理解雇の4要件（又は4要素）の法理（経済的理由による解雇等。6-2-2(2)参照），雇止め制限の法理（7-2参照）等が挙げられます。

このうち，就業規則の不利益変更の法理，解雇権濫用法理，雇止め制限の法理は，労働契約法によって成文化されています。

1-3 労働協約

労働協約とは，使用者と労働組合との間の労働条件その他に関する協約をいいます。労働協約は，書面で作成されること及び両当事者が署名又は記名押印することが必要です（労働組合法14条）。

労働協約は，労働組合の組合員の労働条件を規律し，労働協約に定める基準に違反する労働条件を合意してもその部分は無効となり，労働協約に定める基準が適用されます（労働組合法16条）。また，労働協約の効力は，就業規則にも優先します（労働基準法92条1項）。

Agreement Act, the Minimum Wages Act, the Industrial Safety and Health Act, the Industrial Accident Compensation Insurance Act, the Act on the Welfare of Employees Who Take Care of Children or Other Family Members Including Child Care and Family Care Leave ("Child Care and Family Care Act"), and the Act on Securing, Etc. of Equal Opportunity and Treatment between Men and Women in Employment ("Equal Employment Opportunity Act").

1-2 Doctrines Based on Court Precedents

Although doctrines based on court precedents do not have the binding authority of law, doctrines based on court precedents sometimes serve to compulsorily regulate employee protection. Examples of such doctrines are (i) the Doctrine of Disadvantageous Change of Work Rules (please refer to Section 3), (ii) the Doctrine of an Abuse of the Right to Dismiss Employees (please refer to Section 6-2-2), (iii) the Doctrine of 4 Requirements (or Elements) of Dismissal due to Business Necessity (i.e., dismissals due to financial reasons; please refer to Section 6-2-2(2)), and (iv) the Doctrine of Restriction on Non-Renewal of a Fixed Term Employment Agreement (please refer to Section 7-2).

Some doctrines (e.g., the Doctrine of Disadvantageous Change of Work Rules, the Doctrine of an Abuse of the Right to Dismiss Employees and the Doctrine of Non-Renewal of a Fixed Term Employment Agreement) are codified in the Employment Agreement Act.

1-3 Collective Labor Agreements

"Collective labor agreements" refers to agreements between an employer and a labor union concerning employment conditions, in addition to other matters. Each such agreement must be executed in writing and signed by, or affixed with the names and seals of, both the labor union and the employer (Article 14 of the Labor Union Act). Collective labor agreements govern the employment conditions of the members of a labor union, and if one is in place and a particular employer is a party, agreements on employment conditions between such employer and its employees that do not comply

1-4　就業規則

　就業規則とは，使用者が定める，労働条件や職場規律に関する規則をいいます。就業規則に定める基準に達しない労働条件を合意してもその部分は無効となり，就業規則に定める基準が適用されます（労働契約法12条）。

　後述のとおり，常時10人以上の労働者を使用する使用者は就業規則を作成し，所轄の労働基準監督署長に届け出なければならず，日本の多くの会社において労働条件を規律する重要な規則になっています。

1-5　労働契約

　労働契約は，労働者が使用者に使用されて労働し，使用者がこれに対して賃金を支払う旨の合意です（労働契約法6条）。労働契約法には，大きく分けて期間の定めがない労働契約（無期労働契約）と期間の定めがある労働契約（有期労働契約）があります。また，週の労働時間が通常の労働者より短い労働者として短時間労働者（いわゆるパートタイム労働者）が挙げられます（短時間労働者の雇用管理の改善等に関する法律（パートタイム労働法）2条）。さらに，派遣元事業主により雇用され，派遣先の指揮命令を受け労働に従事する労働者として派遣労働者が挙げられます。派遣労働者については，詳しくは下記9をご参照ください（労働者派遣事業の適正な運営の確保及び派遣労働者の保護等に関する法律（労働者派遣法）2条1号）。

　有期労働契約を締結する労働者，パートタイム労働者及び派遣労働者といっ

with the standards established by the applicable collective labor agreement will be deemed invalid, and the standards established by the applicable collective labor agreement will apply (Article 16 of the Labor Union Act).

In addition, collective labor agreements supersede even the work rules established by employers (Article 92, Paragraph 1 of the Labor Standards Act).

1-4 Work Rules

Work rules refer to regulations established by an employer that prescribe the employment conditions or disciplines for the workplace. If an employer and its employees agree on employment conditions that are less favorable to that employee than the conditions established by the employer's work rules, then such agreed conditions will be deemed invalid, and the standards established by the work rules will apply (Article 12 of the Employment Agreement Act).

As mentioned below, an employer who regularly employs no less than 10 employees is required to draft work rules and submit them to the chief of the local labor standards supervision office; therefore, work rules are important rules that regulate the employment conditions in many Japanese companies.

1-5 Employment Agreement

An employment agreement means an agreement pursuant to which an employee will be employed by an employer and will work for the employer, and the employer will pay wages for such work (Article 6 of the Employment Agreement Act). Employment agreements are classified into those without a fixed term ("Non-Fixed Term Employment Agreement") and those with a fixed term ("Fixed Term Employment Agreement"). In addition, there is a short-working-hours employee whose weekly working hours are shorter than those of ordinary employees (so-called part-time employees) (Article 2 of the Act on Improvement, etc. of Employment Management for Part-Time Workers ("Part-Time Employment Act")). Further, there is a dispatched employee who is employed by the business operator of a dispatching undertaking so as to be engaged in work for a client of the business operator of the dispatching

た，いわゆる非正規社員については，通常の労働者との不合理な待遇差の禁止，有期労働契約の無期労働契約への転換，雇止め制限の法理といった非正規社員を保護する規定が関係法令で定められています。

2．就業規則の作成・変更手続

2-1　就業規則の作成
2-1-1　就業規則の意義
　多数の労働者が就業する職場においては，統一的な労働条件・職場規律を設定する必要があります。このような必要性に基づき，使用者は労働条件や職場規律を定める就業規則を作成し，労働基準法上においてその作成手続・効力が規定されています。

　就業規則か否かは，規程の名称ではなく，その内容によって判断されます。したがって，労働基準法上，就業規則で定めるべき内容を別の名称の規程，例えば「賃金規程」や「退職金規程」等に規定した場合，そのような規程は，労働基準法上の就業規則となります。

2-1-2　就業規則の作成手続
(1)　就業規則の作成・届出義務

undertaking under the client's instruction. For further information regarding dispatched employees, please refer to 9 below (Article 2, Item 1 of the Act for Securing the Proper Operation of Workers Dispatching Undertakings and the Protection of Dispatched Workers ("Worker Dispatching Act")).

For so-called non-regular employees, including employees employed by executing a Fixed Term Employment Agreement, part-time employees, and dispatched employees, pertinent laws provide certain protections to non-regular employees, such as the Prohibition on Imposing Unreasonably Different Employment Conditions due to the Fixed Term, the Conversion of a Fixed Term Employment Agreement to a Non-Fixed Term Employment Agreement, and the Doctrine of Restriction on Non-Renewal of a Fixed Term Employment Agreement.

2. Procedures for Providing and Changing Work Rules

2-1 Providing Work Rules
2-1-1 Work Rules-Defined

In workplaces where the majority of employees work together in one space, it is necessary to establish unified employment conditions and disciplines for the workplace. In order to meet this need, employers provide work rules that prescribe the employment conditions or disciplines for the workplace. The Labor Standards Act sets forth procedures for establishing work rules, as well as the effect of work rules.

Whether certain employer-established regulations are classified as work rules depends not on the title "work rules," but on the contents of the regulations. Accordingly, if certain regulations (e.g., entitled "Wage Rules" or "Retirement Benefit Rules") contain provisions that are required to be provided in work rules under the Labor Standards Act, such regulations are deemed to be work rules.

2-1-2 Procedures for Providing Work Rules
(1) Obligation to Draft and Submit Work Rules

常時10人以上の労働者を使用する使用者は，就業規則を作成し，所轄の労働基準監督署長に届け出なければなりません。この際，以下の点に注意してください。
(a) 「10人以上」とは，会社ごとではなく事業場ごとに判断します。
(b) 就業規則を作成しなければならない場合は，使用する全ての労働者に対し，適用のある就業規則を作成しなければなりません。したがって，例えば正社員と契約社員についての就業規則を別規程にすることは可能ですが，いずれの就業規則の適用もない労働者がいないようにしなければなりません。
(c) 労働基準法上，就業規則に規定すべき事項が定められていますので，この必要記載事項が全て規定されるように就業規則を作成する必要があります。就業規則の記載事項については，第2章「就業規則の記載事項」をご覧ください。もっとも，全てを1つの規程に規定する必要はなく，「就業規則」と「賃金規程」等，別の規程に定めることも可能です。

(2) 労働者の意見聴取義務
就業規則の作成にあたっては，
(a) 当該事業場に労働者の過半数を組織する労働組合がある場合は，当該労働組合
(b) (a)がない場合には，当該事業場の労働者の過半数を代表する者
の意見を聴く必要があります。また，労働基準監督署に就業規則を届け出る際，当該意見を記した書面を添付する必要があります。
あくまでも「意見を聴取する義務」ですので，手続上，(a)又は(b)の同意を得る必要はありません。
なお，(b)の労働者の過半数を代表する者は，次のいずれにも該当する者である必要があります。
（ⅰ） 労働基準法41条2号に規定する監督又は管理の地位にある者でないこと。

Chapter I. Overview of Japanese Employment and Labor Law 11

An employer that regularly employs no less than 10 employees is required to draft written work rules and submit them to the chief of the local labor standards supervision office. Please note the following points regarding this procedure:

(a) the requirement of "no less than 10 employees" is judged on a per workplace basis, not on a per company basis;

(b) work rules must cover all employees so that there is no employee who is not covered by the work rules. An employer may, however, provide a separate set of work rules for different categories of employees (e.g., one set for regular employees and one set for part-time employees); and

(c) work rules must include all the items required to be included under the Labor Standards Act. Please refer to Chapter 2."Work Rules Matters" for descriptions of the items required to be included in the work rules. An employer may have more than one category of rules (e.g., "Work Rules" and "Wage Rules"), and the employer is not required to include all such required items in one rule category if it has more than one rule category, and may provide the required items across several separate rule categories.

(2) Obligation to Solicit Opinions of Employees

When providing work rules, an employer is required to solicit the opinions of either (a) a labor union organized by a majority of the employees at the workplace concerned (where such labor union is organized), or (b) a person representing a majority of the employees at the workplace concerned (where a labor union organized by a majority of the employees at the workplace is not organized). The employer is then required to attach all such opinions in writing to the draft work rules it submits to the local labor standards supervision office.

The obligation is merely to solicit the opinions of the employees, and therefore, it is not necessary to obtain the consent from (a) or (b) from a procedural perspective.

Regarding (b) above, the person representing a majority of the employees must be both:

(i) a person who does not hold a supervisory or management position, as

(ii) 労働者の過半数を代表する者を選出することを明らかにして実施される投票，挙手等の方法による手続により選出された者であること。

　(ii)に関しては，投票・挙手のほか，回覧や電子メールの送信によって投票を行うという方法等，当該事業場の労働者の過半数の支持を得ていると認められる方法である必要があります。

　一方で，使用者が一方的に指名した者，選任手続を得ていない者，一定の範囲の役職者による互選によって選任された者は，(ii)の要件を満たさないと考えられます。

(3) 周知義務

　作成した就業規則は，以下のいずれかの方法で，労働者に周知させる必要があります。

　(a) 常時各作業場の見やすい場所へ掲示し，又は備え付ける。
　(b) 書面を交付する。
　(c) 磁気テープ等に記録し，各作業場にその記録の内容を常時確認できる機器を設置する。

　最近では，社内のイントラネットに就業規則のファイルを掲示することで周知する企業も多くなっています。

2-2　就業規則の変更手続

　就業規則を変更する場合は，以下の手続が必要です。
　(a) 就業規則の変更案を作成する。

prescribed in Article 41, Item 2 of the Labor Standards Act; and

(ii) a person who has been elected by a majority of the employees in accordance with a procedure, such as voting or a show of hands, after the employees have been clearly informed that a person to represent a majority of the employees will be chosen pursuant to such procedure.

With regards to (ii) above, if the procedure used is other than actual voting or a show of hands, it must at a minimum be one by which it can easily be recognized that the elected representative is supported by a majority of the employees in the workplace concerned, such as by passing around a petition among employees or by having employees send e-mails.

A person who is elected by the employer, is not elected through an appropriate procedure, or is elected by only a limited number of employees in the workplace would not meet the requirements as a person representing a majority of the employees.

(3) Obligation to Make Work Rules Known to Employees

An employer is required to make its work rules known and easily accessible to its employees using one of the following methods:

(a) by posting or maintaining a copy of the work rules at a location that is easily accessible to employees at each relevant workplace at all times;

(b) by handing out copies of the work rules to all employees; or

(c) by recording the work rules on magnetic tape or other equivalent media, and providing appliances at each workplace so that the employees can easily access the work rules at all times.

Recently, many Japanese companies post their work rules electronically on their company intranet system as a means of making their work rules known and easily accessible to their employees.

2-2 Procedures for Changing Work Rules

When changing its work rules, an employer is required to abide by the following procedures:

(b) (i)労働者の過半数を組織する労働組合がある場合は，当該労働組合，(ii) (i)がない場合には，労働者の過半数を代表する者の意見を聴取する。
(c) (b)の意見を記した書面を添付して，変更した就業規則を所轄の労働基準監督署長に届け出る。
(d) 変更した就業規則を労働者に周知する。

なお，上記は変更の手続要件であり，当該変更が法的に有効か否かは，後述する就業規則の不利益変更の法理によって判断される点に留意してください。

3．労働条件の（不利益な）変更（特に就業規則の不利益変更の法理）

3-1 就業規則の効力・就業規則の不利益変更の法理

　日本の多くの会社においては，実務上，労働時間・賃金といった労働条件は，個別の労働契約で定められるのではなく，就業規則において統一的に定められています。さらに，前述のように，就業規則に定める基準に達しない労働条件を合意した労働契約は，その部分が無効となり，無効となった部分は，就業規則の基準が適用されます。また，特に労働契約において合意をしていない条件についても就業規則の基準が適用されます。
　では，このように就業規則によって労働条件が規律されている部分について，使用者が就業規則を変更することにより，労働者の同意なく労働条件を一方的に変更すること，特に労働者に不利益に変更することは可能でしょうか。
　この点について，判例は，就業規則を変更することによって労働者の合意な

(a) it must prepare the draft of the changed work rules;
(b) it must solicit the opinions of either (i) a labor union organized by a majority of the employees at the workplace concerned (where such labor union is organized), or (ii) a person representing a majority of the employees (where such labor union is not organized);
(c) it must attach such written opinions to the changed work rules and submit it to the chief of the local labor standards supervision office; and
(d) it must make the changed work rules known and easily accessible to its employees.

The foregoing requirements are merely the procedural requirements for changing work rules; whether the changed work rules are effective is then determined in accordance with the "Doctrine of Disadvantageous Change of Work Rules," which is hereinafter described.

3. (Disadvantageous) Changes to Employment Conditions (in particular, the Doctrine of Disadvantageous Change of Work Rules)

3-1 Effect of Work Rules and the Doctrine of Disadvantageous Change of Work Rules

In practice, many Japanese companies provide for employment conditions, such as working hours and wages, not in individual employment agreements, but in their work rules. As mentioned above, if an employer and its employees agree on employment conditions that are less favorable to that employee than the conditions established by the employer's work rules, then such agreed conditions will be deemed invalid, and the standards established by the work rules will apply. The standards established by the work rules would also apply in the event that the applicable employment agreement is silent as to certain employment conditions.

An important question is whether an employer may change portions of its work rules, thereby changing certain employment conditions, without obtaining consent from its

く労働条件を労働者に不利益に変更することは，原則的に許されないが，変更が合理的なものである限りにおいて許されるとしています。そして，この合理性とは，就業規則変更の必要性及び内容の両面から見て，労働者の受ける不利益の程度を考慮しても，なお内容の合理性を有するものであることをいいます（就業規則の不利益変更の法理）。

就業規則の不利益変更の法理は，労働契約法において下記3-2のように成文化されました。

3-2　就業規則の不利益変更の法理の成文化

労働契約法9条・10条によれば，使用者は，原則として，就業規則を変更することにより，労働者から同意を得ることなく労働条件を労働者の不利益に変更することはできませんが，就業規則の変更が合理的なものであり，変更後の就業規則を労働者に周知させるときは，労働契約の内容である労働条件は，当該変更後の就業規則に定めるところによるものとされています。

変更の合理性は，以下の点に照らして判断されます（労働契約法10条）。

(a)　労働者の受ける不利益の程度
(b)　労働条件の変更の必要性
(c)　変更後の就業規則の内容の相当性
(d)　労働組合等との交渉の状況
(e)　その他の就業規則の変更に係る事情

かかる条項は，就業規則の不利益変更の法理に基づいて成文化されたものであり，具体的な事案において，労働条件の変更が「合理的」といえるか否かについては，過去の判例の基準に照らして検討する必要があります。裁判所は，賃金の減額等労働者の生活に対する影響の大きい就業規則の変更については，合理性を認めず，効力を否定する傾向にありますので，不利益を緩和するため

employees, in particular, if such unilateral change would be disadvantageous to employees.

Court precedents have found that changing work rules, thereby changing employment conditions in a way that is disadvantageous to employees without obtaining their consent, is, in principle, invalid. However, changes may be allowed so long as the changes are "reasonable," determined in light of both the necessity for the changes and the overall contents of the work rules after taking into account the extent of the disadvantage to be incurred by employees. This is referred to as the "Doctrine of Disadvantageous Change of Work Rules."

The Doctrine of Disadvantageous Change of Work Rules was codified in the Employment Agreement Act as described in Section 3-2 below.

3-2 Codification of the Doctrine of Disadvantageous Change of Work Rules

Under Articles 9 and 10 of the Employment Agreement Act, an employer may not change its work rules so as to change employment conditions to the detriment of its employees without obtaining consent from its employees, except where the changes to the work rules are reasonable and the employer makes the changed work rules known and easily accessible to its employees.

The reasonableness of the changes is determined in light of the following (Article 10 of the Employment Agreement Act):

(a) the extent of the disadvantage to be incurred by employees;

(b) the need for changing the employment conditions;

(c) the appropriateness of the content of the changed work rules;

(d) the status of the employer's negotiations with a labor union or the like; and

(e) other relevant circumstances relating to the changes.

The Doctrine of Disadvantageous Change of Work Rules was codified in the Employment Agreement Act based on court precedents; therefore, the analysis of whether changes to work rules in specific cases are "reasonable" should be conducted based on the standards used by the court precedents in those prior cases. Japanese

経過措置を講ずる等の実務上の工夫をすることも考えられます。

4．労働時間

4-1 労働時間とは

　労働基準法上の労働時間とは，使用者の指揮命令下にある時間をいいます。労働時間に該当するか否かは，労働契約や就業規則等の定めのいかんによらず，労働者の行為が使用者の指揮命令下に置かれたものと評価することができるか否かにより客観的に判断されます。使用者の指揮命令は，明示及び黙示の双方を含みます。また，労働者が実際に作業を行ったか否かを問いません。使用者の指示によって行う業務に必要な準備行為（着替え等）や後始末（清掃等），使用者からの指示があった場合に即時の業務従事が求められる待機時間，業務上参加が義務付けられた研修の受講等も労働時間として扱わなければなりません。

4-2 労働時間・休日労働規制

　労働基準法は，労働時間について，原則として1日8時間，1週40時間を上限と定めており，また，原則として毎週1日の休日の付与を義務付けています（第2部第25条第1項及び第26条第1項の解説参照）。この法定労働時間を延長し，又は法定休日に労働させる場合には，あらかじめ労働基準法36条の定めによるいわゆる「三六協定（さぶろく協定）」を締結し，労働基準監督署長へ届

courts tend to deem changes to work rules to be unreasonable (and thus ineffective) if such changes will have a substantial impact on employees' livelihood, such as a reduction of employee wages. One way in which an employer can persuade the courts that changes are reasonable is to provide for a transitional measure for the changes in order to mitigate any detriment to the employees.

4. Working Hours

4-1 Definition of Working Hours

Working hours under the Labor Standards Act means the hours during which employees are acting under their employers' instructions. Whether a certain period is classified as working hours will be objectively determined, depending on whether the employees' acts can be evaluated as being under their employers' instructions, regardless of the provisions of the employment agreement or the work rules, etc. The employers' instructions include both of those indicated and those implied by them. In addition, it does not matter whether employees actually conducted work. Any time spent for preparation (such as changing clothes) or clearing up (such as cleaning) required for the services conducted pursuant to the employers' instructions, the standby time required in order for employees to engage in work immediately when employers instruct them to do so, and time spent for attendance at training and so on in which employees are required to participate for business reasons must also be treated as working hours.

4-2 Regulations on Working Hours and Work on Holidays

The Labor Standards Act provides that the upper limit on the number of working hours will be 8 hours per day and 40 hours per week, in principle, and requires granting 1 day off per week, in principle (see the commentary on Part II, Article 25, Paragraph 1 and Article 26, Paragraph 1). If employees must work more than the statutory working hours or on statutory holidays, it is necessary to execute a labor-management

け出ることが必要です（具体的な三六協定の記載事項については，第3部の書式をご参照ください。）。

　三六協定の締結によって延長できる労働時間は，改正労働基準法において，原則として月45時間，年360時間との限度時間が新たに定められました（改正労働基準法36条3項，4項）。この限度時間を超えて労働時間を延長しなければならない臨時的な特別の事情が予測される場合には，あらかじめ延長する労働時間の限度を定めた特別条項付きの三六協定を締結すれば，1年について6か月以内は，その定めた限度の範囲内で更に労働時間を延長させることができます。この特別条項で定めることができる労働時間の限度は，1か月の時間外労働及び休日労働につき100時間未満，1年の時間外労働につき720時間以内となります（改正労働基準法36条5項）。

　また，実際に三六協定により労働時間を延長し，又は休日に労働させた時間の合計についても，単月100時間未満，複数月（当月以前の2か月から6か月のそれぞれの期間）平均80時間との上限が新たに設けられました（改正労働基準法36条6項2号，3号）。

　これらの上限規制は，平成31年4月1日より，同日以後の期間のみを対象に締結される三六協定について適用されます。ただし，労働基準法138条に規定する中小事業主（原則として，その資本金の額又は出資の総額が3億円以下である事業主又はその常時使用する労働者の数が300人以下である事業主をいい，これは事業場単位ではなく企業単位で判断されます。下表参照）への適用は，平成32年（2020年）4月1日からとされ，建設事業や自動車運転業務，新技術・新商品等の研究開発業務等の事業・業務についても適用が猶予又は除外されています。

agreement with respect to overtime work and work on holidays (*saburoku kyotei*) pursuant to Article 36 of the Labor Standards Act in advance, and to submit it to the Chief of the Labor Standards Supervision Office (for the concrete terms of the labor-management agreement, please see the form in Part III).

The upper limit on the number of working hours by which overtime work can be extended under the labor-management agreement is newly prescribed by the amended Labor Standards Act as 45 hours per month and 360 hours per year, in principle (Article 36, Paragraphs 3 and 4 of the amended Labor Standards Act). In the case of temporary and special circumstances under which working hours may need to be extended in addition to the criteria are expected, however, the labor-management agreement may provide for such additional circumstances with the insertion of a special provision in advance that provides the limit on extended working hours. By executing the labor-management agreement with a special provision, working hours may be further extended within the provided limit, for a period of not more than 6 months per year. The upper limit on the number of working hours that may be provided for in the special provision will be less than 100 hours per month for overtime work and work on holidays, and not more than 720 hours per year for overtime work (Article 36, Paragraph 5 of the amended Labor Standards Act).

In addition, for the total number of working hours actually extended or spent on holidays in accordance with the labor-management agreement, the upper limit has been newly prescribed to be less than 100 hours for a single month and not more than 80 hours per month on average over a two- to six-month period including the current month (Article 36, Paragraph 6, Items 2 and 3 of the amended Labor Standards Act).

On and after April 1, 2019, these upper limit regulations will apply to any labor-management agreement to be executed to cover only periods starting on or after April 1, 2019. However, until April 1, 2020, they will not apply to small and medium-sized employers, as defined in Article 138 of the Labor Standards Act (in principle, small and medium-sized employers are those whose capital/investment is no more than 300 million yen, or who ordinarily employ no more than 300 employees; and whether a certain company is classified as a small or medium-sized employer will be determined

業種	資本金の額又は出資の総額		常時使用する労働者数
原則（下記以外）	3億円以下	又は	300人以下
小売業	5,000万円以下		50人以下
サービス業	5,000万円以下		100人以下
卸売業	1億円以下		100人以下

4-3 労働時間の管理

　使用者は，労働時間を適正に把握する等，労働時間を適切に管理する責務を負っており，厚生労働省が定める「労働時間の適正な把握のために使用者が講ずべき措置に関するガイドライン」（平成29年1月20日策定）において，労働者の労働日ごとの始業・終業時刻を確認し，これを記録することとされています。始業・終業時刻の確認・記録方法としては，原則として，使用者が自ら現認することにより確認・記録する方法か，タイムカード，ICカード，パソコンの使用時間の記録等の客観的な記録を基礎として確認・記録する方法のいずれかによることとされています。これらの方法によることなく，自己申告制により確認・記録を行わざるを得ない場合には，使用者は，労働者や労働時間管理者に対する十分な説明，自己申告による労働時間と実際の労働時間が合致しているかを必要に応じて調査し，補正する等，このガイドラインの内容に沿って自己申告制を適切に運用することとされています。

　なお，使用者は，その労働時間の状況その他の事項が労働者の健康の保持を

Chapter I. Overview of Japanese Employment and Labor Law   23

on a whole-company basis, not based on each workplace. See chart below). Application of these regulations will also be postponed or excluded with respect to certain businesses and services such as construction business, driving services, and research and development services of new technologies or new products.

Type of Business	Total Amount of Capital or Investment		Number of Employees Ordinarily Employed
General Rule (except for below)	No more than 300 million yen	or	No more than 300 people
Retail	No more than 50 million yen		No more than 50 people
Service	No more than 50 million yen		No more than 100 people
Wholesale	No more than 100 million yen		No more than 100 people

4-3 Administration of Working Hours

Employers are responsible for administrating the working hours in an appropriate manner such as by properly keeping track of the working hours, and the "Guidelines for measures that employers should take in order to properly keep track of working hours" (formulated as of January 20, 2017) set forth by the Ministry of Health, Labour and Welfare provides that employers are required to confirm and record the starting time and finishing time of the employee every workday. As a general rule, an employer can confirm and record the starting time and finishing time in person, or can confirm and record using an objective record such as time cards or IC cards, or a record of hours using computers. If an employer cannot utilize the above methods and must confirm and record by requiring its employees to self-report their starting time and finishing time, the employer must properly operate the self-reporting system in line with the instructions provided in the Guidelines, such as by providing sufficient explanation regarding proper self-reporting to its employees and personnel in charge of

考慮して厚生労働省令で定める要件に該当する労働者に対し，医師による面接指導を行わなければならないとされています（労働安全衛生法66条の8）（第2部第85条の解説参照）。平成31年4月1日施行の改正労働安全衛生法では，この面接指導の適切な実施を図るため，使用者は適切な方法により，労働者の労働時間の状況を把握しなければならないこととされました（改正労働安全衛生法66条の8の3）。この労働時間の状況の把握は，管理監督者を含む全ての労働者（ただし，高度プロフェッショナル制度の適用を受ける労働者については，別途健康管理時間の把握が行われるため，ここでは除外されます。）が対象となっています。

5．賃金

5-1　総論

　賃金とは，労働の対償として使用者が労働者に支払うすべてのものであり，賃金，給料，手当，賞与その他名称の如何を問いません（労働基準法11条）。

　賃金の額は，労働者と使用者との間の自由な取引（契約の自由）に委ねられますが，最低賃金法の定める額を下回る額で賃金額を合意した場合，当該賃金額は無効とされ，最低賃金額にまで引き上げられます。また，賃金の支払いについては，労働基準法24条1項により，原則として，①日本国において強制通用力のある貨幣で支払わなければならない（通貨払の原則），②賃金は労働者に直接支払わなければならない（直接払の原則），③賃金はその全額を支払わなければならない（全額払の原則），そして④賃金は毎月1回以上，一定の期日を定めて支払わなければならない（毎月1回以上一定期日払の原則）と定め

administrating working hours, and by conducting an investigation to confirm that the self-reported working hours are consistent with the actual working hours of each employee and making corrections to the working hours, as necessary.

In addition, employers must provide an interview with and guidance from a doctor to those employees whose working hours or other conditions fall under one of the requirements specified by the Ordinance of the Ministry of Health, Labour and Welfare, taking into account the employees' health maintenance (Article 66-8 of the Industrial Safety and Health Act) (see the commentary on Part II, Article 85). The amended Industrial Safety and Health Act to be enforced as of April 1, 2019 provides that, in order to ensure that the interview and guidance are conducted properly, employers must keep track of their employees' working hours using appropriate methods (Article 66-8-3 of the amended Industrial Safety and Health Act). Keeping track of working hours applies to all employees including managers and supervisors (excluding employees who are subject to the Advanced Professionals System, as the monitoring of health management hours is separately conducted for those employees).

5. Wages

5-1 General Introduction

A wage means all types of payment made from an employer to its employees as remuneration for work, including the wage, salary, allowance, bonus, or other name which such payment is given, regardless of names of payment (Article 11 of the Labor Standards Act).

The amount of wages can be freely determined between an employee and an employer (freedom to contract); however, if they agree on a wage amount that is lower than minimum wage amount set forth in the Minimum Wages Act, the wage amount will be held to be invalid and will be increased to the minimum wage amount. In addition, regarding the payment of wages, Article 24, Paragraph 1 of the Labor Standards Act provides that, in principle, wages must be paid (i) using coins and bills that are legal

られています。

5-2 不合理な待遇の相違の禁止

　使用者は，賃金を定める際，パートタイム労働者や有期雇用労働者（いわゆる非正規社員）と通常の労働者（いわゆる正規社員）との間で，不合理な待遇の相違を設けてはなりません。現在，日本では同一労働同一賃金の推進が図られており，正規社員と非正規社員の待遇差を解消するため，パートタイム労働法，労働契約法及び労働者派遣法が改正されます。パートタイム労働法が短時間労働者及び有期雇用労働者の雇用管理の改善等に関する法律（パート有期法）に変更され，パートタイム労働者と有期雇用労働者とが同じ法律によって規律されることになります。パート有期法及び改正労働者派遣法の施行は，平成32年（2020年）4月1日（中小企業主への適用については，平成33年（2021年）4月1日）となっています。

　パート有期法は，非正規社員と正規社員との間の不合理な待遇の相違を禁止し（パート有期法8条），パートタイム労働者・有期雇用労働者が通常の労働者と同視される場合の差別的取扱いを禁止しています（同法9条）。具体的には，パートタイム労働者・有期雇用労働者の待遇毎に，パートタイム労働者・有期雇用労働者の待遇と通常の労働者の待遇を比較し，待遇の性質及び当該待遇を行う目的に照らして，職務内容，職務内容・配置の変更範囲（人材活用の仕組み）及びその他の事情のうち適切と認められるものを考慮し，客観的にみて，不合理と認められるような相違を設けないようにしなければなりません。職務内容又は人材活用の仕組みが異なるのであれば，待遇の相違は許容されやすいものと考えられますが，詳細については，同一労働同一賃金ガイドライン案（厚生労働大臣告示として指針化される予定）をご参照ください。

　また，事業主は，パートタイム労働者及び有期雇用労働者を雇い入れたときは速やかに待遇等に関する説明義務を負うことになり（同法14条1項），パートタイム労働者・有期雇用労働者から求めがあったときは，通常の労働者との

tender in Japan (principle of paying in currency; (ii) directly to employees (principle of direct payment); (iii) in full (principle of paying the entire wage); and (iv) at least once a month on a predetermined date (principle of paying wages more than once a month on definite dates.

5-2 Prohibition on Unreasonably Different Treatment

In prescribing wages, employers must not establish any unreasonably different treatment between part-time employees or fixed-term employees (so-called non-regular employees), and ordinary workers (so-called regular employees). Currently, in Japan, "equal pay for equal work" is being promoted and in order to eradicate different treatment between regular employees and non-regular employees, the Part-Time Employment Act, the Employment Agreement Act, and the Worker Dispatching Act will be amended. The Part-Time Employment Act will be amended to the Act on Improvement, etc. of Employment Management for Part-Time Workers and Fixed-Term Workers ("Part-Time Employment and Fixed-Term Employment Act") to regulate working conditions of part-time employees and fixed-term employees under the same Act. The Part-Time Employment and Fixed-Term Employment Act and the amended Worker Dispatching Act will be enforced as of April 1, 2020 (they will apply to small and medium-sized employers as of April 1, 2021).

The Part-Time Employment and Fixed-Term Employment Act prohibits unreasonably different treatment between non-regular employees and regular employees (Article 8 of the Part-Time Employment and Fixed-Term Employment Act), and also prohibits discriminatory treatment of part-time employees and fixed-term employees who can reasonably be deemed to be equivalent to regular employees (Article 9 of the Part-Time Employment and Fixed-Term Employment Act). More specifically, for each treatment of part-time employees/fixed-term employees, employers need to compare the treatment of part-time employees/fixed-term employees with that of regular employees; and in light of the nature of the treatment and the purpose of granting the relevant treatment, ensure that they do not establish any difference objectively considered unreasonable, taking into consideration the details of duties, the scope of

待遇の相違の内容及び理由等についても説明する義務を負います（同条2項）。

6．労働契約の終了

6-1　解雇以外の労働契約の終了事由
6-1-1　合意解約
　労働契約は，使用者と労働者の合意により，将来に向けて終了します（合意解約）。合意解約は，使用者からの一方的解約ではないため解雇に該当せず，解雇規制（下記6-2-1(a)の解雇手続や下記6-2-2の解雇権濫用法理等）の適用を受けません。
　日本法上，解雇には厳格な要件が課されていることから，実務上はまず希望退職者を募集し，合意によって労働契約を解約する方策を検討することが多くなっています。
　もっとも，民法上の法律行為に関する規定や諸法理の適用は受けることから，例えば使用者が退職合意を強制した場合には，労働者は意思表示の瑕疵に基づき，合意の無効を主張できることになるので留意が必要です。

change in duties or job rotation (the framework for the utilization of personnel), and other circumstances that are deemed applicable. If the details of duties or the framework for the utilization of personnel differ, different treatment would be more permissible; for further information, please refer to the proposed equal pay for equal work guidelines (scheduled to serve as guidelines in the form of a public notice of the Minister of Health, Labour and Welfare).

In addition, employers will be obligated to explain the treatment and other matters promptly when they employ part-time employees and fixed-term employees (Article 14, Paragraph 1 of the Part-Time Employment and Fixed-Term Employment Act); and upon request from part-time employees or fixed-term employees, they will also be obligated to explain the details of and reasons for the treatment differing from that of ordinary workers (Article 14, Paragraph 2 of the Part-Time Employment and Fixed-Term Employment Act).

6. Termination of Employment Agreements

6-1 Events of Termination of Employment Agreements except Dismissal

6-1-1 Termination Based on Agreement

An employment agreement may be terminated prospectively by agreement between an employer and an employee. This type of termination is not a unilateral termination by an employer, and therefore it is not subject to dismissal regulations (e.g., the dismissal procedures mentioned in Section 6-2-1(a) below or the Doctrine of an Abuse of the Right to Dismiss Employees as mentioned in Section 6-2-2 below).

Since dismissals are strictly restricted under Japanese law, it is common practice for an employer to first solicit the voluntary resignation of the employee and to terminate an employment agreement by agreement.

Please note, however, that since the general provisions or principles under the Civil Code regarding juristic acts are applicable, the employee may claim that the termination agreement is null and void because of a defect of intention if the employer

6-1-2 辞　職

辞職とは，労働者による労働契約の解約を意味します。

(a) 無期労働契約である場合は，労働者は，いつでも解約の申入れをすることができます。この場合において，労働契約は，原則として，解約の申入れの日から2週間を経過することによって終了します（民法627条1項）。詳細は，第2部就業規則（本則）19条の解説部分をご参照ください。

(b) 有期労働契約の場合は，労働者は，やむを得ない事由があるときに限り，期間途中での即時解約ができるにすぎず（民法628条），原則として解約はできません。

それゆえ，期間の定めが長期になることは不当な人身拘束になりかねず，3年より長い期間の労働契約は，原則として締結することができないこととされています（労働基準法14条1項）。

6-1-3　期間の満了（有期労働契約）

　有期労働契約は，原則としてその期間の満了によって終了し，労働者から契約更新の申入れがあった場合であっても，更新を受け入れるかどうかは使用者の自由な裁量に委ねられます。

　しかし，一定の場合には，使用者による更新拒絶が「雇止め制限の法理」によって制約されることがあります。この法理は，判例によって確立された後，労働契約法19条に成文化されています。詳しくは，下記7-2をご参照ください。

forced the employee to enter into a termination agreement.

6-1-2 Resignation

Resignation refers to the termination of an employment agreement by an employee.

(a) In the case of a Non-Fixed Term Employment Agreement, the employee may apply for the termination of the employment agreement at any time. In such cases, the employment agreement will, in principle, be terminated on the date 2 weeks after the application (Article 627, Paragraph 1 of the Civil Code). For details, see the commentary on Article 19 in Part II WORK RULES.

(b) In the case of a Fixed Term Employment Agreement, an employee may immediately terminate the employment agreement during the contract term only if there are unavoidable reasons (Article 628 of the Civil Code); however, in principle, an employee may not terminate the employment agreement. Therefore, a long-term employment agreement could become an unfair restraint on an employee, and an employment agreement for a period exceeding 3 years, in principle, may not be executed (Article 14, Paragraph 1 of the Labor Standards Act).

6-1-3 Expiration of the Term of a Fixed Term Employment Agreement

In principle, a Fixed Term Employment Agreement expires when the contract term expires, and employers have the discretion to refuse to renew an employment agreement even if an employee requests it.

However, the employer's renewal of Fixed Term Employment Agreements will be restricted in certain circumstances by the "Doctrine of Restriction on Non-Renewal of a Fixed Term Employment Agreement," which has been established by court precedents and has been codified in Article 19 of the Employment Agreement Act. For further information, please refer to Section 7-2 below.

6-1-4 定　　年

　定年は，一定の年齢に達したことを労働契約の終了事由とするものです。

　なお，定年を60歳未満とすることはできません（高年齢者等の雇用の安定等に関する法律（高年齢者雇用安定法）8条）。また，高年齢者の雇用確保のため，労働者が65歳になるまで下記のいずれかの措置を講ずる必要があります（同法9条1項）。

(a)　定年年齢の引上げ

(b)　継続雇用制度（雇用している労働者の定年後も，当該労働者が希望するときは当該労働者を引き続いて雇用する制度）の導入

(c)　定年の廃止

　多くの会社は，定年を60歳とした上で，上記(b)の継続雇用制度を採用しています。なお，継続雇用制度には，使用者が，一定の関係会社（例えば，親会社や子会社等）との間で，使用者の雇用する高年齢者であってその定年後に雇用されることを希望するものをその定年後に当該関係会社が引き続いて雇用することを約する契約を締結し，当該契約に基づき当該高年齢者の雇用を確保する制度が含まれるものとされています（同法9条2項）。

6-2　解雇による労働契約の終了
6-2-1　解　　雇

　解雇とは，使用者による労働契約の解約を意味します。解雇においては，労働者保護の見地から，労働基準法の定める次の解雇手続や解雇制限を遵守する必要があります。また，無期労働契約においては，解雇権濫用法理により解雇が制限されており，有期労働契約においては，その期間が満了するまでの間，「やむを得ない事由がある場合」でなければ，解雇はできません。

　解雇権濫用法理については，下記6-2-2をご参照ください。

(a)　解雇手続

　　　使用者は，労働者を解雇しようとする場合においては，原則として，少

6-1-4 Retirement Age

"Retirement age" is a system whereby an employment agreement terminates when the employee reaches a certain age. The retirement age shall not be below 60 (Article 8 of the Act on Employment Security, etc. of the Elderly, etc. ("Employment of the Elderly Act")). In addition, the employer shall conduct one of the measures listed below until the employee reaches the age of 65 in order to ensure the protection of employment of older people (Article 9, Paragraph 1 of the Employment of the Elderly Act):

(a) raise the retirement age;

(b) introduce a "continuous employment system" (to employ employees who are to be employed continuously after retirement age); or

(c) abolish the retirement age.

In practice, many companies set retirement age at 60 and introduce a "continuous employment system" as described in (b) above. For this purpose, a "continuous employment system" includes an arrangement in which employers ensure the employment of older employees by concluding an agreement with their parent or subsidiary company or any other certain affiliate company under which they are required to hire employees who have been hired by the original employers and desire to be re-hired after reaching the retirement age (Article 9, Paragraph 2 of the Employment of the Elderly Act).

6-2 Termination of Employment Agreement due to Dismissals
6-2-1 Dismissal

Dismissal is the termination of an employment agreement by the employer. In dismissals, the employer is required to comply with the following procedures and restrictions provided by the Labor Standards Act for the protection of employees. Furthermore, (i) the employers' right to dismiss employees hired under Non-Fixed Term Employment Agreements is restricted by the Doctrine of an Abuse of the Right to Dismiss Employees, and (ii) employers are not allowed to dismiss employees hired under Fixed Term Employment Agreements without "unavoidable reasons" until the expiration of the contract term thereof. Regarding the Doctrine of an Abuse of the

なくとも30日前にその予告をする必要があります（労働基準法20条1項）。予告を短縮する場合には，短縮した日数分の平均賃金を支払わなければなりません（同条2項）。

ただし，（ⅰ）天変事変その他やむを得ない事由のために事業の継続が不可能となった場合，又は（ⅱ）労働者の責めに帰すべき事由に基づいて解雇する場合であって，かつ行政庁の認定を得た場合には，即時解雇が可能です（労働基準法20条3項，1項但書）。

(b) 一定事由・期間における解雇制限

労働者保護の観点から，特に解雇が制限されることがあります。例えば，労働基準法上，業務上災害による療養期間及びその後30日間，産前産後の休業期間及びその後30日間は，原則として，解雇をすることができません（労働基準法19条1項）。

6-2-2 解雇権濫用法理

使用者は，労働者を解雇する場合，上記6-2-1(a)の解雇手続を採る必要があります。また，判例は，使用者の解雇権の行使も，それが客観的に合理的な理由を欠き，又は社会通念上相当として是認することができない場合には，権利の濫用として無効になると判示しています（解雇権濫用法理）。この判例法理は，労働契約法16条に成文化されています。

Right to Dismiss Employees, please refer to Section 6-2-2 below.

(a) Procedures for dismissal

In the case where an employer dismisses an employee, the employer shall provide at least 30 days advance notice (Article 20, Paragraph 1 of the Labor Standards Act). If less than 30 days notice is given, the employer must pay an amount equivalent to the average wages of the employee multiplied by the number of days by which the notice falls short of 30 days (Article 20, Paragraph 2 of the Labor Standards Act). Provided, however, that this shall not apply in the case where (i) the continuance of the business has been made impossible by a natural disaster or other unavoidable reason or (ii) the employee is dismissed for reasons attributable to the employee and the employer obtains the approval of the relevant government agency with respect to the reason (Article 20, Paragraph 3 and the proviso of Article 20, Paragraph 1 of the Labor Standards Act).

(b) Restriction of dismissal due to a specific reason or for a specific period

In some cases, the dismissal is prohibited in order to protect employees. For example, under the Labor Standards Act, an employer shall not, in principle, dismiss an employee during a period of absence from work for medical treatment with respect to work-related injuries or illnesses nor within 30 days thereafter, and shall not dismiss a woman during a period of absence from work before and after childbirth nor within 30 days thereafter (Article 19, Paragraph 1 of the Labor Standards Act).

6-2-2 Doctrine of an Abuse of the Right to Dismiss Employees

In the case where an employer dismisses an employee, the employer shall follow the procedures of dismissal described in Section 6-2-1(a) above. In addition, a court precedent declared that "even when an employer exercises its right of dismissal, it will be void as an abuse of right if it is not based on objectively reasonable grounds or it is not socially acceptable" ("Doctrine of an Abuse of the Right to Dismiss Employees"). This doctrine of the court precedents has been codified into Article 16 of the

(1) 解雇権濫用法理の具体的内容
　(a) 客観的に合理的な理由
　　解雇権濫用法理にいう，解雇の「客観的に合理的な理由」には，主に次のものがあります。
　(i) 労働者の労務提供の不能，適格性の欠如・喪失
　　　傷病や後遺症のための労働能力の喪失，勤務成績の著しい不良，重大な経歴詐称等による信頼関係喪失等が該当します。なお，6-2-1(b)記載のとおり，業務上災害による療養期間及びその後30日間は解雇が禁止されていますので，6-2-1(b)に該当する労働者は，仮にこの(i)の要件に該当したとしても，解雇できません。
　(ii) 労働者の非違行為
　　　業務命令違反，職場規律違反等の非違行為が該当します。
　(iii) 経営上の必要性
　　　合理化による職種の消滅と他職種への配転不能，経営不振による人員整理や，会社の解散等が該当します。経営不振による人員整理については，下記6-2-2(2)をご参照ください。
　(iv) ユニオン・ショップ協定
　　　使用者が，労働組合と締結する労働協約において，自己の雇用する労働者のうち当該労働組合に加入しない者及び当該組合の組合員でなくなったものを解雇する義務を負うことがありますが，かかる協定をユニオン・ショップ協定といいます。かかる協定に基づく解雇も合理性の認められる解雇理由に該当します。
　(b) 社会的相当性
　　解雇が「社会通念上相当」であるとは，解雇理由の程度と解雇処分のバランスがとれていること，解雇が過酷に過ぎないことが必要であることを意味します。そして，裁判例は，労働者に有利な事情を極力考慮して社会的相当性を厳格に解し，解雇を厳しく制限する傾向にあります。
　　例えば，上記6-2-2(1)(a)(i)に記載するような労働者の職務能力に関していえば，単に職務能力が平均的水準に達していないというだけでは不十分

Employment Agreement Act.
(1) Contents of the Doctrine of an Abuse of the Right to Dismiss Employees
 (a) Objectively Reasonable Grounds for Dismissal
  The objectively reasonable grounds for dismissal of the Doctrine of an Abuse of the Right to Dismiss Employees can be generally summarized as follows:
  (i) Employee's inability to provide labor/Lack or loss in aptitude
   For example, an employee's inability to provide labor due to injury, illness, or permanent damage, significantly poor employee performance, or loss of relationship of trust due to material fraud in an application for employment. Please note that, an employer shall not dismiss an employee during a period of absence from work for medical treatment with respect to work-related injuries or illnesses suffered in the course of employment nor within 30 days thereafter as mentioned in Section 6-2-1(b) above, even if the employee falls into category (i);
  (ii) Employee's misconduct
   For example, breach of work orders or disciplines for the workplace;
  (iii) Business necessity
   For example, loss of job responsibility due to rationalization and the inability to rotate employees to a different job, redundancy due to a business downturn or dissolution of the company. Please refer to Section 6-2-2(2) below regarding downsizing due to a business downturn; or
  (iv) Union-Shop Contracts
   In some cases, the employer bears the obligation to dismiss employees who do not join a certain labor union or cease to be a member of such labor union under the collective labor agreement executed with the labor union. This contract is called a "Union Shop Contract." Dismissal due to this contract can be classified as objectively reasonable grounds.
 (b) Social Acceptability
  Social acceptability of dismissal means that the dismissal and the reason for the dismissal are to be balanced, and the dismissal is not to be too harsh for the

であり、また、教育・指導によって能力の向上を図ることができる場合は、解雇は許されません。

(2) 整理解雇の4要件（又は4要素）の法理

　整理解雇とは、使用者の経営上の理由による解雇をいいます。労働者の責めに帰すべき事由による解雇ではなく、使用者の経営上の理由に基づく余剰人員削減のための解雇であるため、判例は、その有効性をより厳格に判断しています。

　具体的には、下記の4つの事由に着目し、判断されることになります（整理解雇の4要件（又は4要素）の法理）。

(a) 人員削減の必要性

　　整理解雇を行うためには、人員削減を行う経営上の必要性が要求されます。これは、倒産必至の状況にあることまでは要しないとされており、また、人員削減の必要性は経営判断事項であることから、裁判所は、経営者の判断を尊重する傾向にあるとされています。もっとも、人員削減の必要性と矛盾する行為、例えば他の労働者の賃上げや、新規採用の実施等は、人員削減の必要性を否定する要素となり得ます。

(b) 解雇回避努力義務

　　人員削減の必要性があったとしても、代替措置として、配転・出向、残業の削減、新規採用の停止、一時帰休、希望退職の募集等の方策もあります。そのため、解雇を行う前に、これらの整理解雇を回避するための努力を尽くすこと（解雇回避努力義務）が必要とされており、かかる努力をなさず行う整理解雇は、権利の濫用として無効となります。

employee. In addition, Japanese courts tend to be pro-labor and to judge the social acceptability of dismissal strictly by taking as many circumstances that are favorable for the employees into account, and limit the effectiveness of dismissal.

For example, regarding the performance of the employee, mentioned in Section 6-2-2(1)(a)(i) above, it is not enough to recognize the social acceptability of a dismissal if the employee's skill is lower than average or if the employee who currently lacks skill may improve his/her skill through training and guidance by the employer.

(2) Doctrine of 4 Requirements (or Elements) of Dismissal due to Business Necessity

Since Dismissal due to Business Necessity (*Seiri-Kaiko*) is caused not by the employee's fault but by business reasons, court precedents judge more strictly the effectiveness of Dismissal due to Business Necessity.

In particular, courts have established the following 4 requirements (or elements) for Dismissal due to Business Necessity ("Doctrine of 4 Requirements (or Elements) of Dismissal due to Business Necessity"):

(a) Necessity to Reduce the Number of Employees

Necessity to reduce the number of employees is required for Dismissal due to Business Necessity. The inevitability of bankruptcy is not required and Japanese courts are said to respect decisions of management because the necessity of reducing the number of employees is considered a business judgment matter. Please note, however, that if employers take actions that are not consistent with the necessity to reduce the number of employees such as increaseing wages or recruiting new employees, it may not be an acceptable reason for reducing the number of employees.

(b) Obligation to Endeavor to Avoid Dismissal

In the case there is a necessity to reduce the number of employees, there are actions the employer can take other than dismissal, such as (job) rotation, secondment, reduction of overtime work, stopping new recruitment, temporary

解雇回避努力義務の程度は，具体的状況に応じて判断され，例えば，経営危機に瀕している状況における整理解雇と，黒字経営下での経営戦略的整理解雇とでは，後者の方が会社により高い解雇回避努力が求められます。

(c) 解雇対象者選定の妥当性

整理解雇が必要であるとしても，解雇される労働者の選定は，客観的で合理的な基準によってなされる必要性があります。

例えば労働組合員や女性であることに基づき解雇する場合には，選定基準の合理性が否定され，整理解雇は無効となります。

(d) 説明・協議等の手続の妥当性

整理解雇に関する適正な手続が履行される必要があり，使用者は，労働組合又は労働者に対して，人員整理について納得を得るよう説明・協議する信義則上の義務があるとされています。

(3) 解雇権の濫用とされた解雇の効力

解雇権の濫用とされた解雇は，無効とされ，解雇された労働者は会社に復職することが可能となります。また，解雇された日から判決までの期間中も，会社との間で労働契約が存続していたこととなるため，原則として，当該期間に対応する賃金を請求できることになります。

Chapter I. Overview of Japanese Employment and Labor Law   41

lay-off, or soliciting voluntary resignation. Therefore, the employer needs to fulfill the obligation of endeavoring to avoid dismissal before dismissal. Without fulfilling this obligation, dismissal shall be judged an abuse of the right of dismissal and shall be null and void.

The degree of the obligation to endeavor to avoid dismissal is judged within respect to specific situations. For example, a higher level of endeavor to avoid dismissal shall be required in situations where the employer has a budget surplus than in a situation where the employer is in a liquidity crisis.

(c) Reasonability of Selecting Person(s) to be Dismissed

In the case where there is necessity for Dismissal due to Business Necessity, the employer shall select the person(s) to be dismissed based on objective and reasonable standards. For example, in the event that an employer dismisses employees due to being female or a member of a labor union, the reasonability of the standards of the dismissal shall be denied and the dismissal shall be deemed null and void.

(d) Proper Procedures (explanation, discussion etc.)

Proper procedures shall be followed, and court precedents show employers have an obligation to enter into good faith discussions with labor unions or employees to explain proposed reductions in numbers of employees in order to obtain their understanding.

(3) Effectiveness of Dismissal Judged as an Abuse of the Right of Dismissal

In the case where an employer abuses the right to terminate employees, the dismissal shall be judged void. Therefore, the employee can come back to the company and can, in principle, demand wage payment for the period of dismissal up to the time of the judgment because the employment agreement is deemed to continue during this period.

6-2-3　有期労働契約における解雇

　有期労働契約の場合，使用者は，その契約期間が満了するまでは，やむを得ない事由がある場合でなければ，労働者を解雇することができません（労働契約法17条1項）。ここでいう「やむを得ない事由」は，解雇権濫用法理における「客観的に合理的な理由」よりも限定的に解釈されているため，使用者が有期労働契約を締結している労働者を契約期間の途中で解雇することは，無期労働契約を締結している労働者を解雇することに比して困難です。

7. 有期労働契約に関する労働契約法上の特則

7-1　有期労働契約の無期労働契約への転換

　有期労働契約が通算で5年を超えて繰り返し更新された場合，労働者は，当該有期労働契約を無期労働契約に転換することができ，労働者が，5年を超えて更新された有期労働契約の契約期間内に，当該有期労働契約が満了した日の翌日を労務提供開始日とする無期労働契約の申込みを行った場合，使用者は当該申込みを承諾したものとみなされます（労働契約法18条1項）。
　なお，5年の通算契約期間は，2013年4月1日以後に締結され又は更新された有期労働契約のみを対象として算定されます。また，一定のクーリング期間（たとえば，契約期間が1年以上の有期労働契約の場合は6か月間）を置いて，有期労働契約が再度締結された場合には，そのクーリング期間前に終了している有期労働契約の契約期間は，5年の契約通算期間には算入されません（労働契約法18条2項）。

6-2-3 Dismissal of Employees Hired under Fixed Term Employment Agreements

Employers may not dismiss employees hired under Fixed Term Employment Agreements without "unavoidable reasons" until the expiration of the contract term thereof (Article 17, Paragraph 1 of the Employment Agreement Act). For the purpose of applying such provision, the requirements to establish "unavoidable reasons" are considered to be more restrictive than those of "objectively reasonable grounds" used when applying the Doctrine of an Abuse of the Right to Dismiss Employees to employees hired under Non-Fixed Term Employment Agreements. Therefore, employers will have more difficulty dismissing employees hired under Fixed Term Employment Agreements during the contract terms thereof than dismissing employees hired under Non-Fixed Term Employment Agreements.

7. Special Provisions on Fixed Term Employment Agreement in the Employment Agreement Act

7-1 Conversion of a Fixed Term Employment Agreement to a Non-Fixed Term Employment Agreement

In cases where a Fixed Term Employment Agreement has been repeatedly renewed and the cumulative working period exceeds 5 years, the employee will obtain an option to convert his/her Fixed Term Employment Agreement to a Non-Fixed Term Employment Agreement. If the employee, during the contract term of a Fixed Term Employment Agreement that has been renewed for over 5 years, makes the employer an offer to enter into the Non-Fixed Term Employment Agreement pursuant to which the employee starts to provide services from the next day after the expiry of his/her Fixed Term Employment Agreement, the employer will be deemed to have accepted such an offer under Article 18, Paragraph 1 of the Employment Agreement Act.

The 5 year period will be counted only in terms of Fixed Term Employment Agreements newly executed or renewed after April 1, 2013. In cases where employers

また、(i)高度な専門的知識等を有する有期雇用労働者及び(ii)定年後引き続いて雇用される有期雇用労働者については、使用者が対象労働者の特性に応じた雇用管理に関する措置についての計画を作成し、労働局長の認定を受けることにより、一定の期間について無期転換申込権が発生しないこととする特例が設けられています（専門的知識等を有する有期雇用労働者等に関する特別措置法）。

7-2 雇止め制限の法理

上記6-1-3で述べたとおり、有期労働契約は、原則としてその期間の満了によって終了しますが、一定の場合には、使用者による更新拒絶が「雇止め制限の法理」（労働契約法19条）によって制約されることがあります。

すなわち、次のいずれかの場合に該当し、かつ、労働者が契約期間内に又は満了後遅滞なく更新の申込みを行ったときには、使用者による更新拒絶が、客観的に合理的な理由に基づき、かつ、社会通念上相当であると認められない限り、従前の労働条件と同一の労働条件において有期労働契約の更新がなされたものとみなされます。

(i) 有期労働契約が過去に反復して更新されており、その契約期間の満了時に当該契約を更新せずに終了させることが、無期労働契約を締結している労働者を解雇することと社会通念上同視できると認められる場合

(ii) 労働者が有期労働契約の契約期間の満了時に当該契約の更新を期待することについて合理的な理由があるものと認められる場合

rehire the same employees after a certain cooling-off period (for example, if the term of a Fixed Term Employment Agreement is 1 year or longer, then 6 months), the terms of any Fixed Term Employment Agreements that have expired before the cooling-off period are excluded from the 5 year period under Article 18, Paragraph 2 of the Employment Agreement Act.

In addition, there is the following exception: regarding (i) a fixed-term employee with advanced expert knowledge and skills and (ii) a fixed-term employee who is continuously employed after reaching the mandatory retirement age, if the employer prepares a plan for measures concerning managing the employment of these employees that matches their characteristics, and the plan is approved by a Director-General of the relevant Labor Bureau, then the option to convert the Fixed Term Employment Agreement to a Non-Fixed Term Employment Agreement will not arise for a specified period (Act on Special Measures Concerning Fixed-term Employees with Expert Knowledge and Skills).

7-2 Doctrine of Restriction of Non-Renewal on a Fixed Term Employment Agreement

As mentioned in Section 6-1-3 above, in principle, a Fixed Term Employment Agreement terminates when the contract term expires, although the renewal by employers of Fixed Term Employment Agreements will be restricted in certain circumstances by the "Doctrine of Restriction on Non-Renewal of a Fixed Term Employment Agreement" provided in Article 19 of the Employment Agreement Act.

The Doctrine provides that unless an employer's non-renewal is based on "objectively reasonable grounds" and is "socially acceptable," the Fixed Term Employment Agreement will be deemed renewed under the same conditions as those before the deemed renewal upon the employee's request during the term of employment or without delay after the expiry, in its following cases:

(i) in cases where a Fixed Term Employment Agreement has been renewed repeatedly and the non-renewal thereof can be reasonably deemed equivalent to the dismissal of an employee with a Non-Fixed Term Employment Agreement;

どのような場合に上記(i)又は(ii)の条件に該当するかについては，労働契約法上も判例上も明確な基準があるわけではありませんが，裁判例上，当該職務・地位が臨時的か常用的か，更新回数，契約存続期間，契約更新手続・実態，雇用の継続性に関する使用者の言動等を総合考慮して個別の事案ごとの判断が行われる傾向があります。

　なお，使用者による更新拒絶が，客観的に合理的な理由に基づくものであるか，あるいは社会通念上相当であると認められるかどうかについては，上記6-2-2(1)の解雇権濫用法理における判断枠組みに準じて判断されることになります。

7-3　期間の定めがあることによる不合理な労働条件の禁止

　使用者が有期労働契約を締結している労働者と無期労働契約を締結している労働者の労働条件との間に期間の定めがあることによる不合理な労働条件の差異を設けることは禁止されています（労働契約法20条）。

　なお，パートタイム労働法がパート有期法に改正され，パートタイム労働者と有期雇用労働者とが同じ法律によって規律されることになり，これに伴い労働契約法20条は削除されます。詳しくは上記5をご参照ください。

or

(ii) in cases where an employee with a Fixed Term Employment Agreement has a reasonable expectation of renewal upon the expiration of his/her Fixed Term Employment Agreement.

Although the Employment Agreement Act does not provide clear criteria regarding the above conditions nor do the court precedents that established this doctrine, judgment tends to be made on a case-by-case basis and based on factors such as whether the job/position was considered to be temporary or regular, how many times the employment agreement was renewed, how long it has been since the employee was hired, whether and how the renewal procedures were conducted, as well as the employer's behavior and conduct regarding the continuity of employment.

For the purpose of applying the Doctrine of Restriction on Non-Renewal of a Fixed Term Employment Agreement, the framework to judge whether an employer's dismissal is based on "objectively reasonable grounds" and "socially acceptable," which is used when applying the Doctrine of an Abuse of the Right to Dismiss Employees (please refer to Section 6-2-2(1) above), will be applied mutatis mutandis for judging whether an employer's non-renewal is based on "objectively reasonable grounds" and "socially acceptable."

7-3 Prohibition on Imposing Unreasonably Different Employment Conditions due to the Fixed Term

Employers are prohibited from creating any unreasonable differences in employment conditions due to difference of existence of an employment term, between employees hired under Fixed Term Employment Agreements and those hired under Non-Fixed Term Employment Agreements under Article 20 of the Employment Agreement Act.

Meanwhile, the Part-Time Employment Act will be amended to the Part-Time Employment and Fixed-Term Employment Act to regulate part-time employees and fixed-term employees under the same Act, as a result of which Article 20 of the Employment Agreement Act will be merged into it and deleted from the Employment Agreement Act. For further information, please refer to 5 above.

8. 競業避止義務・秘密保持義務

8-1 競業避止義務
8-1-1 在職中の競業避止義務
(1) 根　　拠

　競業避止義務とは，労働者が使用者と事業内容や顧客が競合する他社に就職したり，自ら開業したりしない義務をいいます。

　多くの会社では，労働契約・就業規則において在職中の競業避止義務を定めています。もっとも，労働契約・就業規則の明示の根拠規定が存在しない場合であっても，信義則上，在職中の競業避止義務は認められると考えられています。

(2) 競業避止義務が認められる場合の効果

　在職中の労働者に競業避止義務違反の行為があった場合，使用者としては，状況に応じて以下の対応を行うことが考えられます。
　(a) 懲戒処分（懲戒解雇を含む。）
　(b) 解雇
　(c) 損害賠償
　(d) 競業行為の差止請求

8-1-2 労働関係の終了後の競業避止義務

(1) 根　　拠

　労働者は，職業選択の自由・営業の自由を保障されているので，労働関係の終了後は当然に退職した会社に対して競業避止義務を負うことはないと考えら

8. Non-Competition Obligations and Confidentiality Obligations

8-1 Non-Competition Obligations
8-1-1 Non-Competition Obligations During Employment
(1) Basis

A non-competition obligation is an employee's obligation to refrain from working for or managing a company that competes with the business or clients of his/her current or previous employer.

In Japan, many companies require their employees to agree to non-competition covenants during his/her employment either in their respective employment agreements or in the companies' work rules. Based on the principles of faith and trust between a company and its employees, even if the employment agreements and the work rules are silent on non-competition obligations during employment, such obligations are considered to have been imposed on the employees.

(2) Effectiveness of a Non-Competition Obligation

In the event that an employee breaches his/her non-competition obligation during his/her employment, an employer may take any one or more of the following actions, depending on the circumstances:
   (a)　disciplinary action (including disciplinary dismissal);
   (b)　dismissal;
   (c)　demanding compensation for damages; and/or
   (d)　seeking an injunction against competitive action.

8-1-2 Non-Competition Obligations after the Termination of an Employment Relationship
(1) Basis

In principle, employees are not subject to a non-competition obligation after termination of their employment relationship due to the general freedom of choice in

れます。したがって，退職後の労働者に，競業の制限を主張するためには，不正競争防止法等の法令上の根拠，又は契約（就業規則等）の根拠が必要であると考えられます。

また，労働契約・就業規則の根拠規定がある場合であっても，労働者の職業選択の自由・営業の自由に照らして，競業避止義務を課すことについて合理性があると認められる範囲に限り，その労働契約・就業規則の根拠規定の有効性が認められると考えられます。

かかる合理性は，以下のような要素を考慮して判断されます。
(a) 競業制限の目的（使用者が営業秘密・知識の保護に正当な利益を有しているか）
(b) 競業制限の範囲の妥当性（職種・期間・地域等）
(c) 労働者の職務内容・地位
(d) 代償措置の存否及び内容

(2) 競業避止義務が認められる場合の効果

労働関係終了後の労働者に競業避止義務違反の行為があった場合，使用者としては，状況に応じて以下の対応を行うことが考えられます。
(a) 退職金の減額・不支給
(b) 損害賠償
(c) 競業行為の差止請求

8-2　秘密保持義務
8-2-1　在職中の秘密保持義務
(1) 根　　拠

秘密保持義務とは，労働者が使用者の企業秘密を漏洩しない義務をいいます。

employment and the freedom to conduct business that is enjoyed by persons. Therefore, in order to enforce a non-competition obligation on an employee after the termination of an employment relationship, an employer must either rely on the laws and ordinances, such as the Unfair Competition Prevention Act (the "Competition Act") or agree on such obligation with the employee on a contractual basis (including by putting such post-employment requirement in its work rules).

Please note that even if a non-competition covenant after termination of his/her employment relationship exists in an employment agreement or in a company's work rules, such covenant is only valid if it is based on reasonable grounds, sufficient to overcome the presumptions of freedom of choice in employment and freedom to conduct business, taking into consideration the following points:

(a) the purpose of the non-competition obligation (whether the employer has a legitimate interest in the protection of trade secrets or knowledge);
(b) the reasonability of the scope of the non-competition obligation (job category, term, territory, etc.);
(c) the previous duties and position of the employee; and
(d) whether the employee has been compensated for agreeing to the obligation.

(2) Effectiveness of a Non-Competition Obligation

If an employee breaches his/her non-competition obligation after the termination of his/her employment relationship with his/her employer, the employer may take any one or more of the following actions, depending on the circumstances:

(a) reduction or forfeit of severance;
(b) demanding compensation for damages; and/or
(c) seeking an injunction against competitive action.

8-2 Confidentiality Obligations
8-2-1 Confidentiality Obligations During Employment
(1) Basis

A confidentiality obligation is an employee's obligation not to divulge certain

競業避止義務と同様，多くの会社では，労働契約・就業規則において在職中の秘密保持義務を定めていますが，労働契約・就業規則の明示の根拠規定が存在しない場合であっても，信義則上，在職中は，使用者の業務上の秘密を守る義務を負うと解されています。

(2) 秘密保持義務が認められる場合の効果
在職中の労働者に秘密保持義務違反の行為があった場合，使用者としては，状況に応じて以下の対応を行うことが考えられます。
 (a) 懲戒処分（懲戒解雇を含む。）
 (b) 解雇
 (c) 損害賠償
 (d) 秘密保持義務違反行為の差止請求

8-2-2 労働関係の終了後の秘密保持義務

(1) 根　　拠
労働関係終了後においては，労働者に秘密保持義務を課すには，不正競争防止法の要件に該当する場合（詳しくは，下記8-2-3をご参照ください。）を除き，原則として契約（就業規則等）の根拠が必要であると解されています。また，労働契約・就業規則の根拠規定がある場合であっても，労働者の職業選択の自由・営業の自由に照らして，秘密保持義務を課すことについて合理性があると認められる範囲に限り，その労働契約・就業規則の根拠規定の有効性が認められると考えられます。
もっとも，競業避止義務と比べれば，秘密保持義務を課すことが職業選択の自由・営業の自由に及ぼす影響は小さいことから，競業避止義務よりも緩やか

privileged information of his/her employer. Similar to non-competition obligations, many companies require their employees to agree to confidentiality covenants during his/her employment either in their respective employment agreements or in the companies' work rules. Also similar to non-competition obligations, based on the principles of faith and trust between a company and its employees, even if the employment agreements and the work rules are silent on confidentiality obligations during employment, such obligations are considered to have been imposed on the employees.

(2) Effectiveness of a Confidentiality Obligation

If an employee breaches his/her confidentiality obligation during his/her employment, an employer may take any one or more of the following actions, depending on the circumstances:

(a) disciplinary action (including disciplinary dismissal);
(b) dismissal;
(c) demanding compensation for damages; and/or
(d) seeking an injunction against breach of the confidentiality obligation.

8-2-2 Confidentiality Obligations after the Termination of an Employment Relationship

(1) Basis

After the termination of an employment relationship, aside from situations falling under the Competition Act (described further in Section 8-2-3 below), in principle, an employer must agree on such obligation with the employee on a contractual basis (including by putting such a post-employment requirement in its work rules) in order to impose confidentiality obligations on employees.

In addition, even if a confidentiality covenant after the termination of his/her employment exists in an employment agreement or in a company's work rules, such covenant is only valid if it is based on reasonable grounds, sufficient to overcome the presumption of freedom of choice in employment and freedom to conduct business.

に有効性が認められると考えられます。

8-2-3　不正競争防止法

　一定の範囲の企業秘密については，不正競争防止法により，労働関係の存続中・終了後を通じて，労働者が使用・開示することが規制されています。
　具体的には，労働者が，「営業秘密」を不正の競業その他の不正の利益を得る目的又はその保有者に損害を加える目的で使用・開示する行為は営業秘密に関する不正競争とされ（不正競争防止法2条1項7号），使用者は差止（同法3条1項），損害賠償（同法4条）等を求めることができます。「営業秘密」とは，秘密として管理されている生産方法，販売方法その他の事業活動に有用な技術上又は営業上の情報であって，公然と知られていないものをいいます（同法2条6項）。

9．労働者派遣

9-1　労働者派遣の意義

　労働者派遣とは，派遣元事業主が自己の雇用する労働者を，派遣先の指揮命令を受けて，派遣先のために労働に従事させることをいいます（労働者派遣法2条1号）。労働者派遣は，自己の雇用する労働者を他人のために労働させる点で出向や請負に類似しますが，派遣先と労働者との間に雇用関係が成立しない点で出向と区別され，また，労働者は派遣先の指揮命令に従って労働に従事する点で請負とも区別されます。実質的には労働者派遣であるにもかかわらず，形式的に請負契約を締結し，労働者を注文主の指揮命令の下で労働に従事させることを偽装請負といいますが，偽装請負に対しても，労働者派遣法が適用さ

Given that confidentiality obligations have a lesser impact on the freedom of choice in employment or the freedom to conduct business than do non-competition obligations, there tends to be less scrutiny towards the validity of confidentiality obligations.

8-2-3 Unfair Competition Prevention Act

The Competition Act regulates the use and disclosure of certain privileged secrets of a company by its employees both during and after the employment relationship.

In the event that an employee uses or discloses a "trade secret" for the purpose of unfair business competition or for otherwise acquiring an illicit benefit, or to damage an employer, such action falls under the category of "unfair competition" (Article 2, Paragraph 1, Item 7 of the Competition Act), and the employer may seek an injunction (Article 3, Paragraph 1 of the Competition Act), claim damages (Article 4 of the Competition Act) or the like. The term "trade secret" in the Act refers to technical or business information that is useful for commercial activities, such as manufacturing or marketing methods that are managed as secrets and that are not publicly known (Article 2, Paragraph 6 of the Competition Act).

9. Worker Dispatching

9-1 Meaning of Worker Dispatching

"Worker Dispatching" means assigning workers employed by a business operator engaged in worker dispatching (a "Worker Dispatching Business Operator") to engage in work for clients (the "Clients") to whom the Worker Dispatching services are being provided under the instructions of those Clients (Article 2, Item 1 of the Worker Dispatching Act). Even though Worker Dispatching is similar to secondment and contract work in that the workers employed by an entity are assigned to engage in work for another entity, Worker Dispatching is distinguished from secondment in that an employment relationship is not formed between the Clients and the workers, and it is

れ，派遣可能期間の制限（9-2参照）や労働契約申込みみなし制度（9-3参照）の対象となります。

9-2　派遣可能期間の制限

　労働者派遣法は，派遣可能期間について，(1)派遣先の事業所単位の期間制限と(2)派遣労働者の個人単位の期間制限を定めています（労働者派遣法40条の2，同条の3）。かかる派遣可能期間の制限は，労働者派遣法の平成27年改正により定められたもので，改正法の施行日（平成27年9月30日）以降に労働者派遣契約を締結して受け入れた労働者派遣について，その業務の内容を問わず適用されます。もっとも，派遣元事業主と無期雇用契約を締結している労働者を派遣する場合や60歳以上の労働者を派遣する場合等には適用されません（労働者派遣法40条の2第1項）。また，平成27年9月29日までに締結された労働者派遣契約に基づく労働者派遣についても，改正前の期間制限が適用され，以下の(1)及び(2)の期間制限は適用されません。

(1)　事業所単位の期間制限

　派遣先は，派遣先の同一の事業所（工場，事務所，店舗等）において，派遣先で新たな労働者派遣を受け入れてから3年の派遣可能期間を超えて労働者派

also distinguished from contract work in that the workers are engaged in work under the instructions of the Clients. The practice of nominally executing a contract with a worker and referring to the worker as an independent "contractor", despite the worker being engaged in work under the instructions of the assignor in what substantially amounts to a dispatch arrangement is called "disguised contracting" (*giso-ukeoi*). The Worker Dispatching Act also applies to so-called disguised contracting, and such work will be subject to the restrictions on the length of time for dispatch arrangements (see 9-2 below) and the constructive offer of employment (see 9-3 below).

9-2 Restrictions on the Length of Time for Dispatch Arrangements

The Worker Dispatching Act sets forth (1) a restriction on the length of time a worker can be engaged at one particular place of business of the Clients and (2) a restriction on the length of time for dispatch arrangements with respect to individual dispatched workers (Articles 40-2 and 40-3 of the Worker Dispatching Act). Those restrictions on the length of time for dispatch arrangements were established by the amendment to the Worker Dispatching Act in 2015 and apply to worker dispatching based on contracts entered into on and after the date of enforcement of that amendment (September 30, 2015), regardless of the details of the work. However, the restrictions on the length of time for dispatch arrangements do not apply to dispatched workers who executed indefinite employment contracts with the Working Dispatching Business Operator or to dispatched workers who are 60 years of age or older, etc. (Article 40-2, Paragraph 1 of the Worker Dispatching Act). Further, the restrictions on the length of time for dispatch arrangements under (1) and (2) below do not apply to worker dispatching under worker dispatch contracts executed on or before September 29, 2015, as the restrictions on the length of time before the amendment still apply to those dispatch arrangements.

(1) Restrictions on the Length of Time for Dispatch Arrangements with respect to the Place of Business

Clients may not accept dispatched workers for a period exceeding 3 years from the time a new worker commences work at the Client's same place of business (factories,

遣の提供を受けることはできません（労働者派遣法40条の2）。かかる派遣可能期間は，派遣先の事業所の過半数労働組合又は過半数代表者の意見聴取手続を経ることにより3年を上限に延長することができ，その後も同様の手続により，更に延長することができます。かかる意見聴取手続を怠った場合，労働契約申込みみなし制度が適用されます（9-3参照）。なお，労働者派遣の終了後に再び労働者派遣を受け入れる場合，その終了と次の労働者派遣の受入れ開始との間の期間が3か月を超えないときは，労働者派遣の受入れは継続しているものとみなされます（派遣先が講ずべき措置に関する指針（派遣先指針）第2の14(3)）。

(2) 個人単位の期間制限

派遣先は，上記(1)の事業所単位の派遣可能期間が延長された場合であっても，同一の派遣労働者を派遣先の事業所における同一の組織単位で3年を超えて派遣就業させることはできません（労働者派遣法40条の3）。かかる個人単位の期間制限は，上記(1)の事業所単位の期間制限とは異なり，延長することはできません。かかる個人単位の期間制限に違反した場合には，労働契約申込みみなし制度が適用されることになります（9-3参照）。なお，労働者派遣の終了後に再び同一の派遣労働者の派遣を同一の組織で受け入れる場合，その終了と次の労働者派遣の受入れ開始との間の期間が3か月を超えないときは，労働者派遣の受入れは継続しているものとみなされます（派遣先指針第2の14(4)）。

Chapter I. Overview of Japanese Employment and Labor Law 59

offices, stores, etc.) (Article 40-2 of the Worker Dispatching Act). However, restrictions on the length of time may be extended for up to 3 years by holding an opinion hearing procedure with a labor union organized by a majority of the employees or individuals representing the majority of the employees at that Client's place of business, and may be further extended by following a similar procedure thereafter. If the Client fails to follow the opinion hearing procedures, the policy for a constructive offer of employment will apply (see 9-3 below). If the same Client accepts the worker dispatch arrangement again, and the subsequent dispatch arrangement begins within 3 months after the previous dispatch arrangement has terminated, this and any subsequent worker dispatch arrangement will be deemed to be a continuation of the original worker dispatch arrangement (No. 2-14(3) of the Guidelines for Measures to Be Taken by Clients (the "Client Guidelines")).

(2) Restriction on the Length of Time for Dispatch Arrangements with respect to the Individuals

Even where the length of time for the dispatch arrangements with respect to the place of business in (1) above has been extended, the same dispatched worker may not be engaged in dispatch work for a period exceeding 3 years in the same organizational unit at the Client's place of business (Article 40-3 of the Worker Dispatching Act). These restrictions on the length of time for dispatch arrangements with respect to the individuals differs from the restrictions with respect to the place of business in (1) above, and may not be extended. If the restrictions on the length of time for dispatch arrangements with individual workers is violated, the policy for a constructive offer of employment will apply (see 9-3 below). If the same workers are dispatched again to the same organizational unit, and the subsequent dispatch arrangement begins within 3 months after the previous dispatch arrangement has terminated, this and any subsequent worker dispatch arrangement will be deemed to be a continuation of the original worker dispatch arrangement (No. 2-14(4) of the Client Guidelines).

9-3 労働契約申込みみなし制度

　派遣先が次に掲げる違法な労働者派遣を受け入れた場合，派遣先が違法な労働者派遣に該当することを知らず，かつ，知らなかったことに過失がないときを除き，その時点で，派遣先は，当該労働者派遣に係る派遣労働者に対して，当該派遣労働者の当該時点での派遣元事業主における労働条件と同一の労働条件を内容とする労働契約の申込みをしたものとみなされます（労働者派遣法40条の6）。

(a) 労働者派遣の禁止業務（建設業務や港湾運送業務等）に従事させた場合
(b) 労働者派遣事業の許可を得ていない事業主から労働者派遣を受け入れた場合
(c) 事業所単位の期間制限に違反して労働者派遣を受け入れた場合
(d) 個人単位の期間制限に違反して労働者派遣を受け入れた場合
(e) いわゆる偽装請負の場合（労働者派遣法等の規定の適用を免れる目的で，請負等の名目で契約を締結し，労働者派遣の提供を受ける場合）

　労働契約の申込みをしたとみなされた派遣先は，違法な労働者派遣が終了した日から1年経過するまで当該申込みを撤回することができません（労働者派遣法40条の6第2項）。仮に派遣労働者が派遣先による労働契約の申込みを承諾した場合には，違法な労働者派遣が行われた時点での派遣労働者の派遣元における労働条件と同一内容の労働契約が成立します。

9-3 Policy for Constructive Offer of Employment

If a Client engages in one of the following types of illegal worker dispatching, unless the Client did so without knowledge, or was not negligent in failing to acquire that knowledge, the Client will be deemed to have offered an employment contract to the dispatched worker at the time, based on the same employment conditions the dispatched worker is employed under at the Worker Dispatching Business Operator as of the time of the illegal worker dispatching (Article 40-6 of the Worker Dispatching Act).

(a) A Client allows a dispatched worker to engage in statutorily prohibited work for Worker Dispatching (construction work, port transport services, etc.);

(b) a Client accepts a dispatched worker from a business operator that does not have a worker dispatching license;

(c) a Client accepts a dispatched worker, in violation of the restrictions on the length of time for dispatch arrangements with respect to the place of business;

(d) a Client accepts a dispatched worker, in violation of the restrictions on the length of time for dispatch arrangements with respect to the individuals; or

(e) a Client engages in so-called "disguised contracting" (giso-ukeoi) (if a contract is nominally executed as a work contract, etc. and workers are dispatched to circumvent the statutory regulations for the Worker Dispatching Act, etc.).

A Client who is deemed to make an offer of employment may not withdraw that offer until 1 year from the date the illegal worker dispatching activity is terminated (Article 40-6, Paragraph 2 of the Worker Dispatching Act). If the dispatched worker accepts the offer of employment from the Client, an employment contract will be formed, based on the same working conditions that the dispatched worker worked under at the Worker Dispatching Business Operator at the time of the illegal worker dispatching activity.

第2章 就業規則の記載事項

就業規則の記載事項には，労働基準法上記載が求められている「必要的記載事項」と，使用者が任意に就業規則に記載する「任意的記載事項」とがあります。

さらに，就業規則の必要的記載事項には，いかなる場合も必ず記載しなければならない「絶対的必要記載事項」と，制度として実施する場合には記載する必要がある「相対的必要記載事項」とがあります。

1-1 絶対的必要記載事項

1-1-1 労働時間・休日等	
始業及び終業の時刻	始業と終業の時刻を記載する必要があり，「労働時間は1日8時間とする。」という記載では足りません。
休憩時間	休憩時間の長さ，休憩時間の与え方（一斉に与えるか，交代で与えるか）等について規定します。

Chapter II.

Work Rules Matters

Work rules matters consist of (i) "required matters," which are required to be included in the work rules pursuant to the Labor Standards Act, and (ii) "voluntary matters," which employers may, but are not required to, include in the work rules.

The "required matters," in turn, consist of matters that apply at all times under all circumstances (the "Required Matters") and matters that apply only when the employer implements certain matters as a particular system (the "Conditionally Required Matters").

1-1 Required Matters

1-1-1 Working Hours, Holidays and the Like	
Starting time and finishing time	Starting time and finishing time must be expressly provided. This requirement is not met if only the (amount of) "working hours" (e.g., 8 hours a day) is provided.
Breaks	The length of breaks, how breaks are taken (simultaneously or in turns) and the like must be provided.

休日	休日の日数，与える日（土曜日・日曜日等）について規定します。
休暇	法律上定められている年次有給休暇，産前産後休暇，育児介護休業等のほか，会社が独自に定める慶弔休暇等を含みます。
労働者を二組以上に分けて交替に就業させる場合においては就業時転換	交替制を採用する場合には，交代期日，交代順序等に関する事項を規定します。

1-1-2 賃　金

賃金（臨時の賃金等を除きます。以下同じ。）の決定，計算及び支払の方法	決定，計算の方法としては，賃金を決定するために考慮される要素（学歴，年齢，勤続年数等）及びこれらを用いた賃金の計算方法を規定します。 支払の方法としては，直接払い・銀行払い等を規定します。
賃金の締切り及び支払の時期	日給制，週給制，月給制等の区別及び，賃金の算定締切日と支払日を規定します。
昇給	昇給の時期・期間・昇給率・条件等を規定します。

1-1-3 退　職

退職に関する事項（解雇の事由を含む。）	定年，契約期間満了，休職期間満了，解雇合意等について規定します。

Holidays	The number of holidays and the dates there of (e.g., Saturday or Sunday) must be provided.
Leave	Leave includes statutory leave, such as annual paid leave, maternity leave, child care leave, family care leave and the like, and other forms of leave which employers may provide, such as congratulatory or condolence leave.
Shifts when employees work in two or more shifts	If the employer introduces shift work, then a rotation schedule, rotation ordering and the like must be provided.

1-1-2 Wages

Methods for determining, calculating and paying wages (excluding extraordinary wages and the like; hereinafter in this item the same qualification shall apply)	With regard to the method of determining and calculating wages, the elements that are considered in determining wages, such as academic record, age, years of service and the like and the method of calculating wages taking into account these elements must be provided. With regards to the method of payment of wages, the method by which wages will be paid, such as by direct payment, by means of bank transfer or the like, must be provided.
The dates for closing accounts for wages and for payment of wages	The wage payment period (e.g., daily, weekly or monthly), the dates for closing accounts for wages and the dates on which wages are paid must be provided.
Increases in wages	The timing, term, range, conditions and the like for an increase in wages must be provided.

1-1-3 Retirement

Matters relating to retirement (including grounds for dismissal)	Any retirement age, expiration of contractual term, expiration of a period of absence from work, termination agreement and the like must be provided.

1-2 相対的必要記載事項

1-2-1 退職手当	
適用される労働者の範囲	退職手当の適用の対象となる労働者の範囲について規定します。
退職手当の決定，計算及び支払の方法	決定，計算の方法としては，退職手当を決定するために考慮される要素（勤続年数等）及びこれらを用いた退職手当の計算方法を規定します。 支払方法としては，一時金で支払うのか，分割して支払うのかについて規定します。
退職手当の支払の時期	退職手当を受けられるようになってから，いつまでに支払われるかについて規定します。
1-2-2 臨時の賃金等	
臨時の賃金（退職手当を除く。）	支給事由の発生が不確定な賃金，例えば結婚手当，見舞金等について，支給条件，支給額の計算方法を規定します。
最低賃金額	最低賃金の定めを置くときは，その額を規定します。
1-2-3 食費，作業用品その他の負担	
食費，作業用品，その他社宅費等，労働契約によって労働者に経済的負担を課する場合は，負担額，負担方法等を規定します。	
1-2-4 安全及び衛生	

Chapter II. Work Rules Matters 67

1-2 Conditionally Required Matters

1-2-1 Retirement Allowance

The scope of employees covered	The scope of employees covered by the provisions concerning retirement allowance.
Methods of determining, calculating, and paying retirement allowance	With regard to the method of determining and calculating retirement allowance, the elements that are considered in determining the amount of retirement allowance (e.g., years of service) and the methods of calculating the retirement allowance using these elements. With regard to the method of payment of retirement allowance, methods such as lump sum payment, installments or the like.
Timing for payment of retirement allowance	When retirement allowance will be paid once an employee qualifies for the allowance.

1-2-2 Extraordinary Wages, etc.

Extraordinary wages and the like (excluding retirement allowance)	The conditions and methods of calculating certain ad hoc wages (e.g., marriage allowance, visitation allowance).
Minimum wage amounts	If the employer provides regulations concerning minimum wage, the amount of minimum wage.

1-2-3 Obligations Imposed on Employees to Bear Expenses pertaining to Food or Operating Equipment

If, pursuant to the employment agreement, the employer imposes an obligation on the employee to bear the burden of expenses for food, operating equipment or company housing, etc., the amount of each such obligation and the method for making such payment.

1-2-4 Safety and Health

安全・衛生を確保する上で特に定めを置く場合には，これに関する事項について規定します。

1-2-5　職業訓練

職業訓練を行う場合は，職業訓練の種類，内容，訓練期間，訓練を受ける者の範囲等を規定します。

1-2-6　災害補償及び業務外の傷病扶助

業務上の傷病について，労働基準法・労働者災害補償保険法の規定を上回る補償をする場合には，規定します。
業務外の傷病について，使用者が自主的に行う傷病扶助の制度があれば，内容を規定します。

1-2-7　表彰及び制裁

表彰の種類及び程度に関する事項	表彰の種類，事由，手続等について規定します。
制裁の種類及び程度に関する事項	制裁の種類（譴責，減給，出勤停止，降格，懲戒解雇等），事由，手続等について規定します。

1-2-8　その他

前各号に掲げるもののほか，当該事業場の労働者の全てに適用される定めをする場合においては，これに関する事項	労働者の全てに適用される可能性がある定めについて規定します。例えば，配転，出向，休職，福利厚生等があります。

If the employer provides regulations concerning safety and health, specific rules relating to safety and health must be provided.

1-2-5 Vocational Training

If an employer provides regulations concerning vocational training, specific rules setting forth the details of the type and term of training, the scope of employees for vocational training and the like must be provided.

1-2-6 Compensation for Accidents During the Course of Employment and Support for Injury or Illness Outside of Work

If the employer provides regulations concerning accident compensation for accidents occurring during the course of employment which exceed the standards stipulated in the Labor Standards Act and the Industrial Accident Compensation Insurance Act, these details must be provided.

If the employer provides regulations concerning voluntary support for injury or illness occurring outside of work, matters relating thereto must be provided.

1-2-7 Commendations and/or Sanctions

Matters concerning kind and degree of commendations	Matters concerning the kind, degree, procedure and the like for commendations must be provided.
Matters concerning kind and degree of sanctions	Matters concerning the kind (e.g., reprimand, pay reduction, suspension, demotion, disciplinary dismissal), degree, procedure and the like for sanctions must be provided.

1-2-8 Others

If the employer provides regulations applicable to all employees at the workplace in addition to those covered by the preceding items, matters relating thereto.	If the employer provides regulations applicable to all employees at the workplace, the employer needs to provide matters relating thereto in the work rules (e.g., (job) rotation, secondment, leave of absence or welfare benefits).

1-3　任意的記載事項

任意的記載事項の例としては，就業規則の基本精神や解釈適用に関する規定が挙げられます。上記1-2-8の事業場の労働者の全てに適用される定めとの区分についてですが，仮に事業場の労働者の全てに適用される定めであったとしても，労働条件・就業規律に関係しない事項は，任意的記載事項と解されています。

1-3 Voluntary Matters

Examples of voluntary matters are the fundamental spirit of the work rules and matters concerning the interpretation and application of provisions of the work rules. This category differs from the "Others" category in Section 1-2-8 above in that it includes only matters that are applied to all employees in the workplace, but that have nothing to do with employment conditions or work disciplines.

第2部
就業規則（本則）

Part II
WORK RULES

第1章 総　則

第1条　（目　的）
1.　本就業規則は，●●株式会社（以下，「会社」という。）の社員の就業に関する事項を定めるものである。
2.　本就業規則及びその附属規程に定めのない事項については，労働基準法及びその他の関係法令の定めるところによる。

> 就業規則の労働条件の最低基準を定める効力（労働契約法12条）及び法令・労働協約との関係については，第1部第1章1.をご参照ください。

第2条　（就業規則の遵守義務）
　　会社及び社員は，本就業規則及びその附属規程を遵守し，互いに協力して業務の運営に当たらなければならない。

第3条　（社員の定義）
　　本就業規則において，社員とは，第2章第1節に定める採用に関する手続を経て，期間の定めなく正社員として採用された者をいう。

第4条　（適用範囲）
　　本就業規則は前条に定める社員に適用する。契約社員，パートタイマー，臨時社員等として期間を定めて雇用される者又は無期転換社員（労働契約法18条の定めにより有期労働契約から無期労働契約に転換した者）については，本就業規則は適用しない。

Chapter I. General

Article 1. (Purpose)

1. These work rules (the "Work Rules") govern matters relating to the employment and work of the Employees (as defined below) of ●● K.K. (the "Company").
2. For any matters not provided for in the Work Rules and supplementary regulations hereto, the Labor Standards Act and other pertinent laws, ordinances or regulations of Japan shall apply.

> Please refer to Section 1, Chapter I. of Part I with respect to the role of work rules in ensuring a minimum standard of employment conditions (Article 12, Employment Agreement Act), and the relationship between the work rules and laws/collective labor agreements.

Article 2. (Obligation to Observe the Work Rules)

The Company and its Employees shall observe the Work Rules and supplementary regulations hereto, and manage the business in cooperation with each other.

Article 3. (Definition of Employee)

The Employees to which the Work Rules apply are those who are employed by the Company as full-time employees ("Employee(s)") for an indefinite term in accordance with the procedures regarding employment set forth in Chapter II. Section 1.

Article 4. (Scope of Application)

The Work Rules shall be applicable to the Employees described in the preceding article. The Work Rules shall not be applicable to any persons employed for a fixed term such as contract employees, part-time employees, casual employees or employees who have converted their Fixed Term Employment Agreement to a Non-Fixed Term Employment Agreement (employees who have exercised the right to convert their Fixed Term Employment Agreement to a Non-Fixed Term Employment Agreement pursuant to Article

本就業規則の適用対象としない就労形態の労働者（例えば，契約社員等）がいる場合には，当該就労形態の労働者のための就業規則を別途作成し，全ての就労形態の労働者について，適用ある就業規則を作成する必要があります。

▶労働契約法18条による無期労働契約への転換後に適用される就業規則（労働条件）

　労働契約法では，上記第1部解説の「7-1　有期労働契約の無期労働契約への転換」のとおり，有期労働契約が通算で5年を超えて繰り返し更新され，労働者が，5年を超えて更新された有期労働契約の契約期間内に当該有期労働契約が満了する日の翌日を労務提供開始日とする無期労働契約の申込みを行った場合，使用者は当該申込みを承諾したものとみなされます。

　正社員用の就業規則が有期契約社員のみを適用除外としている場合には，労働契約法18条の定めにより有期労働契約から無期労働契約に転換した従業員（無期転換社員）にも正社員用の就業規則が適用される可能性があります。そのため，無期転換社員を正社員と異なる労働条件で規律する場合には，無期転換社員には正社員用の就業規則が適用されないことを規定上も明確化するとともに，無期転換社員用の就業規則を別途整備し，又は，既存の有期契約社員用の就業規則を無期転換社員にも適用する前提で見直す等の対応をとる必要があります。

18 of the Labor Contract Act).

If there are employees to whom these work rules do not apply (e.g., contract employees), the employer needs to provide separate work rules for employees of such employment type. The employer needs to provide applicable work rules for employees of each employment type.
▶Work rules (Employment Conditions) applicable after conversion to a Non-Fixed Term Employment Agreement pursuant to Article 18 of the Labor Contract Act.
According to the Labor Contract Act, as stated in 7-1 Conversion of Fixed Term Employment Agreement to Non-Fixed Term Employment Agreement of Part I COMMENTARY above, where a Fixed Term Employment Agreement has been renewed repeatedly for more than 5 years, and the employee makes the employer, within the contract term of a Fixed Term Employment Agreement that has been renewed exceeding 5 years, an offer to enter into a Non-Fixed Term Employment Agreement pursuant to which the employee will commence providing services from the next date after the expiry of his/her Fixed Term Employment Agreement, the employer shall be deemed to accept such offer.
Where the work rules for regular employees exempt only the employees hired under Fixed Term Employment Agreements, such work rules may apply to employees who have exercised the right to convert their Fixed Term Employment Agreement to a Non-Fixed Term Employment Agreement pursuant to Article 18 of the Labor Contract Act. Therefore, if employers hope to employ employees who have exercised the right to convert their Fixed Term Employment Agreement to a Non-Fixed Term Employment Agreement under Employment Conditions that are different from the Employment Conditions for regular employees, employers should revise the work rules for the regular employees in order to clarify that such work rules does not apply to employees who have exercised the right to convert their Fixed Term Employment Agreement to a Non-Fixed Term Employment Agreement under their work rules. In addition, employers should take countermeasures such as establishing separate work rules for the employees who have exercised the right to convert their Fixed Term Employment Agreement to a Non-Fixed Term Employment Agreement, or revising the current work rules for employees hired under Fixed Term Employment Agreements in order for such work rules to apply to employees who have exercised the right to convert to their Fixed Term Employment Agreement to a Non-Fixed Term Employment Agreement.

第5条　（労働条件の変更）
　　本就業規則に定める労働条件等については，法令の制定・改廃又は経営上の必要性により変更することがある。

> 就業規則の変更手続については，第1部第1章2.をご参照ください。

第2章　人　　事

第1節　採　　用

第●条　（労働条件の明示）
　　会社は，労働者を採用するとき，採用時の賃金，就業場所，従事する業務，労働時間，休日，その他の労働条件を記した労働条件通知書及び本就業規則を交付して労働条件を明示するものとする。

◆　**労働条件の明示**
　労働者の採用に当たり，契約書を作成することは必ずしも必須ではありません。実際，正社員について契約書を締結しない例も多く見られます。しかし，労働基準法により，使用者は，労働契約の期間，労働時間，賃金等の下記の項目の労働条件を，書面の交付により明示する義務を負っています（労働基準法15条1項，同施行規則5条2項，3項）。
(1)　労働契約の期間に関する事項
(2)　期間の定めのある労働契約を更新する場合の基準に関する事項（期間の定めのある労働契約を更新する場合に限る）
(3)　就業の場所及び従事すべき業務に関する事項
(4)　始業及び終業の時刻，所定労働時間を超える労働の有無，休憩時間，休日，休暇並びに労働者を二組以上に分けて就業させる場合における就業時転換に関する事項

Article 5. (Change in Employment Conditions)
Employment conditions, etc. set forth in the Work Rules are subject to change due to the establishment, amendment or abolition of laws and ordinances, or due to management needs.

> Please refer to Section 2, Chapter I. of Part I with respect to procedures for changing the Work Rules.

Chapter II. Personnel Affairs

Section 1. Employment

Article[____] (Clear Statement of the Employment Conditions)
When employing an employee, the Company shall deliver a notice of employment that describes the wages, place of employment, contents of duties, working hours, days off and other initial employment conditions, and these Work Rules, and shall clearly state the employment conditions.

> ◆ **Clear Statement of the Employment Conditions**
> It is not absolutely necessary to enter into an employment agreement in writing when employing an employee. In practice, many companies do not execute an agreement in writing when hiring regular employees. Pursuant to the Labor Standards Act, however, an employer is required to clearly state the following employment conditions, including the employment agreement term, working hours, and wages, by providing a written statement of the foregoing (Article 15, Paragraph 1 of the Labor Standards Act; Article 5, Paragraph 2 and 3 of the Ordinance for Enforcement of the Labor Standards Act).
> (1) matters regarding the term of employment
> (2) matters regarding the criteria for the renewal of a fixed-term employment agreement (only in case of fixed-term employment agreement)
> (3) matters regarding the place of employment and contents of duties
> (4) matters regarding the start and finish time, whether there is overtime work, breaktimes, days off, holidays, and, where a company divides employees into

(5) 賃金（退職手当及び臨時に支払われる賃金を除く。）の決定，計算及び支払の方法，賃金の締切り及び支払の時期並びに昇給に関する事項
(6) 退職に関する事項（解雇の事由を含む。）

◆ **採用内定**

新規学卒者等を採用する場合，採用に先立ち採用内定通知を出すことが一般的です。採用内定の法的性質は，一般的に解約権を留保した労働契約の成立と解されており，内定取消しは契約の解約に当たり，通常の解雇と同様，正当な理由が必要となります。もっとも，実際に働き始めた後の解雇に比べて解約理由が広く認められ，例えば，健康状態の悪化により就業が困難となった場合等には内定取消しが正当と判断され得ます。なお，実際に雇用されるまでの一定の事由の発生（学校を卒業することや，一定の資格を取得すること等）が，内定の前提と解される場合には，当該内定は条件付きの労働契約と解される余地もあります。その場合には，解約権を行使することなく，条件の成就により当然に内定が取り消されることとなります。

◆ **募集・採用に当たっての差別禁止等**

労働者の募集・採用に当たっては，使用者の自由が広く認められていますが，性別による差別及び年齢制限は法律上禁止されています（男女雇用機会均等法5条，雇用対策法10条）。ただし，定年制を採っている場合や法令で年齢制限が定められている場合等一定の場合には，年齢制限禁止の例外が認められています（雇用対策法施行規則1条の3）。また，身体障害者又は知的障害者の雇用を促進するため，事業主には一定の雇用率に達する人数の障害者を雇用すべき義務が課されています（障害者の雇用の促進等に関する法律43条）。

two or more groups to have them work in shifts, matters regarding the shift-work system
(5) matters regarding the method of determination, calculation and payment of wages (excluding retirement allowance and special wages), closing date for wages, pay days, and wage raises
(6) matters regarding resignation (including reasons for dismissal)

◆ Hiring Decision
When hiring a new (college) graduate, it is common to notify such graduate with a "hiring decision" prior to the actual employment date. From a legal perspective, a "hiring decision" is generally interpreted as establishing an employment agreement while reserving the right of the employer to terminate. Revocation of a "hiring decision" is deemed to be a revocation of an agreement, and requires legitimate grounds, as are required for ordinary dismissal. However, there are more possible grounds to revoke a "hiring decision" in comparison to those for dismissing an employee after they have started working. For example, if a person's health deteriorates making it difficult to work, this might be considered to be a legitimate ground for the revocation of a "hiring decision." Further, if the occurrence of certain events are considered to be preconditions for the "hiring decision", and such preconditions must be met prior to actual employment (e.g., graduating from school, obtaining a certain qualification, etc.), then such "hiring decision" may be interpreted as an employment agreement subject to certain conditions precedent. In this case, the "hiring decision" would be automatically revoked when the conditions are/are not met without the need for the employer to exercise the right to terminate, and revocation rights need not be exercised.

◆ Prohibition Against Discrimination During the Offering of Employment and Recruitment
While an employer enjoys broad freedom in soliciting applicants for employment and recruiting, sex-based discrimination or age-based restrictions are prohibited by law (Article 5 of the Act on Securing, Etc. of Equal Opportunity and Treatment between Men and Women in Employment; Article 10 of the Employment Security Act). However, certain exceptions to age restrictions are permitted such as where a retirement age policy exists, or where applicable laws permit age restrictions (Article 1-3 of the Ordinance for Enforcement of the Employment Security Act). Further, in order to encourage employment of physically or mentally handicapped persons, a certain percentage of all employees must be disabled persons (Article 43 of the

第6条　(採用時の提出書類)
1.　会社は，入社希望者のなかから，選考試験に合格し所定の手続を経た者を社員として採用する。社員として採用された者は，採用の日から［10］日以内に次の書類を会社に提出しなければならない。ただし，選考の際に既に提出してあるものは，この限りでない。
　(1)　履歴書
　(2)　写真（［3か月］以内に撮影したもの）
　(3)　会社が適当と認める身元保証人［2］名作成の5年間有効な身元保証書

> 　身元保証書は，近親者等の第三者が，従業員が会社に与えた損害を填補することを誓約する書面です。また，身元保証書は，それに加えて，採用者が従業員としての適格性を有することを保証する趣旨を含むことがあります。

　(4)　住民票記載事項証明書

> 　プライバシー保護を図り，かつ差別を避けるため，年齢，現住所等の確認については，戸籍謄（抄）本及び住民票の写しではなく，「住民票記載事項の証明書」によって処理すべきこととされています。(昭50．2．17基発83号，婦発40号，昭63．3．14基発150号，平11．3．31基発168号)。

　(5)　(前職のあった者全てにつき) 厚生年金保険被保険者証 (又は年金手帳)，雇用保険被保険者証及び源泉徴収票
　(6)　(必要のある者のみにつき) 給与所得の扶養控除等申告書及び健康保険被扶養者届
　(7)　従業員通勤 (交通) 費用報告書
　(8)　誓約書

Services and Supports for Persons with Disabilities Act).

Article 6. (Documents to be Submitted upon Employment)

1. The Company shall hire applicants who have passed the recruitment test and completed the due formalities as Employees. The applicants who have been selected and hired as Employees shall submit the documents listed below to the Company within [ten (10)] days from the date of employment. However, this shall not apply to any documents that have been submitted at the time of the selection.

(1) Resume;

(2) Photograph (taken within [three (3) months]);

(3) Letters of guarantee (*Mimoto-hosho-sho*) which shall be effective for five (5) years and which have been executed by [two (2)] guarantors who are deemed appropriate by the Company;

Mimoto-hosho-sho is a letter in which an individual—for example a close relative, covenants that he/she provides assurance to the employer that he/she will cover damages suffered by the Company caused by the employee. In addition, *Mimoto-hosho-sho* sometimes includes a guarantee of eligibility of the applicant who has passed the recruitment test as an employee.

(4) Certificate as to the matters on the resident card (*Juminhyo-kisaijiko Shomei*);

In order to protect privacy and to avoid discrimination, the age and present address of an employee must be confirmed by a "Certificate as to the matters on the residence registry" (*Juminhyo-kisaijiko Shomei*), not through a copy of an individual's family register or residence register (Circular Notice, Kihatsu, No. 83, Fuhatsu No. 40, February 17, 1975, Circular Notice, Kihatsu, No. 150, Circular Notice, Kihatsu, No.168, March 31, 1999).

(5) Welfare Pension Insurance Certificate (or *Nenkin Techo*), Employment Insurance Certificate and Tax-Withholding Certificate (for those who have held prior jobs);

(6) Statement of the number of dependents for health insurance scheme and tax deduction purposes (if necessary);

> 第3部の書式をご参照ください。

(9) その他会社の指示する書類

> 採用時に調査会社による前歴調査を要求する例がありますが，一般に，使用者には採用の自由があるため，労働者の採否を判断するために一定の調査を行うことも許容されており，調査が社会通念上許容される妥当な方法でなされる限り，いかなる事項につき調査をするかは使用者の裁量に委ねられていると解されています。もっとも，昨今ではプライバシー保護に対する法制度が整備され，社会の意識も高まっていることから，労働者の人権やプライバシーにかかわる態様での調査や，職業上の能力，技能，適格性に関係のない調査については，慎重な対応が求められており，厚生労働省は，就職差別を防止するため，採用選考時に，宗教・思想や本籍・出身地，家族構成や家族の職業等の家庭状況に関する事項等への質問・調査を行わないよう指導しています。

2． 前項に定める提出書類の記載事項に変更が生じた場合，社員は遅滞なく書面で会社に届け出なければならない。

第7条（社員の個人情報等の取扱い）
　会社は，会社への提出書類に係る情報，健康診断に係る健康情報，その他の個人情報及びプライバシーに係る情報は，次の目的のために利用する。
　① 会社の労務管理，賃金管理，健康管理
　② 出向，転籍等のための人事管理

(7) Report on the Employee's commutation (transportation) expenses;
(8) Pledge letter; and

See the form in Part III.

(9) Any other documents as indicated by the Company.

Some companies require potential employees to provide an investigative report from an investigation agency at the time of employment. Generally speaking, employers have freedom to hire, and thus they are permitted to conduct a certain level of investigation to determine whether they wish to hire an individual. It is generally considered that, so long as the investigation method is socially accepted and reasonable, the employer has discretion to determine what items/factors to investigate. Due to the development of laws and regulations regarding privacy protection and its related social awareness, employers need to be careful when conducting investigations in a manner that affects the human rights or privacy of a potential employee, or conducting investigations that are not related to the employee's work performance, competence, or aptitude. The Ministry of Health, Labor and Welfare have advised that questions not be asked and investigations not be conducted regarding religious beliefs/thoughts, domicile/place of birth, family structure, occupation of family members and familial situations of employees at the time of employment.

2. If a change occurs in any of the items mentioned in the documents described in the preceding paragraph, the Employee shall, without delay, report such change to the Company in writing.

Article 7. (Handling of Employees' Personal Information, Etc.)
The Company shall utilize information regarding documents submitted to the Company and health information regarding medical examinations and other personal information and information regarding privacy for the following purposes.
   (i) Company's labor management, wage management, and health management
   (ii) Personnel management for secondment and transfer, etc.

> 　平成27年9月の個人情報保護法の改正により，取り扱う個人情報の多寡を問わず，全ての個人情報取扱事業者（個人情報のデータベース等を事業の用に供している者）において，個人情報を取得し利用する場合には，その利用目的を特定し，当該目的を予め公表していない限り，個人情報の取得の際に，これを本人に通知又は公表することが必要となりました（個人情報保護法15条１項，18条１項）。したがって，会社が社員の個人情報を取得するに際して，就業規則において，その利用目的を特定した上で，予め定めておくことも考えられます。なお，個人情報保護法上の個人情報とは，生存する個人に関する情報であって，当該情報に含まれる氏名，生年月日その他の記述等により特定の個人を識別することができるもの（他の情報と容易に照合することができ，それにより特定の個人を識別することができるものを含む。）又は個人識別符号が含まれるものを指します（個人情報保護法２条１項１号及び２号）。

第８条　（試用期間）

> 　試用期間中の労働契約は，解約権留保付労働契約であると解されており，労働者の適格性を判定する期間であることから，通常の解雇に比べて緩い要件で解雇が認められています。もっとも，試用期間を設けるか否か，また，試用期間中の労働契約をどのような契約内容とするかは，各事業場の実情に応じて定められるもので，必ずしも本条のような規定を設けなくても差し支えありません。

1.　新たに採用された社員は，採用の日から［３］か月間を試用期間とする。

> 　試用期間は３～６か月程度とすることが一般的です。試用期間の長さについて法定の期間はありませんが，合理性のない長期の試用は，労働者の地位を不安定にするため，公序良俗に反して無効とされることがあります。

Pursuant to the amendment of the Act on the Protection of Personal Information in September 2015, regardless of the quantity of personal information to be handled, it is now necessary for all personal information handling business operators (person providing a personal information database, etc. for use in business) to, in the case of acquisition and utilization of personal information except in cases where a utilization purpose has been specified and disclosed in advance to the public, inform a principal of, or disclose to the public, the utilization purpose (Article 15, Paragraph 1 and Article 18, Paragraph 1 of the Act on the Protection of Personal Information). Therefore, upon acquisition of employees' personal information by the Company, it may consider setting forth the utilization purpose in advance in the Work Rules after specifying it. Personal information under the Act on the Protection of Personal Information indicates information relating to a living individual and that containing a name, date of birth, or other descriptions, etc. whereby a specific individual can be identified (including that which can be readily collated with other information and thereby identify a specific individual) and that containing an individual identification code (Article 2, Paragraph 1, Item 1 and Item 2 of the Act on the Protection of Personal Information).

Article 8. (Probation Period)

During the probationary period, an employment agreement is interpreted to have reserved the right of the employer to terminate. Since the probationary period is the period during which the competence of the employee is judged, it is permissible to dismiss such employee during this period based on less strict requirements compared to ordinary dismissals. Whether or not a probationary period is provided, and the details of any probationary period in an employment agreement, can be determined according to the actual situation of each workplace. Therefore, employers need not provide a provision in this form.

1. A newly hired Employee shall be on probation for a period of [three (3)] months from the date of hiring.

It is common to have a three (3) to six (6) months probationary period. There are no legal requirements regarding the length of the probationary period. Please

2. 試用期間は，会社が適当と認めた場合は短縮し，又は設けないことがある。
3. 試用期間は，会社が必要と認めた場合は，［3］か月を限度として延長することがある。

> 　使用者が一方的に試用期間を延ばすことができるように規定しておくことも可能ですが，上記のとおり長期の試用期間は労働者の地位を不安定にするため無効とされることがあります。したがって，試用期間をある程度短期間で区切った上で試用期間の延長を可能とするか，又は無効とならない程度の期間で試用期間を設定して延長を規定しない，といういずれかの対応が望ましいと考えられます。本書では，前者の例を規定しています。また，当初の試用期間では当該労働者の能力を判断することが困難である等の合理的理由がある場合に限って，試用期間を延長するとする運用が妥当と解されています。

4. 会社は，試用期間中の者について，その能力，健康状態，勤務態度等を総合的に判断し，試用期間満了日までに本採用の有無を決定する。会社が，試用期間中の者を社員として不適格と認めた場合，会社は当該試用期間中の者を解雇することがある。

> 　試用期間中の解雇にも合理的理由は必要ですが，上記のとおり，通常の解雇に比べて緩やかな要件で解雇が認められます。会社としては，試用期間満了前に必ず当該労働者の評価を行い，社員としての適格性を確認することが重要です。

5. 試用期間は，これを社員の勤続年数に通算する。

note, however, that an unreasonably long probationary period would be deemed void on grounds of being offensive to public order and morality since it would destabilize an employee's position.

2. The Company may shorten or eliminate the probationary period if it deems appropriate.

3. The Company may extend the probationary period by a maximum of an additional [three (3)] months if it deems necessary.

It is possible to include a provision that enables the employer to unilaterally extend the probationary period. As stated above, however, long probationary periods would be deemed void since they would destabilize an employee's position. Therefore, it is advisable to either designate a relatively short term for the probationary period while reserving the right to extend, or designate a probationary period, without reserving the right to extend, of such a length that it would not be nullified. In addition, it would be appropriate to extend the probationary period only when there is a reasonable ground for extension such as where it is difficult to judge the employee's abilities during the original probationary period.

4. The Company shall comprehensively examine the ability, health condition, and attitude towards work of the Employee under probation and shall decide whether he/she shall be enrolled as an employee of the Company no later than the date of completion of the probation. If the Company deems the Employee under probation to be unqualified for employment, the Company may dismiss his/her employment.

Dismissal during the probationary period still requires reasonable grounds. However, as set forth above, it is possible to dismiss based on broader grounds. It is important for the company to evaluate an employee before his/her probationary period is complete, and to confirm his/her aptitude as an employee.

5. The probationary period shall be included in the length of service of the Employee.

第2節　人事異動等

第9条　（人事異動）

> 　　長期雇用を前提とする正社員については，業務上の必要性に応じて広範囲な配転が行われることが通常であり，判例上，使用者に幅広い配転命令権が認められています。就業規則に根拠規定がなくても，配転を命じることは可能ですが，権利義務関係の明確化のために就業規則に規定しておくほうが望ましいでしょう。労働者との間で職種限定又は職場限定の合意がある場合には，その限定の範囲でしか配転命令権がないと解釈されます。また，使用者に配転命令権があるとしても，①配転に業務上の必要性がない場合，②配転が不当な動機・目的でなされた場合，③配転により通常甘受すべき程度を著しく越える不利益が生じる場合には，判例上，配転命令が権利濫用として無効となります（東亜ペイント事件（最判昭和61年7月14日労判477号6頁））。
>
> 　　配転のうち転勤（勤務地の変更を伴う配転）については，厚生労働省雇用均等・児童家庭局「転勤に関する雇用管理のヒントと手法」において留意すべき点が紹介されており，例えば，労働者の仕事と家庭生活の両立に資する観点から，社内で転勤の態様に関する原則や目安を共有することや，転勤が難しいケースに対応するための仕組みを設けることが望ましいものとされています。また，育児介護休業法26条において，事業主が就労場所の変更を伴う配置の変更をしようとする場合に，これにより育児や介護が困難となる労働者がいるときは，その育児や介護の状況に配慮することが必要と定められています。

1. 会社は，業務の都合又は社員の健康状態により必要がある場合は，社員に対し，職場，部門又は職務の変更その他の異動を命ずることがある。社員は，正当な理由なくかかる異動命令を拒むことはできない。
2. 前項に従い異動を命ぜられた社員は，会社が指定した日までに赴任しなければならない。

Chapter II. Personnel Affairs   91

Section 2. Transfer including Job Rotation, Secondment and Demotion

Article 9. (Intercompany Transfer)

It is common for regular employees, who are retained with the presumption of long-term employment, to experience a broad range of job rotations depending on business necessity. Pursuant to court precedent, an employer has the right to rotate employees within a broad range of jobs. While it is possible to rotate employees despite the absence of any basis in the work rules, it is advisable to provide a provision regarding job rotations in the work rules in order to clarify the rights and duties of the employer and employees. If an employer and employee have agreed to limit the type of jobs/location of workplaces, then a job rotation can only be ordered within such limitations. Also, even if the employer has the right to order a job rotation, pursuant to court precedent, if it is unnecessary to rotate jobs for the business, if an employee is rotated based on unfair motives/purposes, or if a job rotation causes disadvantages which exceed ordinarily tolerable standards, then such job rotation instruction may be deemed to be an abuse of rights and thus void (Toa Paint Case (Judgement of the Supreme Court, July 14, 1986, p.6, Rodo Hanrei No.477)).

In relation to relocation that is job rotations followed by change in workplace, the matters to be noted are introduced in the "Hints and Methods for Employment Management on Transfer" of the Equal Employment and Children and Families Bureau of the Ministry of Health, Labour and Welfare. For example, from the viewpoint of contributing to balancing employees' work and family life, it would be advisable to share principles and standards regarding the manner of relocation followed by change in workplace, and to set forth a response structure in cases where relocation followed by change in workplace is practically difficult. Additionally, in Article 26 of the Act on the Welfare of Employees Who Take Care of Children or Other Family Members Including Child Care and Family Care Leave, it is stipulated that employers must, in making a change to assignment of an employee which results in a change in workplace, give consideration to the employee's situation with regard to childcare or family care, when such a change would make it difficult for the employee to take care of children or other family members.

1. The Company may order an Employee to transfer to another work location, department or job due to the Company's business requirements or the Employee's

第10条　(出　向)

> 　出向とは，会社(使用者)との労働契約を維持したまま，他の使用者の指揮命令下でその業務に従事することをいいます。労働者の予期に反する不利益が生じることもあるため，出向命令を行うためには，就業規則・労働協約上の根拠規定や採用の際の労働者の包括的な同意等が必要となります。出向命令についても，①業務上の必要性，②対象労働者の選定の合理性，③手続の相当性，④出向による著しい不利益等の事情から，判例上出向命令が権利の濫用として無効となる場合があります(労働契約法14条)。
> 　これに対し，転籍とは，元の使用者との労働契約を終了させて新たに他の使用者に採用される場合又は労働契約上の使用者の地位の譲渡を行う場合等，労働者が他の会社へ籍を移してその業務に従事することをいいます。転籍は，労働契約の終了又は労働契約上の地位の譲渡であるため，仮に就業規則に規定されていても一方的に転籍を命じることはできず，労働者の個別同意が必要になります。

1．　会社は，業務上の必要がある場合は，社員に対し，他の会社への出向を命ずることがある。社員は，正当な理由なくかかる出向命令を拒むことはできない。
2．　前項に従い出向を命ぜられた社員は，会社が指定した日までに赴任しなければならない。
3．　社員の出向の条件等については，別途これを定める。

health condition. An Employee may not refuse such transfer without a justifiable reason.

2. An Employee who is required to accept a transfer under the preceding paragraph shall take up the new position no later than the date specified by the Company.

Article 10. (Secondment)

> **Secondment means that an employee maintains an employment agreement with a company (employer), and is engaged in business under the instruction of another employer.** There may be some cases where situations disadvantageous to the employee arise contrary to his/her expectations; therefore, it is necessary that proper grounds for secondment orders be provided in work rules/collective labor agreements, or that comprehensive consent be obtained from employees at the time of employment. There are some court precedents under which a secondment order was deemed void as an abuse of rights, taking into consideration (i) business necessity (to be seconded), (ii) reasonableness in selecting a target employee, (iii) reasonable procedures, and (iv) disadvantage to employees caused by such secondment (Article 14 of the Employment Agreement Act). On the other hand, a transfer (*Tenseki*) means the termination of an employment agreement with a former employer and execution of an employment agreement with a new employer, or an assignment of the employer's position pursuant to an employment agreement. Thus, a transfer indicates that the employee has switched his/her position to work for another company. A transfer is deemed a termination of an employment agreement or an assignment of an employment position pursuant to the employment agreement. Therefore, a transfer may not be unilaterally ordered without the employee's consent even if such provisions exist in the work rules.

1. The Company may order an Employee to accept secondment to another company, due to the Company's business requirements. An Employee may not refuse to accept such secondment without a justifiable reason.

2. The Employee ordered to accept secondment under the preceding paragraph shall take up the new position at the place of secondment no later than the date specified by the Company.

3. Conditions of and matters related to such secondment shall be established separately.

第11条　（業務の引継ぎ）

　　第９条の人事異動又は第10条の出向を命ぜられた者は，後任者に対し指定された日までに業務の引継ぎを終了し，所属長にその旨を報告しなければならない。

第12条　（降　　格）

　　会社は，業務上の必要がある場合，役職罷免，職位の引き下げ等を命ずることがあり，また，社員に勤務成績不良等職務不適格の事由がある場合，資格等級の引き下げを命ずることがある。

> 　降格は職位及び資格等級上の格付けの一方あるいは双方を引き下げることをいい，人事権の行使としてなされる場合と懲戒処分としてなされる場合があります。本条は人事権の行使としてなされる場合について規定しています。降格のうち，職位の引き下げについては，人事権の行使として使用者の大幅な裁量が認められています（もっとも，この場合であっても降格が権利の濫用である場合には無効となります。）。他方で，資格等級上の格付けの引き下げについては，資格等級と給与額が対応している職能資格制度を採用している場合には，賃金上の不利益に直結するため，就業規則上の規定が必要であるとされています。また，国籍，信条，社会的身分を理由とする差別禁止（労働基準法３条），性別を理由とする差別禁止（男女雇用機会均等法６条），組合員を理由とする不利益取扱い及び支配介入の不当労働行為禁止（労働組合法７条１号）の禁止規定等に反する降格は無効となります。

Chapter II. Personnel Affairs   95

Article 11. (Transition of Duties)

An Employee who is ordered to transfer under Article 9 or to accept secondment under Article 10 shall complete the handing over of his/her duties to his/her successor no later than the date specified by the Company and inform his/her supervisor to that effect.

Article 12. (Demotion)

The Company may dismiss an Employee from his/her office or downgrade his/her position due to business necessity, and, if the Company determines that the Employee is no longer qualified to perform his/her duties for reasons such as poor service record, then the Company may downgrade his/her qualification level.

> **Demotion means to lower either or both the employment position and qualification level. It can be conducted either as an exercise of the right over personnel issues or as a disciplinary action. This provision provides for the exercise of the right over personnel issues. An employer has broad discretion to lower an employee's employment position, as it is an exercise of rights to manage personnel (nevertheless, if a demotion is deemed an abuse of rights, it can be nullified). Reducing the qualification level, in contrast, must be based on the work rules, because such action can directly lead to a disadvantage in wages where an employer applies ability-qualification-based policies in which the qualification level corresponds with wages. Further, demotions in breach of the following are prohibited and may be nullified: the prohibition against discrimination based on nationality, belief, or social class (Article 3 of the Labor Standards Act); the prohibition against discrimination based on sex (Article 6 of the Act on Securing, Etc. of Equal Opportunity and Treatment between Men and Women in Employment); and prohibition against unfair labor practices including disadvantageous treatment due to union membership and control/interference with the formation or management of a labor union by employees (Article 7, Item 1 of the Labor Union Act).**

第3節　休職及び復職

> 業務に就くことが不能又は不適当となるような事由が生じた場合であっても，解雇を猶予し，長期雇用を前提として採用した人材を維持することを目的として，休職制度が定められることがあり，多くの会社においてかかる制度が採用されています。休職制度は解雇猶予の趣旨で定められているため，休職制度が定められている場合において，休職制度を適用することなく行った解雇は解雇権濫用として無効と判断されるおそれがあります。

第13条　（休職事由）

> 休職制度は，解雇を猶予し，長期雇用を前提として採用した人材を維持し，復職後も活用することにその目的があるので，本条のように，例えば，会社への貢献度の少ない勤続1年未満の社員や試用期間中の者，復職の見込みのない者については，制度の対象外とすることも考えられます。

1．会社は，社員（試用期間中の場合，勤続年数が［1年］未満の者及び復職の見込みのない場合を除く。）が次の各号の一に該当するときは，休職を命ずることがある。
　(1)　業務外の傷病により，［3か月］を超えて欠勤を継続するとき又は業務外の傷病により休職した者が復職後［1年］以内に同一又は類似の事由により再び欠勤した場合
　(2)　社員の心身の不調，健康状態・体力の減退等により通常の業務に支障を生じると会社が判断するとき（前号とあわせて「私傷病休職」という。）
　(3)　傷病以外の自己の都合により，［1か月］を超えて欠勤を継続するとき（私事休職）
　(4)　議員等の公職に就いて，会社の業務と両立しないと認められるとき（公職休職）
　(5)　第10条に基づき他の会社に出向するとき（出向休職）
　(6)　その他特別の事情で休職させることが相当であると会社が認めたとき

Section 3. Leave of Absence and Resumption of Duties

Leaves of absence are very common among Japanese companies. It postpones the dismissal of an employee, who was hired with the intention of being employed for a long-term, and keeps him/her employed even when it is impossible or inappropriate for him/her to work. Since a leave of absence is provided for the purpose of postponing a dismissal, a dismissal may be void as an abuse of the right to dismiss an employee when the work rules provide for a leave of absence, and an employer dismisses an employee without first granting a leave of absence.

Article 13. (Reasons for Leave of Absence)

Since the purpose of a Leave of Absence is to postpone the dismissal and to keep and make good use of an employee employed, who was hired with the intention of being employed for a long-term, companies may exclude an employee whose contribution to the company is low, such as an Employee whose years of service are less than 1 year, an Employee under a probationary period, or Employees who have no prospect of resuming their duties as in this provision.

1. When an Employee (excluding an Employee under a probationary period, an Employee whose years of service are less than [one (1) year] or Employees who have no prospect of resuming their duties) falls under any of the following categories, the Company may order him/her to be placed on a leave of absence (*Kyushoku*):

    (1) when an Employee continues to be absent from work due to a non-work related injury or illness for a period in excess of [three (3) months], or when an Employee who is placed on a leave of absence due to a non-work related injury or illness is absent from work again for the same or a similar reason within [one (1) year] from the resumption of duties;

    (2) when the Company deems that an Employee is causing difficulties to business operations due to his/her mental and physical disorder, declining health or physical strength, etc., (together with the preceding category, a Leave of Absence for a Non-work Related Injury or Illness);

(特別休職)

> 刑事事件で起訴された場合に関して休職の条項を入れている例もありますが，当該条項は，解雇猶予や懲戒猶予の趣旨が含まれているため，当該条項が定められている場合には，社員が有罪であることが明らかな事案であっても，休職を行わずに行った解雇や懲戒の効力が否定されてしまう可能性がありますので，本規定例では定めていません。仮に，休職させることが適切な場合には第6号の特別休職の条項で対応することになります。

2．前項第1号及び第3号の欠勤は，欠勤の中断期間が休日も含め［1か月］未満の場合は，出勤日数を除いた前後の欠勤期間を通算し1つの継続した欠勤期間とみなすものとする。この場合，通算は複数回にわたっても行われる。また，この場合，次条第1項第1号の「欠勤開始時点」とは，最初の欠勤期間の開始時点をいうものとする。
3．第1項第1号及び第3号の適用においては，［5］時間以上の就業をもって出勤とし，それに満たない場合には欠勤とする。第1項第1号及び第3号に基づく欠勤期間は，年次有給休暇の取得により中断するものではない。
4．第1項各号の場合，社員は会社の要求する書類を速やかに提出するものとする。
5．会社は，第1項による休職の要否及び次条に定める休職期間の判断のために必要な場合は，社員に対し，会社の指定する医師の診断を受け，同医師の作成した診断書を提出することを命じることができる。
6．前項の診断書に関し，会社が診断書を作成した医師又は社員の家族等の関係者に対する面談や情報開示が必要であると判断した場合，社員はその実現に協力しなければならない。

(3) when an Employee continues to be absent from work due to personal reasons other than a non-work related injury or illness for a period in excess of [one (1) month] (Leave of Absence for Personal Reasons);

(4) when an Employee takes office as a member of the Diet or otherwise becomes a public servant, and it is deemed impossible for the Employee to concurrently perform his/her role in and service to the Company (Leave of Absence for Assumption of Public Office);

(5) when an Employee is seconded to another company in accordance with the procedures set forth in Article 10 (Leave of Absence for Secondment); or

(6) in other cases where the Company deems it necessary to grant a leave of absence under special circumstances (Leave of Absence for Special Reasons).

> **There are some examples of work rules that stipulate for a leave of absence to be applied to an employee who has been indicted for a criminal offence; however, this provision does not provide for such a leave of absence because, even if it is obvious that an employee is guilty, dismissal or disciplinary action may be void as an abuse of the right to dismiss or to conduct disciplinary action on the employee when the work rules provide for a leave of absence and an employer dismisses or subjects an employee to disciplinary action without granting a leave of absence since the work rules provide for a leave of absence, which is stipulated as having the purpose of postponing dismissal or disciplinary action. If it is appropriate to grant a leave of absence to an employee, such a case will be dealt with based on item 6, Leave of Absence for Special Reasons.**

2. In applying item 1 and item 3 in the preceding paragraph, when the discontinuation of a period of absence is less than [one (1) month] including holidays, the periods of absence before and after the discontinuation period (excluding numbers of attendances) are aggregated and considered to be continuous. In this case, such aggregation is done more than once and "the Commencement of Absence" prescribed in Article 14, Paragraph 1, Item 1 means the commencement of the first period of absence.

3. In applying item 1 and item 3 in paragraph 1, if an Employee is present for [five (5)] hours or more, the Employee is deemed to be at work that day, and otherwise the

第14条　（休職期間）
1.　休職期間は，前条に定める休職事由を考慮の上，次の期間を限度として会社が定める。休職期間の始期は休職発令日とする。
　(1)　私傷病休職

欠勤開始時点（前条第1項第1号の場合）又は社員の心身の不調，健康状態・体力の減退等により通常の業務に支障を生じると会社が判断した時点（前条第1項第2号の場合）の勤続年数	休職期間
［5］年未満	［3か月］
［10］年未満	［6か月］
［10］年以上	［1年］

　(2)　私事休職　　　［1］か月
　(3)　公職休職　　　その就任期間（ただし，最長［4］年）
　(4)　出向休職　　　会社の命令によるその出向期間
　(5)　特別休職　　　会社が認めた期間

Chapter II. Personnel Affairs 101

Employee is deemed to be absent that day. The period of absence in item 1 and item 3 in paragraph 1 shall not be suspended due to annual paid leave.

4. If any of the events in paragraph 1 occurs, the Employee shall immediately submit any documents that may be required by the Company.

5. If it is necessary in order to consider the necessity of a leave of absence provided in paragraph 1, and the period of a leave of absence provided in Article 14, the Company may order an Employee to be examined by a doctor designated by the Company and to submit a medical certificate from the doctor.

6. With regard to the medical certificate in the preceding paragraph, when the Company considers that an interview with or information disclosure is required from the doctor who issued the medical certificate or the Employee's family, the Employee shall cooperate to ensure the realization thereof.

Article 14. (Leave of Absence Period)

1. The Company shall, considering the reasons for the leave of absence set forth in the preceding article, decide the term of the leave of absence within the limits of the following periods (the commencement date shall be the date when the order for leave of absence is issued):

    (1) Leave of Absence for Non-work Related Injury or Illness:

Years of Service as of the Date of the Commencement of Absence (in case of Article 13, paragraph 1, item 1) or the date the Company deemed that the Employee was causing difficulties for business operations due to his/her mental and physical disorder, declining health or physical strength etc. (in case of Article 13, paragraph 1, item 2)	Period of Leave of Absence
Less than [5] years	[3 months]
Less than [10] years	[6 months]
[10] years or more	[1 year]

    (2) Leave of Absence for Personal Reasons:
      [one (1)] month

    (3) Leave of Absence for Assumption of Public Office:

2. 休職中の社員が，一時出勤した後，同一又は類似の事由により，休日を含め［1年］以内に再び休職する場合には，当該再休職期間は，復職前の休職期間の残期間とする。この場合において，会社が相当と認めるときは，当該残期間が［1か月］未満の場合は，1回に限り，再休職期間を［1か月］とすることができる。

> 休職事由が消滅することなく休職期間が満了する場合には，第16条第6項，第18条第2号により当該社員は退職することになります。復職，休職を繰り返す社員についても，本項で休職期間を通算することにより，同規定を適用することが可能となります。

第15条　（休職期間中の賃金）
　　休職の期間中の社員に対しては賃金を支給しない。ただし，会社が必要と認めた場合には，この限りでない。

第16条　（復　　職）
1. 会社は，休職期間を満了し又は休職事由の消滅した社員に対しては，復職を命じる。ただし，私傷病休職については，会社が特に定めた場合を除き（ⅰ）社員が休職期間の満了前の会社が指定する時期までに主治医の診断書及び主治医宛の医療情報開示同意書を添えて復職を申請し，（ⅱ）社員が会社の指定する医師の診断を受け，同医師において休職事由が消滅したと認め，（ⅲ）会社が，同医師の診断書を踏まえ復職可能と判断した場合に限り，復職を命じる。

The term of the relevant office, up to a maximum period of [four (4)] years.

(4) Leave of Absence for Secondment:
   The term during which the Employee is seconded under the order of the Company.

(5) Leave of Absence for Special Reasons:
   Such period as is deemed necessary by the Company.

2. If an Employee on a leave of absence returns to work, and is subsequently absent again for the same or a similar reason within a [one (1) year] period including holidays, the leave of absence period shall be the remaining period of the previous leave of absence. In this case, if the remaining period is less than [one (1) month], the Company may extend the period of the leave of absence for up to [one (1) month] only once.

If the reason for the leave of absence continues, even after the leave of absence term expires, the employee will be subject to a request from the company to resign pursuant to Article 16, paragraph 6, and Article 18, item 2. By aggregating the leave of absence periods pursuant to this paragraph, these provisions may be applied to an Employee who is on a leave of absence and returns to work repeatedly.

Article 15. (Wages during the Leave of Absence Period)

An Employee on a leave of absence shall not be paid. However, the Employee may be paid if deemed necessary by the Company.

Article 16. (Resumption of Duties)

1. The Company shall order an Employee who has completed the leave of absence, or, for whom the reason for the leave of absence is no longer applicable, to resume work. However, unless the Company deems it unnecessary, in the case of Leave of Absence for Non-work Related Injury or Illness, the Company shall order the Employee to resume work only when: (i) the Employee makes an application, no later than the date specified by the Company which is before the completion of the period of leave of absence, to resume work with a medical certificate from the doctor in charge and an

> 　近年，日本においては，精神疾患の事例が増え，本条を実際に適用する場面が増えています。復職の判断については，医師の診断を参考にしつつも最終的にはあくまで会社が復職の可否を判断するべきものとすることが重要です。

2. 　前項の診断書に関し，会社が診断書を作成した医師又は社員の家族等の関係者に対する面談や情報開示が必要であると判断した場合，社員はその実現に協力しなければならない。
3. 　会社は，復職可否の認定のため，社員に対し，医師の指示の下に，リハビリ勤務を実施することを命じることができる。
4. 　前項に定める復職可否の認定のために医師の指示の下に試行されるリハビリ勤務は，休職期間に通算され，復職就労には該当せず，その間の賃金については，休職前の水準によることなく，その就労実態に応じて，その都度会社が定めるところによるものとする。
5. 　復職後の職務は会社がその都度これを決定するものとする。社員が復職時に休職前と同程度の質・量・密度の業務に服することができず，業務の軽減・時間短縮・責任の軽減等の措置をとる必要がある場合には，会社はその状況に応じた降格・賃金の減額等の調整をなすことがある。
6. 　休職期間満了までに休職事由が消滅しない場合，当該社員は会社から当然に退職するものとする。

> 　休職期間が満了しても休職事由が消滅しない場合，期間満了をもって自動的に退職とするものが一般的であり，本項においてもその旨を定めています。本項とは異なり，休職期間が満了しても休職事由が消滅しない場合には解雇する旨を規定している例もありますが，その場合には，解雇予告等通常の解雇と同様の手続が必要となります。

attached written consent to the disclosure of medical information from the doctor in charge; (ii) the Employee is diagnosed by a doctor designated by the Company, and the doctor recognizes the reason for the leave of absence is no longer applicable, and (iii) the Company recognizes that the Employee can resume work based on the medical certificate from the doctor.

Recently, the number of cases of psychiatric disorders and cases where this provision has been applied has increased. The company should ultimately decide whether an employee may return to work, although it can also refer to the doctor's diagnosis.

2. With regard to the medical certificate in the preceding paragraph, when the Company considers that an interview with or information disclosure is required from the doctor who issued the medical certificate or the Employee's family, the Employee shall cooperate to ensure the realization thereof.

3. The Company may order an Employee to come to the office for rehabilitation under the direction of a doctor, so that the Company can decide whether the Employee can return to work.

4. The period for rehabilitation attempted under the direction of the doctor in order to obtain medical certification to resume work under the preceding paragraph shall be included in the leave of absence period, and is not considered a resumption of work. Wages during the period of rehabilitation shall be decided by the Company on a case-by-case basis in accordance with the Employee's working conditions, not on the basis of the standards before the leave of absence.

5. The Company shall determine the duties of the Employee on a case-by-case basis after he/she resumes work. When the Employee is unable to perform duties of a similar quality, quantity, and density as those before the leave of absence and it is deemed necessary to take measures to reduce the duties, shorten hours, reduce responsibilities, etc., the Company may make adjustments such as demoting the employee and reducing wages, etc. on a case-by-case basis.

6. If the Employee's reason for the leave of absence does not cease even after the

第17条　（勤続年数）
　　休職期間の勤続年数への通算は，原則として次のとおりとする。
　(1)　私傷病休職，私事休職，公職休職の期間は勤続年数に通算しない。
　(2)　出向休職の期間は勤続年数に通算する。
　(3)　特別休職の期間については，その都度定める。

第4節　定年，退職及び解雇

> 労働契約の終了については，第1部第1章4.をご参照ください。

第18条　（退職事由）
　　社員が，次の各号の一に該当するときは，当該日をもって会社から退職し，会社の社員としての地位を喪失するものとする。

completion of the period for the leave of absence, his/her employment with the Company shall be terminated automatically.

> If the reason for the leave of absence continues, even after the leave of absence term expires, it is common to provide that an employee automatically resign from the company at the expiration of the term of the leave of absence. This Paragraph stipulates this automatic resignation as well. However, some work rules stipulate that an employer may dismiss an employee if the reason for the leave of absence continues, even after the leave of absence term expires. In this case, the same procedures as for ordinary dismissal are still required, such as a dismissal notice.

Article 17. (Years of Service)

The leave of absence period shall, in principle, be counted in the Employee's years of service as specified below.

(1) The term of Leave of Absence for Non-work Related Injury or Illness, Leave of Absence for Personal Reasons, and Leave of Absence for Assumption of Public Office shall not be counted in the years of service.

(2) The term of Leave of Absence for Secondment shall be counted in the years of service.

(3) Whether the term of Leave of Absence for Special Reasons should be counted in the years of service shall be decided by the Company on a case-by-case basis.

Section 4. Retirement Age, Resignation and Dismissal

> Please refer to Section 4, Chapter I. of Part I regarding termination of employment agreements.

Article 18. (Reasons for Retirement)

When an Employee falls under any of the following items, he/she shall retire from the Company effective as of the relevant date, and shall lose his/her status as an Employee of

(1) 退職を願い出てこれを会社が承認したとき，又は退職届を提出して14日間を経過したとき。ただし，退職希望日が退職届を提出して15日間を経過したとき以降である場合は，当該退職希望日とする。
(2) 休職事由が消滅することなく，休職期間が満了したとき
(3) 死亡したとき
(4) 会社の取締役に選任されたとき（使用人兼務取締役の場合を除く。）
(5) 会社に連絡なく欠勤する期間が連続［30日］を経過し，会社がその所在を知らないとき
(6) その他本就業規則において別途定めるとき

第19条　（自己都合退職の手続）
1.　社員が自ら退職を希望するときは，原則として退職希望日の［30日］前，少なくとも2週間前までに，書面による退職届を所属長に提出しなければならない。

the Company.

(1) Approval by the Company of a request for retirement, or after fourteen (14) days have passed since the submission of a retirement notice. However, when the requested retirement date is more than fifteen (15) days after the submission of the retirement notice, the effective date shall be the requested retirement date.

(2) Completion of the period of the leave of absence where the reason for the leave of absence continues

(3) Death of the Employee

(4) Appointment as a director of the Company (excluding the case where a director concurrently holds a position as an employee)

(5) Passage of a period of [thirty (30) days] of consecutive absence without the Employee notifying the Company, and where the Company is not informed of the Employee's whereabouts

(6) As separately provided for in the Work Rules

Article 19. (Procedure of Voluntary Retirement)

1. When an Employee wishes to retire voluntarily, he/she must submit a written resignation to the supervisor of his/her department [thirty (30) days] prior to the desired date of retirement in principle, or at least two (2) weeks prior to the desired date of retirement.

民法627条は，労働者が解約申入れ（辞職）を行う場合に適用がありますが，その内容は以下のとおりです。

第1項	当事者が雇用の期間を定めなかった場合は，いつでも解約の申入れをすることができ，この場合，雇用は，解約の申入れの日から2週間を経過することによって終了する。
第2項	期間によって報酬を定めた場合には，解約の申入れは，次期以後に可能であるが，その解約の申入れは，当期の前半にする必要がある（労働者の退職の意思表示の日が給与計算期間の後半初日ならば，最大で46日（31日＋15日）後に退職することになる。）。
第3項	6か月以上の期間によって報酬を定めた場合には，第2項にかかわらず，解約の申入れは，3か月前にする必要がある。

なお，平成32年（2020年）4月1日施行の改正民法では，期間によって報酬を定めたか否かを問わず，労働者はいつでも解約の申入れをすることができ，解約の申入れの日から2週間を経過することによって雇用契約が終了するものとされました（改正民法627条）。

民法627条が強行法規か否かについては争いはあるものの，民法627条が強行法規であるとの見解に従えば，仮に，退職の届出から実際の退職日までの期間を同条の定める期間よりも長く設定したとしても，退職の届出から同条の期間を経過すれば，退職の効力が生じることになります。実務上は，業務引継ぎ等の手続上の必要性から，退職希望日の1か月程度前に届け出るべきことを定める例が多く見られますが，民法627条が強行法規であるとの見解に立てば，解約申入れから2週間の経過により退職の効力が生じることになることには留意が必要です。

本規定例は，原則として30日前までに退職の届出をしなければならないとしつつ，従業員が希望した場合等には，例外的に2週間前に届出を行うことでも退職は可能とすることにより，業務引継ぎ等の手続上の必要性と従業員の利益の双方に配慮し，事後的に紛争になることをできる限り避けることができるような形にしています。

Article 627 of the Civil Code shall apply where an employee resigns from his/her employment, and the contents of Article 627 of the Civil Code are as follows:

Paragraph 1	If the parties have not specified the term of employment, either party may request termination at any time. In such case, employment shall terminate on the expiration of 2 weeks from the day of the request to terminate.
Paragraph 2	If remuneration is specified with reference to a period, the request to terminate may be made with respect to the following period of time onward; provided, however, that the request to terminate must be made in the first half of the current period. (If the day on which an employee manifests the intention to resign is the first day of the second half of the wages calculation period, the employment shall terminate upon the expiration of up to 46 days (31 days plus 15 days) from the day on which the employee manifested the intention to resign).
Paragraph 3	If remuneration is specified with reference to a period of six (6) months or more, notwithstanding Paragraph 2, a request to terminate under the Paragraph 2 must be made three (3) months before the termination.

In addition, pursuant to the amended Civil Code to be enforced on April 1, 2020, an employee will be able to request termination of his/her employment at any time, irrespective of whether remuneration is specified with reference to a period, and the employment shall terminate on the expiration of 2 weeks from the day of the request to terminate. (Article 627 of the amended Civil Code).

Although there are different interpretations of whether or not Article 627 of the Civil Code is compulsory, according to the view that Article 627 of the Civil Code is compulsory, even if there is a provision which provides for a longer period from notice of resignation to the day of actual resignation than the period in Article 627 of the Civil Code, the resignation will become effective after the period in Article 627 of the Civil Code.

In practice, some companies provide that an employee who wishes to resign shall give approximately 1 month notice prior to the resignation date in view of the necessary handoff or other procedures. However, according to the view that

2. 退職届を提出した社員は，会社から別段の指示がある場合を除き，退職日まで通常の職務を遂行しなければならない。

第20条 （定年退職）

> 　定年とは，労働者が一定の年齢に達した時点で当然に労働契約が終了する制度をいいます。定年年齢は60歳以上でなければならず（高年齢者雇用安定法8条），性別により年齢差を設けることはできません（男女雇用機会均等法6条）。また，平成18年4月1日から，段階的に65歳までの高年齢者雇用確保措置をとることが事業主の義務となりました（高年齢者雇用安定法9条1項）。高年齢者雇用確保措置としては，①定年の引上げ，②継続雇用制度の導入，③定年制の廃止の3種類の手法がありますが，②継続雇用制度の導入がもっとも一般的であり，本規定例では②の例を規定しています。
> 　なお，上記②の継続雇用制度には，使用者が，一定の関係会社（例えば，親会社や子会社等）との間で，使用者の雇用する高年齢者であってその定年後に雇用されることを希望する者をその定年後に当該関係会社が引き続いて雇用することを約する契約を締結し，当該契約に基づき当該高年齢者の雇用を確保する制度が含まれるものとされています（同法9条2項）。高年齢者雇用安定法は，制度の導入を求めてはいるものの，労働者の希望に合致した労働条件の提示までは求めておらず，労働者が事業主又は高年齢者雇用安定法第9条第2項に定められる特殊関係事業主が提示する雇用条件に応じない場合に再雇用等を行わないことは直ちには違法ではないと解されてい

Article 627 of the Civil Code is compulsory, please note that the resignation will become effective 2 weeks after such notice has been provided.

In order to give consideration to both the necessity for handoff or other procedures, and for the benefit of the employee, and to prevent ex-post facto conflicts as much as possible, this provision provides that employees must give 30 days notice prior to a termination by resignation in principle, and where an employee makes a special request or other cases, he/she can apply for the termination of an employment agreement by giving 2 weeks prior notice as an exception.

2. Unless otherwise instructed by the Company, an Employee who has submitted his/her written resignation must perform his/her usual duties until the last day of his/her employment.

Article 20. (Retirement due to Retirement Age)

The retirement age system is a policy whereby an employment agreement automatically terminates when an employee reaches a certain age. The retirement age shall be no less than 60 years old (Article 8 of the Employment of Elderly Act), and an employer shall not provide different retirement ages for different sexes (Article 6 of the Act on Securing, Etc. of Equal Opportunity and Treatment between Men and Women in Employment). From April 1, 2006, it has become mandatory for employers to take measures to secure employment opportunities for older employees up to age 65 (Article 9, Paragraph 1 of the Employment of Elderly Act). There are 3 methods to secure employment opportunities for older employees: (i) raising the retirement age, (ii) introducing a continuous employment system, and (iii) abolishing the retirement age. Introducing a continuous employment system is the most common, as in this provision. For this purpose, a "continuous employment system" includes an arrangement in which employers ensure the employment of older employees by concluding an agreement with their parent or subsidiary company or any other affiliate company under which they are required to hire employees who have been hired by the original employers and who desire to be re-hired after reaching the retirement age (Article 9, Paragraph 2 of the Employment of Elderly Act). The Employment of Elderly Act requires employers and affiliate companies provided for in Article 9, Paragraph 2 of the Employment of Elderly Act to provide

> ます(厚生労働省「高年齢者雇用安定法Q&A(高年齢者雇用確保措置関係)」5-4)。

1. 社員の定年は満60歳とし，その誕生［日／日の属する月の末日／日の属する年度の末日］をもって退職とする。
2. 前項による定年により1年以内に退職することが予定されている者が，定年後の雇用を希望した場合には，定年後再雇用規程に基づき継続雇用(高年齢者雇用安定法に定める特殊関係事業主による継続雇用を含む。)する。

第21条 （普通解雇）

> 解雇については，第1部第1章6.をご参照ください。

1. 社員が，次の各号の一に該当するときは，普通解雇する。
   (1) 精神又は身体の障害等により，職務に耐えられないと認められたとき
   (2) 勤務成績又は職務遂行能力が不良で，就業に適しないと認められたとき
   (3) 勤務態度が不良で注意しても改善しないとき
   (4) 協調性を欠き，他の従業員の業務遂行に悪影響を及ぼすとき
   (5) 事業の縮小その他会社の側にやむを得ない事情があるとき
   (6) 試用期間中の者で，会社が社員として不適格と認めたとき
   (7) その他会社の社員として適格性がないと認められたとき

continuous employment opportunities, but it does not require them to propose conditions for employment in accordance with the employees' wishes, and it is understood that it is not automatically illegal not to re-employ or hire employees who have reached the retirement age in the event that such employees do not agree with the conditions proposed by the new employer (The Ministry of Health, Labor and Welfare "Q&A for the Employment of Elderly Act (relating to securing employment opportunities for the elderly"), 5-4).

1. The retirement age of an Employee shall be sixty (60), and the Employee shall be deemed to have retired on [his/her sixtieth (60th) birthday/the last day of the month to which his/her sixtieth (60th) birthday belongs/the last day of the fiscal year to which his/her sixtieth (60th) birthday belongs].

2. Where an Employee, who will retire from the Company within one (1) year by reaching the retirement age prescribed in the preceding paragraph, desires to continue to work in the Company, the Company or the Company's affiliate company (as described in the Employment of Elderly Act) shall re-employ the Employee according to the "Regulations for Re-employment after Retirement".

Article 21. (Ordinary Dismissal)

Please see Section 6, Chapter I. of Part I for dismissal.

1. Employees falling under any of the following items shall be dismissed:
   (1) If he/she becomes mentally or physically disabled or the like, and is considered unfit to perform his/her duties;
   (2) If the quality of work or performance of his/her duties is unsatisfactory, and he/she is considered unfit to work;
   (3) If his/her attitude towards work is unsatisfactory, and does not improve despite warnings;
   (4) If he/she is uncooperative, and negatively influences the performance of other employees;
   (5) If there is a curtailment of the Company's business operations or any other

2. 前項の規定により社員を解雇する場合は，会社は，30日以上前に予告するか，又は平均賃金の30日分の解雇予告手当を支払うものとし，予告日数は，解雇予告手当を支払った日数分だけ短縮するものとする。ただし，次に掲げる場合は，この限りでない。
(1) 試用期間中の者を試用期間開始後14日以内に解雇するとき
(2) 本人の責に帰すべき事由により解雇するとき
(3) 天災事変その他やむを得ない事由のため事業の継続が不可能となったとき

> 解雇を行う場合には，原則として，30日以上前の予告か30日分の解雇予告手当の支払（解雇予告手続）が必要とされていますが（労働基準法20条1項本文），例外的に解雇予告手続をとらなくて良い場合が，労働基準法20条1項但書及び同21条に規定されています。
> 試用期間中の解雇については，最初の14日間以内であれば，労働基準法20条で定められる解雇予告手続をとることなく即時に解雇することができますが，14日間を超えてから解雇する場合は解雇予告手続が必要となります（労働基準法21条4号）。
> なお，労働基準法20条1項但書に定められている事由（すなわち，上記第21条第2項第2号及び第3号の事由）により，解除予告手続なく解雇する場合には，当該事由について行政官庁の認定を受けなければなりません（労働基準法20条3項）。

unavoidable reasons on the part of the Company;

(6) If the Company considers the Employee under probation to be unqualified for employment;

(7) If an Employee is considered unqualified for employment for any other reasons.

2. Where the Company dismisses an Employee in accordance with the provisions of the preceding paragraph, it shall give advance notice to him/her at least thirty (30) days beforehand or pay him/her dismissal notice allowance in the amount equivalent to the Employee's average wage for thirty (30) days. Such period of advance notice shall be shortened by the number of days for which the payment of dismissal notice allowance has been made. However, this paragraph shall not apply to the following cases;

(1) the Company dismisses an Employee under probation within fourteen (14) days after the date of the commencement of the probationary period,

(2) the Company dismisses an Employee for reasons attributable to the Employee, and

(3) it is impossible to continue the enterprise because of a natural disaster or other unavoidable reason.

Where an employer dismisses an employee, in principle, more than 30 days prior notice, or payment of a dismissal notice allowance in the amount equivalent to the average wage for 30 days (dismissal notice procedure) is necessary (the main clause of Article 20, Paragraph 1 of the Labor Standards Act), however, exceptional cases where a dismissal notice procedure is unnecessary are stipulated in the proviso of Article 20, Paragraph 1 and Article 21 of the Labor Standards Act.

Procedures stipulated by Article 20 of the Labor Standards Act are unnecessary for dismissal during the probationary period provided it occurs within the first 14 days and the dismissal can be made immediately. If the dismissal occurs after the first 14 days, however, the dismissal notice procedure is necessary (Article 21, Paragraph 1 of the Labor Standards Act).

Where the employer dismisses an employee without the dismissal notice procedure for reasons stipulated in the proviso of Article 20, Paragraph 1 of the Labor Standards Act (that is, reasons stipulated in item 2 and 3, Paragraph 2, Article 21 above), the employer must obtain the approval of the authorities with

第22条 　（解雇制限）
　1．　会社は，社員が次の各号の一に該当する期間中は，解雇しない。
　(1)　業務上負傷し又は疾病にかかり，療養のために休職する期間及びその後30日間。ただし，社員が，業務上の傷病による療養開始後３年を経過しても治癒せず，労働基準法に基づき打切補償を受領したとき，又は労働者災害補償保険法に基づき療養開始後３年を経過した日において傷病補償年金を受けているとき若しくはその日以後同年金を受けることとなったときは，この限りでない。
　(2)　第44条に定める産前産後の女子社員が休業する期間及びその後30日間。
　2．　前項の規定にかかわらず，会社は，前項に定める期間中に，天災事変その他やむを得ない事由により事業の継続が不可能になった場合は，社員を解雇することができる。

> 　法律上，上記１項に記載されている場合には解雇が禁止されています（労働基準法19条）。
> 　なお，労働基準法19条1項但書後段に定められている事由（すなわち，上記第22条第２項の事由）により解雇する場合には，当該事由について行政官庁の認定を受けなければなりません（労働基準法19条2項）。

第23条 　（業務引継ぎ）
　社員が退職する又は解雇されるときは，会社が指定する日までに，会社が指

Chapter II. Personnel Affairs 119

respect to the reason in question (Article 20, paragraph 3 of the Labor Standards Act).

Article 22. (Restrictions on Dismissal)
1. The Company shall not dismiss an Employee during any of the following periods.
   (1) During the period of his/her leave of absence for medical treatment for work-related injury or disease and for thirty (30) days thereafter. However, if the Employee fails to recover within three (3) years from the date of the commencement of the medical treatment due to a work-related injury or illness, and receives compensation for discontinuance under the Labor Standards Act; or is receiving an illness and injury compensation pension on the day three (3) years after the date of the commencement of medical treatment or becomes eligible to receive such pension after such date under the Industrial Accident Compensation Insurance Act.
   (2) During the period of the leave of absence of a female Employee before and after childbirth as prescribed in Article 44 and for thirty (30) days thereafter.
2. Notwithstanding the preceding paragraph, the Company may dismiss an Employee where it is impossible to continue the enterprise because of a natural disaster or other unavoidable reason within the period set forth in the preceding Paragraph.

Dismissals in the situations stipulated in Paragraph 1 are prohibited by law (Article 19 of the Labor Standards Act).
Where the employer dismisses an employee for reasons stipulated in the second sentence of the provison of Article 19, Paragraph 1 of the Labor Standards Act (that is, reasons stipulated in Paragraph 2, Article 22 above), the employer must obtain the approval of the authorities with respect to the reason in question (Article 19, paragraph 2 of the Labor Standards Act).

Article 23. (Transition of Duties)
An Employee who resigns, retires or is dismissed shall complete the handing over of his/

定する者に完全に業務の引継ぎをしなければならない。

第24条　（社員の会社に対する義務）
1. 　社員が退職し又は解雇されたときは，社員は速やかに身分証明証，健康保険被保険者証及び会社から貸与された財産又は物品の全てを返却するものとする。返却されない品目につき会社は社員に対し補償を求めることがある。
2. 　退職し又は解雇された社員は，その在職中に行った自己の職務に関する責任を免れないものとする。
3. 　退職し又は解雇された社員は，在職中に知り得た機密情報を第三者に開示してはならず，また会社の要請に基づき，機密保持に関する誓約書を提出するものとする。
4. 　退職し又は解雇された社員は，退職後においても会社の営業秘密その他会社の利益を害する不当な競業行為を行ってはならない。

> 退職後の競業避止・秘密保持については，第1部第1章8.及び第3部の書式をご参照ください。

her duties to his/her successor designated by the Company no later than the date designated by the Company.

Article 24. (Employee's Obligations to the Company)

1. When an Employee resigns, retires or is dismissed, he/she shall immediately return his/her company identification card, health insurance certificate and any other property or articles loaned to him/her by the Company. The Company may claim compensation for any items which are not returned by the Employee.
2. An Employee shall not be released, after his/her retirement or dismissal, from any liability arising from his/her conduct during his/her employment with the Company.
3. An Employee shall not, after his/her retirement or dismissal, disclose to any third party any confidential information which he/she has obtained or may have obtained during his/her employment with the Company, and shall submit a pledge of confidentiality upon the Company's request.
4. An Employee shall not engage in competitive acts that are detrimental to trade secrets or other interests of the Company after his/her retirement or dismissal.

See Section 8, Chapter I. of Part I regarding the covenant not to compete/ confidentiality obligations after resignation/retirement.
See the form in Part III.

第3章　勤　　務

第1節　労働時間，休憩及び休日

第25条　（労働時間）
1. 所定労働時間は，原則として1日［8時間］，1週［40時間］とする。ただし，これには次項に定める休憩時間は含まれない。

> 労働基準法32条は，労働時間の長さについて，原則として1日8時間，1週40時間を上限と定めており，これを法定労働時間といいます。これに対し，労働契約において定められた始業時から終業時までの時間から所定の休憩時間を差し引いた時間が所定労働時間であり，所定労働時間は法定労働時間の範囲内で自由に定めることができます。所定労働時間が法定労働時間よりも短く定められている場合，労働基準法上は，法定労働時間を超えた労働（いわゆる法外残業）のみが時間外労働として割増賃金支払の対象となり，所定労働時間を超えて法定労働時間までの時間における労働（いわゆる法内残業）については通常の賃金を支払えばよいこととなっています。

2. 社員の通常の始業及び終業の時刻並びに休憩時間は次のとおりとする。ただし，業務の都合その他やむを得ない事情により，当該労働日の所定労働時間の範囲内で，社員の全部又は一部についてこれを変更することがある。
   (1)　始業時刻　　　午前［9時00分］
   (2)　終業時刻　　　午後［6時00分］
   (3)　休憩時間　　　［正午］から［午後1時00分］まで
3. 始業時刻とは，所定の就業場所で業務（実作業）を開始する時刻をいい，終業時刻とは，業務（実作業）を終了する時刻をいう。
4. 会社は，休憩時間を一斉に与える。ただし，休憩時間の付与に関し，当該事業場に労働者の過半数で組織する労働組合がある場合においてはその労働組合，労働者の過半数で組織する労働組合がない場合においては労働

Chapter III. Performance of Duties

Section 1. Working Hours, Breaks and Holidays

Article 25. (Working Hours)

1. Designated working hours shall be in principle [eight (8)] hours a day, and [forty (40)] hours a week. However, such working hours do not include the break prescribed in the following paragraph.

> **Pursuant to Article 32 of the Labor Standards Act, (8) hours per day, 40 hours per week are stipulated as working hours. This is commonly referred to as "statutory working hours." In contrast, "designated working hours" indicates the period from starting time to finishing time provided in an employment agreement, minus break. Designated working hours may be freely decided provided they are within the scope of statutory working hours. If designated working hours are shorter than statutory working hours, only work during hours which exceed statutory working hours is considered overtime work. Therefore, an employer need only pay ordinary wages for hours which exceed designated working hours but that are within statutory working hours.**

2. The regular starting time, finishing time, and break for Employees shall be as provided below. However, the Company may make changes within the designated working hours of a particular day for all or a portion of the Employees in the case of business necessity or other unavoidable events.
   (1) Starting Time   [9:00]
   (2) Finishing Time   [18:00]
   (3) Break   from [12:00] to [13:00]

3. The starting time means the time to start to engage in the tasks at the work place. The finishing time means the time to finish the tasks.

4. Breaks shall be given to all Employees simultaneously. However, breaks shall be given in rotation if a written agreement has been entered into between (a) a labor union organized by a majority of the employees at the workplace concerned (where

者の過半数を代表する者との間の書面による協定（以下，「労使協定」という。）があるときは，交替で与える。

> 1日の労働時間が6時間を超える場合には少なくとも45分以上，8時間を超える場合には少なくとも1時間以上の休憩時間を，労働時間の途中に与えなければなりません（労働基準法34条1項）。休憩時間は，原則として事業場全ての労働者に一斉に与える必要がありますが，労使協定を締結することにより交替で与えることができます（労働基準法34条2項）。
> また，一斉に休憩を与えることが困難な以下の事業については，例外的に，一斉に休憩を与える必要はありません（労働基準法40条1項，労働基準法施行規則31条）。
> (1) 道路，鉄道，軌道，索道，船舶又は航空機による旅客又は貨物の運送の事業
> (2) 物品の販売，配給，保管若しくは賃貸又は理容の事業
> (3) 金融，保険，媒介，周旋，集金，案内又は広告の事業
> (4) 映画の製作又は映写，演劇その他興行の事業
> (5) 郵便，信書便又は電気通信の事業
> (6) 病者又は虚弱者の治療，看護その他保健衛生の事業
> (7) 旅館，料理店，飲食店，接客業又は娯楽場の事業
> (8) 官公署の事業

第●条　（勤務間インターバル）
 1. いかなる場合も，労働者ごとに1日の勤務終了後，次の勤務の開始までに少なくとも，[11時間]の継続した休息時間を与える。[ただし，災害その他避けることができない場合は，その限りでない。]
 2. 前項の休息時間の満了時刻が，次の勤務の所定始業時刻以降に及ぶ場合，

such labor union is organized), or (b) a person representing a majority of the employees at the workplace concerned (where a labor union organized by a majority of the employees at the workplace is not organized) and the Company ("Labor-Management Agreement") with respect to giving breaks.

> If working hours in 1 working day exceed 6 hours or 8 hours, at least 45 minutes or at least 1 hour of break, respectively, must be granted during the working hours (Article 34, Paragraph 1 of the Labor Standards Act). In principle, breaks must be granted to all employees in a workplace simultaneously. However, breaks can be granted in shifts if it has been agreed as such in a labor-management agreement (Article 34, Paragraph 2 of the Labor Standards Act). It is not necessary to grant a break to all employees simultaneously, as an exception with respect to the following types of businesses where it is difficult to grant a break to all employees simultaneously (Paragraph 1, Article 40 of the Labor Standards Act, Article 31 of the Ordinance for Enforcement of the Labor Standards Act).
> (1) passenger transportation business or cargo transportation business by road, railroad, track, cableway, ship, or air;
> (2) sales business, distribution business, storage business or lease business, or barber business;
> (3) finance business, insurance business, intermediate business, broker business, collection business, guidance business, or advertising business;
> (4) film production business, film projection business, performance business, or entertainment business;
> (5) postal business, mail business, or telecommunication business;
> (6) medical business, nursing business, or health and hygiene business;
> (7) hotel business, restaurant business, hospitality business, or amusement business; or
> (8) businesses of public agencies.

Article [____] (Interval Between Working Days)

1. At all times, a continuous rest of not less than [11 hours] shall be granted to each of the Employees after finishing work for the day and before starting the next period of work. [However, this shall not apply in the case of natural disaster or other unavoidable circumstances.]

当該始業時刻から休息時間の満了時刻までの時間は労働したものとみなす。
3. 社員は，第1項の休息時間の満了時刻が，次の勤務の所定始業時刻以降に及ぶことが見込まれる場合には，所定の手続に従い，事前に所属長に報告するものとする。やむを得ない事情により事前に報告することができない場合には，社員は，遅くとも次の勤務の所定始業時刻までに所属長に報告しなければならない。

◆ 勤務間インターバル

　平成31年4月1日施行の改正労働時間等の設定の改善に関する特別措置法において，事業主は，前日の終業時刻と翌日の始業時刻の間に一定の休息時間（勤務間インターバル）の確保に努めなければならない旨の努力義務が課されることとなりました（改正労働時間等の設定の改善に関する特別措置法2条1項）。

　また，勤務間インターバルの具体的内容についての一般的な規制はありませんので，勤務間インターバル制度の制度設計については，事業主が自由に行うことができます（なお，自動車運転手については，「自動車運転者の労働時間等の改善のための基準（平1.2.9労告7号）」において，勤務終了後，継続8時間以上の休息時間を与えることとされています。）。そのため，勤務間インターバル制度を導入する際には，会社における休息時間に関する状況及び労働者のニーズ等を踏まえて，①対象者の範囲，②休息時間の長さ，③休息時間が次の勤務の所定始業時刻以降に及ぶ場合の勤務時間・賃金の取扱い，④適用除外の有無・範囲，⑤制度の拘束力の有無等を十分に検討して，勤務間インターバルの制度設計を行う必要があります。

　③休息時間が次の勤務の所定始業時刻以降に及ぶ場合の対応については，主に，(i)始業時刻と終業時刻を共に繰り下げるパターン，(ii)所定始業時刻から休息時間の満了までの時間は労働したものとみなす（始業時刻のみを繰り下げ賃金減額は行わない）パターン，(iii)始業時刻のみを繰り下げ賃金減額を行うパターンが考えられます。パターン(i)の場合は，さらに翌日以降の始業・

2. If the rest period set forth in the preceding paragraph extends beyond the prescribed time to start the next period of work, the Employees shall be deemed to have worked during the time between the prescribed starting time and the end of the rest period.
3. If the rest period set forth in paragraph 1 is expected to extend beyond the designated time to start the next period of work, the relevant Employee shall provide a prior report to his/her supervisor in accordance with the prescribed rules. If the Employee is unable to provide such prior report due to unavoidable reasons, the Employee shall provide a report to his/her supervisor not later than the designated time to start the next period of work.

◆ **Interval Between Working Days**
Pursuant to the amended Act on Special Measures for Improvement of Working Hours Arrangements to be enforced on April 1, 2019, an employer will be obligated to make efforts to ensure that regarding an employee there is an interval between working days, where a certain amount of rest between the finishing time on one day and the starting time on the next day is required (Article 2, paragraph 1 of the amended Act on Special Measures for Improvement of Working Hours Arrangements).
Further, because there is no general regulation regarding the interval between working days, an employer can freely design a system for interval between working days (please note that regarding drivers, "Criteria for Improvement of Working Time of Drivers" (Public Notice of the Ministry of Labor No. 7, February 9, 1989) requires that drivers be given more than 8 continuous hours to rest after finishing work). Accordingly, in adopting the system of interval between working days, an employer needs to design the system for interval between working days based on the conditions of rest at the company and employees' needs, etc., and by fully considering (i) the scope of target employees; (ii) the length of the interval; (iii) the handling of working hours and wages where the rest period extends beyond the prescribed time to start the next period of work; (iv) the applicability and scope of exception; and (v) existence or nonexistence of enforceability of the system.
Regarding "(iii) handling of working hours and wages where the rest period extends beyond the designated time to start the next period of work" above, there are the following three patterns for the system of intervals between working days (1) the pattern of deferring both the starting time and the finishing time; (2) the

> 終業時刻が後ろ倒しになることで，業務や生活に支障が生じる可能性があります。また，(iii)については，賃金減額を行うことについて労働者の強い反対が予想され，あまり現実的な制度とはいえません。本規定例では，パターン(ii)を採用していますが，この場合，必要性の乏しい残業を誘発しないよう，残業の必要性を厳格に確認するなどの管理が重要となると考えられます。なお，労働者が各日の始業・終業時刻を自ら決定できるフレックスタイム制（第２部第３章第１節参照）と勤務間インターバルを併用することも効果的と考えられます。

第26条　（休　　日）
1．　社員の休日は，次のとおりとする。
(1)　土曜日
(2)　日曜日
(3)　国民の祝日に関する法律に定められた休日
(4)　年末年始休暇（［12月29日］から［１月３日］）
(5)　夏期休暇（●月●日から●月●日）
(6)　その他会社が指定する日

> 法律上付与が義務付けられているのは毎週１日の法定休日のみであり（労働基準法35条１項），本項で法定休日以外の休日（所定休日）を付与しているのは実務慣行によるものです。使用者は，４週間を通じて４日の法定休日を与える変形週休制をとることも可能です（労働基準法35条２項）。

2．　会社は，業務上の都合その他必要があるときは，前項に定める休日を事前に他の日に振替えることがある。この場合，会社は，別の特定日を振替休日として指定するものとし，休日は４週間を通じ４日を下回ることはないものとする。

pattern of deeming that the employee has worked during the time between the prescribed starting time and the end of the rest period (i.e., only deferring the starting time without reducing wages); and (3) the pattern of only deferring the starting time and reducing wages. In the case of pattern (1), because it is possible that the starting time and the finishing time on the next day and subsequent days will also have to be deferred, business operations and the life of the employee may encounter difficulties. Further, in pattern (3), it is expected that the employees will strongly oppose the wage reduction; accordingly, this cannot be considered a very realistic system. This provision adopts pattern (2); however, in this case, strict confirmation of the necessity for overtime work and other appropriate management may become important so that overtime work that is rarely required might not be encouraged. Please note that it may also be effective to use flexible working hours that allow an employee to determine the starting time and finishing time of each day on their own (see Section 1, Chapter III. of Part II), and the interval between working days, together.

Article 26. (Holidays)

1. Holidays for Employees shall be as follows.

   (1) Saturdays;

   (2) Sundays;

   (3) National Holidays provided for in the Act on National Holidays;

   (4) New Year Holidays (from [December 29] to [January 3]);

   (5) Summer Vacation (from [MM DD] to [MM DD]); and

   (6) Any other days designated by the Company.

Legally, only 1 day per week must be provided as a statutory holiday (Article 35, Paragraph 1 of the Labor Standards Act). This provision provides holidays in addition to those required by law, based on common practice. An employer may implement a modified weekly holidays system by granting 4 statutory holidays within each 4 week period (Article 35, Paragraph 2 of the Labor Standards Act).

2. With prior notice, the Company may transfer the holidays prescribed in the preceding paragraph to another day if necessary for business or other reasons. In such case, the Company shall designate an alternate particular day as a holiday, and holidays shall be no less than four (4) days in a given four (4) week period.

> 本項で定める休日の振替は，所定の休日をあらかじめ他の日に変更して，当初休日とされていた日を休日ではなく労働日とする制度です。次条に定める，休日労働が行われた場合において，その代償として労働日の労働義務を免除するいわゆる「代休」とは異なる制度です。

3. 第１項に定める休日のうち，労働基準法35条の休日（法定休日）は，［日曜日］とする。ただし，社員の就労状況及び業務上の必要に鑑み，変更することがある。

> 就業規則上付与された休日における労働のうち，法定休日における労働のみが労働基準法の休日労働規制の対象となります。法定休日以外の所定休日における労働は休日労働とはならず，法定労働時間を超えた部分が時間外労働となります。平成22年４月１日施行の労働基準法改正により１か月60時間を超える時間外労働の部分にかかる割増賃金率が50％に引き上げられたこととの関連で（第58条の解説参照），１か月の時間外労働時間数に，労働基準法上の法定休日労働の時間は含まれず，法定休日以外の所定休日における労働時間はカウントされることから，就業規則上週休を２日付与している場合には，その一方を法定休日と明確に定めておくことが望ましいとされています。

第27条　（代　　休）
　　休日に８時間以上労働した場合は，本人の請求により，原則として当該休日の属する第51条第１項に定義する賃金締切期間中に１日の代休を与える。代休は無給とする。

> The transfer of holidays mentioned in this paragraph is a policy whereby a designated holiday is changed to an alternative date, and a designated holiday is changed to a working day. This is a different policy from the "compensatory holidays" policy mentioned in the next provision, under which an employee may be exempted from working on a working day as a substitute for working on holidays.

3. Of the holidays provided for in Paragraph 1, the holiday stipulated in Article 35 of the Labor Standards Act (statutory holidays) shall be [Sunday]. However, such holidays may be changed depending on the working conditions of the Employees and business requirements.

> With respect to working on a holiday which has been granted under the work rules, only work done on a statutory holiday is subject to the regulation regarding work on holidays under the Labor Standards Act. Working on designated holidays other than statutory holidays is not considered work on holidays, and only hours which exceed statutory working hours on such days are considered overtime work. Pursuant to the amendment of the Labor Standards Act on April 1, 2010, under which overtime work exceeding 60 hours in any month is subject to an extra wage rate of not less than 50% (see the commentary on Article 58), hours worked on statutory holidays as stipulated under the Labor Standards Act are not included in such calculation, while hours worked on designated holidays other than statutory holidays are included. Accordingly, if two (2) holidays are granted per week in the work rules, it is advisable to clearly provide that one (1) of those days is a statutory holiday.

Article 27. (Compensatory Holidays)
An Employee who has worked for eight (8) hours or longer on a holiday shall be entitled to take one (1) leave day in lieu of the holiday during the Wage Calculation Period, as defined in Article 51, Paragraph 1 hereafter, in which the holiday falls, in principle, upon his/her request. No payment shall be made for such leave in lieu of holiday.

> 　本条で定める代休は，休日労働をした場合に，それに対する代償として労働日の労働義務を免除する措置です。代休付与は法律上の義務ではなく，代休制度を設けないことも可能です。代休は使用者による一方的な労働義務の免除であり，法律上当然には無給とならないため，就業規則で代休は無給である旨を定めておく必要があります。法定休日における労働の場合，無給の代休を与えたとしても，割増賃金支払義務を免れるものではなく，休日労働の割増賃金分（35％以上）を支払わなくてはなりません。

> 　第25条及び第26条は，1日8時間労働，完全週休2日制とする最も典型的な週40時間労働制の規定例です。その他の労働時間制として，労働基準法上，必要に応じて下記のような制度を導入することも可能となっています。

第●条　（1か月単位の変形労働時間制）
1．　第25条第1項の規定にかかわらず，［○○（対象となる労働者の範囲）］の社員の所定労働時間は，［毎月1日］を起算日とする1か月単位の変形労働時間制によるものとする。
2．　前項の場合の所定労働時間は，1か月を平均して週［40時間］以内とし，各日，各週の労働時間は，［前月20日］までに勤務表を作成して，社員に周知する。
3．　第1項の場合の始業・終業時刻，休憩時間は次のパターンの組み合わせによることとする。
　　①　A勤（実働7時間）　　始業時刻　　午前9時00分
　　　　　　　　　　　　　　終業時刻　　午後5時00分
　　　　　　　　　　　　　　休憩時間　　正午から午後1時00分まで
　　②　B勤（実働9時間）　　始業時間　　午前8時00分
　　　　　　　　　　　　　　終業時間　　午後6時00分
　　　　　　　　　　　　　　休憩時間　　正午から午後1時00分まで
4．　1か月単位の変形労働時間制における休日は勤務表によって特定する。

Chapter III. Performance of Duties   133

Compensatory holidays, as stipulated in this provision, are provided to exempt an employee from working on a working day as a substitute for working on a holiday. This policy is not legally required, and it is possible to not provide such a policy. A compensatory holiday is a unilateral exemption by the employer, and it would not legally become an unpaid day automatically. Therefore, it is necessary to provide in the work rules that a compensatory holiday is unpaid. If an employee works on a statutory holiday, the employer remains obligated to pay extra wages for working on holidays (no less than 35%) even if an unpaid compensatory holiday is granted.

Articles 25 and 26 are the most common sections that provide for an 8 hour work day, and holidays of 2 days of weekends per week. An employer may also provide different working hour policies described below as needed pursuant to the Labor Standards Act.

Article [____] (Modified Monthly Working Hours)

1. Notwithstanding the provisions of Article 25, Paragraph 1, the designated working hours of the [(scope of applicable employee)] Employees shall be subject to the Modified Monthly Working Hours starting on the [first day of every month].

2. Designated working hours in the case of the preceding paragraph shall not exceed a one (1) month average of [forty (40) hours] per week, and the Company shall notify Employees of the working hours of each day and each week by preparing a work schedule no later than [the twentieth (20th) day of the preceding month].

3. The starting time, finishing time, and break in the case of Paragraph 1 above shall be one of the following patterns.

  (i)   Work type A (actual working hours: seven (7) hours)
        Starting Time   9:00
        Finishing Time   17:00
        Break   from 12:00 to 13:00
  (ii) Work type B (actual working hours: nine (9) hours)
        Starting Time   8:00

5. 次に定める事由が生じた場合には，社員に事前に通知した上で，第2項の所定労働時間を変更することがある。
 ⑴ ［事故，取引先の緊急発注等により納期が切迫した場合］
 ⑵ ［天災地変等緊急やむを得ない場合］

◆　1か月単位の変形労働時間制
　変形労働時間制は，業務の繁閑や特殊性に応じて労働時間の配分を容易にすることができる制度です。1か月単位の変形労働時間制とは，就業規則等又は労使協定により，1か月以内の一定期間を平均して1週間当たりの労働時間が40時間を超えない定めをした場合には，その定めにより特定された日又は特定された週に8時間又は40時間を超えて労働させることができるという制度です（労働基準法32条の2）。この場合，労使協定は労働基準監督署長に届け出る必要があります。この変形労働時間制を導入する場合には，就業規則において，変形期間の起算日や各日の始業・終業時刻及び各日・各週の労働時間を明確にしておくことが必要です。
　また，1か月単位の変形労働時間制の下において，いったん特定された労働時間の変更に関する条項を就業規則に定め，同条項に基づき労働時間を変更することは，労働基準法32条の2に反するものではありません（下記第5項参照）。もっとも，1か月単位の変形労働時間制の所定労働時間の変更条項は，労働者から見てどのような場合に変更が行われるのかを予測することが可能な程度に変更事由を具体的に定めていないような場合には，労働基準法32条の2の「特定」の要件に欠け，違法・無効なものになるというべきであり，例えば，「業務上の必要がある場合，指定した勤務を変更する」等の規定は，違法・無効なものであるとする裁判例がありますので，留意が必要です（JR東日本（横浜土木技術センター）事件（東京地判平成12年4月27日労判782号6頁））。

Chapter III. Performance of Duties   135

       Finishing Time   18:00
       Break   from 12:00 to 13:00
4. Holidays under the Modified Monthly Working Hours shall be specified by the work schedule.
5. If any one of the following events occurs, the Company may change the designated working hours set forth in Paragraph 2 with prior notice to the Employee.
   (1)   [a deadline is fast approaching because of an accident, urgent order from a customer, or other event]
   (2)   [a natural disaster or other urgent and unavoidable event]

◆ **Modified Monthly Working Hours**
A modified working hour policy facilitates the allocation of working hours depending on the fluctuation or specialization of tasks. A modified monthly working hours policy allows the following: pursuant to the work rules or a labor-management agreement, an employer may have its employees work on a certain day for more than 8 hours or during a certain week for more than 40 hours, so long as the average working hours per week during a certain period within one month do not exceed 40 hours (Article 32-2 of the Labor Standards Act). In such case, an employer needs to file such labor-management agreement with the chief of the labor standards supervision office. When introducing a modified working hour policy, the starting date for the modified term, the starting time/finishing time of the working day, and/or the number of working hours per day/per week need to be clearly provided in the work rules.
Under a modified monthly working hours policy, setting forth a provision to change working hours which have been designated previously, and changing the working hours according to the provision is not in breach of Article 32-2 of the Labor Standards Act (see Paragraph 5 below). However, please note that there is court precedent that indicates that a provision to change the designated working hours of a modified monthly working hours policy should be against the law and invalid as such a provision does not fulfill the requirement of "specification" provided by Article 32-2 of the Labor Standards Act, unless the provision stipulates a reason for the change so specifically that an employee can predict where and when the employer will change the designated working hours, and for example, a provision, such as "the Company may change the designated working hours due to business necessity", is against the law and invalid (East Japan Railway Company case, judgement of Tokyo District Court, April 27, 2000 (p. 6, Rodo Hanrei No. 782)).

第●条 （1年単位の変形労働時間制）
1. 第25条第1項の規定にかかわらず，会社は，社員に対し，1年単位の変形労働時間制に関する労使協定により，毎年4月1日から翌年3月31日までの1年間を平均して1週間当たりの労働時間が40時間を超えない範囲で，特定の週において40時間，特定の日において8時間を超える労働をさせることがある。
2. 前項の1年単位の変形労働時間制による，労働時間，始業・終業時刻，休憩時間及び休日等については，前項の労使協定の定めによる。

◆ 1年単位の変形労働時間制

　1年単位の変形労働時間制は，労使協定により，1か月を超え1年以内の一定期間を平均し，1週間当たりの労働時間が40時間を超えない範囲内において，特定された日又は特定された週に8時間又は40時間を超えて労働させることができるという制度です（労働基準法32条の4）。この場合，労使協定に，対象者の範囲，対象期間及びその起算点，特定期間（対象期間中の特に業務が繁忙な期間），対象期間における労働日及び労働日ごとの所定労働時間，有効期間を定め，労働基準監督署長に届け出る必要があります。本制度を導入する場合，就業規則では，各日の始業・終業時刻及び各日・各週の労働時間等を定めなければなりませんが，上記労使協定を引用する形でも足りるとされています。もっとも，このように就業規則に労使協定を引用する場合は，当該就業規則中に引用すべき労使協定の条文番号を明記し，かつ当該労使協定を就業規則の別紙として添付する必要があるとされている点に留意が必要です（平6.5.31基発330号）。なお，この制度を導入した場合でも，時間外労働等がある場合は，三六協定の締結・届出，割増賃金の支払が必要となります（三六協定等については第1部第1章4-2をご参照ください。）。

Article [____] (Modified Annual Working Hours)

1. Notwithstanding the provisions of Article 25, Paragraph 1, the Company may cause an Employee to work for more than forty (40) hours in a particular week and eight (8) hours in a particular day, provided that the work of the Employee does not exceed an average of forty (40) working hours per week in one (1) year (from April 1 to March 31 every year) under the Labor-Management Agreement with respect to the Modified Annual Working Hours.

2. The working hours, starting time and finishing time of work, break, and holidays, etc. under the Modified Annual Working Hours in the preceding paragraph shall be prescribed by the Labor-Management Agreement referred to in the preceding paragraph.

◆ **Modified Annual Working Hours**
A modified annual working hour policy allows for the following: pursuant to a labor-management agreement, an employer may have its employees work on a certain day for more than 8 hours or in a certain week for more than 40 hours, provided the average working hours per week during a certain period which is more than one month and no longer than one year does not exceed 40 hours (Article 32-4 of the Labor Standards Act). In such case, an employer needs to (i) provide the scope of target employees, the applicable term and its starting date, the specified period (i.e., the period during the applicable term when the work is especially busy), the working days during the applicable term and the designated working hours per working day, and effective time period, and (ii) file such labor-management agreement with the chief of the labor standards supervision office. When introducing this policy, the starting time/finishing time, and the working hours for each day and week need to be clearly provided in the work rules, but such provisions can be quoted from the labor-management agreement. However, in cases where such provisions can be quoted from the labor-management agreement, please note that it is necessary to stipulate a number of Articles in such labor-management agreement and attach it as an annexure to the work rules (Circular Notice, Kihatsu, No. 330, May 31, 1994). Further, even if such policy is introduced, if there is any overtime work, it is necessary to execute and file the labor-management agreement with respect to overtime work and work on holidays, and pay extra wages (see Section 4-2 of Chapter I., Part I regarding "Labor-Management Agreement with respect to Overtime Work and Work on Holidays").

第●条　（フレックスタイム制）
1.　第25条第１項の規定にかかわらず，会社は，労使協定により，フレックスタイム制を採用することがある。フレックスタイム制が適用される社員の始業・終業時刻については，第25条第２項の規定にかかわらず，当該社員の自主的な決定によるものとする。
2.　前項のフレックスタイム制による，始業・終業時刻及び休憩時間等については，前項の労使協定の内容に基づき別途定める規則による。

◆　**フレックスタイム制**
　フレックスタイム制とは，労働者が各日の始業・終業時刻を自ら決定して労働するもので，業務と個人生活の調和を図る制度です（労働基準法32条の３）。フレックスタイム制を導入するためには，就業規則で始業・終業時刻を労働者の決定に委ねる旨を定め，労使協定で下記の事項を定める必要があります（労働基準法32条の３，労働基準法施行規則12条の２第１項，12条の３）。
　①　対象者の範囲
　②　清算期間及びその起算日（フレックスタイム制の単位となる期間で，１か月を上限とする。）
　③　清算期間中に労働すべき総労働時間
　④　標準となる１日の労働時間
　⑤　コアタイム（労働者が必ず労働しなければならない時間帯）を設ける場合はその開始・終了時刻
　⑥　フレキシブルタイム（労働者がその選択により労働することができる時間帯）に制限を設ける場合はその開始・終了時刻
　上記の事項は労使協定で定めれば足りるものですが，実務上フレックスタイム制の運用ルールを定めておくことが望ましいため，上記労使協定の内容に基づき別規程を設ける形にしています。
　なお，平成31年４月１日施行の改正労働基準法により，清算期間の上限が１か月から３か月に拡張されます（改正労働基準法32条の３第１項）。清算期間が１か

Article [___] (Flexible Working Hours)
1. Notwithstanding the provisions of Article 25, Paragraph 1, the Company may adopt Flexible Working Hours under the Labor-Management Agreement. The starting time and finishing time of Employees to whom the Flexible Working Hours are applicable shall be determined by the respective Employee at his/her own discretion, notwithstanding the provisions of Article 25, Paragraph 2.
2. The starting time, finishing time, and break, etc. under Flexible Working Hours referred to in the preceding paragraph shall be prescribed in separate rules based on the content of the Labor-Management Agreement referred to in the preceding paragraph.

◆ Flexible Working Hours
Flexible working hours allow an employee to determine the starting time and finishing time of each day on their own and to balance work and private life (Article 32-3 of the Labor Standards Act). When introducing flexible working hours, the work rules need to provide that employees have discretion to determine the starting time and finishing time, and the following items need to be provided in the labor-management agreement (Article 32-3 of the Labor Standards Act; and Article 12-2, Paragraph 1, and Article 12-3 of the Ordinance for Enforcement of the Labor Standards Act):
① Scope of target employees
② Settlement period and starting date (time period which will be the unit for the flexible working hours up to 1 month)
③ Total amount of required working hours during the settlement period
④ Standard working hours for 1 day
⑤ Starting time and finishing time of the core time (hours when the employees are required to work) if there is any
⑥ Starting time and finishing time of the flexible time hours when employees may choose to work or not) if it is limited

While the above items need to be provided only in the labor-management agreement, from a practical perspective it is advisable to provide regulations regarding flexible working hours, and therefore, this provision is intended to provide separate rules based on such labor-management agreement.
In addition, the amended Labor Standards Act to be enforced on April 1, 2019, will extend the upper limit on the settlement period from 1 month to 3 months (Article

月を超える場合，1週平均50時間（清算期間を1か月毎に区分のうえ算定します。）を超えないことが必要であり（完全週休2日制の場合の上限時間については特例が定められています。），50時間を超えた分については法定割増賃金を支払う必要があります（同条第2項及び第3項）。また，清算期間が1か月を超える場合の上記労使協定は，労働基準監督署長に届け出る必要があります（同条第4項）。

第●条　（専門業務型裁量労働制）
1.　会社は，研究開発の業務等，業務の性質上その遂行を大幅に当該業務に従事する社員の裁量に委ねる必要があるため当該業務の遂行の手段及び時間配分の決定に関し具体的な指示をすることが困難である社員につき，専門業務型裁量労働制に関する労使協定を締結した場合には，当該労使協定に定める時間を労働したとみなすことがある。
2.　前項の裁量労働による適用対象となる業務，労働時間として算定される時間等については，前項の労使協定の内容に基づき別途定める規則による。

◆　**専門業務型裁量労働制**
　裁量労働制とは，業務の性質上，業務遂行の手段や方法，時間配分等を大幅に労働者の裁量に委ねる必要がある業務を労使で定め，労働者を実際にその業務に就かせた場合，労使であらかじめ定めた時間を働いたものとみなす制度です（みなし労働時間制）。裁量労働制には，デザイナーやシステムエンジニア等の専門的な業務に就く者を対象とした専門業務型裁量労働制と，事業運営の企画，立案，調査及び分析の業務を行う者を対象とした企画業務型裁量労働制があります。
　専門業務型裁量労働制を導入するためには，下記の事項を労使協定で定め，労働

32-3, Paragraph 1 of the amended Labor Standards Act). If the settlement period exceeds 1 month, the working hours must not exceed 50 hours per week on average (as calculated for each month of the settlement period) (there are special provisions for the maximum hours permitted in the case of a 5-day work week policy). The statutory extra wages must be paid for any portion exceeding 50 hours per week on average (Article 32-3, Paragraphs 2 and 3 thereof). Further, if the settlement period exceeds 1 month, the labor-management agreement must be filed with the chief of the Labor Standards Supervision Office (Article 32-3, Paragraph 4 thereof).

Article [____]　(Discretionary Working System for Expert Employees)
1. With respect to Employees engaged in work regarding which it is difficult for the Company to provide detailed directives on decisions concerning the means of accomplishment and allocation of time (such as research and development, etc.), because, due to the nature of the work, the methods for accomplishment must be largely left to the discretion of such Employees, if the Company has entered into a Labor-Management Agreement regarding the Discretionary Working System for Expert Employees, the Company may deem such Employees to have worked for the number of hours prescribed in such Labor-Management Agreement, regardless of the actual hours he/she has worked.
2. The type of work, hours to be calculated as working hours, etc. under the Discretionary Working Hours referred to in the preceding paragraph shall be prescribed in separate rules based on the content of the Labor-Management Agreement referred to in the preceding paragraph.

◆ <u>Discretionary Working System for Expert Employees</u>
A discretionary working system is a policy under which a labor-management agreement provides tasks which require the employee's broad discretion due to their nature, procedure/method for performing such work, or allocation of time. If the employee works according to such policy, the actual hours worked are deemed to be working hours provided in the labor-management agreement ("deemed working hours policy"). There are two (2) types of discretionary working systems: (i) discretionary working system for expert employees (i.e., designers, system engineers, etc.); and (ii) discretionary working system for planning employees who engage in

基準監督署長に届け出る必要があります（労働基準法38条の３第１項，労働基準法施行規則24条の２の２第３項）。
① 対象業務
② 労働時間としてみなす時間
③ 対象業務の遂行の手段及び時間配分等に関し労働者に具体的な指示をしないこと
④ 対象業務に従事する労働者の健康・福祉を確保するための措置
⑤ 対象業務に従事する労働者の苦情の処理に関する措置
⑥ 協定の有効期間（不適切に運用されることを防ぐため，３年以内が望ましいとされています（平15．10．22基発1022001号）。）
⑦ 対象業務に従事する労働者の労働時間の状況及び健康福祉・苦情処理の措置の実施状況に係る労働者ごとの記録を協定の有効期間中及びその後３年間保存すること

また，就業規則にも，専門業務型裁量労働制の定めをおく必要がありますが，本規定例では上記労使協定の内容に基づき別規程を定めることとしています。

第●条　（企画業務型裁量労働制）
1. 会社は，事業の運営に関する事項についての企画・立案・調査・分析等，当該業務の性質上これを適切に遂行するにはその遂行の方法を大幅に当該社員の裁量に委ねる必要があるため，当該業務の遂行の手段及び時間配分の決定に関し具体的な指示をしないこととする業務に従事し，当該業務を適切に遂行するための知識，経験等を有する社員につき，次項の企画業務型裁量労働制に関する労使委員会の決議があった場合には，当該決議に定める時間を労働したとみなすことがある。
2. 会社が前項の裁量労働制を導入するためには，事業場において，賃金，

tasks related to the planning, proposing, investigating and analyzing running of a business.
In order to introduce a discretionary working system for expert employees, an employer needs to provide the following items in a labor-management agreement, and file it with the chief of the Labor Standards Supervision Office (Paragraph 1, Article 38-3 of the Labor Standards Act, Paragraph 3, Article 24-2-2 of the Ordinance for Enforcement of the Labor Standards Act):
① target tasks
② hours deemed as working hours
③ the fact that specific instructions will not be given for methods and allocation of time to engage in the target tasks
④ measures to secure health/welfare of the employee engaging in the target tasks
⑤ measures to deal with complaints from the employee engaging in the target tasks
⑥ effective term for the agreement (in order to prevent inappropriate use of the system, a term of 3 years or less is considered to be advisable) (Circular Notice, Kihatsu, No. 1022001, December 22, 2003)
⑦ to record the situation of working hours of employees engaging in the target tasks and measures taken for health and welfare/complaints and preserve it separately for each employee during the effective term of the agreement and three (3) years thereafter
It is necessary to provide a discretionary working system for expert employees in the work rules. This provision is intended to provide separate rules based on the abovementioned items of the labor-management agreement.

Article [____] (Discretionary Working System for Planning Employees)

1. With respect to Employees who have sufficient knowledge and experience to perform work involving Company-management matters such as planning and drawing up plans, surveys and analyses, etc., for which, because the nature of the work requires the Company to widely entrust the method of performance of such tasks to the discretion of the Employees, the Company does not render concrete decisions on how these tasks should be performed and how to allocate the time for the performance of these tasks; if a resolution of a labor-management committee referred to in the following paragraph with respect to the Discretionary Working System for Planning

労働時間その他の当該事業場における労働条件に関する事項を調査審議し，会社に対し当該事項について意見を述べることを目的とする労使委員会を設置し，当該委員会がその委員の5分の4以上の多数による議決により，労働基準法の定める事項につき決議をしなければならない。また，前項の裁量労働制を適用する社員は，労使委員会の決議で規定された社員のうち，その適用について決議に基づく同意をした者とする。

3. 第1項の裁量労働による適用対象となる業務，労働時間として算定される時間等については，前項の労使委員会の決議の内容に基づき別途定める規則による。

◆ **企画業務型裁量労働制**
 企画業務型裁量労働制を導入するためには，労使委員会において，委員の5分の4以上の多数による決議で下記の事項を定め，労働基準監督署長に届け出ることが必要です（労働基準法38条の4第1項，労働基準法施行規則24条の2の3第3項）。

① 対象業務（事業の運営に関する事項についての企画，立案，調査，分析の業務を具体的に定めます。）
② 対象労働者の範囲（対象業務を適切に遂行するために必要となる知識・経験等を有する者である必要があります。）
③ 労働時間としてみなす時間
④ 対象労働者の健康・福祉を確保するための措置（具体的な措置内容）
⑤ 対象労働者の苦情処理の措置（具体的な措置内容）
⑥ 対象労働者の同意を得なければならないこと，及び同意しなかった労働者に対し解雇その他の不利益取扱いをしてはならないこと

Employees has been made, the Company may deem such Employees to have worked the number of hours prescribed in the resolution, regardless of the actual hours they have worked.

2. In order for the Company to adopt the Discretionary Working System described in the preceding paragraph, the Company must establish a labor-management committee in the workplace to investigate wages, working hours and other workplace conditions and make proposals to the Company on these matters, and the committee must resolve certain matters as prescribed under the Labor Standards Act by way of a four-fifths (4/5) or greater majority vote. The Employees to whom the Discretionary Working System in the preceding paragraph is applicable shall be those who are designated by a resolution of the labor-management committee and who have agreed to its application based on the resolution.

3. The type of work, hours to be calculated as working hours, etc. under the Discretionary Working Hours referred to in Paragraph 1 shall be prescribed in separate rules based on the content of the resolution of a labor-management committee referred to in the preceding paragraph.

♦ **Discretionary Working System for Planning Employees**
In order to introduce a discretionary working system for planning employees, the following items must be approved by the resolution of no less than four-fifths 4/5 of the committee members of the labor-management committee and filed with the chief of the Labor Standards Supervision Office (Paragraph 1, Article 38-4 of the Labor Standards Act, Paragraph 3, Article 24-2-3 of the Ordinance for Enforcement of the Labor Standards Act):

① target tasks (the type of planning, proposing, investigating, and analyzing tasks which will be conducted for running the business should be specifically stipulated)
② scope of target employees (these employees need to possess the necessary knowledge/experience to properly perform the target tasks)
③ hours deemed as working hours
④ measures to secure health/welfare of the target employees
⑤ measures to deal with complaints from target employees
⑥ the fact that the employer needs to obtain the consent of target employees and is prohibited from dismissing or treating disadvantageously employees

⑦ 決議の有効期間（不適切に運用されることを防ぐため，3年以内が望ましいとされています（平15.10.22基発第1022001号）。）
⑧ 対象労働者の労働時間の状況，健康福祉・苦情処理の措置の実施状況及び労働者の同意に係る労働者ごとの記録を決議の有効期間中及びその後3年間保存すること

　企画業務型裁量労働制は，対象労働者の同意が要件とされています。また，就業規則にも，企画業務型裁量労働制の定めをおく必要がありますが，本規定例では上記決議の内容に基づき別規程を定めることとしています。
　なお，企画業務型裁量労働制を導入した場合は，対象労働者の労働時間の状況及び当該労働者の健康・福祉確保の措置の実施状況について，決議が行われた日から起算して6か月ごとに1回，労働基準監督署長に報告しなければなりません（労働基準法38条の4第4項，労働基準法施行規則24条の2の5）。

第●条（高度プロフェッショナル制度）
1. 会社は，(i)高度の専門的知識等を必要とし，その性質上従事した時間と従事して得た成果との関連性が通常高くないと認められる業務に従事し，(ii)使用者との書面その他の方法による合意に基づき職務が明確に定められており，かつ，(iii)年間賃金が1075万円以上である社員につき，次項の高度プロフェッショナル制度に関する労使委員会の決議があった場合であって，かつ，本人が同意した場合には，第●条乃至第●条（労働時間，休憩，休日・深夜の割増賃金に関する規定）は適用しない。
2. 会社が前項の高度プロフェッショナル制度を導入するためには，事業場において，賃金，労働時間その他の当該事業場における労働条件に関する事項を調査審議し，会社に対し当該事項について意見を述べることを目的とする労使委員会を設置し，当該委員会がその委員の5分の4以上の多数による議決により，労働基準法の定める事項につき決議をしなければならない。
3. 第1項の高度プロフェッショナル制度を適用する社員は，労使委員会の

Chapter III. Performance of Duties 147

who do not agree
⑦ effective term of the system (in order to prevent inappropriate use of the system, a term of 3 years or less is considered to be advisable) (Circular Notice, Kihatsu, No. 1022001, December 22, 2003)
⑧ to record the situation of working hours of target employees and measures taken for health and welfare/complaints and preserve it separately for each employee during the effective term of the system and for 3 years thereafter.

A discretionary system for planning employees requires the consent of the target employees. It is necessary to provide for a discretionary working system for planning employees in the work rules. These Rules are intended to provide separate rules based on the abovementioned items of the resolution.

If a discretionary working system for planning employees is introduced, the actual hours worked by target employees and the status of measures to secure the health/welfare of such employees must be reported to the chief of the labor standards supervision office every 6 months, counted from the date such introduction is made (Paragraph 4, Article 38-4 of the Labor Standards Act, Article 24-2-5 of the Ordinance for Enforcement of the Labor Standards Act).

Article [____] (Advanced Professionals System)

1. With respect to Employees (i) who are engaged in jobs that require high-level expert knowledge etc. and for which the hours they spent and the results they attained are generally deemed not closely related by the nature of the work, (ii) whose duties are clearly stipulated based on an agreement, in writing or otherwise, with their employers, and (iii) the amount of whose annual wages is not less than JPY 10.75 million, the Company shall not apply Articles ● to ● (provisions regarding working hours, breaks, and extra wages for work on holidays and late hour work) if a resolution of a labor-management committee referred to in the following paragraph with respect to the Advanced Professionals System has been made, and the Employees also agree to the resolution.

2. In order for the Company to adopt the Advanced Professionals System described in the preceding paragraph, the Company must establish a labor-management committee in the workspace to investigate wages, working hours and other workplace conditions and make proposals to the Company on these matters, and the committee must

決議で規定された社員のうち，書面その他労働基準法施行規則で定める方法により同意をした者とする。ただし，当該同意をした者は，会社の指定する方法により，当該同意を撤回することができる。
4. 第1項の高度プロフェッショナル制度の適用対象となる業務，対象労働者の範囲，健康管理時間の把握，対象労働者に取得させる休日，その他当該業務に従事する社員に対して会社が講ずるべき事項等については，前項の労使委員会の決議の内容に基づき別途定める規則による。

◆ **高度プロフェッショナル制度**

平成31年（2019年）4月1日施行予定の改正労働基準法第41条の2により，一定の要件を満たす労働者について，労働基準法第4章で定める労働時間，休憩，休日及び深夜の割増賃金に関する規定を全て適用除外とする高度プロフェッショナル制度が新設されました。

高度プロフェッショナル制度を導入するためには，労使委員会において，委員の5分の4以上の多数による決議で下記の事項を定め，労働基準監督署に届け出ることが必要です（労働基準法41条の2第1項）。

① 対象業務（金融商品の開発業務，ディーリング業務，アナリスト業務，コンサルタント業務，研究開発業務等の厚生労働省令で定める業務に限られます。）

② 対象労働者の範囲（使用者との書面その他の方法による合意に基づき職務が明確に定められていること，年収が1075万円以上であることが必要です。）

③ 健康管理時間（対象業務に従事する対象労働者が，事業場内にいた時間と事業場外において労働した時間の合計時間）を把握する措置

resolve certain matters as prescribed under the Labor Standards Act by way of a four-fifth (4/5) or greater majority vote.

3. The Employees to whom the Advanced Professionals System described in paragraph 1 is applicable shall be those who are designated by a resolution of the labor-management committee and who have agreed to its application based on the resolution in writing or other manner provided by the Ordinance for Enforcement of the Labor Standards Act. However, the Employees who have so agreed may revoke their agreement in a manner prescribed by the Company.

4. Target tasks, scope of target Employees, control of working hours from the viewpoint of health management, number of holidays to be granted to target Employees, and other measures etc. to be taken by the Company for the Employees engaged in such tasks under the Advanced Professionals System referred to in paragraph 1 shall be prescribed in separate rules based on the content of the resolution of a labor-management committee referred in the preceding paragraph.

◆ **Advanced Professionals System**
Pursuant to amendment of Article 41-2 of the Labor Standards Act scheduled to be enforced on April 1, 2019, an advanced professionals system was newly established where employees who satisfy the certain requirements are exempted from all rules on working hours, breaks, and extra wages for work on holidays and late hour work as provided in Chapter 4 of the Labor Standards Act.
In order to introduce an advanced professionals system, the following items must be approved by the resolution of no less than four-fifths (4/5) of the committee members of the labor-management committee and filed with the Labor Standards Supervision Office (Paragraph 1, Article 41-2 of the Labor Standards Act):
① **target tasks (limited to the tasks provided by the Order of the Ministry of Health, Labor and Welfare, such as financial product development, dealing, analyzing, consulting, and research & development)**
② **scope of target employees (whose duties must be clearly stipulated based on an agreement with their employers, in writing or otherwise, and their annual wages must be not less than [10.75 million] yen)**
③ **measures to take control of working hours form the viewpoint of health management of target employees (a total of the hours the target employees**

④ 対象労働者に対して一定の休日を取得させること（1年間を通じ104日以上，かつ，4週間を通じ4日以上）
⑤ 対象労働者に対し，次のいずれかの措置を講じること
　㈰ 始業から24時間を経過するまでに11時間以上の継続した休息時間を確保し，かつ，午後10時から午前5時までの間に労働させる回数を1か月当たり4回以内とすること
　㈪ 健康管理時間を1か月当たり100時間以内，かつ，3か月当たり240時間以内とすること
　㈫ 1年に1回以上，連続2週間（労働者が希望した場合は，1年に2回以上，連続1週間）の休日を与えること
　㈬ 健康管理時間の状況等を考慮して労働者に健康診断を実施すること
⑥ 対象労働者の健康・福祉を確保するための措置（有給休暇の付与，健康診断の実施等）
⑦ 対象労働者の同意の撤回に関する手続
⑧ 対象労働者の苦情処理の措置（具体的な措置内容）
⑨ 同意をしなかった対象労働者に対し解雇その他の不利益取扱いをしてはならないこと
⑩ その他厚生労働省令で定める事項

　また，高度プロフェッショナル制度は，書面等により対象労働者の同意を取得することが要件とされています。さらに，就業規則にも，高度プロフェッショナル制度の定めをおく必要がありますが，本規定例では上記決議に基づき別規程を定めることとしています。

　なお，高度プロフェッショナル制度を導入した場合は，上記④乃至⑥の措置の実施状況を決議が行われた日から起算して6か月ごとに1回，労働基準監督署に報告しなければなりません（労働基準法41条の2第2項）。また，健康管理時間について，1週間当たり40時間を超えた場合のその超えた時間が1か月当たり100時間を超えた対象労働者に対しては，厚生労働省令で定めるところにより，医師による面接指導を行わなければなりません（改正労働安全衛生法66条の8の4第1項）。

were present at their workplace and the hours they worked outside of their workplace, hereinafter "health management hours")

④ granting a certain number of holidays to target employees (104 days or more per year, and four days or more per four weeks)

⑤ taking any of the following measures for target employees:
  (a) to ensure continuous breaks of 11 hours or more per 24 hours from the work starting time, and the times of working from 10 p.m. to 5 a.m. being not more than 4 times per month;
  (b) to restrict health management hours of not more than 100 hours per month and not more than 240 hours per three months;
  (c) to grant holidays once or more per year for two consecutive weeks (or if an employee desires, twice or more per year for one consecutive week); or
  (d) to provide medical examinations to employees considering the status of health management hours etc.

⑥ measures to secure health/welfare of the target employees (such as granting paid leave, and providing medical examinations)

⑦ procedures regarding revocation of the target employee's consent

⑧ measures to deal with complaints from target employees (specific content of measures)

⑨ the representation and warranty that the employer is prohibited from dismissing or treating disadvantageously target employees who do not agree

⑩ other matters provided by the Order of the Ministry of Health, Labor and Welfare.

An advanced professionals system requires the consent of the target employees in writing or otherwise. It is necessary to provide for an advanced professionals system in the working rules. This example provision is intended to provide separate rules based on the abovementioned resolution.

If the advanced professionals system is introduced, the status of measures taken as provided in ④ to ⑥ above must be reported to the Labor Standards Supervision Office every 6 months, counted from the date of such resolution (Paragraph 2, Article 41-2of the Labor Standards Act). In addition, with respect to health management hours, if a target employee's overtime hours [(i.e., hours worked in excess of forty (40) working hours per week) amount to more than one hundred (100) hours in any month], the Company shall provide such target employee with an opportunity of a consultation and guidance by a doctor as stipulated by the Order of the Ministry of Health, Labor and Welfare (Paragraph 1, Article 66-8-4 of the amendment of the Industrial Safety and Health Act).

第2節　事業場外労働及び出張

第28条　（事業場外労働及び出張）
1. 会社は，業務上の必要がある場合は，社員に事業場外労働又は出張を命ずることがある。
2. 社員が前項の命令により，所定労働時間の全部又は一部につき事業場外又は出張で労働した場合であって，労働時間を算定し難いときは，当該社員は第25条第1項に定める所定労働時間を労働したものとみなす。ただし，当該業務を遂行するためには通常所定労働時間を超えて労働することが必要となる場合においては，事業場外労働に関する労使協定において当該業務の遂行に通常必要とされる時間を定め，当該業務に関しては，当該業務の遂行に通常必要とされる時間を労働したものとみなす。

　労働者が使用者の事業場の外で業務に従事し，使用者がその労働時間を算定し難い場合には，一定の時間を労働したものとみなして取り扱うことができます（労働基準法38条の2）。「労働時間を算定し難いこと」とは，事業場の外で働く労働者について労働時間を管理する者がいないため，使用者において具体的な労働時間数を把握できないことを意味しています。次のような場合には，事業場外の労働であっても使用者による具体的な労働時間の把握が可能であり，「労働時間を算定し難いこと」の要件に該当しないこととされています（昭63.1.1基発1号）。
　① 何人かのグループで事業場外労働に従事する場合で，そのメンバーの中に労働時間の管理をする者がいる場合
　② 無線やポケットベル等によって随時使用者の指示を受けながら労働している場合
　③ 事業場において，訪問先，帰社時刻等当日の業務の具体的指示を受けたのち，事業場外で指示どおりに業務に従事し，その後事業場に戻る場合
　なお，みなし労働時間制には，休憩，休日，時間外労働，休日労働，深夜業等の労働基準法上の規制が適用されるため（昭63.1.1基発1号），例えば，

Chapter III. Performance of Duties   153

Section 2. Work Outside of the Workplace and Business Trips

Article 28. (Work Outside of the Workplace and Business Trips)

1. The Company may order Employees to work outside their usual workplace or make business trips as required for the Company's business.

2. Where an Employee has worked all or part of their designated working hours outside of their workplace or on a business trip following the order referred to in the preceding paragraph and such working hours are difficult to compute, such Employee shall be considered to have worked the designated working hours under Article 25, Paragraph 1. However, in the event that it is necessary for such Employee to work longer than the ordinary designated working hours due to the nature of the ordered work, a Labor-Management Agreement regarding Work Outside of the Workplace must designate the hours normally required to perform such work, and the Employee shall be considered to have worked such working hours.

> If an employee works outside of the workplace, and it is difficult for the employer to calculate such working hours, such working hours may be deemed to be a certain amount of hours worked (Article 38-2 of the Labor Standards Act). "Difficulty in calculating working hours" means the case where the working hours of such employee while he/she works outside the workplace cannot be monitored, hence the employer cannot keep track of the specific working hours. In the following cases, an employer can keep track of the specific working hours even if such work was conducted outside the workplace, and these cases do not fall under the category of "difficulty in calculating working hours" (Circular Notice, Kihatsu, No. 1, January 1, 1988):
> ① When several employees work outside the workplace in a group, and one of the group members can administrate the working hours of the other members
> ② When employees are working while receiving instructions from the employer at all times via a wireless device or beeper
> ③ When an employee receives at the workplace specific instructions regarding tasks for the day, including locations to visit and returning time to the workplace, attends to such tasks outside of the workplace pursuant to such instructions, and returns to the workplace afterwards
> Please note that since the provisions regarding breaks, holidays, overtime work

みなし労働時間が8時間を超える場合には，割増賃金の支払い及び三六協定の締結が必要になります。

また，在宅勤務，サテライトオフィス勤務，モバイル勤務等のテレワーク（労働者が情報通信技術を利用して行う事業場外勤務）により，労働者が使用者の事業場の外で業務に従事した場合において，以下の要件をいずれも満たす場合には，労働時間を算定し難いとして，事業場外労働に関するみなし労働時間制が適用されます（情報通信技術を利用した事業場外勤務の適切な導入及び実施のためのガイドライン）。

① 情報通信機器が，使用者の指示により常時通信可能な状態におくこととされていないこと（すなわち，情報通信機器を通じた使用者の指示に即応する義務がない状態であること）

② 随時使用者の具体的な指示に基づいて業務を行っていないこと

このうち，①の「使用者の指示に即応する義務がない状態」とは，使用者が労働者に対して情報通信機器を用いて随時具体的指示を行うことが可能であり，かつ，使用者からの具体的な指示に備えて待機しつつ実作業を行っている状態又は手待ち状態で待機している状態にはないことを指します。例えば，回線が接続されているだけで，労働者が自由に情報通信機器から離れることや通信可能な状態を切断することが認められている場合や，会社支給の携帯電話等を所持していても，労働者の即応の義務が課されていないことが明らかである場合等は「使用者の指示に即応する義務がない」場合に当たります。

and work on holidays and late-hour work, etc., of the Labor Standards Act will be applied to a deemed-working-hours (*minashi rodo jikan*) policy (Circular Notice, Kihatsu, No. 1, January 1, 1988), it is necessary, for example, to pay extra wages and execute a labor-management agreement with respect to overtime work and work on holidays (*saburoku kyotei*) if deemed working hours in one (1) working day exceed 8 hours.

Further, if an employee works outside of his or her usual workplace due to telework such as Work-At-Home, Satellite Office Work, or Mobile Work (employees' work outside their usual workplace using information and communication technology) and fulfills all of the following requirements, a deemed-working-hours (*minashi rodo jikan*) policy regarding work conducted outside the employee's usual workplace is applied as there is a difficulty in calculating work hours (Guidelines for Appropriate Introduction and Implementation of Work Outside Workplace Using Information and Communication Technology).

(i) Information and communication devices are not constantly available for communication, instructed by the employer (i.e., there is no obligation to immediately conform to the direction of the employer through information and communication device); and

(ii) Work is not conducted under the specific direction of the employer at all times.

Out of the foregoing, "there is no obligation to immediately conform to the direction of the employer" in (i) above means that the employers may provide specific direction to the employees using information and communication devices at any time, and the employees are not conducting actual work while waiting in preparation for specific direction of the employer, nor waiting idly. For example, cases where the communication lines are merely connected and employees may be freely removed from information and communication devices cutting off communicable status and cases where it is evident that the employees are not imposed with the obligation to immediately conform, even if they hold mobile phones, etc. supplied by the company, etc. fall under the cases where "there is no obligation to immediately conform to the direction of the employer."

第3節　時間外労働及び休日労働

第29条　（時間外労働，休日労働及び深夜労働）

> 労働時間・休日労働規制については，第1部第1章4-2をご参照ください。

1. 会社は，業務上の必要がある場合は，社員に対し，時間外労働及び休日労働に関する労使協定を締結し，第25条第1項に定める所定労働時間外における労働（以下，「時間外労働」という。），第26条第1項に定める休日における労働（以下，「休日労働」という。）をさせることがある。また，会社は，業務上の必要がある場合は，社員に対し，深夜（午後10時から午前5時までをいう。以下，同じ。）における労働（以下，「深夜労働」という。）をさせることがある。
2. 社員は，所属長の指示又は事前の承認に従い時間外労働，休日労働又は深夜労働を行うものとする。
3. 時間外労働，休日労働及び深夜労働については，第58条から第61条に定める割増賃金を，それぞれ支払うものとする。

> 使用者が労働者に時間外労働又は休日労働をさせた場合には割増賃金を支払わなくてはなりません。割増賃金率は下記のとおりです。
> ① 法定労働時間を超えて働かせた場合（時間外労働）：
> 　1か月60時間を超えない時間外労働については25％以上
> 　1か月60時間を超える時間外労働については50％以上（ただし，中小企業については当分の間適用が猶予されます。詳しくは第58条の解説をご参照ください。）
> ② 法定休日に働かせた場合（休日労働）：35％以上
> ③ 午後10時から午前5時までの深夜に働かせた場合（深夜労働）：25％以上
> ＊時間外労働が深夜に行われた場合には50％以上（①＋③），休日労働が深夜に行われた場合には60％以上（②＋③）となります。

Chapter III. Performance of Duties 157

Section 3. Overtime Work and Work on Holidays

Article 29. (Overtime Work, Work on Holidays and Late Hour Work)

For Regulations on Working Hours and Working on Holidays, please refer to Section 4-2 of Chapter I, Part I.

1. The Company may, due to business necessity, require an Employee to work for hours exceeding the designated working hours under Article 25, Paragraph 1 ("Overtime Work") or perform work on holidays under Article 26, Paragraph 1 ("Work on Holidays"), by entering into a Labor-Management Agreement with respect to Overtime Work and Work on Holidays. The Company may, due to business necessity, also require an Employee to work during late hours (i.e., from 22:00 to 5:00) ("Late Hour Work").
2. An Employee shall perform Overtime Work, Work on Holidays, or Late Hour Work in the workplace following instructions or upon prior approval by his/her supervisor.
3. The Company shall pay the extra wages provided for in Articles 58 to 61 for Overtime Work, Work on Holidays, and Late Hour Work.

> An employer needs to pay employees extra wages for overtime work and work on holidays. The extra wage rates are as follows:
> ① If the employee is requested to work more than the statutory working hours (overtime work):
> No less than 25% for overtime work that does not exceed 60 hours per month
> No less than 50% for overtime work that exceeds 60 hours per month (however, small to medium companies are exempted; please see the commentary on Article 58)
> ② 35% if the employee is requested to work on a statutory holiday (work on holidays)
> ③ 25% if the employee is requested to do late hour work (between 10 p.m. and 5 a.m.)
> * No less than 50% if overtime work was conducted late at night; no less than 60% if work on holidays was conducted late at night

第30条　（非常時及び災害時の例外）
1.　会社は，災害その他避けることのできない事由によって，臨時の必要がある場合においては，事前に所轄労働基準監督署長の許可を受けて（事態急迫のために所轄労働基準監督署長の許可を受ける余裕がない場合においては，事後遅滞なく届け出ることによって），社員に対して所定労働時間を延長し，又は休日労働をさせることがある。
2.　前項の時間外労働については，前条第3項の規定を準用する。

第4節　遅刻，早退，欠勤

第31条　（出　　勤）

> 労働時間の管理については，第1部第1章4-3をご参照ください。

1.　社員は，始業時刻までに仕事場に出勤し，作業準備にかかり，始業時刻と同時に作業に従事し，終業時刻後は特別の指示がない限り速やかに退出しなければならない。
2.　社員は，毎日の出勤及び退出のための所定の手続を遵守しなければならない。

第32条　（遅刻，早退及び私用外出）
1.　社員が所定の始業時刻よりも遅く作業を開始した場合には遅刻とし，社員が所定の終業時刻よりも早く退勤した場合には早退とする。この場合の賃金の支払については第7章の規定による。
2.　社員が遅刻，早退又は私用外出する場合には，所定の手続に従い，所属長の事前の承認を得るものとする。やむを得ない事情により事前の承認を得ることができない場合には，社員は，速やかに所属長の事後の承認を得

Article 30. (Exceptions for Emergencies and Disasters)
1. The Company may require Employees to work in excess of the designated working hours or perform Work on Holidays in the event that it becomes temporarily necessary for the Company due to natural disaster or other unavoidable event, with prior permission of the chief of the labor standards supervision office (in the event that there is no time to obtain prior permission, then by reporting without delay to such person afterwards).
2. The provisions of Paragraph 3 of the preceding article shall apply *mutatis mutandis* to Overtime Work under the preceding paragraph.

Section 4. Late Arrival, Early Departure and Absence

Article 31. (Attendance)

For Administration of Working Hours, please refer to Section 4-3 of Chapter I, Part I.

1. An Employee must arrive at his/her workplace by the prescribed starting time of his/her work day, prepare for the work, start to engage in tasks at the prescribed starting time and leave without delay after the prescribed finishing time of his/her work day unless otherwise specifically instructed by his/her supervisor.
2. Employees must follow the procedures for daily work attendance and departure from the workplace.

Article 32. (Late Arrival, Early Departure and Leaving for Personal Matters)
1. When an Employee starts to engage in tasks later than the starting time, it shall be recorded as a late arrival, and when an Employee leaves work earlier than the finishing time, it shall be recorded as an early departure. In those cases, his/her wage shall be adjusted in accordance with the provisions in Chapter VII.
2. When an Employee intends to arrive at work later than the starting time, to leave work earlier than the finishing time, or to leave the workplace during the working

なければならない。

第33条　(欠　　勤)
1. 社員は，欠勤する場合は，事前にその事由を所属長に届け出て会社の承認を得なければならない。ただし，事前に届け出る余裕がない場合は，社員は所属長に電話その他の方法により連絡し，事後速やかに欠勤事由を届け出なければならない。
2. 社員は，傷病のため欠勤が［１週間］以上にわたる場合，又は会社が必要と認めた場合は，医師の診断書を添えて所属長に届け出なければならない。この場合，会社は指定する医師の診断を受けさせることがある。

第34条　(公民権の行使)
1. 社員が，労働時間中に選挙権その他公民としての権利を行使し，又は公の職務を執行するときは，事前に所属長に届け出なければならない。
2. 会社は，前項の権利の行使又は職務に支障のない範囲において，その時刻を変更させることがある。
3. 第１項の時間については，［無給／有給／○％有給］とする。［ただし，社員が法令に基づき日当を支給されたときは，その金額を控除する。］

> 使用者は，労働者が労働時間中に，選挙権その他公民としての権利を行使し，又は公の職務を執行するために必要な時間を請求した場合においては，それは拒んではならないものとされています（労働基準法７条本文）。ただし，使用者は，権利の行使又は公の職務の執行に妨げがない限り，請求された時刻を変更することができるものとされています（同条但書）。

hours due to personal matters, he/she shall obtain prior approval from his/her supervisor in accordance with the prescribed rules. In the event that he/she is unable to obtain such prior approval due to unavoidable reasons, he/she must obtain approval afterwards from his/her supervisor without delay.

Article 33. (Absence)
1. In the case of an absence from work, an Employee must submit a notification of absence with reasons to his/her supervisor in advance and obtain prior approval from the Company. However, in the event that he/she has no time to submit a notification of absence in advance, he/she must notify his/her supervisor of his/her absence by telephone or any other proper means and promptly submit a notification of absence to his/her supervisor afterwards.
2. In the event that an Employee is absent from work for [one (1) week] or more due to injury or sickness or the Company deems it necessary, he/she must submit a notification of absence with a medical certificate. In such event, the Company may have him/her diagnosed by a doctor designated by the Company.

Article 34. (Exercise of Civil Rights)
1. When an Employee exercises his/her right to vote or other civil rights or discharges his/her public duties during working hours, he/she must report it to his/her supervisor in advance.
2. The Company may order a time-schedule change for the exercise of rights referred to in the preceding paragraph, to the extent that it does not affect the Employee's exercise of civil rights or discharge of public duties provided in the preceding paragraph.
3. For the hours referred to in Paragraph 1, the Employee shall be [unpaid/paid/shall receive percent (____%) payment]. [However, if the employee receives a daily allowance during the leave pursuant to the law, the company shall deduct the daily allowance from the payment.]

ここでいう「公民としての権利」には，公職選挙の選挙権・被選挙権，最高裁判所の裁判官の国民審査，地方自治法上の住民の直接請求，特別法の住民投票が含まれ，「公の職務」には，各種議会の議員，労働委員会の委員，検察審査員，公職選挙の立会人，裁判所・労働委員会の証人，裁判員制度の裁判員などの職務が含まれます。また，公民権行使の場合における欠勤等については，無給とすることも可能です。裁判員休暇など休暇中に労働者が日当等を受ける場合には，当該日当等の額を差し引いた限度で有給とすることも考えられます。

第5節　適用除外

第35条　（適用除外）

　労働基準法41条は，①農業，畜産・養蚕・水産業の労働者，②管理監督の地位にある者又は機密の事務を取り扱う者，③監視又は断続的労働の従事者で行政官庁の許可を受けた者について，法定労働時間や休憩・休日に関する規制条項の適用除外を認めています。これらの者に対しては，労働時間，休憩及び休日の規定が適用されないため，法定労働時間を超える労働や法定休日における労働をした場合でも，労働基準法上，割増賃金を支払う必要はありません。ただし，深夜労働の規制に関する規定はこれらの適用除外者にも適用されると解されているため，深夜労働となる場合には割増賃金の支払が必要です。また，年次有給休暇も適用を排除されません。
　本条で適用除外とされる管理監督者は，労働条件の決定その他労務管理について経営者と一体の立場にある者であり，その名称や就業規則の規定にかかわらず，実態に即して判断すべきこととされています。裁判例や通達によ

When an employee requests necessary time to vote or exercise other civil rights or perform his/her public duties during working hours, the employer should not refuse (Article 7 of the Labor Standards Act). However, the employer may change the time requested by the employee to the extent that the change does not hinder the exercise of the right or the performance of the public duty (the proviso of Article 7 of the Labor Standards Act). "Civil rights" include voting rights and rights to hold office in elections for public office, national review of the judges of the Supreme Court, direct petition from a local resident under the Local Autonomy Act, and a referendum under a special act. "Public duties" include working as a member of various assemblies, a commissioner of a Committee of Labor Affairs, a commissioner of a Committee for an Inquest of Prosecution, an observer for a public office election, a witness in court, or a Committee of Labor Affairs, and a citizen judge.

It is possible for an Employee not to be paid in the case of exercising his/her civil rights. Further, if the employee receives a daily allowance during the leave, e.g., takes leave to serve as a citizen judge, it is possible to deduct the daily allowance from the paid leave.

Section 5. Exception

Article 35. (Exception)

Article 41 of the Labor Standards Act exempts the following from the provisions regarding statutory working hours, breaks/holidays: (i) employees in the agriculture, animal husbandry, silk cultivation, or fisheries industries, (ii) managers and supervisors, or employees who handle confidential work, and (iii) employees under supervision and intermittent employees who have received permission from the authorities. Thus, such employees do not need to be paid extra wages if they work more than the statutory working hours or statutory holidays pursuant to the Labor Standards Act. Regulations regarding late hour work, however, are considered to apply to these exempt persons. Therefore, an employer needs to pay extra wages to such employees for late hour work. Further, annual paid leave requirements are not exempted for such employees. Managers and supervisors who are exempted under this provision are employees who, together with the management of the Company, engage in personnel administration such as determining employment conditions, and who are

ると，①事業主の経営に関する決定に参画し，労務管理に関する指揮監督権限を認められていること，②自己の出退勤をはじめとする労働時間について裁量権を有していること，③地位と権限にふさわしい賃金上の処遇を与えられていることが，管理監督者の要件とされています。

1. 労働基準法第41条第2号に定める監督若しくは管理の地位にある者又は機密の事務を取り扱う者及び労働基準法第41条第3号に定める監視又は断続的労働に従事する者で，会社が所轄労働基準監督署長の許可を受けた者については，本章の労働時間，休憩及び休日に関する規定は適用しない。
2. 第1項に定める者については，第58条から第60条の規定は適用しない。

> required to make immediate decisions on the basis of the actual circumstances regardless of the name of their position or the provisions in work rules. Based on court precedents and official notices, "managers and supervisors" are employees: who participate in employer's management decisions; who are granted authority to instruct and supervise regarding personnel administration; who have discretion to manage his/her own attendance/absence and working hours; or who receive appropriate treatment in connection with the wages for his/her position and authority.

1. The provisions under this Chapter relating to Working Hours, Breaks and Holidays shall not apply to Employees who work as management or administrative staff or who handle confidential affairs under Article 41, Item 2 of the Labor Standards Act; and to Employees who work as staff engaged in monitoring or in intermittent labor, with respect to which the Company has obtained permission from the chief of the labor standards supervision offices, under Article 41, Item 3 of the Labor Standards Act.

2. The provisions of Articles 58 to 60 shall not apply to the Employees stipulated in Paragraph 1.

第4章 休　暇

第36条　（年次有給休暇）

> 労働基準法上，年次有給休暇は，以下のとおり個々の労働者の勤続期間に応じて付与されることとなっています（労働基準法39条）。
>
> | 勤続年数 | 6か月 | 1年6か月 | 2年6か月 | 3年6か月 | 4年6か月 | 5年6か月 | 6年6か月以上 |
> |---|---|---|---|---|---|---|---|
> | 付与日数 | 10日 | 11日 | 12日 | 14日 | 16日 | 18日 | 20日 |
>
> 上記が法律上要求される最低基準ですが，この原則による場合，入社時期の異なる社員ごとに年次有給休暇の発生日が異なり，会社は社員の入社時期に応じて年次有給休暇を付与しなければなりません。社員数がある程度に達する場合には，このような個別の管理は煩雑であるため，労働基準法上の最低基準を上回る内容になることが前提となりますが，一定の基準日を設けて，全社員に対して同日付で一斉に年次有給休暇を付与するという方法も考えられます。本規定例では，基準日を設ける方法での規定例を記載しています。

1. 年次有給休暇は，社員の入社後の経過期間に応じて，以下のとおり与えるものとする。
   (1) 入社後最初の4月1日（4月1日に入社した社員は翌年の4月1日をいう。）までの期間
   　　入社後［3］か月を経過した日を基準日として，以下に規定する入社時期に応じて年次有給休暇を与えるものとする。

Chapter IV. Leave

Article 36. (Annual Paid Leave)

Pursuant to the Labor Standards Act, annual paid leave is granted depending on the employee's length of continuous service, as set forth below (Article 39 of the Labor Standards Act).

Number of years of continuous service	6 months	1 year and 6 months	2 years and 6 months	3 years and 6 months	4 years and 6 months	5 years and 6 months	6 years and 6 months
Number of days granted	10 days	11 days	12 days	14 days	16 days	18 days	20 days

The above is the statutory minimum standard. However, in this case, the date used to calculate the annual paid leave differs for each employee because it depends on when the employee joined the company, and therefore the Company must take the relevant hiring date into consideration when granting annual paid leave to each employee. Since it is difficult to make such arrangements if a company has a large number of employees, the employer may want to designate a certain date, which must exceed the minimum standard under the Labor Standards Act, and grant annual paid leave to all employees simultaneously on such date. This example has employed this method and has designated such a date.

1. Each Employee shall be entitled to Annual Paid Leave according to the time that has passed since his/her joining the Company as follows:

    (1) The period from the date of his/her joining the Company to the first April 1 (which means April 1 of the following year for Employees who joined the Company on April 1)

    Annual Paid Leave shall be granted to the Employee as of the date [three (3)] months after he/she joins the Company, which shall be the base date, according to the time he/she joins the Company, as provided below:

入社時期	入社後［3］か月を経過した日から入社後最初の4月1日までの期間中の有給休暇日数
4月1日から9月30日まで	10日
10月1日から10月31日まで	8日
11月1日から12月31日まで	6日
1月1日から3月31日まで	0日

(2) 入社後最初の4月1日以降

　毎年4月1日から翌年3月31日までの1年間につき，毎年4月1日を基準日として，以下に規定する勤続年数に応じて年次有給休暇を与えるものとする。なお，入社後最初の4月1日が到来した時点で勤続2年として計算する。

勤続年数	有給休暇日数
2年	11日
3年	12日
4年	14日
5年	16日
6年	18日
7年	20日

2.　前項の年次有給休暇は，4月1日から翌年3月31日までの前年度の出勤日数が，休日を除いた所定の総労働日の80％に満たない場合は，当該年度において付与しないものとする。

3.　第1項の年次有給休暇を取得しようとする社員は，予定する休暇の日程及び必要な日数を明記の上，年次有給休暇を取得しようとする［5］日前までに［所属長］に対して書面により届け出るものとする。ただし，社員

Chapter IV. Leave 169

Time of joining the Company	Number of days of Annual Paid Leave from the date [3] months after joining the Company to the first April 1 after joining the Company
From April 1 to September 30	10 days
From October 1 to October 31	8 days
From November 1 to December 31	6 days
From January 1 to March 31	0

(2) The period after the said first April 1

Annual Paid Leave shall be granted as of April 1 every year, which shall be the base date, for the one (1) year period from April 1 every year to March 31 of the following year according to an Employee's total number of service years, as provided below. In addition, his/her length of service shall be counted as two (2) years as of the first April 1 from the time of his/her joining the Company.

Years of service	Number of days of Annual Paid Leave
2 years	11 days
3 years	12 days
4 years	14 days
5 years	16 days
6 years	18 days
7 years	20 days

2. If an Employee whose attendance during the previous one (1) year period from the last April 1 to March 31 of the following year was less than eighty percent (80%) of the total working days excluding designated holidays, the Company shall not grant the Annual Paid Leave provided in the preceding paragraph for that following year.

3. An Employee who intends to take the Annual Paid Leave provided in Paragraph 1 shall submit a written request with his/her vacation schedule and the number of days

が届け出た時季に年次有給休暇を取得することが事業の正常な運営を妨げる場合，会社は社員に対し年次有給休暇の日程の変更を求めることがある。

> 年次有給休暇は，労働者がその始期と終期を指定して使用者に請求すれば，当然にその日が年休日となるのが原則であり，その取得時季については，労働者側に時季指定権があります。代替要員の手配等，使用者として通常可能な配慮をしてもなお，指定した時季に休暇を与えると事業の正常な運営が妨げられる場合にのみ，使用者に休暇時季の変更権が認められます（労働基準法39条5項）。

4．　社員は，年次有給休暇を半日単位で取得することができる（以下，「半日単位年休」という。）。ただし，1年当たり［10］回を限度とする。半日単位年休は，前半休は3時間，後半休は5時間とする。半日単位年休は，2回をもって1日分の年次有給休暇とする。なお，半日単位年休を取得した場合の始業・終業時刻は以下のとおりとする。
　　　前半休　　　［午前9時00分］から［正午］
　　　後半休　　　［午後1時00分］から［午後6時00分］

> 年次有給休暇は日単位で取得することが原則ですが，通達によれば，時間単位の年休に関する労使協定が締結されていない場合であっても，労働者が希望する場合には，日単位での年次有給休暇の取得の阻害とならない範囲で，使用者が任意で半日単位で与えることは可能と解されています（平7.7.27基監発33号）。当該通達でいう「半日」とは午前と午後であるとする見解があり，この見解に従えば，前半休と後半休とで時間数が異なることになりますが，いずれも0.5日分の年休の取得として取り扱われることとされています（安西愈『採用から退職までの法律実務（十四訂）』724頁）。本項は，この見解を踏まえた内容にしています。

5．　年次有給休暇の時間単位の取得に関する労使協定があるときは，社員は，1年で［5］日分を上限として，年次有給休暇を［2］時間単位で取得することができる（以下，「［2］時間単位年休」という。）。［2］時間単位年休は，［4］回をもって1日分の年次有給休暇とする。

to [his/her supervisor] [five (5)] days prior to the date on which he/she wishes to take Annual Paid Leave. However, the Company may require the Employee to change his/her vacation schedule when the Employee taking Annual Paid Leave during the period for which he/she submitted the written request would likely interfere with normal business operations.

> In principle, employees have the right to determine the time of the annual paid leave by designating the start and end dates of the annual paid leave, and employers must grant such request. The employer is allowed to modify the time of the leave only if the requested time would hinder the ordinary operation of business, even after the employer has taken ordinary possible measures such as providing replacement personnel (Article 39, Paragraph 5, Labor Standards Act).

4. Employees may take Annual Paid Leave in half-day units ("Half-Day Leave") with a limit of [ten (10)] times a year. The First Half-Day Leave shall be three (3) hours, a the Second Half-Day Leave shall be five (5) hours. Two (2) Half-Day Leaves shall be counted as one (1) Annual Paid Leave day. When taking Half-Day Leave, the starting time and finishing time are as follows:

   First Half-Day Leave: from [9:00] to [12:00]
   Second Half-Day Leave: from [13:00] to [18:00]

> In principle, annual paid leave may be taken in full day units. However, if an Employee wishes to take a half day of leave, and it does not negatively affect the taking of the Annual Paid Leave in full day units, the Company may allow the Employee to take a half day of leave, even if there is no labor-management agreement with respect to hour-based leave under a circular notice (Circular Notice, Kikanhatsu, No. 33, July 7, 1995). A renowned attorney has stated that a "half day" means either a morning or afternoon. Based on this view, the length of the morning of a half day of leave and the afternoon of a half day of leave might be different; however, the first half-day of leave and second half-day of leave are calculated equally as 0.5 days (pp. 724, Anzai Masaru, "Legal Practice from Employment to Retirement (edition 14)"). This Paragraph takes into account this view.

5. Employees may take Annual Paid Leave in [two (2)]-hour units up to [five (5)] days

> 平成22年4月1日施行の改正労働基準法において，労使協定の締結により年次有給休暇は1年で5日分を上限として，時間単位で取得することが可能となりました（労働基準法39条4項）。

6. 社員は，第4項及び第5項の規定にかかわらず，1日に，半日単位年休と［2］時間単位年休を併用して取得することができないものとする。
7. 未消化の年次有給休暇については翌年度にのみ繰り越すことができる。ただし，翌年度に取得できる［2］時間単位年休は，繰り越し分も含めて5日分を上限とする。
8. 社員は，年次有給休暇の期間につき，通常の賃金の支払を受ける。ただし，半日単位年休及び［2］時間単位年休の場合には，それぞれ次の算式による賃金とする。

　半日単位年休（前半休）　　（［平均賃金］÷年休取得日の所定労働時間数）
　　　　　　　　　　　　　　×［3］時間
　半日単位年休（後半休）　　（［平均賃金］÷年休取得日の所定労働時間数）
　　　　　　　　　　　　　　×［5］時間
　［2］時間単位年休　　　　（［平均賃金］÷年休取得日の所定労働時間数）
　　　　　　　　　　　　　　×［2］時間

> 使用者は，年次有給休暇を取得した労働者に対して，賃金の減額や，皆勤手当・賞与の額の算定に際して年次有給休暇を取得した日を欠勤と同様に扱う等不利益な取扱いをしないようにしなければなりません（労働基準法136条）。

9. 第2項の所定の総労働日とは，会社の所定の労働日の総日数のことであり，その年の出勤率の計算に当たっては，下記のものは出勤したものとして計算する。
　① 年次有給休暇利用日数
　② 振替休日
　［③ 特別有給休暇］
　④ 業務上の傷病により欠勤した期間

in total every year if there is a Labor-Management Agreement providing for such leave ("[Two (2)]-Hour Leave"). [Four (4)] [Two (2)]-Hour Leaves shall be counted as one (1) Annual Paid Leave day.

The amendment of the Labor Standards Act on April 1, 2010, made permissible annual paid leave in hour-based increments, with the maximum amount of days of such annual paid leave being 5 days (Article 39, Paragraph 4 of the Labor Standards Act).

6. Regardless of paragraphs 4 and 5, an Employee may not take Half Day Leave and [Two (2)]-Hour Leave together in a day.

7. Unused Annual Paid Leave may be carried forward only up to the end of the following year. However, [Two (2)]-Hour Leave that Employees are entitled to take during the following year shall be limited to five (5) days, including the days carried forward.

8. Employees will receive normal wages for the period of their Annual Paid Leave. However, the following formula shall apply to Half-Day Leave and [Two (2)]-Hour Leave:

First Half-Day Leave: ([average wage] ÷ designated working hours on the day of Half-Day Leave) × [3] hours

Second Half-Day Leave: ([average wage] ÷ designated working hours on the day of the Half-Day Leave) × [5] hours

[Two]-Hour Leave: ([average wage] ÷ designated working hours on the day of [Two (2)]-Hour Leave) × [Two (2)] hours

Employers must ensure that no employees who have obtained paid annual leave receive a wages deduction or have the days of annual paid leave unfairly treated as days of absence when determining to pay allowance for perfect attendance/ bonus amount (Article 136 of the Labor Standards Act).

9. Total working days prescribed in Paragraph 2 shall be the total number of working days designated by the Company, and when the Company calculates attendance for the year, the following days shall be regarded as days on which Employees reported

⑤ 代替休暇
⑥ 育児・介護休業の期間
⑦ 子の看護休暇
⑧ 介護休暇
⑨ 産前産後休業の期間

> 特別有給休暇の取得日については、出勤率の計算において出勤と扱う義務まではなく、出勤と扱うか欠勤と扱うかは会社が自由に決めることができます。

10. 会社は、労働基準法39条6項に基づく年次有給休暇の計画的付与に関する労使協定があるときは、年次有給休暇のうち、5日を超える部分について計画的に付与することがある。

> 年次有給休暇は労働者個人が自由にその時季を指定して利用するのが原則ですが、労使協定により年休を与える時季についての定めをすれば、その定めに従って使用者が年休を与えることができます。計画年休により具体的な休暇日が決定されれば、当該休暇日が労働者の年休日となり、労働者は別の日を年休日として指定することはできません。労働者の完全な個人的利用のため5日の年休を留保し、5日を超える年休日についてのみ計画的付与が可能となっています（労働基準法39条6項）。

11. 会社は、第1項及び第2項の規定による有給休暇（ただし、これらの規定により会社が与えなければならない有給休暇の日数が10日以上である社員に係るものに限る。以下同様。）の日数のうち5日については、4月1日から1年以内の期間に、事前に社員の希望を聴取の上で、社員毎にその時季を定めることにより与えるものとする。ただし、社員が第3項又は第10項の規定により当該有給休暇を取得した場合、当該社員の有給休暇のうち、当該取得した有給休暇の日数（当該日数が5日を超える場合には、5日とする。）分については、時季を定めることにより与えることを要しない。

Chapter IV. Leave   175

for work:
(1) days taken as Annual Paid Leave
(2) shifted Designated Holidays
[(3) days taken as Special Paid Leave]
(4) days absent from work due to work-related injuries and illnesses
(5) days taken as Substitute Leave
(6) days taken as Child Care/Nursing Care Leave
(7) days taken as Sick/Injured Child Care Leave
(8) days taken as Non-Consecutive Nursing Care Leave
(9) days taken as pre-and post-childbirth leave

Days taken as special paid leave do not need to be categorized as days on which an employee attended work in calculating attendance. It may be freely decided by a company whether days taken as special paid leave need to be treated as days on which an employee attended work or was absent.

10. The Company may grant Annual Paid Leave in a planned manner pursuant to a Labor-Management Agreement providing for such paid leave for the portion of the Annual Paid Leave based on Article 39, paragraph 6 of the Labor Standards Act in excess of five (5) days.

As a general rule, an employee can freely decide the timing and season for taking annual paid leave. However, if the time for taking annual leave is stipulated pursuant to a labor-management agreement, the employer can grant annual leave pursuant to the provisions of such agreement. If specific vacations are determined according to a planned annual leave, such vacations become the respective employee's annual leave, and such employee cannot designate another day as a day(s) for annual leave. An employer needs to reserve 5 days for employees' individual use and may grant annual leave in a planned manner only for leave exceeding 5 days (Article 39, Paragraph 6 of the Labor Standards Act).

11. Regarding 5 days out of the number of days of annual paid leave pursuant to paragraphs 1 and 2 (however, limited to annual paid leave of employees whose number of days of annual paid leave which must be granted by the Company pursuant

> 平成31年4月1日施行の改正労働基準法により，年次有給休暇（年5日）の時季指定義務の規定が追加されました。

第37条　（疾病休暇）

　　業務に起因しない傷病により欠勤する社員は，請求により，毎年［5］日間までの疾病休暇を取得することができる。ただし，未消化の疾病休暇を翌年に繰り越すことはできない。疾病休暇は，無給とする。

> 疾病休暇は法律上付与が義務付けられるものではありませんが，疾病休暇を制度として定める場合は就業規則への記載が必要です。疾病休暇を有給とするか無給とするかは労使の協議又は使用者の判断により決定します。

第38条　（特別有給休暇）

> 特別休暇は法律上付与が義務付けられるものではありませんが，特別休暇を制度として定める場合は就業規則への記載が必要です。特別休暇を有給とするか無給とするかは労使の協議又は使用者の判断により決定します。

1.　社員は，次の各号の一に該当する場合，それぞれに規定する日数を限度として特別有給休暇を取得することができる。
　(1)　結　　婚

to these paragraphs is 10 days or more; and the same shall apply thereafter), the Company shall grant them to each employee within 1 year from April 1 by specifying the period therefor after hearing each employee's wishes in advance. However, if an employee takes annual paid leave pursuant to paragraph 3 or 10, the number of days of annual paid leave taken (considered to be 5 days in cases where the number of days of annual paid leave taken exceeds 5 days) out of the annual paid leave of such employee shall not be required to be specified.

With the amended Labor Standards Act enforced on April 1, 2019, the obligation to designate the period for annual paid leave (5 days per year) was provided for.

Article 37. (Sick Leave)
If an Employee is caused to be absent from work due to non-work related injury or illness, he/she shall be entitled to take a maximum of [five (5)] days' Sick Leave each year. However, unused Sick Leave may not be carried forward to the following year. Sick Leave shall be unpaid.

Sick leave is not required by law. However, if sick leave is implemented as a policy, it must be stipulated in the work rules. The determination of whether sick leave is paid or unpaid may depend on negotiations between labor and management or may be at the employer's discretion.

Article 38. (Special Paid Leave)

Special paid leave is not required by law. However, if special paid leave is implemented as a policy, it must be stipulated in the work rules. The determination of whether special leave is paid or unpaid may depend on negotiations between labor and management or may be at the employer's discretion.

1. If an Employee falls under any of the following items, he/she shall be entitled to take Special Paid Leave up to the maximum number of days as provided below:

① 本人が結婚するとき（ただし入籍日の翌日を起算日として［6か月］以内に取得するものとする。）

　　　　　　　　　　　　　　　　　　　　　　　　　　　　連続［5］日

　② 子（養子を含む。以下，本条において同じ。）が結婚するとき

　　　　　　　　　　　　　　　　　　　　　　　　　　　［連続］［1］日

(2) 配偶者の出産　　　　　　　　　　　　　　　　　［連続］［1］日

(3) 忌　　引

　① 配偶者，父母（養父母を含む。）又は子が死亡したとき

　　　　　　　　　　　　　　　　　　　　　　　　　　　連続［5］日

　② 祖父母（養祖父母を含む。），兄弟姉妹，配偶者の父母，子の配偶者又は孫が死亡したとき

　　本人が喪主である場合　　　　　　　　　　　　　　連続［5］日

　　本人が喪主でない場合　　　　　　　　　　　　　　連続［3］日

　③ 伯叔父母若しくはその配偶者，配偶者の兄弟姉妹，兄弟姉妹の配偶者又は養子の父母が死亡したとき

　　　　　　　　　　　　　　　　　　　　　　　　　　　［連続］［1］日

(4) 法　　事

　社員が実養父母，配偶者，子，兄弟姉妹，実祖父母又は配偶者の父母の一周忌の行事を営む場合

　　　　　　　　　　　　　　　　　　　　　　　　　　　［連続］［1］日

(5) その他の特別休暇

　会社が上記各号に準じて必要と認めたとき

　　　　　　　　　　　　　　　　　　　　　　　　　必要な時間及び日数

2．前項の休暇日数には，第26条第1項に定める休日を含む。

3．社員は，特別有給休暇の期間につき，通常の給与の支払を受ける。

4．第1項の特別有給休暇を取得しようとする社員は，事前に書面にて会社に申し出て，その承認を受け，会社の要求する書類を提出しなければならない。ただし，忌引休暇の場合は，通報の上次の出勤時に所定の手続をとることにより，申出に代えることができる。

Chapter IV. Leave   179

(1) Marriage
  i. Marriage of an Employee (Leave shall be taken within [six (6) months] from the day following the registration of marriage): [five (5)] consecutive days
  ii. Marriage of an Employee's child (including adoptive): [one (1)] day
(2) Child birth of an Employee's spouse: [one (1)] day
(3) Funeral
  i. Death of an Employee's spouse, parent (including adoptive), or child (including adoptive): [five (5)] consecutive days
  ii. Death of an Employee's grand-parent (including adoptive), brother/sister, spouse's parent, child's spouse or grandchild (including adoptive)
  If an Employee is a chief mourner: [five (5)] consecutive days
  If an Employee is not a chief mourner: [three (3)] consecutive days
  iii. Death of an Employee's uncle or aunt or uncle's or aunt's spouse, spouse's brother or sister, brother and sister's spouse, or adopted child's parent: [one (1)] day
(4) Memorial Service for the Deceased
  In case an Employee performs a memorial service for the anniversary of the death (*isshyuki*) of the Employee's parent (including adoptive), spouse, child (including adoptive), brother or sister, grandparent, or the Employee's spouse's parent: [one (1)] day
(5) Other Special Leave
  When the Company deems it necessary: The necessary time or days
2. The number of days taken as Special Leave provided in the preceding paragraph shall include the designated holidays provided in Article 26, Paragraph 1.
3. An Employee may receive his/her normal pay for days taken as Special Paid Leave.
4. If an Employee intends to take Special Paid Leave listed in Paragraph 1, the Employee must submit a written request to the Company in advance for its prior approval, and also submit the documents required by the Company. However, in the case of funeral leave, an Employee may notify the Company, instead of submitting such request for leave, and thereafter take the necessary procedures at the earliest

第39条　（代替休暇）

> 代替休暇は，平成22年4月1日施行の労働基準法改正により導入された制度で，1か月60時間を超える時間外労働部分の割増賃金率が50％に引き上げられたことに伴い，その上積み部分の割増賃金の支払に代えて休暇を付与するものです（労働基準法37条3項）。代替休暇の導入は義務ではないため，本条の規定を設けないこととすることも可能です。なお，中小企業については，1か月60時間を超える時間外労働部分の割増賃金率の引上げの適用が当分の間猶予されているため（第58条の解説参照），当該上積み部分の割増賃金支払義務の存在を前提とする代替休暇の制度も適用されないこととなります。なお，中小企業が任意に1か月60時間を超える時間外労働の割増賃金率を50％以上に引き上げた場合には，代替休暇に相当する制度の導入が可能であるとされています。

会社は，1か月（第51条第1項に定める賃金締切期間）の時間外労働が60時間を超えた社員に対して，第58条第2項第2号に定める時間外労働割増賃金の支払に代えて，労使協定に基づき，次により代替休暇を与えるものとする。

⑴　代替休暇を取得できる期間は，直前の賃金締切日の翌日から起算して翌々月の賃金締切日までの2か月とする。

⑵　代替休暇は，半日又は1日で与える。この場合の半日とは，午前（[午前9時00分]から[午後2時00分]（休憩1時間））又は午後（[午後2時00分]から[午後6時00分]）のことをいう。

⑶　代替休暇の時間数は，1か月60時間を超える時間外労働時間数に換算率を乗じた時間数とする。この場合において，換算率とは，代替休暇を取得しなかった場合に支払う割増賃金率50％から代替休暇を取得した場合に支払う割増賃金率[25]％を差し引いた[25]％とする。また，社員が代替休暇を取得した場合は，取得した時間数を換算率（[25]％）で除した時間数については，[25]％の割増賃金の支払を要しないこととする。

⑷　代替休暇の時間数が半日又は1日に満たない端数がある場合には，その満たない部分については代替休暇を取得することはできず，会社は，これ

time he/she reports to the office.

Article 39. (Substitute Leave)

> **Substitute leave was a policy instituted on April 1, 2010 pursuant to an amendment to the Labor Standards Act.** Since the extra wage rate has been increased to no less than 50 percent for overtime work exceeding 60 hours per month, the amount corresponding to the additional amount of extra wages can be replaced with substitute leave (Article 37, Paragraph 3 of the Labor Standards Act). Introduction of substitute leave is not mandatory, and thus, it is possible to not provide this provision. Further, since small to medium sized companies are exempted from the abovementioned increase in extra wage rate (See the commentary on Article 58), the substitute leave policy does not apply to such companies. (This is because substitute leave requires the existence of a duty to pay a surcharge for extra wages). Further, if a small to medium sized company increases its extra wage rate to more than 50 percent for overtime work, it is deemed acceptable for such company to implement a policy similar to substitute leave.

The Company shall grant to Employees whose overtime work exceeds sixty (60) hours per month (in a Wages Calculation Period, as defined in Article 51, Paragraph 1 hereafter) Substitute Leave in the following manner in accordance with a Labor-Management Agreement, instead of the payment of extra wages for overtime work provided in Article 58, Paragraph 2, Item 2:

(1) The period available for Substitute Leave shall be for two (2) months from the day following the immediate closing day for wages calculation until the closing day for wages calculation in the month following the next month.

(2) Substitute Leave shall be granted in a half-day unit or a full-day unit. In this case, a half-day unit means morning (from [9:00] to [14:00] (including a one-hour break)) or afternoon (from [14:00] to [18:00]).

(3) Number of hours for Substitute Leave shall be the hours for overtime work exceeding sixty (60) hours per month multiplied by a conversion rate. In this case, the "conversion rate" means [twenty five percent (25)%], which is the balance of fifty percent (50%) (extra wage rate payable when Substitute Leave is

に対して割増賃金を支払う。

(5) 代替休暇を取得しようとする社員は，1か月に60時間を超える時間外労働を行った月の賃金締切日の翌日から［5日］以内に，会社に申し出ることとする。代替休暇取得日は，社員の意向を踏まえ決定することとする。

(6) 会社は，前項の申出があった場合には，支払うべき割増賃金額のうち代替休暇に代替される賃金額を除いた部分を通常の賃金支払日に支払うこととする。ただし，当該月の末日の翌日から2か月以内に代替休暇の取得がなされなかった場合には，取得がなされないことが確定した月に係る割増賃金支払日に残りの25％の割増賃金を支払うこととする。

(7) 会社は，第5号に定める期間内に代替休暇の申出がなかった場合は，当該月に行われた時間外労働に係る割増賃金の総額を通常の割増賃金支払日に支払うこととする。

not taken) minus [twenty five percent (25)%] (extra wage rate payable when Substitute Leave is taken). In addition, when an Employee takes Substitute Leave, extra wages at [twenty five percent (25)%] are not required to be paid for the hours after dividing the hours taken by the conversion rate ([twenty five percent (25)%]).

(4) If an Employee earns Substitute Leave hours that are less than a half-day or full-day unit, he/she shall not be entitled to such Substitute Leave, and the Company shall pay extra wages for such hours.

(5) An Employee who intends to take Substitute Leave shall submit a request to the Company within [five (5) days] from the day following the closing day for wages calculation in the month in which he/she worked overtime exceeding sixty (60) hours. Dates of Substitute Leave to be granted shall be determined taking into consideration the Employee's intention.

(6) If an Employee submits a request prescribed in the preceding paragraph, the Company shall pay the amount of extra wages payable minus the wages amount substituted by the Substitute Leave on the usual pay day. However, if the Employee does not take Substitute Leave within two (2) months from the day following the end of the relevant month, the remaining extra wages at twenty five percent (25%) shall be paid on the extra wages pay day of the month in which such leave is determined not to be taken.

(7) If an Employee does not submit a request for Substitute Leave within the period set forth in Item 5 above, the Company shall pay the total amount of extra wages for overtime work in the relevant month on the usual pay day of extra wages.

第5章　母性健康管理の措置

第40条　（労働時間の取扱い）
1. 　会社は，妊娠中の女性社員及び産後1年を経過しない女性社員（以下，「妊産婦」という。）が請求した場合においては，変形労働時間制を採用している場合であっても，当該妊産婦を1週間40時間，1日8時間を超えて労働をさせてはならない。
2. 　会社は，妊産婦が請求した場合は，第29条及び第30条の規定にかかわらず，時間外労働，休日労働，又は深夜労働をさせてはならない。

第41条　（妊娠中の通院等）
　妊産婦が母子保健法による保健指導又は健康診査を受けるために労働時間内に通院する必要がある場合，会社は，妊産婦の請求により遅刻，早退又は離席を認める。通院のため出社不能の場合は，会社は，本人の請求により休暇を与えることがある。

> 事業主は，女性社員が妊産婦のための保険指導又は健康診査（以下，「健康診査等」という。）を受診するために必要な時間を確保することができるようにしなければならないとされています（男女雇用機会均等法12条）。具体的には，事業主は妊娠中である女性社員については，医師又は助産師が異なる指示をした場合を除き，①妊娠23週までは4週間に1回，②妊娠24週から35週までは2週間に1回，③妊娠36週から出産までは週に1回の健康診査等を受診するための必要な時間を確保しなければならないとされており，出産後1年以内の女性社員については，医師又は助産師が健康診査等を受けることを指示したときは，その指示するところにより，当該必要な時間を確保することができるようにしなければならないとされています（男女雇用機会均等法施行規則2条の3）。

Chapter V. Maternal Healthcare

Article 40. (Working Hours in view of Protection)
1. The Company may not request a pregnant female Employee or a female Employees within one year after childbirth ("Expectant or Nursing Mothers") to work more than forty (40) hours a week or eight (8) hours a day if the Expectant or Nursing Mother indicates that she does not wish to work more than forty (40) hours a week or eight (8) hours per day, even if the Company adopts the modified working hours.
2. The Company may not request an Expectant or Nursing Mother perform Overtime Work, Work on Designated Holidays, or Late Hour Work if the Expectant or Nursing Mother indicates that she does not wish to perform such work, notwithstanding the provisions of Articles 29 and 30.

Article 41. (Hospital Visit During Pregnancy)
If an Expectant or Nursing Mother needs to visit a medical doctor to receive health guidance or a physical examination under the Maternal and Child Health Act, the Company shall permit her late arrival, early departure or leaving the premises during the Working Hours upon her request. In the event that an Expectant or Nursing Mother is unable to report to work in order to visit a medical doctor, the Company may grant her leave upon her request.

> **An employer must allow a female Employee the necessary time off so that such female Employee may receive health guidance and medical examinations for an Expectant or Nursing Mother ("Physical Examination") (Article 12 of the Equal Employment Opportunity Act).**
> **Specifically, unless otherwise indicated by a medical doctor or midwife, an employer must allow the necessary time off so that a pregnant female Employee may receive a Physical Examination, (i) once every 4 weeks until 23 weeks of pregnancy, (ii) once every 2 weeks between 24 and 35 weeks of pregnancy, and (iii) once a week after 36 weeks of pregnancy must allow the necessary time off so that a female Employee within one year after childbirth may receive Physical**

> 本規定例は，妊産婦の通院等の機会を確保する観点から，上記規制を一歩前進させ，より妊産婦に配慮した内容としています。

第42条　（通勤緩和の措置）

　　妊娠中の女性社員が，通勤時の混雑が母体の負担になる場合は，本人の請求により，1日合計1時間の範囲で，始業時刻及び終業時刻の繰下げ又は繰上げを行うことができる。

> 　妊娠中及び出産後の女性社員が，健康診査等に基づく指導事項を守ることができるようにするために，事業主は，勤務時間の変更や勤務の軽減等の措置を講じなければならず（男女雇用機会均等法13条），具体的には，①妊娠中の通勤緩和，②妊娠中の休憩に関する措置，③妊娠中又は出産後の症状等に対応する措置を講じる必要があるとされています（妊娠中及び出産後の女性労働者が保健指導又は健康診査に基づく指導事項を守ることができるようにするために事業主が講ずべき措置に関する指針，平9．9．25労働省告示105号）（以下，「平成9年指針」という。）。
> 　このうち通勤緩和の措置については，事業主は，その雇用する妊娠中の女性社員から，通勤に利用する交通機関の混雑の程度が母体又は胎児の健康保持に影響があるとして，医師又は助産師により通勤緩和の指導を受けた旨の申出があった場合には，時差通勤，勤務時間の短縮等の必要な措置を講ずるものとされ，医師又は助産師による具体的な指導がない場合においても，妊娠中の女性社員から通勤緩和の申出があったときは，担当の医師又は助産師と連絡をとり，その判断を求める等適切な対応を図る必要があることとされています（平成9年指針）。
> 　本規定例では，平成9年指針の内容を踏まえて，1日合計1時間の範囲で，始業時間及び終業時間の繰下げ又は繰上げを行うことができることとしています。

Examinations according to the instructions of a medical doctor or midwife (Article 2-3 of the Ordinance for Enforcement of Equal Employment Opportunity Act).
In order to secure opportunities for hospital visits, etc. of Expectant or Nursing Mothers, this provision provides more advantages to Expectant or Nursing Mothers in addition to those under the Equal Employment Opportunity Act.

Article 42. (Commuting Relief)
In the case where congestion during commuting times affects a pregnant female Employee's health, she may alter her starting time or finishing time up to a total of one (1) hour per day upon her request.

An employer must take measures, such as changing work hours and reducing work so that an Expectant or Nursing Mother can comply with instructions based on a Physical Examination (Article 13 of Equal Employment Opportunity Act). Specifically, an employer must take measures for (i) commuting relief for pregnant female Employees, (ii) breaks for pregnant female Employees and (iii) care for symptoms etc. of pregnant and post-childbirth employees (Guidance regarding measures to be taken by employer to make a pregnant female Employee or a female Employees after childbirth complying with instructions based on health guidance and physical examination) (the Guideline; Public Notice of the Ministry of Labor No. 105, September 25, 1997) (the "Guidance").
With respect to (i) commuting relief, an employer must take necessary measures such as staggering commuting hours and shortening work hours, if a pregnant female Employee reports that a medical doctor or midwife gave her instructions regarding commuting relief because the crowded conditions of her means of commuting may affect the health of her body or unborn child. Even if a medical doctor or midwife gives no specific instructions regarding commuting relief, the employer must take appropriate measures such as contacting her medical doctor or midwife and requesting his/her judgement as to whether the pregnant female Employee should be offered commuting relief (the Guidance).
This provision, based on the Guidance, provides that a company must permit a pregnant female Employee to alter her starting time or finishing time up to a total of 1 hour per day upon her request.

第43条　（休憩の措置）

　　妊娠中の女性社員が，勤務中，業務を負担に感じる場合は，本人の請求により適宜休憩することができる。

> 　　妊娠中の女性社員が，健康診査等に基づく指導事項を守ることができるようにするために，事業主は，妊娠中の休憩に関する措置を講じる必要があるとされており（第42条の解説参照），具体的には，その雇用する妊娠中の女性社員から，当該女性社員の作業等が母体又は胎児の健康保持に影響があるとして，医師又は助産師により休憩に関する措置についての指導を受けた旨の申出があった場合には，休憩時間の延長，休憩の回数の増加等の必要な措置を講ずるものとされ，医師又は助産師による具体的な指導がない場合においても，妊娠中の女性社員から休憩に関する措置についての申出があったときは，担当の医師又は助産師と連絡をとり，その判断を求める等適切な対応を図る必要があることとされています（平成9年指針）。
> 　　本規定例では，平成9年指針の内容を踏まえて，妊娠中の女性社員が，勤務中，業務を負担に感じる場合は，本人の請求により適宜休憩することができることとしています。

第44条　（産前・産後休業）
1. 会社は，6週間（多胎妊娠の場合は14週間）以内に出産する予定の女性社員が休業を請求した場合は，就業させないものとする。
2. 会社は，女性社員が出産したときは，産後8週間を経過するまで就業させないものとする。ただし，産後6週間を経過し本人が就業を申し出た場合は，当該社員について会社の指定する医師が支障がないと認めた業務に就業させることがあるものとする。
3. 会社は，妊娠中の女性社員が妊娠期間中他の軽易な業務に従事することを希望する場合は，他の軽易な業務への転換を行うものとする。この場合，会社は，当該担当業務に応じて賃金を変更することがある。

Article 43. (Permission of Breaks)

When a pregnant female Employee considers that her work duties are causing stress affecting her health, she may take necessary breaks upon her request.

> An employer must take measures for breaks for pregnant female Employees so that Expectant or Nursing Mothers can comply with instructions based on a Physical Examination (see commentary on Article 42).
> Specifically, an employer must take necessary measures such as extending break times and increasing the frequency of breaks, if a pregnant female Employee reports that a medical doctor or midwife gave her instructions on matters regarding breaks because her work duties may affect the health of her body or unborn child. Even if a medical doctor or midwife gives no specific instructions regarding breaks for a pregnant female Employee, an employer must take appropriate measures such as contacting her medical doctor or midwife and requesting his/her judgement as to whether a pregnant female Employee should be offered breaks (the Guidance).
> This provision, based on the Guidance, provides that a company must permit necessary breaks upon a pregnant female Employee's request when she considers that her work duties are causing stress affecting her health.

Article 44. (Pre-and Post-Childbirth Leave)

1. In the event that a female Employee requests Pre-Childbirth Leave within six (6) weeks (fourteen (14) weeks in the case of multiple pregnancy) prior to the expected birth, the Company shall not make her work.

2. When an Employee gives birth, the Company shall not make her work before eight (8) weeks have passed after the birth. However, in the event that she requests to return to work six (6) weeks after the birth and a medical doctor designated by the Company recognizes that it would not be harmful for her to work, the Company may allow her to work.

3. In the event that a pregnant Employee requests to be transferred to light work during her pregnancy, the Company shall transfer her to light work. In this case, the Company may change the wages of such employee in accordance with the work she is transferred to.

第45条 （妊娠中及び産後の症状等に対応する措置）
1. 妊産婦が，身体に何らかの症状がある又は症状が発生するおそれがあるとして，医師又は助産師からの指導を受けた場合は，本人の請求により，医師又は助産師の指示に基づく業務内容の軽減，負担の少ない業務への転換，労働時間の短縮等を認める。また，妊産婦が，身体に何らかの症状がある又は症状が発生するおそれがあるとして，医師又は助産師からの指導を受けた場合で，妊産婦の休業が必要な場合は，妊産婦は，本人の請求により，必要日数の休暇を取得することができる。
2. 前項により業務を転換した場合，会社は，当該担当業務に応じて賃金を変更することがある。

> 妊娠中及び出産後の女性社員が，健康診査等に基づく指導事項を守ることができるようにするために，事業主は，妊娠中又は出産後の症状等に対応する措置を講じる必要があるとされており（第42条の解説参照），具体的には，事業主は，その雇用する妊娠中又は出産後の女性社員から，健康診査等に基づき，医師又は助産師によりその症状等に関して指導を受けた旨の申出があった場合には，当該指導に基づき，作業の制限，勤務時間の短縮，休業，作業環境の変更等の必要な措置を講ずるものとされ，医師又は助産師による指導に基づく必要な措置が不明確である場合には，担当の医師又は助産師と連絡をとりその判断を求める等により，作業の制限，勤務時間の短縮，休業，作業環境の変更等の必要な措置を講ずるものとされています（平9年指針，平9．11．4基発695号・女発36号）。
> 本規定例では，平成9年指針の内容を踏まえて，妊産婦の女性社員が，身体に何らかの症状がある又は症状が発生するおそれがあるとして，医師又は助産師からの指導を受けた場合には，本人の請求により，医師又は助産師の指示に基づく業務内容の軽減等がなされることとしています。

Article 45. (Care for Symptoms of Pregnant and After-Childbirth Employees)
1. In the event that an Expectant or Nursing Mother is diagnosed as having or being in danger of having inimical physical symptoms by a medical doctor or midwife, the Company will permit the cutting back of her work load, her transfer to light work, or the shortening of her work hours upon her request in accordance with the instruction of the medical doctor or midwife. In addition, in the event that an Expectant or Nursing Mother is diagnosed as having or being in danger of having inimical physical symptoms by a medical doctor or midwife and she needs an exceptional leave, she may be granted leave of a length deemed necessary upon her request.
2. In the case where the Company permits a pregnant Employee to transfer to light work in accordance with the provisions of the preceding paragraph, the Company may change her wage in accordance with the work she is transferred to.

An employer must take measures to care for symptoms of pregnant and post-childbirth employees so that an Expectant or Nursing Mother can comply with instructions based on a Physical Examination (see commentary on Article 42). Specifically, an employer must take necessary measures such as restricting work, shortening work hours, allowing absence from work, and changing the circumstances of work, if a pregnant female Employee reports that a medical doctor or midwife gave her instructions on matters regarding care for symptoms based on a Physical Examination.
Further, an employer must take necessary measures such as restricting work, shortening work hours, allowing absence from work, and changing the circumstances of work by contacting her medical doctor or midwife, and requesting his/her judgement if appropriate measures based on the instructions of a medical doctor or midwife are unclear (the Guidance, Circular Notice, Kihatsu, No. 695/Jyohatsu, No. 36, November 4, 1997).
This provision, based on the Guidance, provides that upon her request, a company must permit an Expectant or Nursing Mother the cutting back of the work load, etc. in the event that she is diagnosed as having or being in danger of having inimical physical symptoms, in accordance with the instructions of a medical doctor or midwife.

第46条　（育児時間）
　　会社は，生後満1年に達しない子を育てる女性社員が，あらかじめ申し出た場合は，第25条第2項に定める休憩時間の他に，1日につき2回，それぞれ30分間の育児時間を与える。

第47条　（生理休暇）
　　生理日の就業が著しく困難な女性社員は，請求により，必要日数の生理休暇を取得することができる。

第48条　（措置中の待遇）
　　第41条から第47条までに定める休暇，繰下げ又は繰上げ時間，休憩，休業，育児時間の時間ないし期間は，特に定めるもののほか無給とする。

第6章　育児休業及び介護休業等

第49条　（育児休業及び介護休業等）
　　育児休業，介護休業，その他子の養育又は家族の介護については，別途定める「育児・介護休業規程」による。

Article 46. (Childcare Break)
In the event that a female Employee who has a child under one (1) year old requests a childcare break in advance, the Company shall grant her a childcare break (of thirty (30) minutes each) twice a day, in addition to the break provided in Article 25, Paragraph 2.

Article 47. (Menstruation Leave)
A female Employee who finds it extremely difficult to perform her duties during her menstrual periods may take Menstruation Leave of a length deemed necessary upon her request.

Article 48. (Treatment during Maternal Health Care)
The leave, the hours of delay or advance, breaks, absence, or the hours or periods for childcare provided in Articles 41 through 47 shall be granted without pay, unless otherwise stipulated herein.

Chapter VI. Child Care Leave and Nursing Care Leave

Article 49. (Child Care Leave and Nursing Care Leave)
Child Care Leave, Nursing Care Leave, and other nursing of children or family members shall be governed by the "Regulations for Child Care/Nursing Care Leave" to be separately provided.

第7章　賃金，退職金

> 年俸制の場合の規定例としています。

第50条　（賃金の構成）

　賃金の基本的な構成は，次のとおりとする。
(1)　第56条第1項において定義される基本給
(2)　第56条第3項において定義される賞与
(3)　割増賃金手当
　①　時間外労働割増賃金
　②　所定休日労働割増賃金
　③　法定休日労働割増賃金
　④　深夜労働割増賃金
(4)　その他手当
　　通勤手当

> 基本給，賞与及び諸手当を定めるに当たり，パートタイム労働者・有期雇用労働者（いわゆる非正規社員）と通常の労働者（いわゆる正規社員）との間で，不合理と認められる相違を設けることは禁止されています（パート有期法8条）。この点，基本給及び賞与について，非正規社員と正規社員との間では職務内容や人材活用の仕組みが異なることが多く，相違を設けることが比較的許容されやすいものと考えられますが，職務内容等が異ならない場合には，不合理な待遇の相違は禁止されます。一方，諸手当を定めるに当たっては，待遇の相違が裁判所によって違法であると判断されているケースがあるため注意が必要です。たとえば，精皆勤手当，時間外手当といった業務に係る手当について，非正規社員と正規社員との間で設けられた相違が違法であると判断した判例があります。諸手当の目的や性質については各企業に応じて異なりますが，手当の名称ではなく実質に応じて，非正規社員と正規社員との間で設けられた相違が合理的に説明が可能であるか検証する必

Chapter VII. Wages and Retirement Allowance

Stipulated according to an annual wage system.

Article 50. (Structure of Wages)
Wages shall consist of the following:
(1) Basic wage as defined in Article 56, Paragraph 1
(2) Annual bonus as defined in Article 56, Paragraph 3
(3) Extra wage allowance
 (i) Extra wages for Overtime Work
 (ii) Extra wages for Work on Designated Holidays
 (iii) Extra wages for Work on Statutory Holidays
 (iv) Extra wages for Late Hour Work
(4) Other allowances
  Commutation allowance

In prescribing the basic wage, annual bonus, and various allowances, it is prohibited to establish any difference that is considered to be unreasonable between part-time employees or fixed-term employees (so-called non-regular employees), and regular employees (so-called regular employees) (Article 8 of the Part-Time Employment and Fixed-Term Employment Act). In this respect, regarding the basic wage and bonus, it is often the case that duties or the framework for the utilization of personnel differ between non-regular employees and regular employees; accordingly, it would be relatively easily permissible for employers to establish a difference between both types of employees concerning the above matters. However, if there is not any substantial difference regarding duties and the like, unreasonably different treatment will be prohibited. On the other hand, employers need to take care when prescribing various allowances. This is because the courts have considered different treatment concerning various allowances to be illegal in some cases. For example, regarding work-related allowances (such as good or perfect attendance and overtime allowance), there is a court precedent where the difference established between non-regular

要があります。どのような相違が許容され得るものかは，同一労働同一賃金ガイドライン案（厚生労働大臣告示として指針化される予定）を参照してください。

なお，多くの日本型の企業では，就業規則本則とは別に賃金規程が設けられ，役職手当，通勤手当及び地域手当等の諸手当が定められていますが，本書では，外資系企業・グローバル企業を念頭におき，年俸制の場合を想定しており，就業規則本則とは別に賃金規程を設けず，諸手当としては通勤手当のみを定めるなど比較的シンプルな構成としています。

第51条　（賃金の支払）

1. 毎月の賃金の計算期間は，前月［21］日から当月［20］日までとし（以下，「賃金締切期間」という。），毎月［25］日を支払日としてその全額を通貨により直接社員に支払う。ただし，社員の同意を得た場合には，当該社員の指定する本人名義の預金口座に振込むことにより支払う。

　　使用者は，労働者の同意を得た場合には，当該労働者が指定する銀行その他の金融機関の本人口座へ振り込む方法によって賃金を支払うことができることとされています（労働基準法24条1項但書，労働基準法施行規則7条の2）。

　　賃金は現金で支払わなければならず，会社の商品等の現物で支払うことはできません（通貨払いの原則）。ただし，前記のとおり，労働者の同意を得た場合は銀行振込等の方法によることができ，労働協約で定めた場合には現物による支払も可能です。なお，銀行振込による支払にする場合は，前記の労働者の同意に加えて，当該事業場に，労働者の過半数で組織する労働組合がある場合においてはその労働組合，労働者の過半数で組織する労働組合がない場合においては労働者の過半数を代表する者と，①銀行振込みの対象となる労働者の範囲，②銀行振込みの対象となる賃金の範囲及び額，③取扱金

employees and regular employees was considered illegal. The purpose or nature of various allowances differs for respective companies; however, employers need to verify whether they can reasonably explain the difference established between non-regular employees and regular employees, based on the nature of the allowance, rather than its name. For permissible differences, please refer to the proposed equal pay for equal work guidelines (scheduled to serve as guidelines in the form of a public notice of the Minister of Health, Labour and Welfare).

Please note that many Japanese-style companies establish wage rules separately from the main text of the work rules, and prescribe therein various allowances such as managerial position allowance, commutation allowance, and area allowance; however, in this book, we focus on foreign companies and global companies, and assume cases where an annual wage system is used. Accordingly, we take a relatively simple structure; for example, we did not set wage rules separately from the main text of the work rules nor prescribe various allowances other than commutation allowance.

Article 51. (Payment of Wages)

1. Wages per month shall be calculated for a period from the [twenty-first (21st)] day of the previous month to the [twentieth (20th)] day of the current month (a "Wage Calculation Period") and be payable to Employees directly in currency on the [twenty-fifth (25th)] day of every month. However, with the consent of Employees, the Company may pay wages by direct deposit to the bank account in the name of a principal designated by him/her.

> With the consent of the employee, an employer may pay wages via direct deposit to the bank account or other banking establishment account in the name of a principal designated by him/her (proviso of Article 24, Paragraph 1; Article 7-2 of the Ordinance for Enforcement of the Labor Standards Act).
> Wages must be paid in cash, and cannot be paid by the provision of goods, such as the company's products (principle of paying by currency). As above, however, the company may pay by direct deposit if consent from the employee has been obtained. Payment by the provision of goods is permitted if allowed under the collective labor agreement.
> In addition to the above consent of the employee, an employer must execute an agreement regarding (i) the range of employees who are paid by direct deposit to a bank account, (ii) the range and amount of wages paid by bank transfer, (iii) the

> 融機関の範囲，④銀行振込みの実施開始時期について書面による協定を結ぶ必要があります（平13．2．2基発54号）。また，賃金は直接労働者本人に支払わなくてはならず，労働者の親権者その他の法定代理人や，労働者の委任を受けた任意代理人へ支払うことはできません（直接払いの原則）。

2. 基本給の支払の際，次のものを控除する。
   (1) 法令に基づくもの
      ① 源泉所得税
      ② 住民税
      ③ 各種社会保険料
   [(2) 労使協定に基づくもの（もしあれば）]
      ① 組合費
      ② 貸付金
      ③ その他

> 賃金はその全額を労働者に支払わなければならず，「積立金」等の名目で強制的に賃金の一部を控除して支払うことは禁止されています（全額払いの原則）。ただし，所得税や社会保険料等法令で定められているもの及び労使協定により賃金から控除することができることとしたものについては，控除が認められています。

3. 賃金締切期間の中途において入社若しくは退社，又は，休職（第15条但書に基づく場合を除く。）若しくは復職した者に対する当該賃金締切期間における賃金は，日割りで計算して就業日数に応じて支給するものとする。
4. 本就業規則及びその附属規程における1か月平均所定労働時間数は，次の算式により計算する。

$$\frac{(365 - 年間の所定及び法定休日日数) \times 1日の所定労働時間数}{12}$$

5. 第1項に定める支払日が銀行の休業日に当たる場合は，その直前の銀行の営業日をその月の支払日とみなす。
6. 割増賃金手当は当月分を計算し，翌月の支払日に支払うものとする。

range of financial institutions into which wages may be paid, and (iv) the timing for the commencement of the bank transfer, in writing with either (a) a labor union organized by a majority of the employees at the workplace concerned (where such labor union is organized), or (b) a person representing a majority of the employees at the workplace concerned (where a labor union organized by a majority of the employees at the workplace is not organized) in the case where the employer pays wages by direct deposit to bank accounts (Circular Notice, Kihatsu, No. 54, February 2, 2001).

Wages must be paid directly to each employee, and cannot be paid to a legal guardian of the employee, any other legally designated representative, or any agent who has been entrusted by the employee (principle of direct payment).

2. The following shall be deducted from the payment of basic wages:
   (1) As required by laws and ordinances
       (i) Withholding tax
       (ii) Resident tax
       (iii) Social insurance premiums
   [(2) As based on a Labor-Management Agreement, if any]
       (i) Union dues
       (ii) Loans
       (iii) Others

   The entire amount of wages must be paid to the employee, and setting aside a certain amount of wages under the pretext of "deposits" is not permitted (principle of paying the entire wage). However, deductions are permitted under certain circumstances if prescribed by laws, such as income tax and social insurance premiums, or prescribed by labor-management agreements.

3. The wage for an Employee who joins or resigns from the Company, or takes a leave of absence (excluding in the case under the proviso of Article 15) or resumes duties prior to the end of a Wage Calculation Period shall be paid for the relevant period on a pro-rated basis according to the number of days worked.

4. The average designated working hours referred to in the Work Rules and

7. その他手当は毎月基本給と同時に支払うものとする。

第52条 （非常時払）

社員又はその収入によって生計を維持する者が，次のいずれかに該当し，その費用に当てるため，社員から請求があったときは，そのときまでの労働に対する賃金を支払う。
(1) 出産，疾病又は災害の場合
(2) 結婚又は死亡の場合
(3) やむを得ない理由によって1週間以上帰郷する場合

第53条 （欠　勤）

社員が欠勤した場合は，以下の計算式に従って基本給を減額する。

$$\frac{月額基本給 - 第56条第2項に定義する割増賃金相当額}{1か月平均所定労働日数} \times 欠勤日数$$

第54条 （年俸制）

> 日本の会社における基本給の定め方としては，学歴・年齢及び勤続年数によって定まる年齢給（勤続給），当該企業における職務遂行能力の種別であ

supplementary regulations hereto shall be calculated using the following formula:

$$\frac{(365 - \text{No. of designated and statutory holidays per year}) \times \text{Average designated working hours per day}}{12}$$

5. If a pay day set forth in Paragraph 1 falls on a bank holiday, the bank business day immediately preceding that day shall be deemed to be the pay day for that month.
6. Extra wage allowance shall be calculated for the current month, and be paid on the pay day of the following month.
7. Other allowances shall be paid concurrently with the basic wage every month.

Article 52. (Payment upon Emergency)

If an Employee or a person dependent on the Employee's income for their livelihood falls under any of the following, and the Employee requests the emergency payment of wages to cover the necessary cost, the Company shall pay his/her wages according to the number of days worked until the request is made:

(1) In the case of childbirth, sickness, or disaster
(2) In the case of marriage or death
(3) In the case of going home for one (1) week or more for unavoidable reasons.

Article 53. (Absence)

In the case of an Employee's absence, his/her basic wage shall be reduced using the following formula:

$$\frac{\text{Monthly amount of basic wage} - \text{Amount Corresponding to Extra Wages, as defined in Article 56, Paragraph 2 hereafter}}{\text{Average designated working hours per month}} \times \text{No. of days of absence}$$

Article 54. (Annual Wage System)

Common methods of determining wages in Japanese companies include the use of (i) a wage system based on academic background, age, or number of years of

> る職能資格とそのなかでのランクによって定まる職能給等が代表的です（両者が併用されることもあります。）。近年は，いわゆる成果主義や能力主義の人事管理の進展のなかで，職務等級制（企業内の職務を役割や責任の大きさに応じて等級に分類し，等級ごとに給与範囲を設定する制度）等の賃金形態を採用する企業も増えています。
>
> 　年俸制とは，賃金額を年単位で決定する制度であり，その具体的な内容は設計の仕方により異なります。近年は，一年間にわたる仕事の成果等を勘案して，翌年一年間の賃金を決定することにしている企業が多く，このような年俸制は，成果主義的な賃金制度の一つとも言えます。
> 　本規定例においても，年俸制を採用し，労働者の職務遂行能力に加え，労働者の業績等に関する目標の達成度や会社の業務成績等を考慮して，賃金を決定することができることにし，ある程度，仕事の成果等に応じた賃金の設定が可能となるようにしています。

1. 基本給及び賞与は，年俸制で決めるものとする（以下，「年俸額」という。）。
2. 年俸額の計算期間は，1月1日より同年12月31日までとする（以下，「給与年度」という。）。
3. 年俸額のうち16分の12を基本給とし，16分の4を賞与とする。ただし，賞与は第56条第4項に定める条件を満たす者にのみ支給するものとする。

第55条　（年俸額の決め方）

1. 年俸額は，毎年［1］月［1］日に改定する。
2. 年俸額は，職務の内容，責任の大きさ，経験年数，社員の職務遂行能力，前給与年度における本人の目標の達成度，会社への貢献度，職務態度，会社の年間業務成績，同業他社の賃金等を総合的に判断することにより会社

continuous service, or (ii) a wage system based on ability-qualification, that is, the class of the Employee's ability to carry out his/her work in the company and his/her rank in the ability-qualification system (both methods (i) and (ii) can be used together). Recently, there have been developments in managing personnel by performance pay or ability pay, and more companies have used payment structures utilizing a wage system such as a system of classification based on employees' type of office (the policy of grouping employees by class depending on the role or the scope of responsibilities, and stipulating the wage range accordingly).

An annual wage system is a system to determine the amount of wages year by year, and the specific nature of the annual wage system depends on the design of the system. Recently, there are many companies that determine wages for the next year by taking into consideration employees' work performance during the current year. Such an annual wage system may be classified as a system for managing personnel by performance pay.

This provision adopts an annual wage system that enables the company to determine the amount of wages based on employees' work performance by taking into consideration not only an employee's ability to carry out his/her work in the company, but also that employee's level of achievement of his/her goals related to the employee's performance at work, and company performance, etc.

1. The basic wage and bonuses shall be determined under the annual wage system (the "Amount of Annual Wages").

2. The calculation period of the Amount of Annual Wages shall be from January 1 to December 31 of the same year (the "Wage Year").

3. The Amount of Annual Wages shall consist of basic wage (12/16) and bonuses (4/16). However, bonuses shall be payable only to Employees who satisfy the requirements set forth in Article 56, Paragraph 4.

Article 55. (Method for Determining the Amount of Annual Wages)

1. The Amount of Annual Wages shall be revised on January 1 every year.

2. The Amount of Annual Wages shall be determined by the Company, by comprehensively judging the duties, the scale of responsibility, years of service, performance of duties of Employees, the level of accomplishment of the previous

3. 前項の決定に際しては，会社と社員が個別面接を行う。

> 減額の限界を示す観点から，別表を添付し，当該別表において役割等級ごとに基本年俸額を定め，年俸の下限を明確にすることが考えられます。この場合には，会社の裁量の幅が狭くなりすぎないように，就業規則等において，役割等級を会社が柔軟に変更することができるように設計することが考えられます。
>
> なお，決定基準・決定方法を全く定めていなかった事例において，新年度の年俸額についての合意が成立しない場合について，年俸額決定のための成果・業績評価基準，年俸額決定手続，減額の限界の有無，不服申立手続等が制度化されて就業規則等に明示され，かつ，その内容が公正な場合に限り，使用者に評価決定権があるというべきであり，これらの要件が満たされていない場合には，特別の事情が認められない限り，使用者に一方的な評価決定権はないと解するのが相当であるとする裁判例があります（日本システム開発研究所事件（東京高判平成20年4月9日労判959号6頁））。ただし，当該裁判例については，ここで列挙されている内容を，要件として要求するのは厳格にすぎるとし，要素として位置づけるのが妥当との有力な見解があります（荒木尚志『労働法（第3版）』131，132頁）。

第56条　（年俸の配分）

> 年俸の支給方法は，労働基準法24条2項の毎月1回以上払の原則により12分割して毎月支払われるのが一般的ですが，本条のように賞与部分を設ける場合もあります。毎月1回以上支払う限りは，年俸額の分配方法について特に法の定めるものはありません。

Chapter VII. Wages and Retirement Allowance 205

Wage Year, the level of contribution to the Company, Employees' attitudes towards work, annual business results of the Company, the wages of other companies in the same business field, etc.

3. The determination of the Amount of Annual Wages set forth in the preceding paragraph shall be made through an interview between each Employee and the Company.

> **In order to indicate the limit on the amount of deduction, companies may attach a chart that shows the base amount of annual wages for each grade with a lower limit. In this case, companies have an option instead to design work rules, etc., to allow them to change the grade of employees flexibly so that the discretion of the company is not unduly limited.**
>
> **There is a court precedent whereby, where work rules do not stipulate the criteria or method for determining the amount of annual wages, when a company and an employee do not reach an agreement on the amount of annual wages for the next year, companies have the right to determine the amount of annual wages only if assessment criteria for determining the amount of annual wages, a method for determining the amount of annual wages, the presence or absence of the limit of the deduction, an objection process, etc., are institutionalized and stipulated in work rules, etc., and such rules are fair; otherwise, the company does not have the right to unilaterally decide the amount of annual wages unless the circumstances are exceptional (Nihon System Kaihatsu case, Judgement of the Tokyo High Court, April 9, 2008 (pp. 6, Rodo Hanrei No. 959)). However, a renowned professor has commented that this court precedent is too strict in requiring companies to stipulate all these items as requirements; therefore, it is more reasonable to think of these items as factors (pp. 131, 132, Araki Hisashi "Labor Law (3rd Edition)").**

Article 56. (Allocation of Annual Wage)

> **Paying wages once a month by dividing the annual wage into twelve (12) parts, as stipulated in Article 24, Paragraph 2 of the Labor Standards Act, is a common method. It is possible to provide for a bonus, as stipulated in this provision. As long as wages are paid at least once a month, there is no statutory distribution method for disbursing the annual wages.**

1. 基本給は，年俸額の16分の1を毎月支給する。
2. 前項の毎月支給する基本給には，次に定める割増賃金相当額を含むものとする（以下，第1号及び第2号の割増賃金相当額を合わせて「割増賃金相当額」という。）。ただし，一賃金締切期間における現実の時間外労働又は深夜労働の時間数がそれぞれ次に定める時間に満たない場合であっても，基本給は減額しない。
   (1) 第58条第1項に定める時間外労働割増賃金のうち，［30］時間分の時間外労働に対する割増賃金相当額
   (2) 第61条第1項に定める深夜労働割増賃金のうち，［10］時間分の深夜労働に対する割増賃金相当額

> 　年俸制をとった場合でも，割増賃金支払義務は免れず，時間外労働等については割増賃金を支払わなくてはなりません。もっとも，あらかじめ就業規則で定めることにより，年俸額に時間外労働等に対する割増賃金相当額を一定範囲で組み込み，当該範囲の割増賃金は都度払わなくてよいようにすることも可能です。この場合，通常の賃金分と割増賃金分が明確に区分されていなければならないため，年俸額に含まれる割増賃金の範囲を明確に定めておく必要があります。本規定例では，30時間分の時間外労働割増賃金と10時間分の深夜労働割増賃金を年俸額に含めることとし，休日労働割増賃金は年俸額に含めないこととしていますが，この定め方は一例にすぎず，他の定め方をすることも可能です。ただし，組み込まれた割増賃金分を超えた部分については別途割増賃金を計算して支払う必要があることに注意する必要があります。第58条第2項及び第61条第2項ではその計算方法を定めています。

3. 賞与は，年俸額の16分の2を年2回［6月］と［12月］に支給する。
4. 社員が給与年度の途中で退社又は休職（第15条但書に基づく場合を除く。）した場合には，退社日及び休職開始日以降の期間に対応する年俸額は支給しない。
5. 第1項及び第3項の規定にかかわらず，社員が給与年度の途中で退社した場合には，社員（社員が死亡したときはその遺族）の請求により，基本給又は賞与の支給日の前であっても，日割計算により基本給又は賞与を支

1. 1/16th of the Amount of Annual Wages shall be paid monthly as the basic wage.
2. The basic wage to be paid monthly as set forth in the preceding paragraph shall include the amounts corresponding to extra wages set forth in Items 1 and 2 below ("Amount Corresponding to Extra Wages"). However, the basic wage shall not be reduced even if the actual hours of Overtime Work or Late Hour Work are less than the number of hours listed below in one Wage Calculation Period:
   (1) The Amount Corresponding to Extra Wages for [thirty (30)] hours of Overtime Work in the extra wages for Overtime Work set forth in Article 58, Paragraph 1; and
   (2) The Amount Corresponding to Extra Wages for [ten (10)] hours of Late Hour Work out of the extra wages for Late Hour Work set forth in Article 61, Paragraph 1.

> **Even if an annual wage system is used, the employer is not exempted from the duty to pay extra wages and must pay extra wages for overtime work. It is possible to not pay extra wages as they arise, if a certain amount of extra wages for overtime work is included in the annual wage within a certain scope by stipulating this in the work rules in advance. In such a situation, it is necessary to clearly differentiate between ordinary wages and extra wages. In this example, 30 hours' worth of extra wages for overtime work and 10 hours' worth of extra wages for late hour work are included in the annual wage. Extra wages for work on holidays is not included in the annual wage. This provision is only one example, and other arrangements are possible. Please note, however, that any amount that exceeds the predetermined extra wages must be paid separately. A method to calculate such extra wages is set forth in Article 58, Paragraph 2, and Article 61, Paragraph 2.**

3. 2/16ths of the Amount of Annual Wages shall be paid twice per year [in June] and [in December] on the pay day of the relevant month.
4. An Employee who resigns from the Company or takes a leave of absence (excluding in the case under the proviso of Article 15) prior to the end of a Wage Year shall not be entitled to receive the Amount of Annual Wages corresponding to the portion of the Wage Year after his/her resignation date or taking a leave of absence.
5. Notwithstanding the provisions of Paragraph 1 and 3, if an Employee resigns from the Company in the middle of the Wage Year, the basic wages and bonuses shall be paid in an amount calculated on a pro-rated basis even prior to the pay day, upon the

給する。

> 就業規則等において，支給日又は一定の基準日に在籍する者に限り賞与を支給するという取扱いをすることがあり，賞与には，過去の労働に対する報酬としての意味だけでなく，将来の労働に対する意欲向上や支給日又は基準日までの就労確保の狙いもあることから，一般には，このような取扱いも合理的であり有効と解されています。もっとも，本就業規則のように賞与の金額が予め確定している場合には，過去の業績に対する対価としての意味合いが強くなるため，このような場合においては，支給日又は一定の基準日に在籍する者に限り賞与を支給するという取扱いは合理性を有さず，無効であると判断される可能性があります。したがって，本規程例においては，そのような取扱いとはせずに，在籍期間に応じて日割り計算により賞与を支給する取扱いにしています。

第57条　（給与年度内の昇進）
　　給与年度内に職位の昇格又は降格が行われる場合には，残期間の給与は，必要に応じて改訂するものとする。

第58条　（時間外労働割増賃金）

> 中小事業主（第１部第１章４-２参照）の事業については，従前，１か月60時間を超える時間外労働に係る割増賃金率（50％以上）の適用が猶予されていましたが（労働基準法138条），改正労働基準法により猶予措置が廃止され，平成35年（2023年）４月１日より中小事業主にも上記の割増賃金率が適用されることとなりました。

1.　時間外労働割増賃金は，第25条第１項に定める所定労働時間を超え，第29条の定めるところにより所属長の指示により早出，若しくは残業した時間外労働について支給される。
2.　一賃金締切期間の時間外労働の時間数が［30］時間を超える場合，１時

request from the Employee (if the Employee has died, from his/her bereaved family).

It is often stipulated in a company's work rules that bonuses are only paid to employees who are employees of the company as of the bonus payment date, or a certain specified date. Such treatment is generally considered reasonable and valid because bonuses are not only meant to reward for past service, but also to incentivize future service or secure services for the period until such bonus payment date or certain specified date. On the other hand, where the bonus amounts are fixed in advance by a company's work rules, a provision whereby bonuses are only paid to employees who are employees of the company as of the bonus payment date or certain specified date may be deemed unreasonable and invalid. This is because such fixed bonuses, rather than being the incentive mentioned above, are compensation for services already provided in the past. Therefore, this provision does not provide that bonuses are only paid to employees who are employees of the company as of the bonus payment date, but rather that bonuses shall be paid to every employee in an amount calculated on a prorated basis.

Article 57. (Promotion and Demotion within the Wage Year)

In the case where an Employee is promoted or demoted within a Wage Year, his/her wages for the remaining period shall be revised as needed.

Article 58. (Extra Wages for Overtime Work)

Previously, the businesses of small and medium-sized employers (please refer to Section 4-2 of Chapter I, Part I.) were exempted from application of the extra wage rate (no less than 50%) for overtime work that exceeds 60 hours per month (Article 138 of the Labor Standards Act). However, the amendment of the Labor Standards Act will abolish the exemption, and the extra wage rate above will also apply to small and medium-sized employers from April 1, 2023.

1. Extra wages for Overtime Work shall be paid for the hours of Overtime Work exceeding the designated working hours set forth in Article 25, Paragraph 1 to an Employee who comes to work early or works overtime due to his/her supervisor's instruction pursuant to Article 29.

間につき次の計算方式により算定される時間外労働割増賃金を支給する。

(1) 1か月60時間以下の時間外労働

$$\frac{月額基本給 - 第56条第２項に定義する割増賃金相当額}{1か月平均所定労働時間} \times 1.25$$

(2) 1か月60時間を超える時間外労働

$$\frac{月額基本給 - 第56条第２項に定義する割増賃金相当額}{1か月平均所定労働時間} \times 1.50$$

　1か月60時間の計算においては，時間外労働の時間数は法定労働時間を超える時間外労働の時間数だけをカウントし，所定労働時間を超えて法定労働時間までの時間（法内残業）及び法定休日労働の時間は含まれません。法定休日以外の休日（所定休日）における労働時間で法定労働時間を超えるものはカウントされます（第26条第３項の解説参照）。また，1か月の起算日は，就業規則に定めがあればその起算日となりますが，特に定めがない場合は賃金締切期間の初日を起算日とすることになっています（平21.5.29基発0529001号）。

　割増賃金の計算の基礎となる賃金は「通常の労働時間又は労働日の賃金」であり，①家族手当，通勤手当，別居手当，子女教育手当，住宅手当（これらは労働の量や質と関係なく労働者の個人的事情に基づき支給されるものであり，名称のいかんを問わず，実質的に判断されます。），②臨時に支払われた賃金（なお，年度当初に年俸額を決定し，その一部を賞与として支払う年俸制における賞与はこれに該当しないとされています。），③1か月を超える期間ごとに支払われる賃金（賞与や勤続手当等）は算定の基礎から除外されます。本規定例では，30時間分の時間外労働割増賃金と10時間分の深夜労働割増賃金を年俸額に含めることとしている関係上，基本給からこれら

Chapter VII. Wages and Retirement Allowance 211

2. Where the hours of Overtime Work exceed [thirty (30)] hours in one Wage Calculation Period, extra wages for Overtime Work calculated using the following formula per hour shall be paid:

(1) For Overtime Work of sixty (60) hours or less in one (1) month

$$\frac{\text{Monthly amount of basic wage} - \text{Amount Corresponding to Extra Wages as defined in Article 56, Paragraph 2 hereafter}}{\text{Average designated working hours per month}} \times 1.25$$

(2) For Overtime Work of more than sixty (60) hours in one (1) month

$$\frac{\text{Monthly amount of basic wage} - \text{Amount Corresponding to Extra Wages as defined in Article 56, Paragraph 2 hereafter}}{\text{Average designated working hours per month}} \times 1.50$$

When calculating the 60 hours per month, the number of overtime work hours should only be counted if the number of overtime work hours exceeds the statutory working hours. (i) The number of working hours that exceeds the designated working hours, but does not exceed the statutory working hours, and (ii) working hours during statutory holidays, are not counted. Working hours during holidays other than statutory holidays (i.e., designated holidays), and which exceed statutory working hours, are counted (see the commentary on Article 26, Paragraph 3). Further, the starting date of one month is considered to be the first day of the month for which the wages are calculated unless otherwise provided in the work rules (Circular Notice, Kihatsu, No. 0529001, May 29, 2009).

The base wage for the purpose of calculating extra wages is limited to "wages for working during ordinary working hours or working days." (i) Family allowances, commuting allowances, allowances for living separately from the family, education allowances, living allowances (these allowances shall be paid due to reasons of an individual employee irrespective of the quantity and quality of the employee's work, and whether any allowance falls under this category of allowances shall be judged substantially and irrespective of their name), (ii) extraordinary wages (further, bonuses which are paid as part of the Amount of Annual Wages which is determined from the beginning of the year are not included), and (iii) wages paid for a time period that exceeds 1 month (including

の割増賃金の額を差し引いて1か月平均所定労働時間で除した額が，割増賃金の計算の基礎となります。なお，この場合，割増賃金の計算の基礎となる額（1時間当たりの単価）は，次の計算式により導くことができます。すなわち，割増賃金の計算の基礎となる額をAとし，1か月平均所定労働時間をHとすると，A＝{月額基本給−（A×1.25×30＋A×0.25×10)}／Hとなり，これを整理すると，A＝月額基本給／（H＋40）となります。

また，近時の判例（最判平成24年3月8日集民240号121頁）には，櫻井裁判官による，便宜的に毎月の給与のなかにあらかじめ一定時間の残業手当が算入されているものとして給与が支払われている場合（いわゆる定額残業制の場合）には，①一定時間の残業手当が算入されている旨が雇用契約上も明確であり，②支給時に支給対象の時間外労働の時間数と残業手当の額が当然に労働者に明示され，③①で示した一定時間を超えて残業が行われた場合には別途上乗せして残業手当を支給する旨があらかじめ明らかにされていなければならないという補足意見が付されているため留意が必要です。

第59条　（所定休日労働割増賃金）

> 労働基準法上休日労働割増賃金の支払が必要になるのは，法定休日に労働した場合のみです。法定休日以外の所定休日における労働については，法定労働時間を超えた部分について，時間外労働として25％以上の割増賃金率で割増賃金を支払うこととなります。

1. 所定休日労働割増賃金は，法定休日以外の所定休日に労働した場合に支給される。
2. 前項の手当は，1時間につき，次の計算方式により算定される。

bonuses and money paid for continued service), are all excluded from the basis of calculation. In this provision, 30 hours' worth of extra wages for overtime work and ten (10) hours' worth of extra wages for late hour work are included in the annual wage. Therefore, the basic wages for late hour work are included in the annual wage. Therefore, the base wage for the purpose of calculating extra wages is the amount calculated by deducting the extra wages from the basic wage, and then dividing by the average designated working hours per month. In this case, the amount serving as a basis for the calculation of extra wages (i.e., an amount per hour) can be determined using the following formula: Assuming that the amount serving as a basis for the calculation of extra wages is "A" and the average designated working hours per month is "H," A = {monthly amount of basic wage − (A×1.25×30 + A×0.25×10)}/H; in other words, A = monthly amount of basic wage/(H + 40).

Further, please note the supporting opinion by judge Sakurai in a court precedent (Judgement of the Supreme Court, March 8, 2012) which states that in the case of a monthly salary which includes an allowance for overtime work for a certain period (the "Certain Period") (in the case of so-called flat-rate overtime work), (i) it shall be stated clearly in the employment agreement that salary includes allowances for overtime work for the Certain Period, (ii) the number of hours for overtime work and allowance for overtime work to be paid shall be stated clearly at the time of payment of salary to employees, and (iii) it shall be stated clearly in advance that an employer must pay an additional allowance for overtime work beyond the Certain Period in the case where an employee works overtime beyond the Certain Period.

Article 59. (Extra Wages for Work on Designated Holidays)

An employer needs to pay extra wages for holiday work pursuant to the Labor Standards Act only if an employee has worked on a statutory holiday. An employer needs to pay an extra wage rate of not less than 25% for overtime work if an employee has worked on a designated holiday other than a statutory holiday; such a payment will be made for the portion that exceeded the statutory working hours.

1. Extra Wages for Work on Designated Holidays shall be paid when an Employee works on designated holidays excluding statutory holidays.

$$\frac{\text{月額基本給} - \text{第56条第2項に定義する割増賃金相当額}}{1\text{か月平均所定労働時間}} \times 1.25$$

第60条 （法定休日労働割増賃金）
1. 法定休日労働割増賃金は，第26条第3項に定める法定休日に労働した場合に支給される。
2. 前項の手当は，1時間につき，次の計算方式により算定される。

$$\frac{\text{月額基本給} - \text{第56条第2項に定義する割増賃金相当額}}{1\text{か月平均所定労働時間}} \times 1.35$$

第61条 （深夜労働割増賃金）
1. 深夜労働割増賃金は，午後10時以降午前5時までの間に労働した場合に支給される。
2. 一賃金締切期間の深夜労働の時間数が［10］時間を超える場合，1時間につき次の計算方式により算定される深夜労働割増賃金を支給する。

$$\frac{\text{月額基本給} - \text{第56条第2項に定義する割増賃金相当額}}{1\text{か月平均所定労働時間}} \times 1.25$$

> 深夜労働と時間外労働又は休日労働が重なる場合は，深夜労働の割増賃金率に時間外労働又は休日労働の割増賃金率が加算されます（第29条第3項の解説参照）。また，管理監督者等の労働時間規制の適用除外者であっても深夜割増賃金の支払は必要とされています（第35条の解説参照）。

2. Allowances under the preceding paragraph shall be calculated using the following formula per hour:

$$\frac{\text{Monthly amount of basic wage} - \text{Amount Corresponding to Extra Wages as defined in Article 56, Paragraph 2 hereafter}}{\text{Average designated working hours per month}} \times 1.25$$

Article 60. (Extra Wages for Work on Statutory Holidays)

1. Extra Wages for Statutory Work on Holidays shall be paid when an Employee works on the statutory holidays prescribed in Article 26, Paragraph 3.
2. Allowances under the preceding paragraph shall be calculated using the following formula per hour:

$$\frac{\text{Monthly amount of basic wage} - \text{Amount Corresponding to Extra Wages as defined in Article 56, Paragraph 2 hereafter}}{\text{Average designated working hours per month}} \times 1.35$$

Article 61. (Extra Wages for Late Hour Work)

1. Extra wages for Late Hour Work shall be paid when an Employee works between the hours of 22:00 and 5:00.
2. Where the hours of Late Hour Work exceed [ten (10)] hours in one Wage Calculation Period, extra wages for Late Hour Work calculated using the following formula per hour shall be paid:

$$\frac{\text{Monthly amount of basic wage} - \text{Amount Corresponding to Extra Wages as defined in Article 56, Paragraph 2 hereafter}}{\text{Average designated working hours per month}} \times 1.25$$

> **If there is an overlap in late hour work and either (i) overtime work, or (ii) work on holidays, the extra wage rate for work on holidays or overtime work is added to the extra wage rate for late hour work (see the commentary on Article 29, Paragraph 3). Even if the employee is exempted from the working hour policies due to his/her being in a managerial and supervisory position, it is still necessary to pay extra wages for late hour work (see the commentary on Article 35).**

第62条　（割増賃金手当の計算方法）
　　第58条から第61条において，1か月における時間外労働，休日労働及び深夜労働に対する割増賃金手当の総額に1円未満の端数が生じた場合，1円に切り上げる。

第63条　（通勤手当）
　　通勤手当は，社員の住所から勤務先までの最も合理的な経路及び方法により公共交通機関を利用した場合に要する1か月の定期券代を毎月支給する。

第64条　（退　職　金）
　　退職金の決定，計算及び支払等に関する細則は，別途定める「退職金規程」による。

> 　日本法において，使用者には退職金の支払義務はなく，退職金制度を設けるか否かは使用者の判断に委ねられています。退職金制度を設ける場合には就業規則への記載が必要となりますが，規定が詳細になるため別途退職金規程を設けるのが一般的です。退職金規程に定めるべき事項は次のとおりです。
> 　・目的
> 　・適用される労働者の範囲
> 　・退職金の受給資格
> 　・退職金の額の算定方法
> 　・勤続年数の計算方法，上限
> 　・特別功労加算金
> 　・支給制限（不支給・減額事由）と退職金の返還
> 　・支給時期，支給方法
> 　・端数処理

Chapter VII. Wages and Retirement Allowance   217

Article 62. (Method of Calculation of Extra Wage Allowance)
With respect to Articles 58 through 61, if there is a fraction of less than one (1) yen in the total amount of extra wage allowance for Overtime Work, Work on Holidays, and Late Hour Work, the fraction shall be rounded up to one (1) yen.

Article 63. (Commuting Allowance)
Commuting allowance shall be paid every month in an amount equal to the cost of a one (1)-month commuter pass required to commute from the domicile of the Employee to the workplace calculated by the most reasonable route and method using public transportation.

Article 64. (Retirement Allowance)
Details regarding determination, calculation, and payment, etc. of the retirement allowance shall be provided separately in the "Retirement Allowance Regulations."

> An employer does not need to pay any retirement allowances under Japanese law, and it has discretion to decide whether to provide a retirement allowance. It is necessary to stipulate in the work rules if an employer wishes to establish a retirement allowance policy. Since the details of such policies are very specific, it is common to separately stipulate rules regarding retirement allowances. Rules regarding retirement allowances should specify the following items:
> · Purpose
> · Scope of applicable employees
> · Qualifications necessary to receive retirement allowance
> · Calculation method of retirement allowance
> · Calculation method of number of years worked, upper limit
> · Additional amount for distinguished service
> · Limitation of payment (non-payment, reasons for deduction) and returning retirement allowances
> · Payment timing and method
> · How to deal with fractions

第8章　服務規律

> 服務規律に関する事項は，必ず定めなければならないものではありませんが，定めた場合には，就業規則への記載が必要となります。会社の秩序維持のために必要不可欠であり，懲戒処分の根拠となるため，就業規則において服務規律を定める例が一般的です。

第65条　（服務の原則）
1. 社員は，本就業規則に定めるほか，所属長の指示命令に従い，自己の業務に専念し，創意を発揮して能力向上に努めるとともに，互いに協力して職場の秩序を維持向上しなければならない。
2. 所属長は，その所属社員の人格を尊重し誠意をもって指導し，率先してその職責を遂行しなければならない。

第66条　（一般禁止行為）
社員は，次の各号に掲げる行為をしてはならない。
(1) 会社の事前の承認なしに，会社の機密情報又は書類を第三者に開示すること
(2) 個人情報の取扱いに関して法令・社内規程等に違反すること
(3) 会社の内外を問わず，会社の評判や信用を損うこと

> 会社外での労働者の行為は，原則として会社の支配が及ばないものであるため，それが事業活動に直接関連を有するものである場合又は会社の社会的評価の毀損をもたらすものである場合に限り，服務規律違反として懲戒の対象となると限定的に解されています。

(4) 会社における地位や権限を利用して自己の利益を図り若しくは会社に損

Chapter VIII. Work Discipline

> Items regarding work discipline do not need to be provided. If they are stipulated, however, these items must be provided in the work rules. It is common to stipulate disciplinary provisions in the work rules since these are indispensable for maintaining order within the company, and the items can serve as a basis for disciplinary action.

Article 65. (Observance of Discipline)

1. Employees must devote themselves to their own duties by observing the Work Rules and following their supervisor's instructions, improve their capabilities by making the best use of their ingenuity, and maintain and improve the order of the workplace by cooperating with each other.

2. The supervisor must instruct each Employee under his/her management with faithfulness by honoring the personality of each Employee, and shall take the initiative in performing his/her own duties.

Article 66. (Generally Prohibited Acts)

Employees shall not commit any of the following acts:

(1) To disclose confidential information or documents of the Company to a third party without the Company's prior approval;

(2) To violate laws, regulations, internal rules, or the like related to the handling of personal information;

(3) To damage the reputation and trustworthiness of the Company within or outside of the Company;

> Behavior of employees outside of the company is, in principle, not subject to the company's control. Therefore, an employee is considered to be subject to disciplinary action due to a violation of the disciplinary provisions only if such behavior directly affects the business activities of the company, or damages the

害を与えること，又は会社の許可なく会社の金品若しくは文書類を持ち出し，使用し又は他者に貸与，交付若しくは提示すること
(5) 勤務時間中に特別な用事がないのに職場をしばしば離れること
(6) 勤務時間中に会社の敷地内で政治的活動に従事すること
(7) 事前の承認なく会社の敷地内で集会を開き，演説を行い，掲示を貼付し又はチラシを頒布すること
(8) 勤務時間中に会社の敷地内で，金銭の貸借をし，物品の売買を行い，他の従業員に寄附を強要し，その他会社の事業以外の事業を行うこと
(9) 会社での現在又は過去の職務遂行中に考案した発明に関し，会社の明示の承認なしに，特許その他の権利（工業所有権を含む。）の出願をすること
(10) セクシュアルハラスメントを行うこと。なおセクシュアルハラスメントの詳細については，「ハラスメント防止規程」により別途定める。
(11) パワーハラスメントを行うこと。なおパワーハラスメントの詳細については，「ハラスメント防止規程」により別途定める。
(12) 妊娠・出産・育児休業・介護休業等に関するハラスメントを行うこと。なお，妊娠・出産・育児休業・介護休業等に関するハラスメントの詳細については，「ハラスメント防止規程」により別途定める。
(13) 会社の規程，指示・命令に反する行為を行うこと
(14) その他前各号に準ずる行為を行うこと

第67条　（副業・兼業）
1. 社員は，勤務時間外において，他の会社等の業務に従事することができ

social reputation of the company.

(4) To act in order to pursue one's personal interest by taking advantage of one's position and authority within the Company or cause damage to the Company, or remove or utilize or lend, deliver or present to others, the Company's money, goods or documents without the Company's permission;

(5) To leave the workplace during work hours repeatedly without any good reasons;

(6) To engage in any political activities during work hours and on the Company's premises;

(7) To organize rallies, make speeches, post notices, or distribute handbills on the Company's premises without prior approval;

(8) To make a loan or borrow money, sell or buy goods, coerce other employees into making donations or conduct any business other than the Company's during work hours and on the Company's premises;

(9) To apply for any patent or other right (including industrial property rights) relating to an invention developed during his/her past or present employment with the Company without the Company's express approval;

(10) To commit sexual harassment. Details of sexual harassment shall be separately provided in the "Regulations on the Prevention of Harassment";

(11) To commit power harassment. Details of power harassment shall be separately provided in the "Regulations on the Prevention of Harassment";

(12) To commit harassment related to pregnancy, childbirth, child-care leave, family care leave, or the like. Details of harassment related to pregnancy, childbirth, child-care leave, family care leave, or the like shall be separately provided in the "Regulations on the Preveution of Harrassment."

(13) To commit any acts against regulations, instructions or orders of the Company; or

(14) To commit any acts similar to any of the foregoing items.

Article 67. (Secondary Occupation/Side Occupation)

1. Employees may engage in the business of another employer or the like outside the

る。
2. 社員は，前項の業務に従事するにあたっては，事前に，会社に所定の届出を行うものとする。
3. 第1項の業務に従事することにより，次の各号のいずれかに該当する場合には，会社は，これを禁止又は制限することができる。
 (1) 労務提供上の支障がある場合
 (2) 会社の秘密が漏洩する場合
 (3) 会社の名誉や信用を損なう行為や，信頼関係を破壊する行為がある場合
 (4) 競業その他の事情により，会社の利益を害するおそれがある場合
4. 社員が，他の会社等の業務に従事する場合には，会社の求めるところに従い，他の会社等の業務に従事した時間等につき報告するものとする。

　憲法上職業の自由が保障されていることから，業務に支障を来さない限り，副業・兼業を行うか否かは原則として労働者の自由に委ねられていると解されています。平成30年1月に公表された厚生労働省のモデル就業規則では，副業・兼業に関する規定振りが大きく変わり，原則として副業・兼業が労働者の自由になし得ることが確認されました。もっとも，使用者が就業規則や契約によって労働者の副業・兼業を禁止又は制限することが認められる場合も存在しており，例えば，裁判例においては，3項に列挙したような場合において，副業・兼業に対する禁止又は制限が有効とされています。なお，3項1号の「労務提供上の支障がある場合」については，「副業・兼業が原因で自社の業務が十分に行えない場合」や「長時間労働など労働者の健康に影響が生じるおそれがある場合」が含まれると解されています。
　使用者が労働者の副業・兼業を認める場合，労務提供上の支障や会社の秘密の漏洩がないか等を確認するため，2項のように，事前に届出を行わせることが一般的です。また，労働者が自社及び副業・兼業先の両方で「雇用」されている場合には，「労働時間は，事業場を異にする場合においても，労働時間に関する規定の適用については通算する」と規定する労基法38条等を踏まえ，時間外労働等に係る労働時間管理を行うため，4項のように，副業・兼業先での労働時間等につき報告を行わせることが望ましいと考えられます。
　使用者が，労働者の副業・兼業について事前の承認を要求する場合，本条

Chapter VIII. Work Discipline

working hours of the Company;

2. Employees shall submit a designated notification to the Company in advance when engaging in the business provided in the preceding paragraph;

3. If an Employee's engaging in the business provided in paragraph 1 falls under any of the following items, the Company may prohibit or limit it:

   (1) Where the provision of services to the Company is hindered;

   (2) Where the Company's secrets are divulged;

   (3) Where there are acts damaging the reputation and trustworthiness of the Company or destroying the relationship of trust; or

   (4) Where interests of the Company may be harmed due to competition or other circumstances.

4. If an Employee engages in the business of another employer or the like, the Employee shall report on the working hours engaged in the business of another employer or the like according to the Company's request.

> **From the viewpoint of the constitutional right to choose one's own job, it is interpreted that, in general, employees are free to choose whether to engage in secondary occupations/side occupations, as long as such engagement does not obstacle his/her job in the company. The Model Work Rules of the Ministry of Health, Labour and Welfare published in January 2018 were a major revision of provisions related to secondary occupations/side occupations and confirmed that, in general, employees may freely engage in secondary occupations/side occupations. However, there are cases where an employer may prohibit or limit its employees' secondary occupations/side occupations by work rules or contract: for example, court precedents indicate that in such cases listed in paragraph 3 above, the prohibition or limitation of secondary occupations/side occupations could be valid. In addition, the case "where the provision of services to the company is hindered" provided in paragraph 3 above, item 1 is interpreted to include the case "where secondary occupations/side occupations lead to insufficient performance of services for the company" and the case "where it may result in long working hours or other circumstances likely to affect employees' health."**
>
> **If an employer permits its employees to engage in secondary occupations/side occupations, in order to ensure that provision of services to the company is not hindered and the company's secrets are not divulged, typically it will have its**

> （第67条（副業・兼業））を次のように改めるか，第66条（一般的禁止行為）に事前の承認を得ない兼業行為を加えることとなります。
> 　第67条（副業・兼業）
> 　1．社員は，会社の事前の承認なしに，他の職業に従事してはならない。
> 　2．社員が，他の会社等の業務に従事する場合には，会社の求めるところに従い，他の会社等の業務に従事した時間等につき報告するものとする。
> 　ただし，就業規則の定めをこのように整理したとしても，副業・兼業を行うか否かが原則として労働者の自由に委ねられているという点に変わりはありませんので，注意が必要です。

第68条　（就業禁止）
1．次の各号の一に該当する社員は，会社の敷地に立ち入ることを禁じられることがある。かかる就業禁止の間は無給とする。
　(1)　精神的疾患のため就業が適当でない社員
　(2)　第87条各号に定める病者の就業禁止事由に該当する社員
　(3)　就業により悪化する可能性のある疾病に罹患している社員
　(4)　前各号の他，心身の状況が就業に適当でないと会社が判断した社員
2．前項の就業禁止を命ぜられた社員が勤務を再開しようとするときは，全快を証する会社の指定する医師の証明書を会社に提出することを求められる。

employees submit an advance notification as provided in paragraph 2 above. Further, if an employee is "employed" by both the company and another company of secondary occupations/side occupations, based on Article 38 of the Labor Standards Act which provides that "As far as application of the provisions on working hours is concerned, the total hours worked shall be aggregated, even if the hours worked were at different workplaces" and so on, then in order to manage working hours including overtime work, it is desirable to have its employees report on working hours worked at another company of secondary occupations/side occupations as provided in paragraph 4 above.

If an employer requires prior approval when its employees engage in secondary occupations/side occupations, this Article (Article 67. (Secondary Occupation/Side Occupation)) must be changed to the following stipulation or the item (which prohibits secondary occupations/side occupations without prior approval) must be included in Article 66. (Generally Prohibited Acts):

 Article 67. (Secondary Occupation/Side Occupation)
 1. An Employee shall not engage in other occupations without the Company's prior approval.
 2. If an Employee engages in the business of another employer or the like, the Employee shall report on the working hours engaged in the business of another employer or the like according to the Company's request.

However, please note that even if the Work Rules contain the above stipulations, there are no differences concerning the point that employees may, in general, freely engage in secondary occupations/side occupations.

Article 68. (Work Suspension)

1. Employees who fall under any of the following items may be prohibited from entering the Company's premises. No payment shall be made during the period of work suspension:

    (1) Employees who are unfit for work due to mental illness;

    (2) Employees who fall under any of the causes of suspension of work for sick persons under each item of Article 87;

    (3) Employees who suffer from a disease which may be aggravated by working; or

    (4) Employees whose mental and physical condition is deemed to be unfit for work by the Company.

2. If Employees who have been suspended from work under the preceding paragraph

第69条　（電子端末の利用）

> 　業務用の電子端末については，業務外使用の問題や，会社のモニタリング（閲覧）によるプライバシーの問題が生じることがあるため，使用基準や会社による閲覧の可能性があることをあらかじめ規定しておくことが望ましいといえます。電子端末使用規程には，使用にあたっての遵守事項や禁止事項，会社によるデータ閲覧，紛失・破損・情報漏洩の場合の報告義務等を定めます。

1. 社員は，会社が貸与したパソコン，携帯電話等の電子端末（以下，「電子端末」という。）を業務上必要な範囲で使用するものとし，私的に利用してはならない。
2. 会社は，必要と認める場合には，社員に貸与した電子端末内に蓄積されたデータ等を，当該社員の承諾なく閲覧することがある。
3. その他会社が貸与する電子端末の使用基準については別途定める規則による。

第70条　（所持品検査及び会社が貸与した物品の喪失）

> 　所持品検査が適法とされるためには，判例上，①就業規則その他の明示の根拠に基づくこと，②検査を必要とする合理的理由があること，③検査方法が一般的に妥当な方法及び程度であること，④検査が制度として労働者に対して画一的に実施されることが要件とされています。検査の対象が労働者個人の所持品であり，会社が貸与したパソコンの閲覧よりもプライバシー侵害の程度が大きいため，要件が厳しくなっています。

1. 会社は，必要と認める場合，職場への入退出の際，社員が所持している物品を検査することがある。社員は，正当な理由なくかかる検査を拒むこ

Chapter VIII. Work Discipline 227

intend to resume work, they shall be required to submit to the Company a certificate made by a medical doctor designated by the Company attesting to their complete recovery.

Article 69. (Use of Electronic Devices)

It is advisable to stipulate in advance the manner of use of electronic devices, and the possibility of inspecting workplace electronic devices in order to deal with problems regarding usage for purposes other than work, and privacy problems related to monitoring. Provisions regarding electronic device usage should stipulate items to be observed and prohibited items, data monitoring by the company, and the mandatory duty to report in the event of loss, damage, or information divulgation.

1. Employees shall use the electronic devices such as PCs or mobiles ("Electronic Devices") lent by the Company only to the extent required for work, and not for private use.
2. The Company may access data, etc., which are stored in the Electronic Devices lent to the Employees without the relevant Employee's approval when it considers necessary.
3. Any other matters relating to the use of Electronic Devices lent by the Company shall be prescribed by the rules to be established separately.

Article 70. (Inspection of Belongings and Loss of Articles Lent by the Company)

In order to legally conduct an inspection of belongings, court precedents dictate that (i) such an inspection must be based on clear provisions including work rules, (ii) there must be reasonable grounds for conducting such an inspection, (iii) the method and degree of inspection must be generally considered reasonable, and (iv) the inspection must be conducted as a universal policy among all employees. If the targets of inspections are the employees' belongings, there is a higher possibility of violating the employee's privacy; and as such, criteria for such inspections are more strict than those for the inspection of PCs that belong to the company.

1. The Company may inspect articles being carried by Employees upon their entry into

とができない。
2. 会社は，社員が会社から貸与を受けた物品を故意又は過失により紛失した場合，その損失に対する適切な補償を求めることがある。

第9章　職務発明

第71条　（知的財産権の帰属）
1. 社員が，その性質上会社の業務範囲に属し，かつ，その発明をするに至った行為が会社におけるその社員の現在又は過去の職務に属する発明等（以下，「職務発明」という。）をなした場合，別途定める規則に従い，内外国の特許，実用新案登録又は意匠登録を受ける権利は会社に承継されるものとする。
2. 前項の規定にかかわらず，社員が職務発明について自ら出願し，内外国の特許権，実用新案権，又は意匠権を取得したときは，別途定める規則に従い，当該権利は会社に承継されるものとする。
3. 本条に定めるほか，社員がその職務に関連して行った発明については，別途定める規則による。

> 職務発明については，あらかじめ就業規則等に規定することによって，会社が当該発明にかかる権利を譲り受けることができますが，別途労働者に相当の対価を支払う必要があります（例えば特許法35条）。かかる対価の支払方法等を含め，別途職務発明規程を整備する例が一般的です。職務発明規程には，発明の届出手続，職務発明の認定手続，権利の承継・処分，対価の算定方法・支払時期，発明者からの意見聴取，発明委員会の設置・審議事項，秘密保持等を定めます。

and upon leaving the workplace when it considers necessary. Employees shall not refuse such an inspection without justifiable reason.

2. If Employees intentionally or negligently lose articles lent by the Company, they may be required to make appropriate compensation for the loss to the Company.

Chapter IX. Employee Inventions

Article 71. (Attribution of Intellectual Property Rights)

1. If any Employee makes an invention, etc., which is within the scope of business due to the nature of the invention, etc., and pertains to the present or past duties of the Employee ("Employee Invention(s)"), the Employee shall immediately transfer to the Company the rights to obtain both domestic and international patent rights, and registrations of utility models or design rights to the Company, pursuant to the rule separately provided.

2. Notwithstanding the preceding paragraph, if any Employee has applied for and obtained domestic or international patent rights, utility model rights or design rights with respect to any Employee Invention, such rights shall be transferred to the Company, pursuant to the rule separately provided.

3. Any other matters relating to inventions made in connection with the Employee's duties shall be prescribed by the rules to be established separately.

> **By providing for employee inventions in advance in the work rules, the company may receive the rights related to such inventions. However, the company needs to pay sufficient consideration (e.g., Article 35 of the Patent Act). It is common to stipulate separate rules regarding employee inventions, including the method of payment of such consideration. Such rules should specify procedures for reporting the invention; procedures for receiving approval of payment for such employee invention; transfer/disposal of rights; method of calculating consideration/timing of payment; conducting a hearing with the inventor; establishing an invention committee/items to be considered by such committee; and confidentiality obligations.**

第10章　社員福利厚生及び訓練

第72条　（福利厚生）
　社員は，別途定める規則の規定に従い，福利厚生制度の適用を受けることができる。

> 　福利厚生制度については，別規程で具体的な福利厚生の内容，利用手続等を設ける例が一般的です。例えば，社内預金規程，住宅資金融資規程，慶弔見舞金規程，社宅入居規程等があります。

第73条　（訓　　練）
1.　会社は，社員の技能及び知識の発展・向上を図るために必要な訓練及び教育を行う。
2.　社員は，会社が企画・実行する訓練・教育プログラムに進んで参加し，技能の向上に専心しなければならない。

第11章　表　　彰

> 　表彰制度は，導入する場合には就業規則に定める必要がありますが，導入しないことも可能です。また，表彰の内容については，下記にかかわらず会社が設計することが可能です。

Chapter X. Employees Welfare Benefits and Training

Article 72. (Welfare Benefits)

Employees are entitled to welfare benefits according to the rules to be separately prescribed.

> It is common to provide a separate provision regarding specific details of the welfare benefits and the procedures for utilizing the benefits. For example, there may be provisions regarding the following: company savings plans, financing of home loans, celebration and condolence payments, and moving into company-owned housing.

Article 73. (Training)

1. The Company will provide Employees with training and education necessary for the development and improvement of their skills and knowledge.
2. Employees shall, on their own initiative, participate in the training and education program(s) planned and carried out by the Company, and they shall devote themselves to the improvement of their skills.

Chapter XI. Commendation

> It is necessary to stipulate under the work rules if the employer introduces a commendation policy. It is also possible to not introduce such a policy. The company may choose the manner of commendation, and it is not limited to the example provisions below.

第74条　（表彰の基準）
　次の各号の一に該当する社員又はその集団で，他にとって模範になると認められる者は，これを表彰する。
　(1)　社員又はその集団の業績又は技能が優れ，その行動が他の従業員にとって模範となる場合
　(2)　社員又はその集団が会社に恩恵をもたらす発明，改良その他の工夫をした場合
　(3)　永年誠実に勤務（勤続各10年目，15年目，20年目，25年目，30年目，35年目）した社員
　(4)　社員又はその集団が顕著な社会奉仕活動を行い，会社及び社員の評判を高めた場合
　(5)　社員又はその集団が災害・事故の発生を防止し，又は模範的な行動をして緊急時に社員及び会社に利益をもたらした場合
　(6)　社員又はその集団が会社の利益の大幅増加，売上の拡大等に大いに貢献した場合
　(7)　その他社員が会社から表彰されるに値する事由がある場合

第75条　（表彰の方法）
　表彰は，次の各号の一，二ないしそれ以上の物を社員又はその集団に授与する方法によって行う。
　(1)　賞状
　(2)　商品又は賞金
　(3)　特別昇給
　(4)　特別有給休暇

Article 74. (Commendation Criteria)

An Employee, or a group of Employees, who falls under any of the following items and who is recognized as a model Employee, or a model group of Employees, for others, shall be commended:

(1) In the case where the work performance or skill of the Employee or group of Employees is excellent and his/her/their behavior will be a model for other employees;

(2) In the case where the Employee or group of Employees has made inventions, improvements or other devices beneficial to the Company;

(3) In the case where the Employee has served faithfully for years with the Company (at the tenth (10th), fifteenth (15th), twentieth (20th), thirtieth (30th) and thirty-fifth (35th) year of service);

(4) In the case where the Employee or group of Employees has rendered outstanding social service that elevates the reputation of the Company and its Employees;

(5) In the case where the Employee or group of Employees has prevented a disaster or accident from occurring or has conducted him/her/themselves in an exemplary manner resulting in benefits to Employees and the Company in the event of an emergency;

(6) In the case where the Employee or group of Employees has greatly contributed to the Company's substantial profit growth or sales expansion, etc.; or

(7) In the case where there are other reasons for which the Employee or group of Employees deserves commendation from the Company.

Article 75. (Commendation Methods)

The commendation shall be provided by means of awarding the relevant Employee or group of Employees with one, two, or more of the following items:

(1) Letter of Commendation
(2) Prize Article or Prize Money
(3) Special Pay Increase
(4) Special Paid Leave

第12章 懲　　戒

　懲戒処分を行うには，就業規則上の根拠が必要であり，懲戒事由及び懲戒処分の種類・程度を就業規則に定めておかなくてはなりません。懲戒処分を行うときは，弁明の機会を与え，事情をよく聴取する等，適正な手続による必要があります。使用者が懲戒することができる場合であっても，その懲戒が客観的に合理的な理由を欠き，社会通念上相当であると認められない場合には，権利濫用に該当するものとして無効となる場合があります（労働契約法15条）。懲戒の対象者に対しては，規律違反の程度に応じて過去の同種の事例における処分の程度等を考慮して公正な処分を行うことが必要となります。また，懲戒規定が設けられる以前の行為に遡って懲戒処分を行うことや，同一の事案に対し２回懲戒処分を行うことはできないとされています。

　実務上，懲戒に該当する疑いのある行為を行った労働者に対しては，事実調査のため，自宅待機（有給）を命じることが多くみられます。就業規則にこのような自宅待機の規定を設ける例もありますが，労働者には就労請求権はないとするのが通説ですので，有給とする限り特段の規定がなくても自宅待機を命じることは可能です。
　また，「当該労働者を就労させないことにつき，不正行為の再発，証拠隠滅のおそれなどの緊急かつ合理的な理由が存する」場合には，無給での自宅待機命令も可能とする裁判例があります（日通名古屋製鉄作業事件・名古屋地判平成３年７月22日労判608号59頁）。

　就業規則に懲戒処分の手続に関する規定をおく例もありますが，その場合には，所定の手続を遵守しなかっただけで懲戒処分が無効となる可能性があります。本規定例では，柔軟な運用の余地を残すために，手続規定を定めていません。

Chapter XII. Disciplinary Action

In order for employers to take disciplinary action, the grounds for such action must be included in the work rules. The reasons for disciplinary action, the types of disciplinary action and their degree must be specified in the work rules. It is necessary to take appropriate measures before taking disciplinary action, such as by giving employees an opportunity to explain and conducting hearings regarding facts. Even in the case where an employer rightfully conducts disciplinary action, if such discipline lacks reasonable grounds from a rational perspective and is unacceptable based on social policy, it may be considered null and void as an abuse of rights (Article 15 of the Employment Agreement Act.) An employee should be fairly disciplined based on the degree of the violation and the degree of the disciplinary action that was taken in previous similar events. Disciplinary action may not be taken in the event that the action subject to disciplinary action occurred before disciplinary provisions were stipulated. Further, disciplinary action may not be taken twice for the same infraction.

In practice, there are many instances when (paid) standby at home is ordered for employees who may be subject to disciplinary action. Some work rules stipulate standby at home as a disciplinary action. However, employees are commonly considered to have no right to request to be at work; therefore, provided the employee is paid during such time period, ordering standby at home is possible without having such specific stipulations in the work rules.
There is a court precedent that states: in the case where "there are urgent and reasonable grounds for standby at home, e.g., if there is a possibility of recurrence of misconduct or destruction of evidence," it is possible for the company to order standby at home without the payment of salary (Nittsu Nagoya Seitetsu Sagyo case, Judgement of the Nagoya District Court, July 22, 1991 (p. 59, Rodo Hanrei No. 608)).

Some work rules provide procedures for disciplinary actions. In such cases, a disciplinary action may be invalidated if the specified procedure is not observed. Under the below provisions, specific procedures are not specified, which allows employers flexible use.

第76条　（懲戒の種類）
　懲戒の種類及び程度は，次のとおりとする。
　(1)　譴　　責　　始末書を徴して将来を戒める。
　(2)　減　　給　　始末書を徴するほか，1回につき平均賃金1日分の2分の1以内を減給し将来を戒める。ただし，2回以上にわたる場合においてもその総額が一賃金支払期における賃金総額の10分の1以内で減給するものとする。

> 　減給については，1回の事案に対する減給の額が平均賃金の1日分の半分を超えてはならず，また，一賃金支払期に複数事案に対する減給を行う場合は，その総額が一賃金支払期における賃金の総額の10分の1を超えてはならないこととされています（労働基準法91条）。したがって，複数事案に対する減給を行う場合であって，減給の総額が一賃金支払期における賃金の総額の10分の1を超える場合は，当該超過する額の減給を次期の賃金支払期に行わなければなりません。
> 　なお，労働基準法91条は制裁としての賞与の減額にも適用されます（昭63．3．14基発150号）。すなわち，1回の事案に対する制裁としての賞与の減額は，平均賃金の1日分の半分を超えてはならず，また，総額は，「一賃金支払期における賃金」，すなわち賞与額の10分の1を超えてはならないとされています（昭63．3．14基発150号）。
> 　また，懲戒処分として出勤停止となった場合，出勤停止期間中に無給となること（昭23．7．3基収2177号）や懲戒処分として降格しその職務変更に伴い賃金が下がること（昭37．9．6基発917号）は，労働基準法91条の減給制裁に該当しないとされています。

　(3)　出勤停止　　始末書を徴するほか，［7日］を限度として出勤を停止し，その期間の賃金は支給しない。

Article 76. (Types of Disciplinary Action)

Types and degree of disciplinary action shall be as follows:

(1) Reprimand: The Company will require a letter of apology and caution the Employee against future misconduct;

(2) Pay Cut: The Company will, in addition to requiring a letter of apology, reduce the Employee's wages, the amount of which shall not exceed one half (1/2) of the relevant Employee's daily average wage, for a single incident and will caution the Employee against future misconduct; however, when the said wage reduction is required two (2) times or more, the total amount of such wage reduction shall not exceed ten percent (10%) of the total wages due in a single wage period;

> **The amount of a pay cut per one instance of disciplinary action may not exceed half of 1 day's worth of average wages. In the case where the employer reduces the employee's wages for 2 incidents or more in 1 wage period, the total amount of the pay cut may not exceed more than one-tenth of the total amount of wages paid for a single wage period (Article 91 of the Labor Standards Act). Therefore, in the case where the employer reduces the employee's wages for 2 incidents or more, and the total amount of the pay cut exceeds one-tenth of the total amount of wages paid for a single wage period, the employer must impose the remainder of the pay cut from wages paid for the next wage period.**
>
> **Article 91 of the Labor Standards Act must also be applied to the reduction of bonuses as a sanction (Circular Notice, Kihatsu, No. 150, March 14, 1988). Therefore, the amount of a bonus cut per one instance of disciplinary action may not exceed half of 1 day's worth of average wages, and the total amount of the bonus cut may not exceed "one-tenth of the total amount of wages paid for a single wage period," which means, in this case, one-tenth of the total amout of the bonus (Circular Notice, Kihatsu, No. 150, March 14, 1988).**
>
> **Article 91 of the Labor Standards Act does not prohibit the payment of no wages during a period of suspension in the case where the employee has been disciplined by means of suspension (Circular Notice, Kishu, No. 2177, March 7, 1948), or the lowering of wages with job modification because of demotion as a disciplinary action (Circular Notice, Kihatsu, No. 917, June 9, 1962).**

(3) Suspension: The Company will, in addition to requiring a letter of apology, suspend Employees from work for any period up to [seven (7) days] without paying wages therefor;

> 出勤停止期間の上限について，あまりに長期間である場合に公序良俗による制限がある他は，明示の法規制はありませんが，7日から30日以内で定める例が一般的です。

(4) 降　　格　　始末書を徴するほか，職位を解任若しくは引き下げ，及び職能資格制度上の資格・等級の引き下げのいずれか，又は双方を行う。

> 降格に伴って将来の賃金が減額される結果になることも多いですが，これは降格の結果生じるものにすぎないため，労働基準法上の減給の規制は受けません。ただし，その減額の幅は権利濫用の考慮要素の1つとなります。

(5) 諭旨解雇　　退職願を提出するように勧告する。ただし，勧告に応じない場合は，懲戒解雇とする。諭旨解雇となる者には，その状況を勘案して退職金の一部を支給しないことがある。

(6) 懲戒解雇　　予告期間を設けることなく即時解雇する。ただし，所轄労働基準監督署長の認定を受けたときは，解雇予告手当を支給しない。懲戒解雇となる者又は在職中に懲戒解雇相当事由を行った者には，その状況を勘案して退職金の全部又は一部を支給しない。

> There are no clear laws or regulations regarding the upper limit of a suspension term, although an extremely long term may be limited in the interest of public policy. It is common to prescribe a suspension period of 7 to 30 days.

(4) Demotion: The Company will, in addition to requiring a letter of apology, remove or lower the job title of the Employee and/or lower the Employee's qualification or class under the ability qualification system;

> It is common for a company to decrease future wages pursuant to a demotion. This reduction of future wages occurs only as a result of a demotion and therefore is not subject to the regulation regarding pay cuts under the Labor Standards Act described in Item 2 above. However, the amount of the reduction of wages is one of the factors a court will consider when determining whether or not an employer has abused its rights.

(5) Counseled Dismissal: The Company will advise the Employee to submit a request for retirement. However, if such advice is not followed, the Employee shall be given a disciplinary dismissal. Depending on the circumstances, part of the retirement allowances may not be paid to Employees who are subject to counseled dismissal; and

(6) Disciplinary Dismissal: The Company will dismiss the Employee immediately, without providing any notification period. However, if the approval of the chief of the Labor Standards Supervision Office is obtained, the Company shall not be required to pay a dismissal notice allowance. In consideration of the circumstances, all or part of the retirement allowances shall not be paid to Employees who are subject to disciplinary dismissal or have engaged in activities that may lead to disciplinary dismissal.

> 懲戒解雇の場合も，原則として労働基準法20条の解雇予告手当の規定が適用され，30日前の予告か予告手当の支払が必要となります。ただし，労働者の責めに帰すべき事由に基づく解雇の場合は，労働基準監督署長の認定を受けると解雇予告義務が免除されます。解雇予告手当を支払わず即時に懲戒解雇する場合には，あらかじめ労働基準監督署長の認定を受ける必要があります。懲戒解雇についても解雇権濫用法理（労働契約法16条）の適用があります。

> 懲戒解雇の場合に退職金の全部又は一部を不支給とすることがありますが，そのためには退職金規程等に明示することが必要です。ただし，判例上，退職金不支給規定を有効に適用できるのは，労働者のそれまでの勤続の功を抹消・減殺してしまう程の著しく信義に反する行為があった場合に限られると解されており，退職金不支給の有効性は懲戒解雇の有効性よりもさらに制限的に判断されることとなります。

第77条　（譴責，減給，出勤停止及び降格の事由）
　社員が次の各号の一に該当するときは，その情状に応じ，譴責，減給，出勤停止，降格に処する。ただし，反則の程度や情状に応じて懲戒を免じ訓戒とすることがある。
　⑴　社員が会社の規則（本就業規則その他の規程・内規を含む。），指示又は通知に違反したとき
　⑵　正当な事由なくして遅刻，早退，私用外出若しくは無届欠勤したとき，又はしばしば職場を離脱して業務に支障をきたしたとき
　⑶　勤務に関する手続若しくは届出を偽り，又は怠ったとき
　⑷　故意に会社の業務効率を害し，又は会社の業務を妨害しようとしたとき

As a general rule, provisions regarding dismissal notice allowance (i.e., under Article 20 of the Labor Standards Act) will apply even in the case of disciplinary dismissal. Therefore, 30 days prior notice or a notice payment must be provided. However, if the dismissal is made due to the fault of the employee and if the chief of the Labor Standards Supervision Office approves, the employer will be exempted from the duty to notify the employee of the dismissal. It is necessary to obtain approval from the chief of the Labor Standards Supervision Office beforehand if the employer immediately dismisses an employee for disciplinary reasons without paying a dismissal notice allowance. The doctrine of abuse of the right to dismiss employees (Article 16 of the Employment Agreement Act) applies to disciplinary dismissal as well.

In the event of disciplinary dismissal, employers may withhold all or part of the retirement allowance if provided for in the rules regarding retirement allowances. According to court precedents, however, in order for the employer to withhold payment of retirement allowance, the employee must have engaged in an act that nullifies or cancels his/her past continuous service. Therefore, the situations where withholding of retirement allowance will be valid are even more limited than those where disciplinary dismissal will be valid.

Article 77. (Grounds for Reprimand, Pay Cut, Suspension, and Demotion)
An Employee shall be disciplined by means of reprimand, pay cut, suspension, or demotion, according to the circumstances, in the following cases; however, the Company may reduce the disciplinary action to a warning based on the degree or circumstances of the contravention:

(1) Where the Employee violates rules (including the Work Rules, other provisions, and internal rules), instructions or notices of the Company;

(2) Where the Employee arrives late, leaves early, leaves the workplace for private reasons or does not come to work without notice, without a justifiable reason, or repeatedly leaves the workplace and thereby causes difficulties in business

(5) 業務に対する誠意を欠き，職務怠慢と認められるとき
(6) 正当な理由なく職場配置，配転，出張，転勤，出向又は職位決定等の人事命令を拒否したとき
(7) 業務上の書類，伝票等を改変し，若しくは虚偽の申告，届出をし，又は会社の掲示を汚損，改変若しくは破棄したとき
(8) 職場の内外において，他の従業員に対しセクシュアルハラスメント，パワーハラスメント又は妊娠・出産・育児休業・介護休業等に関するハラスメントをして職場の風紀・秩序を乱し，他の従業員の就業を妨げたとき
(9) 他の従業員に対し暴行，脅迫を加え，又は社内において賭博その他これに類する行為をなす等，社内の風紀・秩序を乱したとき
(10) 勤務時間中に会社の承認なく私用を行ったとき
(11) 故意，過失，怠慢若しくは監督不行届きによって災害，傷害，その他の事故を発生させ，又は会社の設備，器具を破損したとき
(12) 所属長又は関連上長の業務上の指示・命令に従わないとき
(13) 業務外の非行行為により会社の名誉・信用を損ない，又は会社に損害を及ぼしたとき，その他，業務外の非行行為により企業秩序が乱されたとき
(14) 社員が，他人を教唆又は幇助して前各号に該当する行為をさせたとき
(15) その他前各号に準ずる程度の不都合な行為があったとき

operations;

(3) Where the Employee falsifies or neglects the procedures or notifications relating to his/her duties;

(4) Where the Employee intentionally impairs the efficiency of the Company's work or attempts to interfere with the Company's business;

(5) Where the Employee is considered not to be sufficiently serious about his/her work and is neglectful of his/her duties;

(6) Where the Employee refuses, without reasonable grounds, personnel orders regarding job placement, job rotation, business trips, relocation, secondment or decisions regarding job titles;

(7) Where the Employee alters business documents or vouchers, etc., makes any false notifications or submittals, or defaces, alters or destroys any notices of the Company;

(8) Where the Employee disturbs the morale and order in the office by engagird in sexual harassment, power harassment or harassment concerning pregnancy, childbirth, child care leave, and nursing care leave, etc. against other employees within or outside the workplace and therefore interferes with the work of other employees;

(9) Where the Employee disturbs Company morale and order by the use of violence threatening other employees, or in gambling or any other similar acts in the Company;

(10) Where the Employee engages in his/her personal business during work hours without the Company's approval;

(11) Where the Employee causes casualties, disorder or any other accidents or damages any items, facilities or equipment of the Company due to willful misconduct, negligence, omission or lack of supervision;

(12) Where the Employee disobeys instructions or orders from his/her supervisor or relevant superiors;

(13) Where the Employee damages the reputation and trustworthiness of the Company or causes damage to the Company by work-unrelated delinquent actions, or where

第78条　（諭旨解雇及び懲戒解雇の事由）
　　社員が次の各号の一に該当するときは，その情状に応じ，諭旨解雇又は懲戒解雇に処する。ただし，反則の程度や情状に応じて，譴責，減給，出勤停止，降格の処分にとどめることがある。
　(1)　会社の規則・命令の重大な違反若しくは前条各号に規定された行為が再度に及ぶとき，又は情状重大と認められるとき
　(2)　前条各号に該当する事由で懲戒処分を受けた者が，同種又は類似の行為を行ったとき
　(3)　重要な経歴を偽り，その他不正な方法を用いて採用されたとき
　(4)　正当な理由なく，無断欠勤が連続14日以上に及んだとき
　(5)　殺人，傷害，暴行，脅迫，強盗，窃盗，横領その他重大な刑法犯に該当する行為があったとき
　(6)　業務外の非行行為により，会社の名誉・信用を著しく損ない，又は会社に重大な損害を及ぼした場合，その他，企業秩序が著しく乱された場合でその行為態様が悪質なとき
　(7)　会社の営業秘密を不正な目的で利用若しくは漏洩し，又は利用若しくは漏洩しようとしたとき
　(8)　会社やその経営・業務に関して故意に虚偽の事実を宣伝流布する等の行為により，会社の信頼，名誉や信用を害したとき
　(9)　社員が，他人を教唆又は幇助して前各号に該当する行為をさせたとき
　(10)　その他前各号に準ずる程度の不都合な行為があったとき

the Employee disturbs the order of the Company by delinquent actions unrelated to work;

(14) Where the Employee solicits or helps someone to commit any act in the item adove; and

(15) Where the Employee engager in misconduct similar to any of the types of misconduct detailed in each of the foregoing items.

Article 78. (Grounds for Counseled Dismissal and Disciplinary Dismissal)
In the case where an Employee falls under any of the following items, the Employee shall be subject to counseled dismissal or disciplinary dismissal according to the circumstances thereof. However, depending on the degree of the violation and extenuating circumstances, the punishment may be reduced to that of reprimand, pay cut, suspension, or demotion:

(1) Where the Employee commits serious violations of the Company's rules, regulations or orders; or commits any of the acts detailed in each of the items in the preceding article more than once, or if the manner in which the Employee has committed the same is considered to be serious;

(2) Where the Employee has already been disciplined and commits the same or a similar act;

(3) Where the Employee is hired by the Company as a result of his/her having falsified important biographical details or using any other improper means;

(4) Where the Employee is absent from work without notice or permission and without justifiable cause for fourteen (14) consecutive days or more;

(5) Where the Employee commits murder, willful injury, assault, intimidation, robbery, theft, embezzlement or any other serious criminal offense;

(6) Where the Employee significantly damages the reputation and trustworthiness of the Company or causes serious damage to the Company by delinquent actions unrelated to work, or in any other case where the Employee significantly disturbs the order of the Company willfully;

(7) Where the Employee uses or divulges, or intends to use or divulge, the Company's

第79条　（損害賠償）
　社員の故意又は過失により会社が損害を被った場合，会社は当該社員に対し損害の全部又は一部の賠償を求めることがある。ただし，これによって当該社員が第77条及び第78条に定める懲戒処分の対象となるのを免れるものではない。

> 　判例上，使用者の労働者に対する損害賠償請求又は求償請求は制限的に解されており，損害の公平な分担という見地から信義則上相当と認められる限度においてのみ，使用者は労働者に対して損害賠償等を請求することができることとされています（茨城石炭商事事件（最判昭和51年7月8日民集30巻7号689頁））。

business secrets for illegal purposes;

(8) Where the Employee impairs the integrity, reputation and trustworthiness of the Company by spreading intentionally false information with respect to the Company, its management or business;

(9) Where the Employee solicits or helps someone to commit any act in the item above; or

(10) Where the Employee engages in misconduct similar to any of the types of misconduct detailed in each of the foregoing items.

Article 79. (Compensation for Damage)
In the event that the Company suffers damages due to an intentional or negligent act by an Employee, the Company may demand compensation from the Employee for all or part of such damages; however, this shall not exempt the Employee from the disciplinary actions prescribed in Articles 77 and 78.

> **Based on court precedents, requests for compensation or claims for damages by employers against employees are interpreted in a limited way. Employers may claim for damages against employees only within the scope that is acceptable based on the principles of faith and trust from the perspective of sharing a fair burden of the damages (Ibaraki Sekitan Shoji Case, Judgement of the Supreme Court, July 8, 1976 (p.689, Saikosaibansho Minji Hanreishu Vol. 30-7)).**

第13章 安全及び衛生

> 安全衛生について定める場合には，就業規則への記載が必要ですが，就業規則本体では基本的な事項を定め，詳細な定めを要する場合には別規程を設けることが一般的です。定めるべき事項は，①遵守義務，②安全衛生管理体制，③安全衛生教育，④健康診断，⑤医師による面接指導，⑥ストレスチェック，⑦自己保健義務，⑧就業制限・禁止，⑨各企業・各事業場で必要となる安全衛生基準，⑩健康管理制度等です。会社の規模によっては，安全委員会の設置等が義務付けられる場合があります。なお，就業規則や別規程において労働安全衛生法上の諸基準を網羅的に定める必要はなく，当該事業場の安全衛生上特に必要な事項を定めることとされています。

第1節 安　全

第80条　（安全の確保）

　　会社は，人命尊重と資産保護のために安全施設及び安全規則を設けて災害防止に努めるものとする。

第81条　（安全の心得）

　　社員は，安全担当者その他の関係者の指示に従い，安全維持及び災害の防止に努めなければならない。

第2節 衛　生

第82条　（衛生の確保）

　　会社は，社員の保健衛生に関する事項につき注意を払い，社員の健康の維持増進を図ることに努めるものとする。

Chapter XIII. Safety and Sanitation

> If employers provide regulations regarding safety and sanitation, such provisions must be included in the work rules. However, it is common to stipulate basic factors in the work rules and provide for separate rules regarding specific stipulations. Items that would be provided include: (i) obligations that should be followed; (ii) policy for managing safety and health; (iii) safety and health education; (iv) medical examination; (v) face-to-face guidance by a doctor; (vi) stress check; (vii) self-insurance duty; (viii) restrictions/prohibition on work; (ix) safety standards necessary for each workplace; (x) health management policy, etc. Depending on the size of the company, it may be mandatory to set up a safety committee. It is not necessary to comprehensively stipulate standards pursuant to the Industrial Safety and Health Act in the work rules or other rules, and it is sufficient to stipulate in the work rules or other rules factors which are especially necessary from the perspective of safety and sanitation in the workplace.

Section 1. Safety

Article 80. (Ensuring Safety)

The Company shall endeavor to provide safe facilities and establish safety rules to prevent accidents for the purpose of preserving human life and protecting property.

Article 81. (Safety Readiness)

Employees shall, subject to instructions from the person in change of safety and other related persons, make efforts to maintain safety and prevent accidents.

Section 2. Sanitation

Article 82. (Sanitation)

The Company shall be mindful of matters related to the health and sanitation of Employees and endeavor to maintain and improve the health of Employees.

第83条　（衛生担当者）
　　社員は，常に衛生担当者その他の関係者の指示に従い，保健及び衛生に関する事項を守り，健康維持増進に努めなければならない。

第84条　（衛生のための遵守事項）
　　社員は，保健衛生のために，法令又は会社が定めた諸規程を守るとともに，次の事項を遵守しなければならない。
　(1)　常に職場を整理整頓し清潔に保つこと
　(2)　定期健康診断及び会社が必要に応じて行う健康診断を受けること
　(3)　その他，衛生に関する責任者及び上長の指示，注意を遵守すること

第85条　（健康診断）
　1．　会社は，次の健康診断を実施する。社員は，正当な理由なくかかる健康診断を拒むことはできない。
　(1)　入社時健康診断　　社員の勤務開始に際して実施する。
　(2)　定期健康診断　　　年1回定期的に実施する。
　(3)　臨時健康診断　　　感染症が発生し若しくは発生するおそれがあるとき，又は特に必要と認められたときは，臨時に健康診断を行うことがある。
　2．　会社は，1週間当たり40時間を超えて行う労働が1か月当たり［80時間／100時間　※解説参照］を超え，疲労の蓄積が認められる社員について，当該社員からの申出があった場合には，会社の指定する医師による面接指導を行う。ただし，前1か月以内に面接指導を受けた者その他これに類する者で医師が必要ないと認めた者は除く。
　3．　会社は，第1項の健康診断の結果に基づき，就業の場所又は業務の転換，労働時間の短縮，その他，社員の健康維持に必要な措置を命じることができる。社員は，正当な理由なくかかる措置を拒むことはできない。

Article 83. (Person in Charge of Sanitation)
Employees shall obey the instructions of the person in charge of sanitation and other related persons at all times, observe the matters related to health and sanitation, and endeavor to maintain and improve their health.

Article 84. (Matters to be Observed for Sanitation)
Employees shall observe the laws and the rules and regulations prescribed by the Company and also:
(1) Keep the workplace clean and tidy;
(2) Take a periodic medical examination and other medical examinations as required by the Company; and
(3) Comply with other instructions and cautions given by managers and superiors in relation to sanitation.

Article 85. (Medical Examination)
1. The Company shall provide the following medical examinations. Employees may not refuse to take such medical examinations without a justifiable reason.
   (1) Medical examination upon starting work (carried out when a new Employee starts working);
   (2) Periodic medical examination (regularly carried out on an annual basis); and
   (3) Special medical examination (carried out when an infectious disease breaks out or is likely to break out or when the Company deems it especially necessary).
2. If an Employee's overtime working hours (i.e., hours worked in excess of forty (40) working hours per week) amount to more than [eighty (80)/one hundred (100) hours *see the commentary] in any month, and he/she is deemed to be suffering from fatigue as a result of excessive working hours, and upon his/her request, the Company shall provide face-to-face guidance by a doctor designated by the Company. This shall not apply to Employees who have undertaken the face-to-face guidance within the past one (1) month and for whom the doctor determines there is no need to do so.
3. The Company may order that measures necessary to maintain the health of an

事業者は，労働者の1週間当たり40時間を超えて行う労働が1か月当たり100時間を超える者で，疲労の蓄積があると認められる者（ただし，前1か月以内に面接指導を受けた者その他これに類する者で医師が必要ないと認めた者を除く。）から申出があった場合には，医師による面接指導を実施しなければなりません（労働安全衛生法66条の8，労働安全衛生規則52条の2，52条の3）。また，「疲労の蓄積」は，通常，他者には認知しにくい自覚症状として現れるものであることから，労働安全衛生規則52条の3に基づく申出の手続をとった労働者については，「疲労の蓄積があると認められる者」として取り扱うこととされています（平18.2.24基発0224003号）。

　なお，現行の労働安全衛生規則は，上記のとおり，当該面接指導の対象となる労働者を，1週間当たり40時間を超えて行う労働が1か月当たり100時間を超える者と定めていますが，今後，同規則が改正され，1か月当たりの超過時間が80時間に変更される予定です。また，平成31年（2019年）4月施行の改正労働安全衛生法においては，新たに研究開発業務に従事する者で，1週間当たり40時間を超えて行う労働が1か月当たり100時間を超えた者に対しては，労働者からの申出がない場合でも，医師による面接指導が義務付けられることとなりました（改正労働安全衛生法66条の8の2第1項）。また，同改正によって，事業者は医師による面接指導を実施するため，管理監督者を含む全ての労働者の労働時間を把握することが義務付けられましたが（改正労働安全衛生法66条の8の2第1項），詳細については第1部第1章4.4-3をご参照ください。

Employee be taken, such as change of workplace, change of work contents or reduction in working hours, in accordance with the results of the medical examinations set forth in Paragraph 1. The Employee shall not refuse such measures without a justifiable reason.

Employers must be provided face-to-face guidance by a doctor in the case where an employee whose overtime hours (i.e., hours worked in excess of 40 working hours per week) amount to more than 100 hours in any month, and who is deemed to be suffering from fatigue as a result of excessive working hours (excluding an employee who has undertaken face-to-face guidance within the past month and for whom the doctor determines there is no need for further consultation), upon the employee's request (Article 66-8 of the Industrial Safety and Health Act, Articles 52-2 and 52-3 of the Ordinance on Industrial Safety and Health). Since "to be suffering from fatigue as a result of excessive working hours" is generally a subjective assessment, the symptoms of which are invisible to others, an employee who makes a request pursuant to Article 52-3 of the Ordinance on Industrial Safety and Health shall be treated as an employee "who is deemed to be suffering from fatigue as a result of excessive working hours" (Circular Notice, Kihatsu, No. 0224003, February 24, 2006).
Although the current Ordinance on Industrial Safety and Health designates an employee whose overtime working hours (i.e., hours worked in excess of 40 working hours per week) exceed 100 hours in any month as an employee to whom the employer must provide the face-to-face guidance as described above, the ordinance is scheduled to be amended and the definition of the employee to whom the face-to-face guidance should be provided is to be changed to those employees whose overtime working hours exceed 80 hours in any month. Further, the amended Industrial Safety and Health Act to be enforced in April 2019 is to newly require the employer to provide face-to-face guidance by a doctor in the case where an employee who is engaged in research and development and whose overtime working hours (i.e., hours worked in excess of 40 working hours per week) amount to more than 100 hours in any month, even if there is no request from the employee (Article 66-8-2, Paragraph 1 of the amended Industrial Safety and Health Act). In addition, the amended Industrial Safety and Health Act is to require the employer to monitor the working hours of all the employees including managers and supervisors, in order to provide face-to-face guidance by a doctor (Article 66-8-2, Paragraph 1 of the amended Industrial Safety and Health Act). For detailed information relating to the new duty, please see Part I, Chapter I, 4. 4-3.

第86条（ストレスチェック）
1. 会社は，社員に対し，年1回定期的に，会社の指定する医師，保健師等による心理的な負担の程度を把握するための検査（ストレスチェック）を実施する。
2. 会社は，前項のストレスチェックの結果，ストレスが高く，面接指導が必要であると医師，保健師等が認定した社員について，当該社員からの申出があった場合には，会社の指定する医師による面接指導を実施する。
3. 会社は，前項の面接指導の結果に基づき，就業の場所又は業務の転換，労働時間の短縮，その他必要な措置を命ずることがある。社員は，正当な理由なくかかる措置を拒むことはできない。

　事業者は，心理的な負担の程度を把握するための検査（ストレスチェック）を1年に1回定期的に実施する必要があり（労働安全衛生法66条の10第1項），ストレスチェック及びその結果を踏まえた面接指導の費用は事業者が負担するべきものと考えられています。
　また，ストレスチェックの結果は，医師，保健師等から労働者に直接通知されなければならず，労働者本人の同意がない限り，事業主は把握してはならないこととされています（労働安全衛生法66条の10第2項）。したがって，ストレスチェックの結果，医師，保健師等が，ストレスが高く，面接指導が必要であると認めた労働者については，事業者がその結果を把握しているとは限らないため，当該労働者からの申出があって初めて，事業者には医師による面接指導を実施する義務が生じます（労働安全衛生法66条の10第3項）。
　事業者は，上記面接指導を実施した医師からその結果の提供を受けることができますが，事業者が選任している産業医等（労働安全衛生法13条1項）以外の外部の医師，保健師等が面接指導を実施した場合には，当該面接指導を受けた労働者の同意が必要とされています（厚生労働省「心理的な負担の程度を把握するための検査及び面接指導の実施並びに面接指導結果に基づき事業者が講ずべき措置に関する指針」）。そして，事業主には，当該面接指導の結果を踏まえ，作業の転換，労働時間の短縮，深夜業の回数の減少等の措置を講じることが義務付けられています（労働安全衛生法66条の10第5項，第6項）。

Article 86. (Stress Check)

1. For each Employee, the Company shall periodically (i.e., once a year) perform a test by a doctor or a public health nurse, etc. to assess the degree of the Employee's psychological burden (stress check), as designated by the Company.
2. As a result of the stress check set forth in the preceding paragraph, if the doctor or the public health nurse, etc., decides that the Employee is under a high level of stress and accordingly is required to be provided with face-to-face guidance, the Company shall provide the Employee with face-to-face guidance by a doctor designated by the Company upon the Employee's request.
3. The Company may order that necessary measures be taken, such as change of workplace or work contents or reduction in working hours, in accordance with the results of the face-to-face guidance set forth in the preceding paragraph. The Employee shall not refuse such measures without a justifiable reason.

Employers must periodically perform a test annually to assess the degree of the employees' psychological burden (stress check) (Article 66-10, Paragraph 1 of the Industrial Safety and Health Act). And it is considered that the cost of performing the stress check and providing employees with face-to-face guidance should be borne by employers based on the results of the stress check.
The results of the stress check must be notified directly to the employees by a doctor or a public health nurse, etc. And the employers shall be prohibited from ascertaining the result, without obtaining the relevant employees' consent (Article 66-10, Paragraph 2 of the Industrial Safety and Health Act). Accordingly, where, as a result of the stress check, the doctor or the public health nurse, etc., decides that the relevant employee is under a high level of stress and accordingly is required to be provided with face-to-face guidance, the employer shall be obligated to provide the employee with face-to-face guidance by a doctor only upon the employee's request because the employer has not necessarily ascertained the results of the stress check (Article 66-10, Paragraph 3 of the Industrial Safety and Health Act).
The employer can receive the results of the face-to-face guidance described above from the doctor who conducted them; however, if an external doctor or public health nurse, etc., other than the industrial physician, etc. appointed by the employer (Article 13, Paragraph 1 of the Industrial Safety and Health Act) has provided the face-to-face guidance, the consent of the employee who received

第87条（健康管理上の個人情報の取扱い）
1. ストレスチェックを実施した医師，保健師等から社員のストレスチェックの結果を入手する場合には，あらかじめ本人の同意を得るものとする。ただし，社員が前条第2項の面接指導を申し出た場合には，同意が得られたものとみなす。
2. 社員の定期健康診断の結果，社員から提出された診断書，医師等（歯科医師を含む。）からの意見書，第85条第2項の面接指導の結果，ストレスチェックの結果，前条第2項の面接指導の結果その他社員の健康管理に関する情報は，社員の健康管理のために利用するとともに，必要な場合には医師等に対し意見聴取等のために提供するものとする。
3. 健康診断，第85条第2項の面接指導，ストレスチェック及び第86条第2項の面接指導の実施の事務に従事した者は，その事務に従事したことによって知り得た社員の秘密を漏らしてはならない。

> ストレスチェックを実施する医師，保健師等が，労働者の同意を得ないでストレスチェックの結果を事業者に提供することは禁止されていますが（労働安全衛生法66条の10第2項），労働者が面接指導を申し出た場合には，同意が得られたものとみなすことが可能です（厚生労働省「心理的な負担の程度を把握するための検査及び面接指導の実施並びに面接指導結果に基づき事業者が講ずべき措置に関する指針」）。
> また，健康診断等の事務に従事した者は，実施によって知った労働者の秘密を漏らしてはならないこととなっています（労働安全衛生法104条）。

the face-to-face guidance shall be required (the Ministry of Health, Labour and Welfare, "Guidelines concerning the Test to Assess the Degree of the Psychological Burden, Provision of the Face to Face Guidance, and the Measures to Be Taken by Employers Based on the Results of the Face to Face Guidance"). And the employer shall be required to take measures such as change of work contents, reduction in working hours, and reduction in night work frequency, in accordance with the results of the face-to-face guidance (Article 66-10, Paragraphs 5 and 6 of the Industrial Safety and Health Act).

Article 87. (Handling of Personal Information for Health Management Purposes)

1. If the Company receives the results of an Employee's stress check from a doctor or a public health nurse, etc., who conducted the stress check, the Company shall obtain the Employee's consent in advance. However, if an Employee requests face-to-face guidance under Paragraph 2 of the preceding Article, the Company shall be deemed to have obtained the Employee's consent.

2. Information concerning Employees' health management, including the results of Employees' periodic medical examinations, medical certificates submitted by Employees, the opinions from doctors, etc. (including dentists), the results of the face-to-face guidance under Article 85, Paragraph 2, the results of the stress checks, and the results of the face-to-face guidance under Paragraph 2 of the preceding Article, shall be utilized for the Employees' health management; and when necessary, the Company shall provide that information to doctors, etc. to hear their opinions and for other similar purposes.

3. The person who conducted clerical work for execution of the medical examination, the face-to-face guidance under Article 85, Paragraph 2, the stress check, and/or the face-to-face guidance under Article 86, Paragraph 2, shall not disclose the confidential information that he/she has learnt while conducting the above.

A doctor and a public health nurse, etc., who conduct a stress check are prohibited from providing the results of the stress check to the employer without obtaining the employee's consent (Article 66-10, Paragraph 2 of the Industrial Safety and Health Act); however, if the employee requests face-to-face guidance,

第88条　（応急処置）
 1．　社員は，勤務中に傷病のため職務の遂行に支障をきたした場合は，直ちにその旨を申し出て所属長の指示に従わなければならない。
 2．　他の者の急病を知ったときは，直ちに応急の措置をとり所属長に報告しなければならない。

第89条　（病者の就業禁止）
　会社は，社員が次の各号の一に該当するときは，会社の指定する医師の意見を聴取の上，就業を禁止する。
 (1)　法定感染症患者及びその保菌者
 (2)　勤務のため，病気が悪化するおそれのある者及び病気治療後回復せず，通常勤務が困難と認められる者
 (3)　その他，法令に定める病気にかかった者

第90条　（法定感染症発生時の措置）
　社員の自宅・近隣に法定感染症が発生若しくは発生の疑いがあったり，感染症患者に接触したりしたときは，直ちに所属長に届け出なければならない。

the doctor and the public health nurse, etc., can be deemed to have obtained the employee's consent (the Ministry of Health, Labour and Welfare, "Guidelines concerning the Test to Assess the Degree of the Psychological Burden, Provision of the Face to Face Guidance, and the Measures to Be Taken by Employers Based on the Results of the Face to Face Guidance").

The person who conducted clerical work for execution of the medical examination and the like shall not disclose the confidential information that he/she has learnt while conducting the above (Article 104 of the Industrial Safety and Health Act).

Article 88. (Emergency Measures)

1. In the event an Employee experiences difficulty performing his/her work duties due to illnesses or injuries sustained at work, the Employee shall report the circumstances to their supervisor and follow their instructions.

2. In the event an Employee becomes aware of a sudden illness of another Employee, the Employee shall provide first aid and report such illness to their supervisor.

Article 89. (Compulsory Leave for Sick Persons)

In the event that any of the following items is applicable to an Employee, the Company shall suspend the Employee from work after hearing the opinion of a medical doctor designated by the Company:

(1) The Employee suffers from a disease legally designated as infectious or is a carrier of such disease;

(2) The Employee is likely to have his/her illness aggravated by working and experience difficulty in ordinary work because he/she did not recover after the medical treatment; and

(3) The Employee suffers from any other disease designated by law.

Article 90. (Measures in the Event of the Occurrence of Infectious Diseases)

In the event that a disease legally designated as infectious breaks out or is in danger of breaking out at the residence of an Employee or in the surrounding area, or in the event that an Employee has contact with persons suffering from an infectious disease, the

第91条　（安全・衛生教育）
　　会社は，新たに社員を採用又は社員の作業内容を変更したときは，当該社員に対して遅滞なく，安全・衛生に関する教育を行う。この場合，社員は，進んでこれを受けなければならない。

Employee shall immediately report the circumstances to his/her supervisor.

Article 91. (Safety and Health Training)

When the Company hires a new Employee or changes the work of an Employee, the Company shall immediately provide safety and health training to the Employee. In such case, the Employee shall voluntarily take such training.

第14章　災害補償

> 　労働基準法は，労働者が業務上負傷し，又は疾病にかかった場合，使用者に災害補償義務を課しています。使用者の災害補償義務は無過失責任であり，実際には，労働者災害補償保険（以下，「労災保険」という。）制度による保険給付により補償がなされています。ただし，労働災害により休業する場合の最初の３日間は，労災保険からの休業補償給付が行われないため，使用者は労働基準法76条に基づき平均賃金の60％以上を補償しなければなりません。労災保険制度は政府管掌の災害補償制度で，労働者を使用する全ての使用者（一部の農林・畜産・水産事業を除く。）は，労災保険に加入しなければなりません。なお，通勤災害は，業務上の災害ではなく，労働基準法の災害補償条項の適用はありませんが，労働者保護のため，労災保険による保険給付の対象とされています。

第92条　（災害補償）
1.　社員が業務上負傷し，疾病にかかり，又は死亡したときは，労働者災害補償保険法により補償給付を受ける。
2.　社員が業務上の負傷又は疾病による療養のため労働することができないために賃金を受けない最初の３日間については，労働者災害補償保険法による補償給付の対象とならないため，会社が労働基準法に基づき補償を行う。
3.　第１項の補償が行われる場合には，会社はその限度で労働基準法上の補償の義務を負わない。

Chapter XIV. Accident Compensation

Pursuant to the Labor Standards Act, an employer is required to compensate an employee if the employee suffers a job-related injury or becomes sick. The employer is responsible regardless of fault, and in reality, the workers' accident compensation insurance (the "Workers' Compensation Insurance") policy compensates by providing insurance proceeds. However, if an employee takes a leave of absence due to a job-related accident, he/she does not receive absence compensation payment, from the Workers' Compensation Insurance for the first three (3) days. Therefore, pursuant to Article 76 of the Labor Standards Act, the employer is required to compensate at least 60% of the average wages of such employee during those first three days. The Workers' Compensation Insurance Policy is an accident compensation policy administered by the government, and any employer with employees (except for certain forestry, dairy, and fisheries industries) must carry Workers' Compensation Insurance. Further, accidents during commuting are not considered job-related accidents and do not fall under the accident compensation provision of the Labor Standards Act. However, in the interest of protecting employees, such accidents are subject to insurance payments from the Workers' Compensation Insurance.

Article 92. (Accident Compensation)

1. When an Employee suffers a work-related injury or illness, or an Employee dies due to such injury or illness, the government shall provide the Employee or his/her survivor, with accident compensation pursuant to the Industrial Accident Compensation Insurance Act.

2. During the first three (3) days when an Employee fails to receive wages because of his/her inability to work due to medical treatment for a work-related injury or illness, the Company shall provide the Employee with accident compensation pursuant to the Labor Standards Act because the government shall not provide the Employee with accident compensation pursuant to the Industrial Accident Compensation Insurance Act.

3. In the case described in paragraph 1, if insurance benefits shall be provided, the

第93条　（療養義務）
　　社員は，業務上負傷し，又は疾病にかかった場合で，前条の補償を受けているときは，療養に努めなければならない。

第94条　（通勤災害）
　　社員が通勤により負傷し，疾病にかかり，又は死亡したときは，労働者災害補償保険法により保険給付を受ける。

第15章　附　　則

第95条　（施　行　日）
　　本就業規則は，平成〇年〇月〇日から施行する。

Company shall not assume a duty under the Labor Standards Act to compensate for the amount provided.

Article 93. (Obligation to Undergo Medical Treatment)
An Employee shall endeavor to undergo medical treatment when he/she has suffered a work-related injury or illness and shall receive the compensation prescribed in the preceding article.

Article 94. (Commuting-Related Accidents)
When an Employee suffers a commuting-related injury or illness, or an Employee dies due to such injury or illness, the government shall provide the Employee or his/her survivor, with insurance benefits.

Chapter XV. Supplementary Provisions

Article 95. (Date of Enforcement)
These Work Rules shall come into force as of MM/DD/YY.

第3部
附属規程・書式

Part III
SUPPLEMENTARY REGULATIONS / FORMS

育児・介護休業規程

本規程は，特段の記載がない限り，育児休業，介護休業等育児又は家族介護を行う労働者の福祉に関する法律（以下，「法」といいます。）等の法令が要求する最低限度の基準で作成した規程例となっています。

第1章　目　的

第1条　（目　的）

　　本規程は，従業員の育児・介護休業，子の看護休暇，介護休暇，育児・介護のための所定外労働の免除，育児・介護のための時間外労働及び深夜業の制限並びに育児・介護短時間勤務等に関する取扱いについて定めるものである。

第2章　育児休業制度

第2条　（育児休業の対象者）
1. 育児のために休業することを希望する従業員（日雇従業員を除く。）で

Regulations for Child Care/ Nursing Care Leave

> Please note that, unless otherwise specified, these Regulations have been drafted as sample regulations which satisfy the minimum requirements of the Act on the Welfare of Employees Who Take Care of Children or Other Family Members Including Child Care and Family Care Leave (the "Act") and any other applicable laws.

Chapter I. Purpose

Article 1. (Purpose)

These Regulations prescribe the handling of child care/nursing care leave, sick/injured child care leave, non-consecutive nursing care leave, exemption from work outside the designated working hours due to child care/nursing care, limitations on overtime work and late hour work for child care/nursing care, shortened working hours for child care/nursing, and other related matters pertaining to employees.

Chapter II. Child Care Leave System

Article 2. (Eligible Employees)
1. Employees who live with and raise a child aged less than one (1) year and who

あって，1歳に満たない子と同居し，養育する者は，本規程に定めるところにより育児休業をすることができる。ただし，有期労働契約社員にあっては，申出時点において，次のいずれにも該当する者に限り育児休業をすることができる。
 (1) 入社1年以上であること。
 (2) 子が1歳6か月（本条第5項の申出にあっては2歳）に達する日までに労働契約期間が満了し，更新されないことが明らかでないこと。
2.　前項にかかわらず，労使協定により除外された次の従業員からの休業の申出は拒むことができる。

> 本項に基づき一定の労働者を除外するためには労使協定を締結する必要があります。

 (1) 入社1年未満の従業員
 (2) 申出の日から1年以内に雇用関係が終了することが明らかな従業員
 (3) 1週間の所定労働日数が2日以下の従業員
3.　配偶者が従業員と同じ日から又は従業員より先に育児休業をしている場合，従業員は，子が1歳2か月に達するまでの間で，出生日以後の産前・産後休業期間と育児休業期間との合計が1年を限度として，育児休業をすることができる。
4.　次のいずれにも該当する従業員は，子が1歳6か月に達するまでの間で必要な日数について育児休業をすることができる。なお，育児休業を開始しようとする日は，原則として子の1歳の誕生日に限るものとする。
 (1) 従業員又は配偶者（内縁を含む。以下同じ。）が原則として子の1歳の誕生日の前日に育児休業をしていること
 (2) 次のいずれかの事情があること
　　(ｱ) 保育所に入所を希望しているが，入所できない場合
　　(ｲ) 従業員の配偶者であって育児休業の対象となる子の親であり，1歳以降育児に当たる予定であった者が，死亡，負傷，疾病等の事情により子を養育することが困難になった場合
5.　次のいずれにも該当する従業員は，子が2歳に達するまでの間で必要な

request leave for child care (excluding employees hired on a daily basis) may take child care leave pursuant to the provisions of these Regulations. Fixed Term Employees may only take child care leave if they satisfy all of the following conditions at the time they submit a request:

(1) At least one (1) year has passed since the employee joined the Company;

(2) It is not evident that the term of his/her employment agreement will expire by the date on which the child becomes one (1) year and six (6) months old (two (2) years old for the request pursuant to Paragraph 5 of this Article) and will not be renewed.

2. Notwithstanding the preceding paragraph, the Company may reject a request for child care leave of an employee excluded pursuant to the Labor-Management Agreement who falls under any of Items 1 through 3 below:

A labor-management agreement will be required in order to exclude certain employees pursuant to this paragraph.

(1) An employee who has served in the Company for less than one (1) year;

(2) An employee whose employment is to evidently end within one (1) year from the date of request; or

(3) An employee whose designated working days are not more than two (2) days per week.

3. In the case of an employee whose spouse commences or has already been on child care leave on the date on which the employee's child care leave commences, the employee may take child care leave until the child becomes one (1) year and two (2) months old, provided that the total period of the employee's pre- and post-childbirth leave and child care leave shall not exceed one (1) year.

4. Employees who satisfy both of the following conditions may take child care leave for the number of days required until the child becomes one (1) year and six (6) months old. The date on which the child care leave commences shall, in principle, be the first birthday of the child.

(1) In principle, the employee or his/her spouse (including common-law marriage;

日数について育児休業をすることができる。なお,育児休業を開始しようとする日は,原則として子の1歳6か月の誕生日に限るものとする。

(1) 従業員又は配偶者が原則として子の1歳6か月の誕生日の前日に育児休業をしていること
(2) 次のいずれかの事情があること
　ア　保育所に入所を希望しているが,入所できない場合
　イ　従業員の配偶者であって育児休業の対象となる子の親であり,1歳6か月以降育児に当たる予定であった者が,死亡,負傷,疾病等の事情により子を養育することが困難になった場合
6．第4項及び前項にかかわらず,労使協定により除外された次の従業員からの休業の申出は拒むことができる。

> 本項に基づき一定の労働者を除外するためには労使協定を締結する必要があります。

(1) 入社1年未満の従業員
(2) 申出の日から6か月以内に雇用関係が終了することが明らかな従業員
(3) 1週間の所定労働日数が2日以下の従業員

hereinafter in these Regulations, the same qualification shall apply) is on child care leave on the date immediately prior to the first birthday of the child, and

(2) Either of the following circumstances applies:
  (i) The child's application for admission to a nursery has not been accepted; or
  (ii) The employee's spouse who is a parent of the relevant child and was to nurse the child when and after the child becomes one (1) year old is no longer able to do so due to death, injury, illness or other similar reasons.

5. Employees who satisfy both of the following conditions may take child care leave for the number of days required until the child becomes two (2) years old. The date on which the child care leave commences shall, in principle, be the first and half-birthday of the child.

  (1) In principle, the employee or his/her spouse is on child care leave on the date immediately prior to the first and half-birthday of the child, and
  (2) Either of the following circumstances applies:
    (i) The child's application for admission to a nursery has not been accepted; or
    (ii) The employee's spouse who is a parent of the relevant child and was to nurse the child when and after the child becomes one (1) year and six (6) months old is no longer able to do so due to death, injury, illness or other similar reasons.

6. Notwithstanding Paragraph 4 and the preceding paragraph, the Company may reject a request for child care leave of an employee excluded pursuant to the Labor-Management Agreement who falls under any of Items 1 through 3 below:

A labor-management agreement will be required in order to exclude certain employees pursuant to this paragraph.

  (1) An employee who has served in the Company for less than one (1) year;
  (2) An employee whose employment is to evidently end within six (6) months from the date of request; or
  (3) An employee whose designated working days are not more than two (2) days per week.

第3条 （育児休業の申出の手続等）
1. 育児休業をすることを希望する従業員は，原則として育児休業を開始しようとする日（以下，「育児休業開始予定日」という。）の1か月前（第2条第4項及び第5項に基づく1歳及び1歳6か月を超える休業の場合は，2週間前。）までに育児休業申出書を会社に提出することにより申し出るものとする。なお，育児休業中の有期労働契約社員が労働契約を更新するに当たり，引き続き休業を希望する場合には，更新された労働契約期間の初日を育児休業開始予定日として，育児休業申出書により再度の申出を行うものとする。
2. 申出は，次のいずれかに該当する場合を除き，一子につき1回限りとする。ただし，産後休業をしていない従業員が，子の出生日又は出産予定日のいずれか遅い方から8週間以内にした最初の育児休業については，1回の申出にカウントしない。
　⑴ 第2条第1項に基づく休業をした者が同条第4項又は第5項に基づく休業の申出をしようとする場合又は本条第1項後段の申出をしようとする場合
　⑵ 第2条第4項に基づく休業をした者が同条第5項に基づく休業の申出をしようとする場合又は本条第1項後段の申出をしようとする場合
　⑶ 配偶者の死亡等特別の事情がある場合
3. 会社は，育児休業申出書を受け取るに当たり，必要最小限度の各種証明書の提出を求めることがある。
4. 会社は，育児休業申出書が提出されたときは，速やかに当該育児休業申出書を提出した者（以下，この章において「申出者」という。）に対し，育児休業取扱通知書を交付する。

> 休業中における待遇や休業後における労働条件等に関する取扱いを明示した育児休業取扱通知書の交付は努力義務とされています（法21条2項）。ただし，事業主は，育児休業の申出に対して，①育児休業申出を受けた旨，②育児休業開始予定日及び育児休業終了予定日，③育児休業申出を拒む場合には，その旨及び理由を速やかに通知しなければならないこととされており

Article 3. (Procedures for Requesting Child Care Leave)

1. An employee who requests child care leave shall make a request by submitting to the Company a request for child care leave at least, in principle, one (1) month (or two (2) weeks in the case of leave that extends beyond the first birthday and the first and half-birthday of the child pursuant to Article 2, Paragraph 4 or 5) prior to the date on which the employee intends to commence the child care leave (the "Scheduled Commencement Date of Child Care Leave"). If a Fixed Term Employee on child care leave requests to continue the child care leave at the time his/her employment agreement is renewed, the first date of the renewed term of the employment agreement shall be the Scheduled Commencement Date of Child Care Leave, and a new request for child care leave shall be submitted accordingly.

2. A request for child care leave may be made only once per child, except for either of the following cases; provided, however, that a request for child care leave made for the first time within eight (8) weeks from the latter of the date of childbirth or the expected date of childbirth by an employee who has not taken post-childbirth leave shall not be counted as one (1) request:

    (1) An employee on child care leave under Article 2, Paragraph 1 makes a request for child care leave pursuant to Article 2, Paragraph 4 or 5, or makes a request as provided for in the second sentence of Paragraph 1 of this article;

    (2) An employee on child care leave under Article 2, Paragraph 4 makes a request for child care leave pursuant to Article 2, Paragraph 5, or makes a request as provided for in the second sentence of Paragraph 1 of this Article; or

    (3) There are special circumstances including, without limitation, death of the employee's spouse.

3. Prior to accepting a request for child care leave, the Company may request that the employee submit several kinds of certifications as the Company may deem are minimum requirements.

4. Upon receipt of a request for child care leave, the Company shall promptly deliver a notice of handling child care leave to the employee who submitted the request (in this Chapter, an "Applicant").

> （同法施行規則（以下，「規則」といいます。）５条４項），これらの事項のみを通知書に盛り込むことでも差し支えないこととされています。

5. 申出者は，申出の日後に申出に係る子が出生したときは，出生後２週間以内に会社に育児休業対象児出生届を提出しなければならない。

第４条　（育児休業の申出の撤回等）
1. 申出者は，育児休業開始予定日の前日までは，育児休業申出撤回届を会社に提出することにより，育児休業の申出を撤回することができる。
2. 会社は，育児休業申出撤回届が提出されたときは，速やかに当該育児休業申出撤回届を提出した者に対し，育児休業取扱通知書を交付する。
3. 育児休業の申出を撤回した者は，特別の事情がない限り同一の子については再度申出をすることができない。ただし，第２条第１項に基づく休業の申出を撤回した者であっても，同条第４項及び第５項に基づく休業の申出をすることができ，第２条第４項に基づく休業の申出を撤回した者であっても，同条第５項に基づく休業の申出をすることができる。
4. 育児休業開始予定日の前日までに，子の死亡等により申出者が休業申出に係る子を養育しないこととなった場合には，育児休業の申出はされなかったものとみなす。この場合において，申出者は，原則として当該事由が発生した日に，会社にその旨を通知しなければならない。

> An employer has a duty to use efforts to deliver a notice of handling child care leave expressly stating the employee's treatment during the leave and post-leave employment conditions, etc. (Article 21, Paragraph 2 of the Act). However, an employer may also sufficiently perform the duty by including in the notice only the following matters of which the employer is required to notify the applicant promptly upon receipt of a request for child care leave: (i) that the employer has received the request for child care leave; (ii) the Scheduled Commencement Date of Child Care Leave and the Scheduled Termination Date of Child Care Leave (as defined below); and (iii) if the employer rejects the request for child care leave, the rejection and reasons therefore (Article 5, Paragraph 4 of the Ordinance for Enforcement of the Act (the "Ordinance")).

5. When the child subject to the request is born after the request date, the Applicant shall submit to the Company a report of childbirth eligible for child care leave within two (2) weeks of the birth.

Article 4. (Withdrawal of Request for Child Care Leave)
1. An Applicant may withdraw a request for child care leave by submitting to the Company a notice of withdrawal of request for child care leave by the date immediately preceding the Scheduled Commencement Date of Child Care Leave.
2. Upon receipt of a notice of withdrawal of request for child care leave, the Company shall promptly deliver a notice of handling child care leave to the Applicant who submitted the notice.
3. The Applicant who withdrew a request for child care leave shall not resubmit a request for child care leave for the same child, unless there are special circumstances. Notwithstanding the foregoing, an Applicant who withdrew a request for child care leave pursuant to Article 2, Paragraph 1 may submit a request for child care leave pursuant to Article 2, Paragraph 4 or 5, and an Applicant who withdrew a request for child care leave pursuant to Ariticle 2, Paragraph 4 may submit a request for child care leave pursuant to Article 2, Paragraph 5.
4. In the event that, on or before the day preceding the Scheduled Commencement Date of Child Care Leave, the Applicant no longer needs to raise the child who is the

第5条　（育児休業の期間等）
1. 　育児休業の期間は，原則として，子が1歳に達するまで（第2条第3項，第4項及び第5項に基づく休業の場合は，それぞれ定められた時期まで。）を限度として育児休業申出書に記載された期間とする。
2. 　前項にかかわらず，会社は，育児・介護休業法の定めるところにより育児休業開始予定日の指定を行うことができる。
3. 　従業員は，育児休業期間変更申出書により会社に，育児休業開始予定日の1週間前までに申し出ることにより，育児休業開始予定日の繰り上げ変更を，また，育児休業を終了しようとする日（以下，「育児休業終了予定日」という。）の1か月前（第2条第4項及び第5項に基づく休業をしている場合は，2週間前。）までに申し出ることにより，育児休業終了予定日の繰り下げ変更を行うことができる。
　　　育児休業開始予定日の繰り上げ変更及び育児休業終了予定日の繰り下げ変更とも，原則として1回に限り行うことができるが，第2条第4項及び第5項に基づく休業の場合には，第2条第1項に基づく休業とは別に，子が1歳から1歳6か月に達するまで及び1歳6か月から2歳に達するまでの期間内で，1回，育児休業終了予定日の繰り下げ変更を行うことができる。
4. 　育児休業期間変更申出書が提出されたときは，会社は速やかに当該育児休業期間変更申出書を提出した者に対し，育児休業取扱通知書を交付する。
5. 　次の各号に掲げるいずれかの事由が生じた場合には，育児休業は終了するものとし，当該育児休業の終了日は当該各号に掲げる日とする。
(1) 子の死亡等育児休業に係る子を養育しないこととなった場合
　　当該事由が発生した日（なお，この場合において本人が出勤する日は，事由発生の日から2週間以内であって，会社と本人が話し合いの上決定した日とする。）

subject of the request for any reason including the child's death, the request shall be deemed not to have been made. In the above case, the Applicant shall, in principle, notify the Company thereof on the day when such event occurs.

Article 5. (Period of Child Care Leave)

1. The period of child care leave shall, in principle, be the period set forth in the request for child care leave, which shall not exceed the date on which the child becomes one (1) year old (or the date respectively designated in the case of leave under Article 2, Paragraph 3, 4 or 5).
2. Notwithstanding the preceding paragraph, the Company may designate the Scheduled Commencement Date of Child Care Leave pursuant to the Act.
3. An employee may advance the Scheduled Commencement Date of Child Care Leave and defer the Scheduled Termination Date of Child Care Leave (as defined below) by submitting to the Company a notice of change of child care leave period at least one (1) week prior to the Scheduled Commencement Date of Child Care Leave, and at least one (1) month (or two (2) weeks in the case of leave under Article 2, Paragraph 4 or 5) prior to the date on which the employee intends to end the child care leave (the "Scheduled Termination Date of Child Care Leave"), respectively. The advancement of the Scheduled Commencement Date of Child Care Leave and the deferment of the Scheduled Termination Date of Child Care Leave may, in principle, be made only once respectively. In the case of leave under Article 2, Paragraph 4 or 5, and apart from the leave under Article 2, Paragraph 1, the Scheduled Termination Date of Child Care Leave may be deferred only once within the period from the date on which the child becomes one (1) year old to the date on which the child becomes one (1) year and six (6) months old or one (1) year and six (6) months old to the date on which the child becomes two (2) years old.
4. Upon receipt of a notice of change of child care leave period, the Company shall promptly deliver a notice of handling child care leave to the employee who submitted the notice.
5. If any of the events specified in the following items occurs, the child care leave shall

(2) 育児休業に係る子が1歳に達した場合等

　　子が1歳に達した日（第2条第3項に基づく休業の場合を除く。第2条第4項に基づく休業の場合は，子が1歳6か月に達した日。第2条第5項に基づく休業の場合は，子が2歳に達した日。）

(3) 申出者について，産前産後休業，介護休業又は新たな育児休業期間が始まった場合

　　産前産後休業，介護休業又は新たな育児休業の開始日の前日

(4) 第2条第3項に基づく休業において，出生日以後の産前・産後休業期間と育児休業期間との合計が1年に達した場合

　　当該1年に達した日

6. 前項第1号の事由が生じた場合には，申出者は原則として当該事由が生じた日に会社にその旨を通知しなければならない。

第3章　介護休業制度

第6条　（介護休業の対象者）

1. 要介護状態にある家族を介護する従業員（日雇従業員を除く。）は，本

be terminated and the date of termination of such child care leave shall be the date stated in the respective items concerned:

(1) In the event that the Applicant no longer needs to raise the child who is the subject of the request for any reason, including the child's death:

The date on which such event occurs (in that case, the date on which the employee resumes work shall be the date within two (2) weeks of the date of occurrence of the event as determined through discussions between the Company and the employee).

(2) In the event the child who is the subject of the child care leave becomes one (1) year old:

The date on which the child has become one (1) year old (excluding in the case of leave under Article 2, Paragraph 3), the date on which the child has become one (1) year and six (6) months old in the case of leave under Article 2, Paragraph 4, or the date on which the child has become two (2) years old in the case of leave under Article 2, Paragraph 5.

(3) In the event that pre- and post-childbirth leave, nursing care leave or new child care leave commences with respect to the Applicant:

The date immediately preceding the date of commencement of the pre- and post-childbirth leave, nursing care leave or new child care leave.

(4) In the case of leave under Article 2, Paragraph 3, the total period of the Applicant's pre- and post-childbirth leave and child care leave has reached one (1) year:

The date on which the total period has reached one (1) year.

6. In the event of Paragraph 5, Item 1, the Applicant shall, in principle, notify the Company thereof on the date on which such event occurs.

Chapter III. Nursing Care Leave System

Article 6. (Eligible Employees)

1. Employees who nurse a family member requiring nursing (excluding employees hired

規程に定めるところにより介護休業をすることができる。ただし，有期労働契約社員にあっては，申出時点において，次のいずれにも該当する者に限り介護休業をすることができる。
(1) 入社１年以上であること。
(2) 介護休業を開始しようとする日（以下，「介護休業開始予定日」という。）から93日を経過する日から６か月を経過する日までに労働契約期間が満了し，更新されないことが明らかでないこと。
2. 前項にかかわらず，労使協定により除外された次の従業員からの休業の申出は拒むことができる。

> 本項に基づき一定の労働者を除外するためには労使協定を締結する必要があります。

(1) 入社１年未満の従業員
(2) 申出の日から93日以内に雇用関係が終了することが明らかな従業員
(3) １週間の所定労働日数が２日以下の従業員
3. この要介護状態にある家族とは，負傷，疾病又は身体上若しくは精神上の障害により，２週間以上の期間にわたり常時介護を必要とする状態にある次の者をいう。
(1) 配偶者
(2) 父母
(3) 子
(4) 配偶者の父母
(5) 祖父母，兄弟姉妹又は孫

第７条　（介護休業の申出の手続等）
1. 介護休業をすることを希望する従業員は，原則として介護休業開始予定

on a daily basis) may take nursing care leave pursuant to the provisions of these Regulations. Fixed Term Employees may only take nursing care leave if they satisfy all of the following conditions at the time they submit a request:

(1) At least one (1) year has passed since the employee joined the Company; and
(2) It is not evident that the term of his/her employment agreement will expire by the day six months have passed since the date on which 93 days have elapsed since the date on which he/she was to commence nursing care leave (the "Scheduled Commencement Date of Nursing Care Leave") and will not be renewed.

2. Notwithstanding the preceding paragraph, the Company may reject a request for nursing care leave of an employee excluded pursuant to the Labor-Management Agreement who falls under any of Items 1 through 3 below:

A labor-management agreement will be required in order to exclude certain employees pursuant to this paragraph.

(1) An employee who has served in the Company for less than one (1) year;
(2) An employee whose employment is to evidently end within ninety three (93) days from the date of request; or
(3) An employee whose designated working days are not more than two (2) days per week.

3. A family member requiring nursing shall mean any of an employee's family members set forth below who requires nursing at all times over a period of at least two (2) weeks due to injury, illness, or physical or mental disability:

(1) Spouse;
(2) Parent;
(3) Child;
(4) Spouse's parent; or
(5) Grandparent, sibling or grandchild.

Article 7. (Procedures for Requesting Nursing Care Leave)
1. An employee who requests nursing care leave shall make a request by submitting to

日の２週間前までに，介護休業申出書を会社に提出することにより申し出るものとする。なお，介護休業中の期間契約従業員が労働契約を更新するに当たり，引き続き休業を希望する場合には，更新された労働契約期間の初日を介護休業開始予定日として，介護休業申出書により再度の申出を行うものとする。

2. 申出は，対象家族１人につき３回までとする。ただし，前項後段の申出をしようとする場合にあっては，この限りでない。
3. 会社は，介護休業申出書を受け取るに当たり，必要最小限度の各種証明書の提出を求めることがある。
4. 介護休業申出書が提出されたときは，会社は速やかに当該介護休業申出書を提出した者（以下，この章において「申出者」という。）に対し，介護休業取扱通知書を交付する。

> 　育児休業の場合と同様に，休業中における待遇や休業後における労働条件等に関する取扱いを明示した介護休業取扱通知書の交付は努力義務とされています（法21条２項）。ただし，事業主は，介護休業の申出に対して，①介護休業申出を受けた旨，②介護休業開始予定日及び介護休業終了予定日，③介護休業申出を拒む場合には，その旨及び理由を速やかに通知しなければならないこととされており（規則22条２項），これらの事項のみを通知書に盛り込むことでも差し支えないこととされています。

第８条　（介護休業の申出の撤回等）
1. 申出者は，介護休業開始予定日の前日までは，介護休業申出撤回届を会

the Company a request for nursing care leave at least, in principle, two (2) weeks prior to the Scheduled Commencement Date of Nursing Care Leave. If a term contract employee on nursing care leave requests continuation of the nursing care leave at the time his/her employment agreement is renewed, the first date of the renewed term of the employment agreement shall be the Scheduled Commencement Date of Nursing Care Leave, and a new request for nursing care leave shall be submitted accordingly.

2. A request for nursing care leave may be made up to three (3) times for a family member for a particular care-requiring condition; provided, however, that this provision shall not apply in the case of a request provided for in the second sentence of the preceding paragraph.
3. Prior to accepting a request for nursing care leave, the Company may request that the employee submit several kinds of certifications as the Company may deem are minimum requirements.
4. Upon receipt of a request for nursing care leave, the Company shall promptly deliver a notice of handling nursing care leave to the employee who submitted the request (in this Chapter, an "Applicant").

As in the case of child care leave, an employer has a duty to use efforts to deliver a notice of handling nursing care leave expressly stating the employee's treatment during the leave and post-leave employment conditions, etc. (Article 21, Paragraph 2 of the Act). However, an employer may also sufficiently perform the duty by including in the notice only the following matters of which the employer is required to notify the applicant promptly upon receipt of a request for nursing care leave: (i) that the employer has received the request for nursing care leave; (ii) the Scheduled Commencement Date of Nursing Care Leave and the Scheduled Termination Date of Nursing Care Leave (as defined below); and (iii) if the employer rejects the request for nursing care leave, the rejection and reasons therefor (Article 22, Paragraph 2 of the Ordinance).

Article 8. (Withdrawal of Request for Nursing Care Leave)
1. An Applicant may withdraw a request for nursing care leave by submitting to the

社に提出することにより，介護休業の申出を撤回することができる。
2. 介護休業申出撤回届が提出されたときは，会社は速やかに当該介護休業申出撤回届を提出した者に対し，介護休業取扱通知書を交付する。
3. 同一対象家族について2回連続して介護休業の申出を撤回した者について，当該家族について再度の申出はすることができない。ただし，会社がこれを適当と認めた場合には，申し出ることができるものとする。

> 法14条2項では，2回連続して介護休業の申出が撤回された場合に，会社はこれ以降の申出を拒むことができることとなっており，ただし書は削除することも可能です。

4. 介護休業開始予定日の前日までに，申出に係る家族の死亡等により申出者が家族を介護しないこととなった場合には，介護休業の申出はされなかったものとみなす。この場合において，申出者は，原則として当該事由が発生した日に，会社にその旨を通知しなければならない。

第9条　（介護休業の期間等）
1. 介護休業の期間は，対象家族1人につき，原則として，通算93日間の範囲内で，介護休業申出書に記載された期間とする。
2. 前項にかかわらず，会社は，育児・介護休業法の定めるところにより介護休業開始予定日の指定を行うことができる。
3. 従業員は，介護休業期間変更申出書により，介護休業を終了しようとする日（以下，「介護休業終了予定日」という。）の2週間前までに会社に申し出ることにより，1回に限り，介護休業終了予定日の繰下げ変更を行うことができる。
　　この場合において，介護休業開始予定日から変更後の介護休業終了予定日までの期間は通算93日の範囲を超えないことを原則とする。

Company a notice of withdrawal of request for nursing care leave by the date immediately preceding the Scheduled Commencement Date of Nursing Care Leave.

2. Upon receipt of a notice of withdrawal of request for nursing care leave, the Company shall promptly deliver a notice of handling nursing care leave to the Applicant who submitted the notice.

3. The Applicant who has withdrawn a request for nursing care leave twice consecutively may not make an additional request for nursing care leave for the same family member. However, if the Company deems it appropriate, the Applicant may make the additional request.

Article 14, Paragraph 2 of the Act provides that where a request for nursing care leave is withdrawn twice consecutively, the company may refuse any further request. It is therefore possible to delete the proviso.

4. In the event that, on or before the day preceding the Scheduled Commencement Date of Nursing Care Leave, the Applicant no longer needs to nurse the family member who is the subject of the request, for any reason including the family member's death, the request shall be deemed not to have been made. In the above case, the Applicant shall, in principle, notify the Company thereof on the day when such event occurs.

Article 9. (Period of Nursing Care Leave)

1. The period of nursing care leave shall, in principle, be the period set forth in the request for nursing care leave, which shall not exceed ninety-three (93) days in total.

2. Notwithstanding the preceding paragraph, the Company may designate the Scheduled Commencement Date of Nursing Care Leave pursuant to the Act.

3. An employee may defer the date on which the employee intends to end the nursing care leave (the "Scheduled Termination Date of Nursing Care Leave") by submitting to the Company a notice of change of nursing care leave period at least two (2) weeks prior to the Scheduled Termination Date of Nursing Care Leave. In that case, the period from the Scheduled Commencement Date of Nursing Care Leave to the Scheduled Termination Date of Nursing Care Leave shall, in principle, not exceed

4. 介護休業期間変更申出書が提出されたときは，会社は速やかに当該介護休業期間変更申出書を提出した者に対し，介護休業取扱通知書を交付する。
5. 次の各号に掲げるいずれかの事由が生じた場合には，介護休業は終了するものとし，当該介護休業の終了日は当該各号に掲げる日とする。
  (1) 家族の死亡等介護休業に係る家族を介護しないこととなった場合
    当該事由が発生した日（なお，この場合において本人が出勤する日は，事由発生の日から2週間以内であって，会社と本人が話し合いの上決定した日とする。）
  (2) 申出者について，産前産後休業，育児休業又は新たな介護休業が始まった場合
    産前産後休業，育児休業又は新たな介護休業の開始日の前日
6. 前項第1号の事由が生じた場合には，申出者は原則として当該事由が生じた日に会社にその旨を通知しなければならない。

第4章　子の看護休暇

第10条　（子の看護休暇）
1. 小学校就学の始期に達するまでの子を養育する従業員（日雇従業員を除く。）は，負傷し，又は疾病にかかった当該子の世話をするために，又は当該子に予防接種や健康診断を受けさせるために，就業規則第36条に規定する年次有給休暇とは別に，当該子が1人の場合は1年間につき5日，2人以上の場合は1年間につき10日を限度として，子の看護休暇を取得することができる。この場合の1年間とは，［4月1日から翌年3月31日］ま

ninety-three (93) days in total.

4. Upon receipt of a notice of change of nursing care leave period, the Company shall promptly deliver a notice of handling nursing care leave to the employee who submitted the notice.

5. In either of the events specified in the following items, the nursing care leave shall be terminated and the date of termination of such nursing care leave shall be the date stated in the respective items concerned:

  (1) In the event that the Applicant no longer needs to nurse the family member who is the subject of the request for any reason, including the family member's death:
  The date on which such event occurs (in that case, the date on which the employee resumes work shall be the date within two (2) weeks of the date of occurrence of the event as determined through discussions between the Company and the employee).

  (2) In the event that pre- and post-childbirth leave, child care leave or new nursing care leave commences with respect to the Applicant:
  The date immediately preceding the date of commencement of the pre- and post-childbirth leave, child care leave or new nursing care leave.

6. In the event that Paragraph 5, Item 1 is applicable, the Applicant shall, in principle, notify the Company thereof on the date on which such event occurs.

Chapter IV. Sick/Injured Child Care Leave

Article 10. (Sick/Injured Child Care Leave)

1. Apart from the annual paid leave prescribed in Article 36 of the Work Rules, employees who raise a child(ren) younger than the primary school age (excluding employees hired on a daily basis) may take leave for nursing their injured or sick child(ren) or for having the child(ren) receive vaccination or medical examination, for not more than five (5) days a year if there is one (1) such child and not more than ten (10) days a year if there are two (2) or more such children. For the purpose of this

での期間とする。ただし，労使協定によって除外された次の従業員からの子の看護休暇の申出は拒むことができる。

> 本項に基づき一定の労働者を除外するためには労使協定を締結する必要があります。

　(1)　入社６か月未満の従業員
　(2)　１週間の所定労働日数が２日以下の従業員
２．　子の看護休暇は半日単位で取得することができる。
　(1)　従業員のうち，勤務時間が午前［９時］～午後［６時］の従業員の半日単位となる時間数は，労使協定により始業時刻から［３時間］又は終業時刻までの［５時間］とする。休暇１日当たりの時間数は，［８時間］とする。ただし，１日の所定労働時間が４時間以下である従業員は１日単位とする。
　(2)　上記以外の従業員については，半日単位となる時間数は１日の所定労働時間の２分の１とし，始業時刻から連続し，又は終業時刻まで連続するものとする。

> 平成29年１月１日施行の法の改正により，子の看護休暇の半日単位での取得が可能となりました。なお，「半日」の定義につきまして，原則として１日の所定労働時間の２分の１と定められていますが（法施行規則34条１項），労使協定を締結することにより，これ以外の時間数を「半日」と定めることができることとされています（同条２項）。本書式は，就業規則25条２項に定められた労働時間を前提に，午前と午後の勤務時間をそれぞれ「半日」とする旨の労使協定を締結した場合を想定して記載しています。

３．　子の看護休暇を取得しようとする者は，原則として，子の看護休暇申出書を事前に会社に提出するものとする。

paragraph, one year shall be the term [from April 1 to March 31 of the following year]. Notwithstanding the foregoing, the Company may reject a request for sick/injured child care leave of an employee excluded pursuant to the Labor-Management Agreement who falls under either of Items 1 or 2 below:

A labor-management agreement will be required in order to exclude certain employees pursuant to this paragraph.

(1) An employee who has served in the Company for less than six (6) months; or
(2) An employee whose designated working days are not more than two (2) days per week.

2. Employees may take sick/injured child care leave on a half-day basis.
(1) For those employees whose working hours are from [9:00] a.m. to [6:00] p.m., the number of hours constituting a half day shall be [three (3) hours] from the starting time or [five (5) hours] till the finishing time based on a labor-management agreement. The number of hours constituting one (1) day of leave shall be [eight (8)] hours. However, employees whose designated working hours per day are four (4) hours or less may take such leave only on a daily basis.
(2) For those employees other than the above, the number of hours constituting a half day shall be half (1/2) of the designated working hours per day that are consecutive from the starting time or till the finishing time.

The amendment of the Act enforced on January 1, 2017 enabled employees to take sick/injured child care leave on a half-day basis. In principle, a "half day" is defined as half (1/2) of the designated working hours per day (Article 34, Paragraph 1 of the Ordinance for Enforcement of the Act); however, the number of hours other than this may be defined as a "half day" by executing a labor-management agreement (Paragraph 2 of the same Article). This Form describes cases where a labor-management agreement is executed providing that the working hours in the morning and those in the afternoon are respectively defined as a "half day" based on the working hours prescribed in Article 25, paragraph 2 of the Work Rules.

3. Employees who request sick/injured child care leave shall, in principle, submit a

第5章　介護休暇

第11条　（介護休暇）
1. 要介護状態にある家族の介護その他の世話をする従業員（日雇従業員を除く。）は，就業規則第36条に規定する年次有給休暇とは別に，当該対象家族が1人の場合は1年間につき5日，2人以上の場合は1年間につき10日を限度として，介護休暇を取得することができる。この場合の1年間とは，［4月1日から翌年3月31日］までの期間とする。ただし，労使協定によって除外された次の従業員からの介護休暇の申出は拒むことができる。

> 本項に基づき一定の労働者を除外するためには労使協定を締結する必要があります。

   (1)　入社6か月未満の従業員
   (2)　1週間の所定労働日数が2日以下の従業員
2. 介護休暇は半日単位で取得することができる。
   (1)　従業員のうち，勤務時間が午前［9時］～午後［6時］の従業員の半日単位となる時間数は，労使協定により始業時刻から［3時間］又は終業時刻までの［5時間］とする。休暇1日当たりの時間数は，［8時間］とする。ただし，1日の所定労働時間が4時間以下である従業員は1日単位とする。
   (2)　上記以外の従業員については，半日単位となる時間数は1日の所定労働時間の2分の1とし，始業時刻から連続し，又は終業時刻まで連続するものとする。

> 前条の解説と同様，介護休暇につきましても，平成29年1月1日施行の法の改正により，半日単位での取得が可能となりました。1日の所定労働時間の2分の1以外の時間数を「半日」とする場合，労使協定の締結が必要である点も前条と同様です。

request for sick/injured child care leave to the Company in advance.

Chapter V. Non-Consecutive Nursing Care Leave

Article 11. (Non-Consecutive Nursing Care Leave)

1. Apart from the annual paid leave prescribed in Article 36 of the Work Rules, employees who nurse or otherwise care for a family member(s) requiring nursing (excluding employees hired on a daily basis) may take non-consecutive nursing care leave, for not more than five (5) days a year if there is one (1) such family member and not more than ten (10) days a year if there are two (2) or more such family members. For the purpose of this paragraph, one year shall be the term [from April 1 to March 31 of the following year]. Notwithstanding the foregoing, the Company may reject a request for non-consecutive nursing care leave of an employee excluded pursuant to the Labor-Management Agreement who falls under either of Items 1 or 2 below:

A labor-management agreement will be required in order to exclude certain employees pursuant to this paragraph.

(1) An employee who has served in the Company for less than six (6) months; or
(2) An employee whose designated working days are not more than two (2) days per week.

2. Employees may take non-consecutive nursing care leave on a half-day basis.
   (1) For those employees whose working hours are from [9:00] a.m. to [6:00] p.m., the number of hours constituting a half day shall be [three (3) hours] from the starting time or [five (5) hours] till the finishing time based on a labor-management agreement. The number of hours constituting one (1) day of leave shall be [eight (8)] hours. However, employees whose designated working hours per day are four (4) hours or less may take such leave only on a daily basis.
   (2) For those employees other than the above, the number of hours constituting a half day shall be half (1/2) of the designated working hours per day that are

3. 介護休暇を取得しようとする者は、原則として、事前に会社に申し出るものとする。

第6章　所定外労働の免除

第12条　（育児・介護のための所定外労働の免除）
1. 3歳に満たない子を養育する従業員（日雇従業員を除く。）が当該子を養育するために申し出た場合、又は要介護状態にある家族を介護する従業員（日雇従業員を除く。）が当該家族を介護するために申し出た場合には、事業の正常な運営に支障がある場合を除き、所定労働時間を超えて労働をさせることはない。
2. 前項にかかわらず、労使協定によって除外された次の従業員からの所定外労働の免除の申出は拒むことができる。

> 本項に基づき一定の労働者を除外するためには労使協定を締結する必要があります。

    (1) 入社1年未満の従業員
    (2) 1週間の所定労働日数が2日以下の従業員
3. 申出をしようとする者は、1回につき、1か月以上1年以内の期間（以下、この条において「免除期間」という。）について、免除を開始しようとする日（以下、この条において「免除開始予定日」という。）及び免除を終了しようとする日を明らかにして、原則として、免除開始予定日の1

consecutive from the starting time or till the finishing time.

> The same as with our comment for the preceding Article, due to the amendment of the Act enforced on January 1, 2017, non-consecutive nursing care leave may be taken on a half-day basis as well. Similar to the preceding Article, the number of hours constituting a half day shall be half (1/2) of the designated working hours per day, and a labor-management agreement must be executed.

3. Employees who request non-consecutive nursing care leave shall, in principle, submit a request to the Company in advance.

Chapter VI. Exemption From Work Outside Designated Working Hours

Article 12. (Exemption from Work Outside Designated Working Hours for Child Care/Nursing Care)

1. Employees who raise a child younger than three (3) years old (excluding employees hired on a daily basis) or nurse a family member requiring nursing (excluding employees hired on a daily basis), shall, upon request to the Company in order to raise the child or nurse the family member, not be required to work outside the designated working hours, except in a case which may hinder the normal business operation.

2. Notwithstanding the preceding paragraph, the Company may reject a request for exemption from work outside the designated working hours of an employee excluded pursuant to the Labor-Management Agreement who falls under either of Items 1 or 2 below:

> A labor-management agreement will be required in order to exclude certain employees pursuant to this paragraph.

   (1) An employee who has served in the Company for less than one (1) year; or
   (2) An employee whose designated working days are not more than two (2) days per

か月前までに，育児・介護のための所定外労働免除申出書を会社に提出するものとする。この場合において，免除期間は，次条第3項に規定する制限期間と重複しないようにしなければならない。
4. 会社は，所定外労働免除申出書を受け取るに当たり，必要最小限度の各種証明書の提出を求めることがある。
5. 申出の日後に申出に係る子が出生したときは，所定外労働免除申出書を提出した者（以下，この条において「申出者」という。）は，出生後2週間以内に会社に所定外労働免除対象児出生届を提出しなければならない。
6. 免除開始予定日の前日までに，申出に係る子又は家族の死亡等により申出者が子を養育又は家族を介護しないこととなった場合には，申出されなかったものとみなす。この場合において，申出者は，原則として当該事由が発生した日に，会社にその旨を通知しなければならない。
7. 次の各号に掲げるいずれかの事由が生じた場合には，免除期間は終了するものとし，当該免除期間の終了日は当該各号に掲げる日とする。
 (1) 子又は家族の死亡等免除に係る子を養育又は家族を介護しないこととなった場合
    当該事由が発生した日
 (2) 免除に係る子が3歳に達した場合
    当該3歳に達した日
 (3) 申出者について，産前産後休業，育児休業又は介護休業が始まった場合
    産前産後休業，育児休業又は介護休業の開始日の前日
8. 第7項第1号の事由が生じた場合には，申出者は原則として当該事由が生じた日に，会社にその旨を通知しなければならない。

week.

3. An employee who intends to request the exemption shall, per request for a period not less than one (1) month and not more than one (1) year (in this article, the "Exemption Period") submit a request for exemption from work outside the designated working hours for child care/nursing care to the Company at least one (1) month before the day when the employee intends to commence the exemption (hereinafter in this article, the "Scheduled Commencement Date of Exemption") by specifying the Scheduled Commencement Date of Exemption and the day when the employee intends to terminate the exemption, in principle. In this case, the Exemption Period should not overlap with the Limitation Period prescribed in Paragraph 3 of the following Article.

4. Prior to accepting a request for exemption from work outside the designated working hours, the Company may request that the employee submit several kinds of certifications as the Company may deem to be minimum requirements.

5. When the child subject to the request is born after the request date, the employee who submitted the request for exemption from work outside the designated working hours (in this article, the "Applicant") shall submit to the Company a report of childbirth eligible for exemption from work outside the designated working hours within two (2) weeks of the birth.

6. In the event that, on or before the preceding day of the Scheduled Commencement Date of Exemption, the Applicant no longer needs to raise the child or nurse the family member who is the subject of the request due to the death of the child or family member, etc., the request shall be deemed not to have been made. In such event, the Applicant shall, in principle, notify the Company thereof on the date on which such event occurs.

7. If any of the events specified in the following items occurs, the Exemption Period shall be terminated and the date of termination of such Exemption Period shall be the date stated in the respective items concerned:

   (1) In the event that the Applicant no longer needs to raise the child or nurse the family member who is the subject of the exemption for any reason, including the child's or the family member's death:

第7章　時間外労働の制限

第13条　（育児・介護のための時間外労働の制限）
1. 小学校就学の始期に達するまでの子を養育する従業員（日雇従業員を除く。）が当該子を養育するため又は要介護状態にある家族を介護する従業員（日雇従業員を除く。）が当該家族を介護するために申し出た場合には，就業規則第29条の規定及び時間外労働に関する協定にかかわらず，事業の正常な運営に支障がある場合を除き，1か月について24時間，1年について150時間を超えて時間外労働をさせることはない。
2. 前項にかかわらず，次のいずれかに該当する従業員からの時間外労働の制限の申出は拒むことができる。
   (1) 入社1年未満の従業員
   (2) 1週間の所定労働日数が2日以下の従業員
3. 申出をしようとする者は，1回につき，1か月以上1年以内の期間（以下，この条において「制限期間」という。）について，制限を開始しようとする日（以下，この条において「制限開始予定日」という。）及び制限を終了しようとする日を明らかにして，原則として，制限開始予定日の1か月前までに，育児・介護のための時間外労働制限申出書を会社に提出す

The day on which such event occurs.

(2) In the event the child who is the subject of the exemption becomes three (3) years old:

The date on which the child becomes three (3) years old.

(3) In the event that pre- and post-childbirth leave, child care leave or nursing care leave commences with respect to the Applicant:

The day immediately preceding the date of commencement of the pre- and post-childbirth leave, child care leave or nursing care leave.

8. In the event of Paragraph 7, Item 1, the Applicant shall, in principle, notify the Company thereof on the date on which such event occurs.

Chapter VII. Limitations on Overtime Work

Article 13. (Limitations on Overtime Work for Child Care/Nursing Care)

1. Notwithstanding the provisions of Article 29 of the Work Rules or the agreement concerning overtime work, employees who raise a child younger than primary school age (excluding employees hired on a daily basis) or who nurse a family member requiring nursing (excluding employees hired on a daily basis) shall, upon request to the Company in order to raise the child or to nurse the family member, not be required to work overtime for more than twenty four (24) hours a month or one hundred fifty (150) hours a year, except where this may hinder the normal business operations.

2. Notwithstanding the preceding paragraph, the Company may reject a request for limitations on overtime work from an employee who falls under either of Items 1 or 2 below:

(1) An employee who has served in the Company for less than one (1) year; or

(2) An employee whose designated working days are not more than two (2) days per week.

3. An employee who intends to request limitations shall, per request for periods of not less than one (1) month and not more than one (1) year (in this article, the "Limitation

るものとする。この場合において，制限期間は，前条第3項に規定する免除期間と重複しないようにしなければならない。
4. 会社は，時間外労働制限申出書を受け取るに当たり，必要最小限度の各種証明書の提出を求めることがある。
5. 申出の日後に申出に係る子が出生したときは，時間外労働制限申出書を提出した者（以下，この条において「申出者」という。）は，出生後2週間以内に会社に時間外労働制限対象児出生届を提出しなければならない。
6. 制限開始予定日の前日までに，申出に係る子又は家族の死亡等により申出者が子を養育又は家族を介護しないこととなった場合には，申出されなかったものとみなす。この場合において，申出者は，原則として当該事由が発生した日に，会社にその旨を通知しなければならない。
7. 次の各号に掲げるいずれかの事由が生じた場合には，制限期間は終了するものとし，当該制限期間の終了日は当該各号に掲げる日とする。
 (1) 子又は家族の死亡等制限に係る子を養育又は家族を介護しないこととなった場合
　　当該事由が発生した日
 (2) 制限に係る子が小学校就学の始期に達した場合
　　子が6歳に達する日の属する年度の3月31日
 (3) 申出者について，産前産後休業，育児休業又は介護休業が始まった場合
　　産前産後休業，育児休業又は介護休業の開始日の前日
8. 前項第1号の事由が生じた場合には，申出者は原則として当該事由が生じた日に，会社にその旨を通知しなければならない。

Period"), submit a request for limitations on overtime work for child care/nursing care to the Company at least one (1) month before the day when the employee intends to commence the limitations (in this article, the "Scheduled Commencement Date of Limitations") by specifying the Scheduled Commencement Date of Limitations and the day when the employee intends to terminate the limitations, in principle. In this case, the Limitation Period should not overlap with the Exemption Period prescribed in Article 12, Paragraph 3.

4. Prior to accepting a request for limitations on overtime work, the Company may request that the employee submit several kinds of certifications as the Company may deem to be minimum requirements.

5. When the child subject to the request is born after the request date, the employee who submitted the request for limitations on overtime work (in this article, the "Applicant") shall submit to the Company a report of childbirth eligible for limitations on overtime work within two (2) weeks of the birth.

6. In the event that, on or before the day preceding the Scheduled Commencement Date of Limitations, the Applicant no longer needs to raise the child or nurse the family member who is the subject of the request due to the death of the child or the family member, etc., the request shall be deemed not to have been made. In such event, the Applicant shall, in principle, notify the Company thereof on the date on which such event occurs.

7. If any of the events specified in the following items occurs, the Limitation Period shall be terminated and the date of termination of such Limitation Period shall be the date stated in the respective items concerned:

   (1) In the event that the Applicant no longer needs to raise the child or nurse the family member who is the subject of the limitations for any reason, including the child's or the family member's death:

   The day on which such event occurs.

   (2) In the event the child who is the subject of the limitations reaches the primary school age:

   March 31 of the school year including the date on which the child becomes six (6)

第8章　深夜業の制限

第14条　（育児・介護のための深夜業の制限）
1. 小学校就学の始期に達するまでの子を養育する従業員（日雇従業員を除く。）が当該子を養育するため又は要介護状態にある家族を介護する従業員（日雇従業員を除く。）が当該家族を介護するために申し出た場合には，就業規則第29条の規定にかかわらず，事業の正常な運営に支障がある場合を除き，午後10時から午前5時までの間（以下，「深夜」という。）に労働させることはない。
2. 前項にかかわらず，次のいずれかに該当する従業員からの深夜業の制限の申出は拒むことができる。
　(1)　入社1年未満の従業員
　(2)　申出に係る家族の16歳以上の同居の家族が次のいずれにも該当する従業員
　　(ｱ)　深夜において就業していない者（1か月について深夜における就業が3日以下の者を含む。）であること。
　　(ｲ)　心身の状況が申出に係る子の保育又は家族の介護をすることができる者であること。
　　(ｳ)　6週間（多胎妊娠の場合にあっては，14週間。）以内に出産予定でなく，かつ産後8週間以内でない者であること。
　(3)　1週間の所定労働日数が2日以下の従業員

years old.

(3) In the event that pre- and post-childbirth leave, child care leave or nursing care leave commences with respect to the Applicant:

The day immediately preceding the date of commencement of such pre- and post-childbirth leave, child care leave or nursing care leave.

8. In the event that Paragraph 7, Item 1 is applicable, the Applicant shall, in principle, notify the Company thereof on the date on which such event occurs.

Chapter VIII. Limitations on Late Hour Work

Article 14. (Limitations on Late Hour Work for Child Care/Nursing Care)

1. Notwithstanding the provisions of Article 29 of the Work Rules, employees who raise a child younger than primary school age (excluding employees hired on a daily basis) or who need to nurse a family member requiring nursing (excluding employees hired on a daily basis) shall, upon request to the Company in order to raise the child or to nurse the family member, not be required to work anytime between 10:00 p.m. and 5:00 a.m. (the "Late Hours"), except where this may hinder the normal business operations.

2. Notwithstanding the preceding paragraph, the Company may reject a request for limitations on late hour work from an employee who falls under any of the following items:

(1) An employee who has served in the Company for less than one (1) year;

(2) An employee whose family member of not less than sixteen (16) years old, that lives with the family member subject to the request, falls under all of the following:

   (i) A person not working in Late Hours (including those whose work at Late Hours does not exceed three (3) days a month);

   (ii) A person with such mental and physical capacity as may enable him/her to raise the child or nurse the family member concerning the request;

   (iii) Neither a person who is expected to give birth within six (6) weeks (within

(4) 所定労働時間の全部が深夜にある従業員
3．申出をしようとする者は，1回につき，1か月以上6か月以内の期間（以下，この条において「制限期間」という。）について，制限を開始しようとする日（以下，この条において「制限開始予定日」という。）及び制限を終了しようとする日を明らかにして，原則として，制限開始予定日の1か月前までに，育児・介護のための深夜業制限申出書を会社に提出するものとする。
4．会社は，深夜業制限申出書を受け取るに当たり，必要最小限度の各種証明書の提出を求めることがある。
5．申出の日後に申出に係る子が出生したときは，深夜業制限申出書を提出した者（以下，この条において「申出者」という。）は，出生後2週間以内に会社に深夜業制限対象児出生届を提出しなければならない。
6．制限開始予定日の前日までに，申出に係る子又は家族の死亡等により申出者が子を養育又は家族を介護しないこととなった場合には，申出されなかったものとみなす。この場合において，申出者は，原則として当該事由が発生した日に，会社にその旨を通知しなければならない。
7．次の各号に掲げるいずれかの事由が生じた場合には，制限期間は終了するものとし，当該制限期間の終了日は当該各号に掲げる日とする。
　(1) 子又は家族の死亡等制限に係る子を養育又は家族を介護しないこととなった場合
　　当該事由が発生した日
　(2) 制限に係る子が小学校就学の始期に達した場合
　　子が6歳に達する日の属する年度の3月31日
　(3) 申出者について，産前産後休業，育児休業又は介護休業が始まった場合
　　産前産後休業，育児休業又は介護休業の開始日の前
8．前項第1号の事由が生じた場合には，申出者は原則として当該事由が生じた日に，会社にその旨を通知しなければならない。
9．深夜業の制限を受ける従業員に対して，会社は必要に応じて昼間勤務へ転換させることがある。

fourteen (14) weeks, in case of multiple birth children) nor a person who gave birth less than eight (8) weeks previously;

(3) An employee whose designated working days are not more than two (2) days per week; and

(4) An employee whose designated working hours are all Late Hours.

3. An employee who intends to request limitations shall, per request for periods of not less than one (1) month and not more than six (6) months (in this article, the "Limitation Period") submit a request for limitations on late hour work for child care/nursing care to the Company at least one (1) month before the day when the employee intends to commence the limitations (in this article, the "Scheduled Commencement Date of Limitations") by specifying the Scheduled Commencement Date of Limitations and the day when the employee intends to terminate the limitations, in principle.

4. Prior to accepting a request for limitations on late hour work, the Company may request that the employee submit several kinds of certifications as the Company may deem to be minimum requirements.

5. When the child subject to the request is born after the request date, the employee who submitted the request for limitations on the late hour work (in this article, the "Applicant") shall submit to the Company a report of childbirth eligible for limitations on late hour work within two (2) weeks of the birth.

6. In the event that, on or before the preceding day of the Scheduled Commencement Date of Limitations, the Applicant no longer needs to raise the child or nurse the family member who is the subject of the request for any reason including the child's or the family member's death, the request shall be deemed not to have been made. In the above case, the Applicant shall, in principle, notify the Company thereof on the day when the relevant event has occurred.

7. If any of the events specified in the following items occurs, the Limitation Period shall be terminated and the date of termination of such Limitation Period shall be the date stated in the respective items concerned.

(1) In the event that the Applicant no longer needs to raise the child or nurse the

第9章　所定労働時間の短縮措置等

第15条　（育児短時間勤務）
1. 　3歳に満たない子を養育する従業員（日雇従業員を除く。）は，申し出ることにより，就業規則第25条の所定労働時間について，以下のように変更することができる。
　　 所定労働時間を［午前9時］から［午後4時］まで（うち休憩時間は，［午前12時］から［午後1時］までの1時間とする。）の6時間とする（1歳に満たない子を育てる女性従業員は更に別途30分ずつ2回の育児時間を請求することができる。）。

family member who is the subject of the limitations for any reason, including the child's or the family member's death:

The day on which such event occurs.

(2) In the event that the child who is the subject of the limitations reaches the primary school age:

March 31 of the school year including the date on which the child becomes six (6) years old.

(3) In the event that pre- and post-childbirth leave, child care leave or nursing care leave commences with respect to the Applicant:

The day immediately preceding the date of commencement of such pre- and post-childbirth leave, child care leave or nursing care leave.

8. In the event that Paragraph 7, Item 1 is applicable, the Applicant shall, in principle, notify the Company thereof on the date on which such event occurs.

9. The Company may shift an employee, whose late hour work is limited, to daytime work, as deemed necessary.

Chapter IX. Measures Such as Shortening of Designated Working Hours

Article 15. (Shortened Working Hours for Child Care)

1. Employees who raise a child who is less than three (3) years old (excluding employees hired on a daily basis) may make a request to the Company that the designated working hours set forth in Article 25 of the Work Rules be changed as follows:

The designated working hours shall be six (6) hours from [9:00 a.m.] to [4:00 p.m.] (excluding a break of one hour from [noon] to [1:00 p.m.]) (in addition, a female employee taking care of her child who is less than one (1) year old may request two (2) thirty (30)-minute child care breaks).

> 　所定労働時間の短縮措置としては，原則として1日の所定労働時間を6時間としなければなりません（規則34条1項）。1日の所定労働時間を5時間や7時間等とする選択肢を設けることも可能ですが，その場合であっても，1日の所定時間を6時間とする選択肢も設けなければなりません。

2. 前項にかかわらず，次のいずれかに該当する従業員からの育児短時間勤務の申出は拒むことができる。

> 　本項に基づき一定の労働者を除外するためには労使協定を締結する必要があります。

(1) 1日の所定労働時間が6時間以下である従業員
(2) 労使協定によって除外された次の従業員
　(ア) 入社1年未満の従業員
　(イ) 1週間の所定労働日数が2日以下の従業員
　(ウ) 業務の性質又は業務の実施体制に照らして所定労働時間の短縮措置を講ずることが困難と認められる業務として別に定める業務に従事する従業員
3. 申出をしようとする者は，1回につき，1か月以上1年以内の期間について，短縮を開始しようとする日及び短縮を終了しようとする日を明らかにして，原則として，短縮開始予定日の1か月前までに，育児短時間勤務申出書により会社に申し出なければならない。申出書が提出されたときは，会社は速やかに申出者に対し，育児短時間勤務取扱通知書を交付する。その他適用のための手続等については，第3条から第5条までの規定（第3条第2項及び第4条第3項を除く。）を準用する。

As a measure to shorten designated working hours, the designated working hours per day shall be set at 6 hours, in principle (Article 34, Paragraph 1 of the Ordinance). There are other options, such as setting the designated working hours per day at 5 or 7 hours, etc., but when doing so, there must be an option to set the designated working hours per day at 6 hours.

2. Notwithstanding the preceding paragraph, the Company may reject a request for shortened working hours for child care from an employee who falls under any of the following items:

A labor-management agreement will be required in order to exclude certain employees pursuant to this paragraph.

(1) An employee whose designated working hours are not more than six (6) hours per day;

(2) The following employees who are excluded pursuant to the Labor-Management Agreement:

(i) An employee who has served in the Company for less than one (1) year;

(ii) An employee whose designated working days are not more than two (2) days per week; and

(iii) An employee who takes charge of any of the duties separately designated as duties for which taking measures to shorten the designated working hours is deemed to be difficult in light of the nature or the performance of the duties.

3. An employee who intends to request shortened working hours for child care shall, per request for periods of not less than one (1) month and not more than one (1) year, submit a request for shortened working hours for child care to the Company at least one (1) month before the day when the employee intends to commence the shortened working hours by specifying the scheduled commencement date of shortened working hours and the day when the employee intends to terminate shortened working hours, in principle. When the request is submitted, the Company shall promptly issue a notice of handling shortened working hours for child care to the employee who submitted such request. As for other procedures, etc. for the application of this

第15条の2 (業務上育児短時間勤務が困難な従業員に対する代替措置)

> 業務上育児短時間勤務が困難な労働者（指針第2の9(3)：例えば，a．国際路線等に就航する航空機において従事する客室乗務員等，b．労働者数が少ない事業所において，当該業務に従事し得る労働者数が著しく少ない業務に従事する者，c．流れ作業方式による製造業であって，短時間勤務の者を勤務体制に組み込むことが困難な業務に従事する者等。）に対しては，代替措置として，①育児休業，②フレックスタイム制，③始業・終業時刻の繰上げ・繰下げ，④保育施設の運営その他これに準じる便宜の供与のいずれかの措置を講じなければなりません（法23条2項，規則34条2項）。本規程例では③を導入する例を記載しています。

1.　前条第2項(2)ウの従業員（日雇従業員を除く。）は，申し出ることにより，子が3歳に達するまでの間，就業規則第25条の始業及び終業時刻について，以下のように変更することができる。

　　　通常勤務：　　午前［9時00分］始業，午後［6時00分］終業
　　　時差出勤A：　午前［8時30分］始業，午後［5時30分］終業
　　　時差出勤B：　午前［9時30分］始業，午後［6時30分］終業

2.　申出をしようとする者は，1回につき，1年以内の期間について，制度の適用を開始しようとする日及び終了しようとする日並びに時差勤務A又は時差勤務Bのいずれに変更するかを明らかにして，原則として適用開始予定日の1か月前までに，育児時差出勤申出書により会社に申し出なければならない。申出書が提出されたときは，会社は速やかに申出者に対し，育児時差出勤取扱通知書を交付する。その他適用のための手続等については，第3条から第5条までの規定（第3条2項及び第4条3項を除く。）を準用する。

system, the provisions of Articles 3 through 5 (excluding Article 3, Paragraph 2, and Article 4, Paragraph 3) shall apply, *mutatis mutandis*.

Article 15-2. (Alternative Measures for Employees Who Take Charge of Duties for which Shortening of Working Hours for Child Care is Difficult)

> One of the following alternative measures must be taken for those employees who are in charge of duties for which the shortening of working hours for child care is difficult (Part 2-9(3) of the Guideline: employees such as (a) flight attendants who work on aircrafts flying foreign routes, etc.; (b) employees who, at a workplace at which there is a small number of employees, are in charge of duties which a materially small number of employees can be in charge of; and (c) employees who, at a manufacturing business which adopts an assembly-line system, are in charge of duties for which it would be difficult to incorporate shortened working hours into the work schedule): (i) child care leave; (ii) flextime system; (iii) advancement/delay of the starting/finishing time; and (iv) operation of a child care center or provision of a similar facility (Article 23, Paragraph 2 of the Act; and Article 34, Paragraph 2 of the Ordinance). Specified in these Regulations is an example of applicable provisions when alternative measures (iii) are adopted.

1. Employees who fall under Article 15, Paragraph 2, Item (2)(iii) (excluding employees hired on a daily basis) may make a request to the Company that the starting time and the finishing time set forth in Article 25 of the Work Rules should be changed as follows until the child reaches three (3) years of age:

    Regular working hours:
    Starting at [9:00] a.m., finishing at [6:00] p.m.
    Staggered working hours type A:
    Starting at [8:30] a.m., finishing at [5:30] p.m.
    Staggered working hours type B:
    Starting at [9:30] a.m., finishing at [6:30] p.m.

2. An employee who intends to request staggered working hours for child care shall, per request for periods of not more than one (1) year, submit a request for staggered working hours for child care to the Company at least one (1) month before the day when the employee intends to commence staggered working hours by specifying the

第16条　（介護短時間勤務）

> 事業主は，要介護状態にある家族を介護する労働者に対して，①短時間勤務の制度，②フレックスタイム制，③始業・終業時刻の繰上げ・繰下げ，④労働者が利用する介護サービスの費用の助成その他これに準ずる制度のうちいずれかの措置を講じなければなりません（法23条3項，規則34条3項）。本規程例では①を導入する例を記載しています。

1. 要介護状態にある家族を介護する従業員（日雇従業員を除く。）は，申し出ることにより，対象家族1人当たり利用開始の日から3年の間で2回までの範囲内を原則として，就業規則第25条の所定労働時間について，以下のように変更することができる。
　　所定労働時間を［午前9時］から［午後4時］まで（うち休憩時間は，［午前12時］から［午後1時］までの1時間とする。）の［6時間］とする。
2. 申出をしようとする者は，短縮を開始しようとする日及び短縮を終了しようとする日を明らかにして，原則として，短縮開始予定日の2週間前までに，介護短時間勤務申出書により会社に申し出なければならない。申出書が提出されたときは，会社は速やかに申出者に対し，介護短時間勤務取扱通知書を交付する。その他適用のための手続等については，第7条から第9条までの規定を準用する。

scheduled commencement date and the day when the employee intends to terminate staggered working hours, as well as which of the staggered working hours type A or staggered working hours type B the employee requests a change to, in principle. When the request is submitted, the Company shall promptly issue a notice of handling staggered working hours for child care to the employee who submitted such request. As for other procedures, etc. for the application of this system, the provisions of Articles 3 through 5 (excluding Article 3, Paragraph 2, and Article 4, Paragraph 3) shall apply, *mutatis mutandis*.

Article 16. (Shortened Working Hours for Nursing)

An employer must take one of the following measures for those employees who nurse family members requiring nursing: (i) shortened working hour system; (ii) flextime system; (iii) advancement/delay of the starting/finishing time; and (iv) subsidizing of expenses for a nursing service used by an employee, or a similar system (Article 23, Paragraph 3 of the Act; and Article 34, Paragraph 3 of the Ordinance). Specified in these Regulations is an example of provisions applicable where measure (i) is adopted.

1. An employee who nurses family members requiring nursing (excluding employees hired on a daily basis) may make a request to the Company that the designated working hours set forth in Article 25 of the Work Rules be changed as follows up to two (2) times within three (3) years from the date using this system per family member subject to such request, in principle:
The designated working hours shall be [six (6) hours] from [9:00 a.m.] to [4:00 p.m.] (excluding a break of an hour from [noon] to [1:00 p.m.]).
2. An employee who intends to request shortened working hours for nursing shall, submit a request for shortened working hours for nursing to the Company at least two (2) weeks before the day when the employee intends to commence the shortened working hours by specifying the scheduled commencement date of shortened working hours and the day when the employee intends to terminate shortened working hours, in principle. When the request for shortened working hours is submitted, the

第10章　その他の事項

第17条　（給与等の取扱い）

> 育児・介護休業の期間を無給とすること等，労務を提供しなかった期間を働かなかったものとして取り扱うことは差し支えありません（指針（平9.9.25労告105号）第2の11⑶ハ⑷）。もっとも，育児・介護休業の申出，取得等を理由として，不利益な取扱いをしてはならないこととされています（法10条，法16条，法16条の4，法16条の7，法16条の9等）。

1. 育児・介護休業の期間については，基本給その他の月毎に支払われる給与は支給しない。
2. 賞与については，その算定対象期間に育児・介護休業をした期間が含まれる場合には，出勤日数により日割りで計算した額を支給する。
3. 定期昇給は，育児・介護休業の期間中は行わないものとし，育児・介護休業期間中に定期昇給日が到来した者については，復職後に昇給させるものとする。
4. 退職金の算定に当たっては，育児・介護休業をした期間を勤務したものとして勤続年数を計算するものとする。

Company shall promptly issue a notice of handling shortened working hours for nursing to the employee who submitted such request. As for other procedures, etc. for the application of this system, the provisions of Articles 7 through 9 shall apply, *mutatis mutandis*.

Chapter X. Other Matters

Article 17. (Handling of Wages, etc.)

Paying no wages or similar treatment by deeming that an employee has not worked during the term of child care/nursing care leave during which the employee did not provide service is in itself acceptable (Part 2-11(3)*ha(i)* of the Guideline (Notification No.105 of the Ministry of Health, Labor and Welfare, 9/25/1997)). However, the Act stipulates that an employer must not treat a worker disadvantageously by reason of the worker's making an application for child care/nursing leave or taking child care/nursing care leave, etc. (Articles 10, 16, 16-4, 16-7, and 16-9 of the Act, etc.).

1. No basic salary and other monthly allowances shall be paid during the term of child care/nursing care leave.
2. Where the bonus calculation period includes the term during which child care/nursing care leave is taken, the Company shall pay the bonus in the amount calculated on a pro rata basis based on the number of working days.
3. No periodic increase in wages shall be paid during the term of child care/nursing care leave. For those employees whose date of periodic increase comes during the term of child care/nursing care leave, their wages shall be increased after they resume working.
4. In calculating the retirement allowance, an employee shall be deemed to have served in the Company during the term of child care/nursing care leave for the purpose of calculating his/her service years.

第18条　(介護休業期間中の社会保険料の取扱い)

> 育児休業を取得した場合には，健康保険，厚生年金保険の被保険者負担分，事業主負担分ともに保険料が免除されますが，介護休業については免除されません。

　介護休業により給与が支払われない月における社会保険料の被保険者負担分は，各月に会社が納付した額を翌月〇日までに従業員に請求するものとし，従業員は会社が指定する日までに支払うものとする。

第19条　(円滑な取得及び職場復帰支援)
　会社は，育児休業又は介護休業等の取得を希望する従業員に対して，円滑な取得及び職場復帰を支援するために，当該従業員ごとに育休復帰支援プラン又は介護支援プランを作成し，同プランに基づく措置を実施する。なお，同プランに基づく措置は，業務の整理・引継ぎに係る支援，育児休業中又は介護休業中の職場に関する情報及び資料の提供など，育児休業又は介護休業等を取得する従業員との面談により把握したニーズに合わせて定め，これを実施する。

第20条　(復職後の勤務)
1. 育児・介護休業後の勤務は，原則として，休業直前の部署及び職務とする。
2. 前項にかかわらず，本人の希望がある場合及び組織の変更等やむを得ない事情がある場合には，部署及び職務の変更を行うことがある。この場合は，育児休業終了予定日の1か月前又は介護休業終了予定日の2週間前までに正式に決定し通知する。

Article 18.　(Handling of Social Insurance Premium during the Nursing Care Leave)

No social insurance premium shall be exempted during nursing care leave, whereas both an employee's portion and the employer's portion of the health insurance premium and employee's pension insurance premium shall be exempted during child care leave.

An employee's portion of the social insurance premium, which accrues during the months included in the nursing care leave when the employee is not paid wages, shall be invoiced to the employee by the [＿]th day of the succeeding month in such an amount as has been paid by the Company in each of such months. The employee shall pay the invoiced amount by the date designated by the Company.

Article 19.　(Support for efficient taking of leave and returning to work)
For employees who desire to take child care/nursing care leave etc., the Company shall prepare a support plan for returning from child care/nursing care leave for each employees to support each of them efficiently taking such leave and returning to work and take measures based on each plan. The measures based on the plan shall include support for organizing and taking over business, provision of information and materials related to their workplace during the term of child care/nursing care leave based on the needs ascertained during individual interviews with employees who will take child care/nursing care leave.

Article 20.　(Work Duties after Returning to Work)
1. Work subsequent to child care/nursing care leave shall be in the same section and of the same content as it was immediately before taking the leave, in principle.
2. Notwithstanding the preceding paragraph, the employee's section or work duties may be changed in the event that the employee so desires, or in the event of an unavoidable situation, such as a change in the Company's organization. In such event, the Company shall formally decide and notify such employee of the change no later than one (1) month prior to the Scheduled Termination Date of Child Care Leave

第21条　（年次有給休暇）
　年次有給休暇の権利発生のための出勤率の算定に当たっては，育児・介護休業をした日は出勤したものとみなす。

第22条　（法令との関係）
　育児・介護休業，子の看護休暇，介護休暇，育児・介護のための所定外労働の免除，育児・介護のための時間外労働及び深夜業の制限並びに所定労働時間の短縮措置等に関して，本規程に定めのないことについては，育児・介護休業法その他の法令の定めるところによる。

第●条　（育児目的休暇）
1．　小学校就学の始期に達するまでの子を養育する従業員（日雇従業員を除く）は，養育のために，就業規則第36条に規定する年次有給休暇とは別に，当該子が1人の場合は1年間につき●日，2人以上の場合は1年間につき●日を限度として，育児目的休暇を取得することができる。この場合の1年間とは，4月1日から翌年3月31日までの期間とする。
2．　前記育児目的休暇を取得しようとする者は，原則として，育児目的休暇申出書を事前に会社に申し出るものとする。

> 事業主は，小学校就学の始期に達するまでの子を養育する労働者が，育児に関する目的で利用できる休暇制度の措置を設けるよう努めるとされています（法24条）。育児目的休暇は，子の看護休暇，介護休暇及び年次有給休暇とは別に設ける必要があり，具体的な例としては，いわゆる配偶者出産休暇や，入園式，卒園式などの行事参加も含めた育児にも利用できる多目的休暇などが挙げられるとされています。

or two (2) weeks prior to the Scheduled Termination Date of Nursing Care Leave.

Article 21. (Annual Paid Leave)
In calculating the attendance ratio for entitlement to annual paid leave, days on child care leave or nursing care leave shall be deemed to be days on which the employee attended work.

Article 22. (Relationship with Laws)
Any matters not provided for in these Regulations with regard to child care/nursing care leave, sick/injured child care leave, non-consecutive nursing care leave, exemption from work outside the designated working hours for child care/nursing care, limitations on overtime work and late hour work for child care/nursing care, and measures to shorten the designated working hours for child care/nursing care, shall be governed by the Act and other applicable laws.

Article ● (Child-rearing leave)
1. Apart from the annual paid leave prescribed in Article 36 of the Work Rules, employees who raise a child(ren) younger than the primary school age (excluding employees hired on a daily basis) may take child-rearing leave (ikuji mokuteki kyuka), for not more than ● days a year if there is one (1) such child and not more than ● days a year if there are two (2) or more such children. For the purpose of this paragraph, one (1) year shall be the term from April 1 to March 31 of the following year.
2. Employees who request child-rearing leave above shall, in principle, submit a request for taking child-rearing leave to the Company in advance.

> **The Act provides that employers must, regarding employees who raise children younger than the primary school age, endeavor to take measures to establish a system available to them for taking leave related to child-rearing (Article 24 of the Act). Child-rearing leave must be established separately from sick/injured child care leave, nursing care leave, and annual paid leave; more specific examples**

附　則
　　1．（施行日）
　　　　本規程は，平成〇年〇月〇日から施行する。

are so-called leave for spouse's childbirth, multi-purpose leave that are available for child-rearing, including attendance at events such as nursery entrance or graduation ceremonies, etc.

Supplementary Provisions

1. (Date of Enforcement)

These Regulations shall be in force as of MM/DD/YY.

ハラスメント防止規程

第1条　（目　　的）
　本規程は，職場におけるハラスメント行為を防止するため，従業員が遵守すべき事項及び雇用管理上の措置等を定める。

第2条　（定　　義）
　1．　本規程においてセクシュアルハラスメント（以下「セクハラ行為」という。）とは，従業員の職場における性的な言動に対する他の従業員の対応等により，当該従業員の労働条件に関して不利益を与えること，又は，性的な言動により他の従業員（直接的に性的な言動の相手方となった被害者に限らない。）の就業環境を害する行為をいう。また，相手の性的指向又は性自認の状況にかかわらない他，異性に対する言動だけでなく，同性に対する言動も該当する。
　2．　本規程においてパワーハラスメント（以下「パワハラ行為」という。）とは，職務上の地位や人間関係などの職場内の優位性を背景に，業務の適正な範囲を超えて，同じ職場で働く者に対して精神的・身体的苦痛を与える行為又は職場環境を悪化させる行為をいう。
　3．　本規程において，妊娠・出産・育児休業・介護休業等に関するハラスメント（以下「マタハラ等行為」といい，セクハラ行為及びパワハラ行為と併せて「ハラスメント行為」という。）とは，他の従業員に対する以下の各行為をいう。ただし，以下の各行為のうち，業務分担や安全配慮等の観点から，客観的にみて，業務上の必要性に基づく言動によるものについては，マタハラ等行為には該当しないものとする。

Regulations on the Prevention of Harassment

Article 1. (Purpose)

These Regulations prescribe the matters to be observed by employees and the measures to be taken for employment management purposes, in order to prevent harassment from occurring in the workplace.

Article 2. (Definitions)

1. In these Regulations, "sexual harassment" ("Sexual Harassment") means an act by an employee that subjects another employee to adverse employment conditions due to his/her response to the employee's sexual behavior in the workplace, etc. or an act that disrupts the working environment of other employees (not limited to the aggrieved employee who was directly subject to the sexual behavior) because of the employee's sexual behavior. Whether an act is classified as Sexual Harassment will be determined regardless of the aggrieved employee's sexual orientation or gender identity. Sexual Harassment covers not only behavior toward persons of a different gender but also that toward persons of the same gender.

2. In these Regulations, "power harassment" ("Power Harassment") means an act by an employee inflicting mental or physical distress on workers in the same workplace or worsening the working environment beyond the appropriate scope of business, by utilizing the employee's superiority based on seniority or personal relationships, etc. in the workplace.

3. In these Regulations, "harassment concerning pregnancy, childbirth, child care leave, and nursing care leave, etc." ("Maternity Harassment, etc."; collectively with Sexual Harassment and Power Harassment, "Harassment") means each of the following acts

(1) 従業員の、他の従業員が就業規則第5章又は第6章に定める制度又は措置（以下「妊娠・出産・育児休業・介護休業等に関する制度」という。）を利用したことに関する言動により、当該他の従業員の就業環境が害されるもの
(2) 従業員の、他の女性従業員が妊娠したこと、出産したことその他の妊娠又は出産に関する事由（雇用の分野における男女の均等な機会及び待遇の確保等に関する法律施行規則（昭和61年1月27日労働省令第2号）第2条の2各号に列挙される事由を含む。）（以下「妊娠等の事由」という。）に対する言動により、当該他の従業員の就業環境が害されるもの
4. 本規程における職場とは、勤務部店のみならず、従業員が業務を遂行する全ての場所をいい、また、就業時間内における場所に限らず、実質的に職場の延長とみなされる就業時間外の時間における場所を含むものとする。

第3条 （禁止行為）
 1. 従業員は、次に掲げるセクハラ行為を行ってはならない。
  (1) 交際・性的関係の強要
  (2) 容姿及び身体上の事柄・特徴に関する不必要な質問・発言
  (3) 性的な漫画や雑誌、写真等を見せること、及びわいせつ図画の閲覧、配布、掲示
  (4) 性的冗談や性的うわさの流布
  (5) 不必要な身体への接触

by an employee toward other employees. However, among the following acts, from the perspective of task assignment or safety consideration, among others, those that are objectively considered to have resulted from behavior based on business necessity do not fall under the category of Maternity Harassment, etc.

(1) An act by an employee toward another employee who uses the system or measures set forth in Chapter V or VI of the Work Rules ("Systems Concerning Pregnancy, Childbirth, Child Care Leave, and Nursing Care Leave, etc."), and which disrupts the working environment of the latter employee due to the employee's behavior regarding such use; and

(2) An act by an employee toward another female employee who is pregnant or gave birth, and which disrupts the working environment of that female employee due to the employee's behavior regarding such fact or other events relating to her pregnancy or childbirth (including the events listed in each Item of Article 2-2 of the Ordinance for Enforcement of the Act on Ensuring Equal Opportunities for and Treatment of Men and Women in Employment (Ordinance of the Ministry of Labour No. 2, January 27, 1986)) ("Events of Pregnancy, etc.").

4. The "workplace" mentioned in these Regulations refers not only to employees' own departments but also all of the places in which employees perform their duties, and is not limited to the places during business hours but includes the places during non-business hours when employees engage in any matters deemed substantially to be an extension of their workplaces.

Article 3. (Prohibited Acts)

1. Employees shall not commit the acts of Sexual Harassment listed below:
   (1) Force an employee to date or have a sexual relationship with him/her;
   (2) Make unwanted questions or remarks about an employee's appearance and physical aspects or features;
   (3) Show sexual cartoons, magazines or photos to an employee; view, distribute or post obscene images;
   (4) Spread sexual jokes or sexual rumors about an employee;

(6)　のぞき見や盗撮を行い又は体を凝視すること
　(7)　性的な言動により，他の従業員の就業意欲を低下せしめ，又は能力の発揮を阻害する行為
　(8)　性的な言動への相談，抗議又は拒否等を行った従業員に対して，解雇，不当な人事考課，配転等の不利益を与える行為
　(9)　その他，相手方及び他の従業員に不快感を与える性的な言動
2.　従業員は，次に掲げるパワハラ行為を行ってはならない。
　(1)　暴行・傷害等身体的な攻撃を行うこと
　(2)　脅迫・名誉棄損・侮辱・ひどい暴言等精神的な攻撃を行うこと
　(3)　隔離・仲間外し・無視等人間関係からの切り離しを行うこと
　(4)　業務上明らかに不要なことや遂行不可能なことの強制，仕事の妨害等を行うこと
　(5)　業務上の合理性なく，能力や経験とかけ離れた程度の低い仕事を命じることや仕事を与えないこと
　(6)　私的なことに過度に立ち入ること
　(7)　その他前各号に準ずる行為
3.　従業員は，次に掲げるマタハラ等行為を行ってはならない。
　(1)　妊娠・出産・育児休業・介護休業等に関する制度の利用を請求した従業員，又は当該制度を利用した従業員に対して，解雇，不当な人事考課，配転等の不利益を示唆する言動
　(2)　妊娠・出産・育児休業・介護休業等に関する制度の利用の請求や，当該制度の利用を阻害する言動
　(3)　妊娠・出産・育児休業・介護休業等に関する制度を利用したことにより，繰り返し又は継続的に嫌がらせ的な言動を行い，業務に従事させなくさせ，又は専ら雑務に従事させる等の行為
　(4)　妊娠等の事由が生じた女性従業員に対して，解雇，不当な人事考課，配転等の不利益を示唆する言動
　(5)　妊娠等の事由によって，繰り返し又は継続的に嫌がらせ的な言動を行い，業務に従事させなくさせ，又は専ら雑務に従事させる等の行為
　(6)　その他前各号に準ずる行為

(5) Make unwanted physical contact with an employee;
(6) Take a peep at or sneak camera shots of an employee, or stare at an employee's body;
(7) Exhibit sexual behavior which decreases other employees' motivation to work or prevents them from exercising their professional abilities;
(8) Conduct acts disadvantageous to an employee who consults on, protests against or refuses to accept the sexual behavior, such as dismissal, unfair performance rating, or job rotation; and
(9) Exhibit other sexual behavior which annoys or offends the person subjected to the sexual behavior and other employees.

2. Employees shall not engage in the Power Harassment listed below:
(1) assault, injure, or engage in other physical attacks toward other employees;
(2) intimidate, defame, insult, use significantly abusive language, or engage in other mental attacks toward other employees;
(3) isolate, ostracize, ignore, or otherwise separate an employee from personal relationships;
(4) force an employee to do work that is apparently unnecessary in the course of business or impossible for him/her to perform, or interfere with the performance of his/her work;
(5) without any business-related justification, order an employee to do work that is significantly low-level regarding his/her ability or experience, or provide no work for him/her;
(6) excessively intrude into an employee's private life; or
(7) conduct any act similar to each item above.

3. Employees shall not engage in the Maternity Harassment, etc. listed below:
(1) behave in a manner to imply any disadvantageous treatment of an employee such as dismissal, unfair performance rating, or job rotation, who requested to use or used the Systems Concerning Pregnancy, Childbirth, Child Care Leave, and Nursing Care Leave, etc.;
(2) behave in a manner to prevent an employee from requesting to use or using the

4. 上司は，部下である従業員がハラスメント行為を受けている事実を知りながら，これを黙認する行為をしてはならない。

第4条　（管理監督者の注意義務）
1. 管理監督者は，良好な職場環境を確保するため，日常の教育・指導等により，ハラスメント行為の防止及び排除に努めなければならない。
2. 管理監督者は，ハラスメント行為に関する苦情・相談を申し出たこと，ハラスメント行為に関する調査に協力したこと，その他ハラスメント行為に対する職員の対応に起因して，当該職員が職場において不利益な取扱を受けることがないよう配慮しなければならない。

第5条　（懲戒）
　　第3条に該当する事実が認められた場合は，会社は，就業規則に基づく懲戒処分を含む人事上必要な措置を行う。

Systems Concerning Pregnancy, Childbirth, Child Care Leave, and Nursing Care Leave, etc.;

(3) repeatedly or continuously behave in a manner to harass an employee, prevent him/her from engaging in work, or have him/her engage solely in ad hoc tasks, due to his/her using the Systems Concerning Pregnancy, Childbirth, Child Care Leave, and Nursing Care Leave, etc.;

(4) behave in a manner to imply any disadvantageous treatment of a female employee such as dismissal, unfair performance rating, or job rotation, to whom Events of Pregnancy, etc. occurred;

(5) repeatedly or continuously behave in a manner to harass a female employee, prevent her from engaging in work, or have her engage solely in ad hoc tasks, due to Events of Pregnancy, etc.; or

(6) conduct any act similar to each item above.

4. The superior of an employee who is subjected to Harassment shall not tolerate the Harassment if he/she is aware of it.

Article 4. (Managers and Supervisor's Duty of Care)

1. In order to ensure a good working environment, the managers and supervisors shall try to prevent and eliminate Harassment by providing daily education or guidance, etc.

2. The managers and supervisors shall consider that employees who have raised complaints or consultation requests regarding Harassment, who have cooperated in the investigation of Harassment, or who have otherwise responded to Harassment will not be treated in a disadvantageous manner in their workplace due to these acts.

Article 5. (Disciplinary Action)

If any fact falling under Article 3 is found, the Company shall take all necessary action in terms of personnel affairs, including disciplinary action in accordance with the Work Rules.

> 具体的には，行為者と被害者の職場を分けるための配転や，行為者に対する被害者への謝罪要求等が考えられます。

第6条　（ハラスメント行為の相談及び苦情への対応）
1. ハラスメント行為に関する相談及び苦情処理の窓口は，[本社及び各事業場]に設ける。会社は，窓口担当者が，相談に対し，その内容や状況に応じ適切に対応できるよう，窓口担当者の研修その他必要な体制を整える。
2. ハラスメント行為の被害者に限らず，全ての従業員は，ハラスメント行為に関する相談及び苦情を窓口担当者に申し出ることができる。
3. 会社は，職場におけるハラスメント行為に係る相談の申出があった場合において，その事案に係る事実関係を迅速かつ正確に確認するため，相談者の人権・プライバシーに十分配慮した上で，関係者からの事情聴取を含む事実調査を行うものとする。かかる聴取を求められた従業員は正当な理由なくこれを拒むことはできない。
4. 苦情・相談を受けた者及び調査に協力した者は，ハラスメント行為に関し知り得た情報を，第三者に開示・漏洩してはならない。
5. 会社は，職場におけるハラスメント行為が行われたか又は行われようとしていた事実を確認した場合は，行為者に対する措置及び被害を受けた従業員に対する措置をそれぞれ適正に行う。
6. 相談及び苦情の対応に当たっては，関係者のプライバシーは保護される。また，会社は，ハラスメント行為に関し相談したこと又は事実関係の調査に協力したことをもって，不利益な取扱いを行わない。

> Specific actions will include job rotation in order to separate an offender's workplace from that of the aggrieved employee, and a request for an apology from the offender to the aggrieved, etc.

Article 6. (Handling of Consultation Requests and Complaints regarding Harassment)

1. A contact center for handling consultation requests and complaints regarding Harassment shall be established at [the head office and each workplace]. The Company shall provide training for responsible persons at the contact center or develop a necessary system so that the responsible persons may handle consultation requests in an appropriate manner depending on the subject matter and the circumstances.

2. Not only the employee aggrieved by Harassment but also any employees may submit consultation requests or complaints regarding Harassment to the responsible persons at the contact center.

3. If the Company receives from an employee a consultation request regarding Harassment in the workplace, the Company shall question the persons involved in the Harassment and conduct the necessary investigation to promptly and accurately ascertain the facts regarding the issue, in consideration of the human rights of the employee who requested the consultation. Employees who are requested to be questioned shall not refuse the request without a justifiable reason.

4. Employees who receive any complaint or consultation request and employees who cooperated in the investigation shall not disclose or divulge any information that comes to their knowledge to any third party.

5. If the Company acknowledges that Harassment was committed or was attempted to be committed in the workplace, it shall take action with respect to the employee(s) who committed or attempted to commit the Harassment and the aggrieved employee thereby in an appropriate manner.

6. In handling consultation requests and complaints, the privacy of the persons involved shall be protected. The Company shall not treat the persons involved in a

第7条　（従業員研修等）
　　会社は，ハラスメントに関する知識や対応能力を向上させ，社内におけるハラスメント行為を事前に防止するために，管理職の従業員及びその他の従業員に対して必要な研修等を行う。

> 従業員に対する研修等は，管理職の従業員とその他の従業員に分けての研修が効果的です。もっとも，企業規模に応じて，研修を纏めて行うことも考えられます。

第8条　（再発防止）
　　会社は，ハラスメント行為に係る相談の申出があった場合は，ハラスメント行為に関する方針の周知及び啓発の再徹底，研修の実施等の再発防止に向けた措置を講ずる。

附　則
　1．（施行日）
　　　この規程は，平成○年○月○日から施行する。

disadvantageous manner because they consulted with or cooperated in the fact-finding investigation with the Company regarding Harassment.

Article 7. (Training for Employees etc.)
The company shall provide necessary training, etc. for managerial employees and other employees in order to improve their knowledge and response capability regarding Harassment, and to prevent Harassment in the company beforehand.

> **Regarding training, etc. for employees, it is effective to provide it separately to managerial employees and other employees. However, depending on the size of the company, training will possibly be provided to all employees collectively.**

Article 8. (Recurrence Prevention)
When the Company receives a consultation request regarding Harassment, it shall take measures to prevent recurrence thereof, including making the Harassment policy known company-wide, developing employees' awareness or providing training, etc.

Supplementary Provisions
1. (Date of Enforcement)
These Regulations shall be in force as of MM/DD/YY.

定年後再雇用規程

第1条（目　　的）
　本規程は，就業規則第20条第2項に基づき，●●株式会社（以下，「会社」という。）の定年後再雇用制度について定めるものである。

第2条（再雇用等の手続）
　1．　社員（就業規則第3条に定めるものをいう。以下同じ。）のうち，1年以内に定年退職することが予定されている者が，第3項の規定に従い，引き続き会社で勤務することを希望した場合には，会社は，当該希望者を再雇用し，又は，高齢者雇用安定法9条2項に定められる特殊関係事業主との間で特殊関係事業主が当該希望者を引き続き雇用することを内容とする契約を締結するものとする（再雇用及び特殊関係事業主による雇用の継続を，個別に又は総称して，以下，「再雇用等」といい，再雇用等に係る契約を以下，「再雇用等契約」という。また，再雇用等された社員を以下，「定年後再雇用者」という。）。再雇用等契約の期間は，原則として1年とする。
　2．　前項の規定にかかわらず，就業規則第21条及び第77条に定める解雇事由又は就業規則第18条に定める退職事由に該当する場合は，会社又は特殊関係事業主は再雇用等をしない。ただし，これらの規定中，「社員」は，「定年後再雇用者」と読み替える。

> 就業規則に定める解雇事由又は退職事由（年齢に関するものを除きます。）に該当する場合には，再雇用等しないことができますが，再雇用等をしない

Regulations for Re-employment after Retirement

Article 1. (Purpose)

These Regulations prescribe the system for post-retirement re-employment of workers at ●●K.K. (the "Company") in accordance with Article 20, Paragraph 2 of the Work Rules.

Article 2. (Procedure for Re-employment)
1. In the case where an Employee (as defined in Article 3 of the Work Rules; the same shall apply hereinafter), who will retire from the Company within one (1) year by reaching the retirement age, desires to continue to work for the Company, according to the rules prescribed in Paragraph 3 below, the Company shall re-employ the Employee or shall conclude an agreement with the Company's affiliate company provided for in Article 9, Paragraph 2 of the Act on Employment Security, etc., of the Elderly, etc. (the "Employment of Elderly Act"; such company as, the "Affiliate Company") under which the Affiliate Company is required to continue to employ the Employee (the "Re-employment" individually and collectively means re-employment by the Company and continued employment by the Affiliate Company; the "Re-employment Agreement" means an agreement related to Re-employment; and the "Re-employed Retired Employee" means an Employee who is on Re-employment by the Company or the Affiliate Company). The period of the Re-employment Agreement shall be one (1) year, in principle.
2. Notwithstanding the preceding paragraph, in the case where the Employee is subject to any grounds for dismissal as prescribed in Article 21 or Article 77 of the Work Rules, or for retirement as prescribed in Article 18 thereof, the Company and the

> ことについては、客観的に合理的な理由があり、社会通念上相当であることが求められると考えられております（高年齢者雇用確保措置の実施及び運用に関する指針（平成24年厚生労働省告示第560号）第2,2）。
> 　就業規則や労使協定等において、会社自ら雇用するか、又は一定の関係会社をして雇用させるかを判断するための基準を定めることも可能です。仮に、会社が、一定の関係会社により雇用を確保しようとする場合は、その雇用する高年齢者を当該一定の関係会社が引き続いて雇用することを約する契約を、当該一定の関係会社との間で締結する必要があります（同指針第2,2）。

3. 社員のうち、定年後も引き続き会社で勤務することを希望する者は、定年到達日の［6］か月前までに、［所定の様式］により、［所属長／●●部長／●●課］に申し出るものとする。
4. 会社又は特殊関係事業主が、定年後も引き続き会社で勤務することを希望する社員に対して、内定等の通知を出した後であっても、定年までの間に、就業規則第21条及び第77条に定める解雇事由又は就業規則第18条に定める退職事由に該当することとなった場合又は該当することが判明した場合には、会社又は特殊関係事業主は、かかる内定等の通知を撤回する。
5. 再雇用等を希望する社員が、会社又は特殊関係事業主の提示する雇用条件に合意しない場合は、会社又は特殊関係事業主は、再雇用等をする義務を負わないものとする。

> 　高年齢者雇用安定法は、労働者の希望に合致した労働条件の提示までは求められておらず、労働者が会社又は特殊関係事業主が提示する雇用条件に応じない場合に再雇用等を行わないことは直ちには違法ではないと解されていますので（厚生労働省「高年齢者雇用安定法Q&A（高年齢者雇用確保措置関係）」（以下、「高年法Q&A」といいます。）5-4）、本項のように、この点を明示的に規定しておくことが考えられます。
> 　ただし、高年齢者雇用安定法の趣旨を没却するような雇用条件を提示する場合には、かかる提示が会社又は特殊関係事業主の裁量の範囲を超えると判

Affiliate Company shall not provide Re-employment. For the purpose of these Regulations, the term "Employee(s)" in these Articles shall be deemed to be replaced with "Re-employed Retired Employee(s)."

> **In the case where an employee is subject to any grounds for dismissal or for retirement (excepting any grounds relevant to age), the employer shall not be required to provide continuous employment opportunities; however, please note that it is necessary for the dismissal or retirement to have objectively reasonable grounds, and to be socially acceptable ("The Guideline Related to Enforcement and Operation of Securing Employment Opportunities for the Elderly" (Public Notice of the Ministry of Health, Labor and Welfare No. 560, 2012), 2-2).**
> **An employer may set a standard in the work rules or labor-management agreement, etc. by which either the employer itself re-employs the employee, or it causes an affiliate company to employ the employee, after reaching the retirement age. If an employer intends to cause a certain affiliate company to employ older employees, the employer needs to conclude an agreement with the affiliate company under which the affiliate company agrees to take over the employment of older employees after their retirement from the employer (The aforementioned guideline, 2-2).**

3. An Employee who desires to continue to work for the Company after reaching the retirement age shall make a request of [his/her supervisor/ ●● Manager/ ●● Section] using [a designated form], at least [six (6)] months prior to the date on which the Employee reaches the retirement age.

4. Even after the Company or the Affiliate Company, as the case may be, provides an offer letter to the Employee who desires to continue to work for the Company after his/her retirement, in the event where such Employee becomes subject to any grounds for dismissal as prescribed in Article 21 or Article 77 of the Work Rules, or for retirement as prescribed in Article 18 thereof, or where it turns out that such Employee has become subject to such grounds before reaching the retirement age, the Company or the Affiliate Company, as the case may be, may withdraw the offer letter.

5. The Company and the Affiliate Company shall not be required to provide Re-employment in the event where an Employee who desires Re-employment does not agree to the conditions for employment which the Company or the Affiliate Company

> 断され，違法と解される可能性がありますので，留意が必要です。

第3条　（再雇用等契約の更新）
1. 定年後再雇用者が，第2条第1項の再雇用期間満了後も引き続き会社又は特殊関係事業主で勤務することを希望する場合には，会社は，再雇用等契約を自ら又は特殊関係事業主をして，1年間，更新し又は更新させるものとし，以後同様とする。ただし，65歳に到達する［日／日の属する月の末日／日の属する年度末日］を更新の限度とする。
2. 前項の規定にかかわらず，就業規則第21条及び第77条に定める解雇事由又は就業規則第18条に定める退職事由に該当する場合は，会社及び特殊関係事業主は再雇用等契約を更新しない。ただし，これらの規定中，「社員」は，「定年後再雇用者」と読み替える。

> 1年間ごとに雇用契約を更新する形態の場合については，65歳を下回る上限年齢が設定されていないことが必要であり，また，65歳までは原則として契約が更新されることが必要となります。他方で，能力など年齢以外を理由として契約を更新しないことは，客観的に合理的な理由を欠き，社会通念上相当であると認められないときを除き，認められます（高年法 Q&A 1

has proposed.

The Employment of Elderly Act does not require employers or certain affiliate companies to propose conditions for employment which conform to the employee's request, and it is understood that it is not automatically illegal not to re-employ or hire the employee after reaching the retirement age, in the event that he/she does not agree to the conditions that the employer or the affiliate company proposes (The Ministry of Health, Labor and Welfare; "Q&A for the Employment of Elderly Act (relating to securing employment opportunities for the elderly)" (the "Q&A for Employment of Elderly"), 5-4). Therefore, as prescribed in this paragraph, it is advisable to include an express provision to this effect.
However, please note that in the case where the employer or a certain affiliate company proposes conditions for employment which disregard the spirit of the Employment of Elderly Act, such proposals may be held to be an abuse of discretion by the employer and the affiliate and to be illegal.

Article 3. (Renewal of a Re-employment Agreement)

1. When a Re-employed Retired Employee desires to continue to work for the Company or the Affiliate Company after the term of the Re-employment Agreement prescribed in Article 2, Paragraph 1 hereof, the Company shall renew or cause the Affiliate Company to renew the Re-employment Agreement for one (1) additional year, and the same shall apply thereafter. However, [his/her sixty fifth (65th) birthday/the last day of the month to which his/her sixty fifth (65th) birthday belongs/the last day of the fiscal year to which his/her sixty fifth (65th) birthday belongs] shall be the limit of any renewed term of the Re-employment Agreement.

2. Notwithstanding the preceding paragraph, in the case where the Re-employed Retired Employee becomes subject to any grounds for dismissal as prescribed in Article 21 or Article 77 of the Work Rules, or for retirement as prescribed in Article 18 thereof, the Company or the Affiliate Company, as the case may be, shall not renew the Re-employment Agreement. For the purpose of these Regulations, the term "Employee(s)" in these Articles shall be deemed to be replaced with "Re-employed Retired Employee(s)."

-4)。

　なお，定年後再雇用者も要件を備えれば無期転換権（労働契約法18条1項，第1部解説7-1参照）を取得するため，そのような事態を避ける観点から，65歳を更新の限度として，再雇用契約や就業規則に明示的に規定しておくことが考えられます（第1項参照）。

3. 　第1項の規定にかかわらず，次表の左欄に記載された特例期間中に，それに対応する右欄の年齢以上の者との再雇用等契約を更新する場合には，当該事業場に，労働者の過半数で組織する労働組合がある場合においてはその労働組合，労働者の過半数で組織する労働組合がない場合においては労働者の過半数を代表する者との間の書面による協定に定められた以下の各号の基準を，［定年到達時／再雇用等契約の更新時］においてすべて満たした者のみを対象とする。

In the case where the re-employment agreement is renewed every year, the employer and the certain affiliate company are not permitted to limit the employee's age to an age under 65 years old, and are required to renew the re-employment agreement in principle until the employee's 65th birthday. On the other hand, the employer and the certain affiliate company are permitted to refuse to renew the re-employment agreement because of reasons other than age, except in the case where the refusal of continued employment is based on objectively reasonable grounds and is considered socially acceptable (Q&A for Employment of Elderly, 1-4).

In the case where an older employee who was re-employed continuously after reaching the retirement age fulfills the necessary conditions, the Re-employed Retired Employee will also retain the option to convert the Fixed Term Employment Agreement to a Non-Fixed Term Employment Agreement (Article 18, Paragraph 1 of the Labor Contract Act; please refer to Section 7-1 of Part I Commentary). Therefore, if employers wish to avoid such situations, it is advisable to expressly set the age of 65 as the limit of renewal in the re-employment agreement and the work rules (please refer to Paragraph 1 above).

3. Notwithstanding Paragraph 1, during the period prescribed in the left-hand column of the following table, when the Company or the Affiliate Company renews the Re-employment Agreement with a Re-employed Retired Employee at or above the age prescribed in the right-hand column of the same line of the following table, the Company or the Affiliate Company shall renew only the Re-employment Agreement with the Re-employed Retired Employee who meets all of the following criteria set forth in a written agreement between the Company, and either a labor union organized by a majority of the workers at the workplace (in the case where such labor union is organized), or a person representing a majority of the workers thereat (in the case where such labor union is not organized) [when the employee reaches his/her retirement age/when the Re-employment Agreement is renewed].

期間	年齢
平成25年4月1日から平成28年3月31日まで	61歳
平成28年4月1日から平成31年3月31日まで	62歳
平成31年4月1日から平成34年3月31日まで	63歳
平成34年4月1日から平成37年3月31日まで	64歳

(1)　直近の健康診断の結果により健康面において業務遂行に支障がなく，前年と同様に勤務できると認められる者
(2)　過去［3］年間の出勤率が［90］％以上の者
(3)　過去［3］年間に就業規則に定める減給以上の処分を受けたことのない者
(4)　過去［3］年間，人事評価が［標準］以上と評価されていた者
(5)　会社における勤続期間が通算［10］年以上である者
(6)　過去［3］年間，無断欠勤がない者

　　改正高年齢者雇用安定法が施行されるまで（平成25年3月31日まで），高齢者雇用安定法上，労使協定により，継続雇用制度の対象となる高年齢者を限定することができると定められていました（平成24年法律第78号「高年齢者等の雇用の安定等に関する法律の一部を改正する法律」による改正前の高齢者雇用安定法9条2項）が，改正高年齢者雇用安定法では，かかる基準は廃止されています。もっとも，経過措置として平成37年3月31日までは，一定の年齢以上の者に当該基準を適用することができるとされています（平成24年法律第78号「高年齢者等の雇用の安定等に関する法律の一部を改正する法律」附則3条）。なお，経過措置により継続雇用制度の対象者を限定する基準を定めることができるのは，改正高年齢者雇用安定法が施行されるまで（平成25年3月31日まで）に労使協定により継続雇用制度の対象者を限定する基準を定めていた事業主に限られます（高年法Q&A 3－1）。
　　労使協定で定める基準の内容については，原則として労使に委ねられるものとされておりますが，労使で十分に協議の上定められたものであっても，会社が恣意的に継続雇用を排除しようとするなど高年齢者雇用安定法の改正の趣旨や他の労働関連法規に反する又は公序良俗に反するものは認めら

Period	Age
2013/4/1～2016/3/31	61 years old
2016/4/1～2019/3/31	62 years old
2019/4/1～2022/3/31	63 years old
2022/4/1～2025/3/31	64 years old

For the purpose of Article 3, Paragraph 3 above, a Re-employed Retired Employee who meets the following criteria is one:

(1) who is deemed to have no difficulties in performing the tasks required of him/her in respect of health, and to be able able to work as he/she did in the previous year pursuant to the results of the latest medical examination,

(2) whose attendance rate in the last [three (3)] years has been [ninety (90)]% or higher,

(3) who has not been subject to a pay reduction as set forth in the Work Rules or a more severe disciplinary action in the last [three (3)] years,

(4) whose personal evaluations in the last [three (3)] years have been higher than [average],

(5) whose total duration of service in the Company is [ten (10)] years or longer; and

(6) who has never been absent from work without notice or permission in the last [three (3)] years.

Although it was possible under the Employment of Elderly Act for employers to exclude some of their elderly employees from the coverage of their continued employment system by means of standards that they established through a Labor-Management Agreement until the enforcement of the Employment of Elderly Act (until March 3, 2013) (Article 9, Paragraph 2 of the Employment of Elderly Act before amendment by the "Act on the Partial Revision of the Act on Employment Security, etc. of the Elderly, etc." (Act No. 78 of 2012)), the amended Act abolished such rule. However, until March 31, 2025, the Employment of Elderly Act provides a transitional measure that allows employers to continue to apply the standards they have set for Re-employed RetiredEmployees who have reached a certain age (Article 3, Supplementary Provisions to the "Act on the Partial Revision of the Act on Employment Security, etc. of the Elderly, etc." (Act No. 78 of 2012)).

れません（高年法 Q&A4-1）。また，かかる基準は具体性と客観性を備えているものが望ましいとされています（高年法 Q&A4-1）。

　労使協定で定める基準に該当するか否かの判断時点については，労使に委ねられるものとされていますので（高年法 Q&A3-4），定年到達時とすることや再雇用等契約の更新時とすることが考えられます。再雇用等契約の更新時を判断時点とする場合には，直近の時点までの出勤状況や人事評価等をもとに再雇用等契約の更新の可否を決することが可能となります。他方で，定年後再雇用者については人事評価を行わない場合，正社員とは異なる評価制度を用いる場合，定年後再雇用者は所定労働時間が短い場合等の理由により定年後再雇用者の出席率と正社員の出席率を同視することができない場合等には，判断基準を再雇用等契約の更新時とすると，基準を適切に適用できないという不都合が生じる可能性がありますので，そのような場合には，定年到達時を判断時点とすることが考えられます。

4．　再雇用等契約を更新する手続等に関しては，第2条第3項及び第4項を準用する。

Only employers which had established standards for excluding some of their employees from the coverage of their continued employment system through a Labor Management Agreement before and until the enforcement of the Act (i.e., until March 31, 2013) may establish standards for excluding some of their employees from the coverage of their continued employment system as a transitional measure (Q&A for Employment of Elderly, 3-1). It is generally considered that the employer and employees have discretion to determine what standards shall be stipulated in a Labor-Management Agreement, in principle. However, it is not acceptable to set standards against the spirit of the amendment to the Employment of Elderly Act, other labor-related laws, or public policy, such as where the employer intends to exclude employees from the continuous re-employment system in an arbitrary manner, even where such standards are determined upon sufficient consultation between the employer and the employees (Q&A for Employment of Elderly, 4-1). Moreover, it is desirable that such standards be specific and objective (Q&A for Employment of Elderly, 4-1).

It is generally considered that the employer and employees have discretion to determine a base point in time to judge whether an employee meets the standards stipulated in the Labor-Management Agreement (Q&A for Employment of Elderly, 3-4), and it may be an option to stipulate the time when an employee reaches the retirement age or the time when the re-employment agreement is renewed as the base point in time. In the case where the employer and employees stipulate that the base point in time is when the re-employment agreement is renewed, the employer may decide whether to renew the re-employment agreement or not based on the latest attendance and personal evaluation of the employee, etc. However, in a case such as where an employer does not evaluate Re-employed Retired Employees, or applies to Re-employed Retired Employees an evaluation system different from that which is applied to regular employees, or where it is impossible to treat the attendance rate of a Re-employed Retired Employee as comparable to the attendance rate of regular employees due to a reason such as the designated working hours of Re-employed Retired Employees being short, since stipulating that the base point in time is when the re-employment agreement is renewed is likely to lead to undesirable consequences such as the employer not being able to apply the standards to Re-employed Retired Employees appropriately, it may be an option to stipulate that the base point in time is when the employee reaches the retirement age.

4. The provisions of Article 2, Paragraphs 3 and 4 hereof shall apply *mutatis mutandis* to the procedures for renewing a Re-employment Agreement.

5. 再雇用等の更新を希望する者が，会社又は特殊関係事業主の提示する雇用条件に合意しない場合は，会社又は特殊関係事業主は，再雇用等の更新をする義務を負わない。

附　則
1. （施 行 日）
　　本規程は，平成○年○月○日から施行する。

5. The Company or the Affiliate Company shall not be required to renew a Re-employment Agreement where a Re-employed Retired Employee who requests a renewal of his/her Re-employment Agreement does not agree to the employment conditions which the Company or the Affiliate Company has proposed.

Supplementary Provisions

1. (Date of Enforcement)

These Regulations shall be in force as of MM/DD/YY.

労働条件通知書

（一般労働者用；常用，有期雇用型）

労働条件通知書

　　　　　　　　　　　　　　　　　　　　　　　　　年　　月　　日

	＿＿＿＿＿＿＿殿 事業場名称・所在地 使用者職氏名
契約期間	期間の定めなし，期間の定めあり（　年　月　日～　年　月　日） 【有期雇用特別措置法による特例の対象者の場合】 無期転換申込権が発生しない期間：Ⅰ（高度専門）・Ⅱ（定年後の高齢者） 　Ⅰ　特定有期業務の開始から完了までの期間（　年　か月（上限10年）） 　Ⅱ　定年後引き続いて雇用されている期間
就業の場所	就業場所や職種を限定して労働者を雇い入れた場合，労働者の同意がない限り，限定された当該就業場所又は職種以外への配転はできません。その反面，解雇の場面においては，当該就業場所や職種以外への配転が制限されるため，解雇回避努力義務が軽減され，比較的緩やかに解雇が認められる傾向にあります。就業場所等を限定する場合は，労働条件通知書に特定の就業場所等を記載すると共に，当該就業場所等に限定する旨を明記する必要があります。
従事すべき業務の内容	【有期雇用特別措置法による特例の対象者（高度専門）の場合】 ・特定有期業務（　　　　　　　開始日：　　　完了日：　　　）
始業・終業の時刻，休憩時間，就業時転換（(1)～(5)のうち該当するもの一つに○を付けること。），所定時間外労働の有無に関する事項	1　始業・終業の時刻等 　(1) 始業（　時　分）終業（　時　分） 【以下のような制度が労働者に適用される場合】 　(2) 変形労働時間制等；（　）単位の変形労働時間制・交替制として，次の勤務時間の組み合わせによる。 　　　　始業（　時　分）終業（　時　分）（適用日　　） 　　　　始業（　時　分）終業（　時　分）（適用日　　） 　　　　始業（　時　分）終業（　時　分）（適用日　　） 　(3) フレックスタイム制；始業及び終業の時刻は労働者の決定に委ねる。 　　　　（ただし，フレキシブルタイム　（始業）　時　分から　時　分， 　　　　　　　　　　　　　　　　　　　（終業）　時　分から　時　分， 　　　　　コアタイム　　　　　　　　　　　　　時　分から　時　分） 　(4) 事業場外みなし労働時間制；始業（　時　分）終業（　時　分） 　(5) 裁量労働制；始業（　時　分）終業（　時　分）を基本とし，労働者の決定に委ねる。 　(6) 高度プロフェッショナル制度；労働時間，休憩，休日及び深夜の割増賃金に関する規定の適用を受けない。 ○詳細は，就業規則第　条～第　条，第　条～第　条，第　条～第　条 2　休憩時間（　）分 3　所定時間外労働の有無（有，無）
休　　日	・定例日；毎週　　曜日，国民の祝日，その他（　　　　　　　　　　　） ・非定例日；週・月当たり　　日，その他（　　　　　　　　　　　　） ・1年単位の変形労働時間制の場合―年間　　　日 ○詳細は，就業規則第　条～第　条，第　条，第　条

（次頁に続く）

休　　暇	1　年次有給休暇　6か月継続勤務した場合→　　　　　日 　　　　　　　　　継続勤務6か月以内の年次有給休暇　(有，無) 　　　　　　　　　→　　　　　　か月経過で　　　　　日 2　その他の休暇　有給（　　　　　　　　　） 　　　　　　　　　無給（　　　　　　　　　） ○詳細は，就業規則第　　条〜第　　条，第　　条〜第　　条
賃　　金	1　基本賃金　イ　月給（　　　　　円）ロ　日給（　　　　　円） 　　　　　　　ハ　時間給（　　　　　円） 　　　　　　　ニ　出来高給（基本単価　　　　円，保障給　　　　円） 　　　　　　　ホ　その他（　　　　　円） 　　　　　　　ヘ　就業規則に規定されている賃金等級等 　　　　　　　　　┌─────────────────────────┐ 　　　　　　　　　└─────────────────────────┘ 2　諸手当の額及び計算方法 　　イ（　　　　　手当　　　　　円　／計算方法：　　　　　） 　　ロ（　　　　　手当　　　　　円　／計算方法：　　　　　） 　　ハ（　　　　　手当　　　　　円　／計算方法：　　　　　） 　　ニ（　　　　　手当　　　　　円　／計算方法：　　　　　） 3　所定時間外，休日又は深夜労働に対して支払われる割増賃金率 　　イ　所定時間外，法定超　月60時間以内　　（　　　）％ 　　　　　　　　　　　　　月60時間超　　　（　　　）％ 　　　　　　　　　所定超　　　　　　　　　（　　　）％ 　　ロ　休日　法定休日（　　　）％，法定外休日（　　　）％ 　　ハ　深夜（　　　　　）％ 4　賃金締切日（　　　）―毎月　　日，（　　　）―毎月　　日 5　賃金支払日（　　　）―毎月　　日，（　　　）―毎月　　日 ┌────────────────────────────────┐ │6　労使協定に基づく賃金支払時の控除（無，有（　　　　　　　））│ │7　昇給　（時期等　　　　　　　　　　　　　　　　　　　　　　）│ │8　賞与　（有（時期，金額等　　　　　　　　　　　　　　　　，無）│ │9　退職金（有（時期，金額等　　　　　　　　　　　　　　　　，無）│ └────────────────────────────────┘
退　職　に 関する事項	1　定年制　(有（　　歳），無) 2　自己都合退職の手続（退職する　　　　日以上前に届け出ること） 3　解雇の事由及び手続 　┌　　　　　　　　　　　　　　　　　　　　　　　　　　　　　　┐ 　└　　　　　　　　　　　　　　　　　　　　　　　　　　　　　　┘ ○詳細は，就業規則第　　条〜第　　条，第　　条〜第　　条
その他	・社会保険の加入状況（厚生年金　健康保険　厚生年金基金 　　　　　　　　　　　その他（　　　　　　　　　）） ・雇用保険の適用　(有，無) ・雇用管理の改善等に関する事項に係る相談窓口 　　部署名　　　　　担当者職氏名　　　　　（連絡先　　　　　） 　従来はパートタイム労働者について求められていたものですが，パート有期法において有期雇用労働者についても求められることとなりました。 ・その他［　　　　　　　　　　　　　　　　　　　　　　　　　］ ※ 以下は，「契約期間」について「期間の定めあり」とした場合に記入 1　契約更新の有無 ［自動的に更新する・更新する場合があり得る・契約の更新はしない・その他（　　　　　）］ 2　契約の更新は次により判断する。 ・契約期間満了時の業務量　　・勤務成績，態度　　・能力 ・会社の経営状況　　・従事している業務の進捗状況

(次頁に続く)

その他	・その他（　　　　　　　　　　　　）
	※ 以下は，「契約期間」について「期間の定めあり」とした場合についての説明です。 　労働契約法第18条の規定により，有期労働契約（平成25年4月1日以降に開始するもの）の契約期間が通算5年を超える場合には，労働契約の期間の末日までに労働者から申込みをすることにより，当該労働契約の期間の末日の翌日から期間の定めのない労働契約に転換されます。 　ただし，有期雇用特別措置法による特例の対象となる場合は，この「5年」という期間は，本通知書の「契約期間」欄に明示したとおりとなります。

※　以上の他は，当社就業規則による。

Notification of Employment Conditions

(For regular employee; non-fixed term and fixed-term contracts)

Notification of Employment Conditions

Date:
Name of employee:
Name of employer and address:
Person in charge:

Contract term	No fixed term Fixed term (From: To:) [When the employee is eligible for an exception under the Act on Special Measures Concerning Fixed-Term Employees with Expert Knowledge and Skills.] Period in which the right to apply for conversion to indefinite term status is not granted: I. (highly skilled professional), II. (elderly person after retirement age) I. Period from the beginning to the end of specified fixed-term task (months from ___[maximum of 10 years]) II. Period of continuous employment after reaching mandatory retirement age
Workplace	**If the employee's employment by the employer is subject to a limitation on the workplace or job type, the employer cannot transfer the employee to any other workplace or job-type other than that which is specified. In the meantime, in the context of dismissal, since a transfer to another workplace or job type is limited, the level of the employer's obligation to make an effort to avoid dismissal would be lowered; there is a tendency for dismissals to be effectuated comparatively leniently. When limiting the workplace, etc. the employer must state in the Notification of Employment Conditions the specific workplace, etc., and note that the employee's workplace, etc. is limited to such a place, etc.**
Contents of duties	[When the employee is eligible for an exception under the Act on Special Measures Concerning Fixed-Term Employees with Expert Knowledge and Skills. (highly skilled professional)] •Specified fixed-term task ([ ]; Start date: [ ] End date: [ ])

Working hours
 	
Break time
 	
Variation of working hours (please circle, from 1) to 5) the one that is most appropriate)
 	
Matters regarding overtime work
	1. Working hours, etc.
	1) From: ( ) To: ( )
	
	[When the following systems apply to an employee]
	2) Non-fixed working hours/Working in shifts
	   Combining the following working hours.
	   From: ( ) To: ( ) Days applied: ( )
	   From: ( ) To: ( ) Days applied: ( )
	   From: ( ) To: ( ) Days applied: ( )
	
	3) Flexitime: Start and end times are decided by the employee
	   Flexible time: (Start) From: To: (End) From: To:
	   Core time: From: ( ) To: ( )
	
	4) Work outside the office: From: ( ) To: ( )
	
	5) Self-decided working hours
	   Basic hours: From: ( ) To: ( )
	   Other than that, left to the employee's discretion
	6) Advanced Professionals System: Provisions regarding working hours, break time, extra wage for work on holidays and late hour work are not applicable.
	⇒ For further details, please refer to the Work Rules.
	
	2. Break time: ( ) minutes
	
	3. Whether there is overtime work: ( )

Notification of Employment Conditions

Holidays	•Regular week holiday: day, national holiday, others ( ) •Non-regular holiday: days per week/month, others ( ) •When working under non-fixed working hours: days per year ⇒ For further details, please refer to the Work Rules.
Leave	1. **Annual paid-leave:** If having worked continuously for 6 months: (days) Whether there is annual paid-leave for service of less than 6 months ( ) 2. **Other types of leave** Paid: ( ) Non-paid: ( ) ⇒ For further details, please refer to the Work Rules.

Wage	1. **Basic wage**
	A) Per month: ( )
	B) Per day: ( )
	C) Per hour: ( )
	D) Piecework (Basic wage: Guaranteed wage:)
	E) Others: ( )
	F) Wage ranking as stipulated in the Work Rules:
	[ ]
	2. **Amount and calculation method of various allowances:**
	[ ]
	3. **Increase rate for overtime work, work on holidays and late hour work**
	A) Overtime work:
	    Above legal limit: 60 hours or less per month (%)
	    More than 60 hours per month (%)
	    Above agreed limit: (%)
	B) Work on holidays
	    On statutory holidays: (%)
	    On designated holidays: (%)
	C) Late hour work: (%)
	
	4. **Closing date for payment:**
	[ ]
	
	5. **Day of payment:**
	[ ]
	
	6. **Whether there is a deduction in payment based on the agreement of the union and management:** ( )
	7. **Pay rise:** ( )
	8. **Bonus:** ( )
	9. **Retirement allowance:** ( )

Termination of contract	1. **Retirement age:** ( ) 2. **Procedure for voluntary retirement:** (notice of more than days) 3. **Procedure and reason for dismissal:** [ ] ⇒ For further details, please refer to the Work Rules.

Other matters	•Social insurance:
	    Welfare pension, health insurance, welfare pension foundation, others: ( )
	•Unemployment insurance: ( )
	•Consultation desk for matters concerning the improvement of employment management
	    Dept. name: _____ Contact person's name: _____
	    Contact information: _____
	
	This provision has been traditionally required for part-time workers; however, it is now also required for Fixed-Term Employees under the amended Act on Improvement, etc. of Employment Management for Part-Time Workers and Fixed-Term Workers.
	
	•Other matters:

Other matters	※The following are stated when the "Contract term" is "Fixed term" 1. Renewal of contract [The contract shall automatically be renewed/may be renewed/shall not be renewed/Others ( )] 2. Renewal of the contract will be determined based on the following: - Business volume at the time of expiration of the contract term - Employee's performance, attitude toward work - Employee's ability - The Company's business condition - Progress of business in which an employee is engaged - Others ( ) ※ The following are explanations when the "Contract term" is "Fixed Term" In accordance with Article 18 of the Employment Agreement Act, if the contract term of a fixed-term employment agreement (only those starting on and after April 1, 2013) exceeds five (5) years in total, such an agreement will be converted into a non-fixed term employment agreement as of the day following the last day of the fixed-term agreement, upon application by an employee at the end of the agreement term. However, when the employee is eligible for an exception under the Act on Special Measures Concerning Fixed-Term Employees with Expert Knowledge and Skills, this period of "five (5) years" will become the period provided for the "Contract Term" in this Notice.

※ Matters not stated above shall be governed by the Company's Work Rules.

契約社員雇用契約書

本書式は，有期雇用契約である契約社員の雇用契約書のひな形です。有期雇用契約については，第1部第1章7.を参照してください。

●●株式会社（以下「甲」という。）と●●（以下「乙」という。）は，次のとおり契約社員雇用契約（以下「本契約」という。）を締結する。

第1条　（雇用期間等）

　　甲は乙を次の各号の条件により，契約社員として雇用し，乙は甲の契約社員就業規則その他諸規程及び指揮命令に従い，誠実に勤務する。

① 雇用期間（以下「雇用期間」という。）

　　●年●月●日より●年●月●日まで

② 就業場所

　　●●

③ 所属

　　●●

④ 役職

　　●●

⑤ 業務内容

　　●●

Contract Employee Employment Agreement

This is a sample Employment Agreement for contract employees under a Fixed Term Employment Agreement. For the Fixed Term Employment Agreement, please refer to Section 7, Chapter 1 of Part I.

This Contract Employee Employment Agreement (this "Agreement") is entered into between ●● K.K. (the "Company") and ●● (the "Employee") as follows:

Article 1. (Employment Period, etc.)
The Company shall employ the Employee as a contract employee on the following conditions, and the Employee shall work for the Company in good faith pursuant to the Company's Work Rules for Contract Employees, and other regulations, and at the Company's directive and instruction.

(1) Employment period (the "Employment Period")
From [MM/DD/YY] to [MM/DD/YY]
(2) Workplace

(3) Division/Department

(4) Title

(5) Contents of Duties

> 　正社員とは別に有期雇用の社員を適用対象とする就業規則を設ける場合には，正社員との労働条件の相違点を整理して規定する必要があります。具体的には，更新の有無，更新がある場合の更新基準等，有期雇用契約に特有の事項を定めると共に，試用期間の有無，所定労働時間・休憩・休日，異動・職種変更の有無，休職制度，賃金及び各種手当，退職金の有無，解雇事由等の各労働条件について，正社員と異なる条件を設定するか否かを検討し，異なる条件については有期雇用社員の就業規則に規定することが必要です。もっとも，正社員と異なる労働条件を設定する場合，その相違は，職務の内容・性質，責任の程度，職務内容の変更や配置転換の範囲その他の事情を考慮して，不合理と認められるものであってはならないとされています（労働契約法20条）。なお，本条は削除され，パート有期法8条に統合される予定です。詳しくは上記5-2をご参照ください。
> 　一般に長期雇用を前提とする休職制度及び試用期間については，有期雇用では期間満了毎に更新の有無を決定することができるため，実務上はこれらの制度を設けないことが多いと考えられます。

第2条　（更　　新）

　本契約の更新の有無及び更新後の雇用条件は，甲の業績及び業務量並びに乙の業務能力，勤務成績，勤務態度その他諸般の事情を総合して，甲が判断する。ただし，更新後の雇用期間は，更新前の雇用期間と通算して5年を超えないものとする。

In order to establish work rules applicable to employees under a Fixed Term Employment Agreement, separately from regular employees, it is necessary to provide employment conditions focusing on the differences between Fixed Term Employees and regular employees. More specifically, the employer must establish matters specific to a Fixed Term Employment Agreement, such as whether to renew the agreement, and if so, renewal standards. Furthermore, the employer shall determine if it will establish employment conditions different from regular employees, such as with or without a probationary period, designated working hours, breaks, holidays, possibility of intercompany transfer or change of work type, a leave of absence system, wages and allowances, possibility of retirement allowance, reasons for dismissal, etc., and if so, the employer must provide such different conditions in the work rules applicable to Fixed Term Employees. However, when establishing employment conditions different from regular employees, such conditions may not be unreasonable taking into consideration the details, nature of duties, degree of responsibility, the scope of change in duties or job rotation, and other circumstance (Article 20 of the Employment Agreement Act). Article 20 of the Employment Agreement Act will be delated and will be integrated into Article 8 on the Part-Time Employment and Fixed-Term Employment Act. For futher information, please rafer to 5-2 above.

Generally speaking, regarding a leave of absence system and a probation period both of which are premised on long-term employment, the employer may decide whether to renew an employment agreement upon expiration of each employment period; therefore, in most cases, these systems are not established in the work rules applicable to Fixed Term Employees.

Article 2. (Renewal)

The Company will decide whether to renew this Agreement and the employment conditions after renewal by comprehensively considering the Company's performance and business volume, and the Employee's business ability, performance, attitude toward work, and other circumstances. However, the Employment Period after renewal shall not exceed five (5) years including the Employment Period before renewal.

> 有期雇用契約が通算で5年を超えて繰り返し更新された場合，労働者は，当該有期雇用契約を無期雇用契約に転換することができ，労働者が5年を超えて更新された有期雇用契約の契約期間内に申し込みを行うことにより，当該有期雇用契約が満了した日の翌日を労務提供開始日とする無期雇用契約が締結されたものとみなされます(労働契約法18条1項)。この関係で，使用者が，雇用調整の必要性に鑑み，無期雇用契約への転換がない純粋な有期雇用契約とすることを望む場合には，あらかじめ契約の更新がない旨又は更新後の雇用期間が更新前の雇用期間と通算して5年を超えない旨を明記しておくことが考えられます。

第3条　（勤務時間・休憩時間・休日・休暇）
　　乙の勤務時間及び休憩時間並びに休日及び休暇は契約社員就業規則による。

> ここでは契約社員就業規則によることとしていますが，有期雇用の場合，各社員毎に条件が異なることも多いため，就業規則では個別の労働契約に委任する旨を規定し，雇用契約書において具体的に定めることも可能です。

第4条　（時間外労働）
　　乙は，甲が業務の都合により必要と認めた場合，所定勤務時間を超え又は所定休日に勤務しなければならない。

> If a fixed-term employment agreement has been repeatedly renewed for more than 5 years in total, an employee will obtain an option to convert such fixed-term employment agreement to a non-fixed term employment agreement. If the employee files an application within the Employment Period of the fixed-term employment agreement renewed for more than 5 years, it is considered that a non-fixed term employment agreement is deemed to have been entered into on the day following the expiration of such fixed-term employment agreement as the commencement date of providing labor (Article 18, paragraph 1 of the Employment Agreement Act). In connection to this, if an employer wishes to execute a genuine fixed-term employment agreement that cannot be converted into a non-fixed term employment agreement when considering the necessity of employment adjustment, it is advisable to specify in advance that no renewal is planned, or the Employment Period after renewal shall not exceed 5 years including the Employment Period before renewal.

Article 3.   (Work Hours, Breaks, Holidays, and Leave)

Work hours, breaks, holidays, and leave regarding the Employee shall be governed by the Company's Work Rules for Contract Employees.

> It is described here that these shall be governed by the Contract Employee Work Rules; however, in the case of a Fixed Term Employment, in many cases, the employment conditions may differ for each employee. As such, it is advisable to provide in the Work Rules that this will be addressed in an individual employment agreement, and then provide specific matters in such employment agreement.

Article 4.   (Overtime Work)

If the Company deems that it is necessary for business reasons, the Employee shall work any hours exceeding the designated work hours or perform work on designated holidays.

第5条（賃　　金）
1． 基本賃金は，月給●●円とする。
2． 時間外勤務手当，休日勤務手当，深夜勤務手当その他手当及び控除費用については契約社員就業規則によるものとする。
3． 退職手当は，支給しないものとする。
4． 賞与は，甲の業績並びに乙の業務能力，勤務成績及び態度を考慮し，甲が支給の有無及び金額を決定する。

第6条（所属異動等）
　　甲は，業務の都合により必要と認めた場合，乙に所属の異動及び役職の変更を命ずることができるものとする。

第7条（退職事由）
　　乙は次の各号の一に該当するときは，その日を退職日とし，その翌日に契約社員としての身分を失う。
① 乙が死亡した場合。
② 雇用期間が満了した場合。
③ 行方不明となり1か月が経過したとき。
④ 乙が自身の都合により退職を申し出て，甲がこれを承認した場合。なお，乙は，退職日の30日前迄に退職願を提出する必要がある。

第8条（解雇事由）
　　乙が次の各号の一に該当するときは，雇用期間中である場合にも，甲は本契約を終了させ，乙を解雇することができる。

Article 5. (Wages)

1. The basic wage shall be ●● yen per month.
2. Overtime work allowance, holiday work allowance, extra wages for late hour work, and other allowances and deductions shall be governed by the Work Rules for Contract Employees.
3. Retirement allowance shall not be paid.
4. The Company will decide whether it will pay a bonus, and the amount of bonus, if any, after considering the Company's performance and the Employee's business ability, performance, and attitude toward work.

Article 6. (Change in Division/Department, etc.)
If the Company deems that it is necessary for business reasons, it may order the Employee to change the division or department that he/she belongs to, or his/her title.

Article 7. (Grounds for Retirement)
When the Employee falls under any of the following items, he/she shall retire from the Company effective as of the relevant date, and shall lose his/her status as a contract employee of the Company as of the day following such date.
   (1) Death of the Employee;
   (2) Expiration of the Employment Period;
   (3) Passage of a period of one (1) month without the Employee's whereabouts being known; or
   (4) Approval by the Company of the Employee's request for retirement for personal reasons. The Employee shall submit the request for retirement no later than thirty (30) days before the requested retirement date.

Article 8. (Grounds for Dismissal)
When the Employee falls under any of the following items, the Company may terminate this Agreement and dismiss the Employee during the Employment Period.

① 乙の精神若しくは身体に障害があり又は虚弱老衰のため業務に耐えられないと認められるとき。
② 業務上の傷病の為，療養開始後3年を経過し，なお療養及び休業を必要として長期傷病補償給付が行なわれる事になった場合。
③ 乙の業務能力が著しく劣り，勤務成績が不良のとき。
④ 甲の業績が著しく低下した場合，その他やむを得ない事業上の都合により，乙の雇用を必要としなくなった場合。
⑤ 前各号以外の事由で，契約社員就業規則による懲戒解雇事由に該当する場合。
⑥ その他やむを得ない事由がある場合。

第9条 （本契約に定めのない事項）
　本契約に定めのない事項は，契約社員就業規則に従うものとする。

(1) If the Employee becomes mentally or physically disabled, is in delicate health or becomes senile, and is considered to be unable to perform his/her duties;

(2) If even after three (3) years from the date of commencement of medical treatment due to work-related injury or disease, the Employee still requires medical treatment and a leave of absence, and will receive long-term illness and injury compensation benefits;

(3) If the Employee's business ability is significantly lowered, and performance is poor;

(4) If the Company's performance significantly declines, or the employment of the Employee is no longer necessary for unavoidable business reasons;

(5) If the Employee falls under the items subject to disciplinary dismissal listed in the Work Rules for Contract Employees, other than any of the foregoing; or

(6) If there are other unavoidable reasons.

Article 9. (Matters not Provided for Herein)

Matters not provided for herein shall be governed by the Work Rules for Contract Employees.

本契約の成立を証すため本契約書を2通作成し，記名押印の上，甲乙が各1通を保有するものとする。

●年●月●日

甲　　住所

　　　氏名　　　　　　　　　　　　　　　㊞

乙　　住所

　　　氏名　　　　　　　　　　　　　　　㊞

IN WITNESS WHEREOF, the Company and the Employee shall execute this Agreement in duplicate, affix their names and seal impressions hereto, and retain one copy each.

MM/DD/YY

The Company   Address:

                Name: (seal)

The Employee   Address:

                Name: (seal)

嘱託社員雇用契約書

本書式は，定年後再雇用制度に基づき，定年退職した者を嘱託社員として再雇用する場合の雇用契約書のひな形です。定年後再雇用制度については，第２部の就業規則（本則）第20条及び第３部の定年後再雇用規程の解説も併せて参照してください。

●●株式会社（以下「甲」という。）と●●（以下「乙」という。）は，定年後再雇用制度に基づき，次のとおり嘱託社員雇用契約（以下「本契約」という。）を締結する。

第１条 （雇用期間等）

 甲は乙を次の各号の条件により，嘱託社員として雇用し，乙は甲の定年後再雇用規程，契約社員就業規則その他諸規程及び指揮命令に従い，誠実に勤務する。

① 雇用期間（以下「雇用期間」という。）

 ●年●月●日より●年●月●日までの１年とする。ただし，その期間の満了が満65歳を超えるときは，65歳に到達する日の属する月の末日までの期間とする。

SHOKUTAKU Worker Employment Agreement

This is a sample Employment Agreement if the company re-employs retirees based on the system for post-retirement re-employment of workers. For the system for post-retirement re-employment of workers, please refer to commentaries in Article 20 of the Work Rules in Part II; and the Regulations for Re-employment after Retirement in Part III (the "Regulations").

This *Shokutaku* Worker Employment Agreement (this "Agreement") is entered into between ●● K.K. (the "Company") and ●● (the "Employee") based on the system for post-retirement re-employment of workers as follows:

Article 1. (Employment Period, etc.)

The Company shall employ the Employee as a *shokutaku* (short-term contract) worker ("*Shokutaku* Worker") upon the following conditions, and the Employee shall work for the Company in good faith pursuant to the Company's Regulations for Re-employment after Retirement, the Work Rules for Contract Employees, and other regulations, and at the Company's directive and instruction.

(1) Employment period (the "Employment Period")

The Employment Period shall be one (1) year from [MM/DD/YY] to [MM/DD/YY]; however, where the Employment Period expires after the Employee's sixty fifth (65th) birthday, the period shall end on the last day of the month to which his/her sixty fifth (65th) birthday belongs.

> 定年後雇用規程第2条1項に合わせて，雇用期間を1年としていますが，異なる期間を定めることも可能です。また，同規程第3条第1項及び本書式第2条1項において65歳に到達する日の属する月の末日を更新の限度とする旨定めた場合は，同規程に基づき，限度とされた日を以て最終更新後の雇用期間が満了するよう定める必要があります。上記のただし書きに代えて，最終更新後の雇用契約書において，個別の雇用期間の末日（65歳に到達する日の属する月の末日）を記入することも考えられます。

② 就業場所
●●
③ 所属
●●
④ 業務内容
●●

第2条 （更　新）
1. 乙が，第1条第1項の雇用期間満了後も引き続き甲で勤務することを希望する場合には，甲は，本契約を1年間更新し，以後同様とする。ただし，65歳に到達する日の属する月の末日を更新の限度とする。
2. 前項の規定にかかわらず，就業規則第21条及び第77条に定める解雇事由又は就業規則第18条に定める退職事由に該当する場合は，甲は，本契約を更新しない場合もありうる。ただし，これらの規定中，「社員」は，「定年後再雇用者」と読み替える。

The Employment Period is for one (1) year in accordance with Article 2, Paragraph 1 of the Regulations; however, it is possible for there to be a different period. Where it is provided in Article 3, Paragraph 1 of the Regulations and Article 2, Paragraph 1 of this form that the last day of the month to which his/her 65th birthday belongs is the limit for renewing the re-employment agreement, it is necessary to state that based on the Regulations, the Employment Period after the last renewal shall expire on that day. In the last-updated employment agreement, instead of the above-mentioned proviso, it is possible to state the last day of the respective Employment Period (the last day of the month to which his/her 65th birthday belongs.)

(2) Workplace

(3) Division/Department

(4) Contents of Duties

Article 2. (Renewal)

1. When the Employee desires to continue to work for the Company after the expiration of the Employment Period in Article 1, Paragraph 1 hereof, the Company shall renew the Agreement for one (1) additional year; the same shall apply thereafter. However, the last day of the month to which his/her sixty fifth (65th) birthday belongs shall be the limit of any renewed term of the Agreement.

2. Notwithstanding the preceding paragraph, in the event that the Employee becomes subject to any grounds for dismissal as prescribed in Article 21 or Article 77 of the Work Rules, or for retirement as prescribed in Article 18 thereof, the Company, as the case may be, shall not renew the Agreement. The term "Employee(s)" in these Articles shall be deemed to be replaced with "Re-employed Older Employee(s)."

> 定年後雇用規程第3条1項に合わせて更新の限度を定めていますが,更新の限度を「65歳に到達する日」又は「65歳に到達する日の属する年度末」と定めることも考えられます。最終更新後の雇用契約書においては,本条において雇用契約を更新しない旨を定めることがより明確であるといえます。

第3条 (勤務時間・休憩時間・休日・休暇)
　乙の勤務時間及び休憩時間並びに休日及び休暇は契約社員就業規則による。

第4条 (時間外労働)
　乙は,甲が業務の都合により必要と認めた場合,所定勤務時間を超え又は所定休日に勤務しなければならない。

第5条 (賃　　金)
　1. 基本賃金は,月給●●円とする。
　2. 時間外勤務手当,休日勤務手当,深夜勤務手当その他手当及び控除費用については契約社員就業規則によるものとする。
　3. 退職手当は,支給しないものとする。
　4. 賞与は,甲の業績並びに乙の業務能力,勤務成績及び態度を考慮し,甲が支給の有無及び金額を決定する。

> パート有期法8条は,パートタイム労働者・有期雇用労働者(いわゆる非正規社員)と通常の労働者(いわゆる正規社員)との間の不合理な待遇の相違を禁止しています。定年後再雇用者についても,パートタイム労働契約・有期雇用契約が締結される限り,同条の適用対象となり,通常の労働者との間で不合理な待遇の相違を設けることが禁止されます。なお,定年後再雇用者の賃金と通常の労働者の賃金とを比較する際,定年後再雇用者を長期間雇用することは通常予定されていないこと,定年退職するまでの間,無期雇用労働者として賃金の支給を受けており,また,一定の要件を満たせば老齢厚

> The limitation to renewal is provided here in accordance with Article 3, Paragraph 1 of the Regulations; and, it is also possible to state that the limit of renewal shall be "his/her 65th birthday" or "the last day of the fiscal year to which his/her 65th birthday belongs." It would be clearer to state that the employment agreement shall not be renewed in the corresponding article of the employment agreement after the last renewal.

Article 3. (Work Hours, Breaks, Holidays, and Leave)

Work hours, breaks, holidays, and leave regarding the Employee shall be governed by the Company's Work Rules for Contract Employees.

Article 4. (Overtime Work)

If the Company deems that it is necessary for business reasons, the Employee shall work any hours exceeding the designated work hours or perform work on designated holidays.

Article 5. (Wages)

1. The basic wage shall be ●● yen per month.
2. Overtime work allowance, holiday work allowance, extra wages for late hour work, and other allowances and deductions shall be governed by the Work Rules for Contract Employees.
3. Retirement allowance shall not be paid.
4. The Company will decide whether it will pay a bonus, and if it decides to make such payment, it shall determine the bonus amount upon consideration of the Company's performance, the Employee's quality of work or performance and the Employee's attitude toward work.

> Article 8 of the Part-Time Employment and Fixed-Term Employment Act prohibits unreasonably different treatment between part-time employees or fixed-term employees (so-called non-regular employees), and ordinary workers (so-called regular employees). The Article also applies to re-employed retired employees as long as they execute a part-time employment agreement or a fixed-

> 生年金の支給を受けることも予定されていること等の事情を考慮することが可能です。

第6条　（所属異動）
　　甲は，業務の都合により必要と認めた場合，乙に所属の変更を命ずることができるものとする。

第7条　（退職事由）
　　乙は次の各号の一に該当するときは，その日を退職日とし，その翌日に嘱託社員としての身分を失う。
　①　乙が死亡した場合。
　②　雇用期間が満了した場合。
　③　行方不明となり1か月が経過したとき。
　④　乙が自身の都合により退職を申し出て，甲がこれを承認した場合。なお，乙は，退職日の30日前迄に退職願を提出する必要がある。

第8条　（解雇事由）
　　乙が次の各号の一に該当するときは，雇用期間中である場合にも，甲は本契約を終了させ，乙を解雇することができる。
　①　乙の精神若しくは身体に障害があり又は虚弱老衰のため業務に耐えられないと認められるとき。
　②　業務上の傷病の為，療養開始後3年を経過し，なお，療養及び休業を必

term employment agreement ; thus, any unreasonably different treatment from regular employees is prohibited. When comparing the wages of re-employed retired employees and those of regular employees, it is possible for the employer to consider circumstances such as that employing re-employed retired employees for a long period is not usually unexpected; or that wages are paid to them as non-fixed term employees until their retirement due to them reaching retirement age and they also plan to receive an old-age welfare pension, subject to meeting certain requirements.

Article 6. (Change in Division/Department)

If the Company deems that it is necessary for business reasons, it may order the Employee to change the division or department where the Employee works.

Article 7. (Grounds for Retirement)

When the Employee falls under any of the following items, he/she shall retire from the Company effective as of the relevant date, and shall lose his/her status as a *Shokutaku* Worker of the Company as of the day following such date.

(1) Death of the Employee;

(2) Expiration of the Employment Period;

(3) Passage of a period of one (1) month without the Employee's whereabouts being known; or

(4) Approval by the Company of the Employee's request for retirement for personal reasons. The Employee shall submit the request for retirement no later than thirty (30) days before the requested retirement date.

Article 8. (Grounds for Dismissal)

When the Employee falls under any of the following items, the Company may terminate the Agreement and dismiss the Employee during the Employment Period.

(1) If the Employee becomes mentally or physically disabled, fragile or senile, and is considered to be unable to perform his/her duties;

(2) If even after three (3) years from the date of commencement of medical treatment

要として長期傷病補償給付が行なわれる事になった場合。
③　乙の業務能力が著しく劣り，勤務成績が不良のとき。
④　甲の業績が著しく低下した場合，その他やむを得ない事業上の都合により，乙の雇用を必要としなくなった場合。
⑤　前各号以外の事由で，契約社員就業規則による懲戒解雇事由に該当する場合。
⑥　その他やむを得ない事由がある場合。

第9条　（本契約に定めのない事項）
　　本契約に定めのない事項は，契約社員就業規則に従うものとする。

　本契約の成立を証すため本契約書を2通作成し，記名押印の上，甲乙が各1通を保有するものとする。

　　●年●月●日

　　甲　住所

　　　　氏名　　　　　　　　　　　　　　㊞

　　乙　住所

　　　　氏名　　　　　　　　　　　　　　㊞

due to work-related injury or disease, the Employee still requires medical treatment and a leave of absence, and will receive long-term illness and injury compensation benefits;

(3) If the Employee's business ability is significantly lowered, and performance is poor;

(4) If the Company's performance significantly declines, or the employment of the Employee is no longer necessary for unavoidable business reasons;

(5) If the Employee falls under the items subject to disciplinary dismissal listed in the Work Rules for Contract Employees, other than any of the foregoing; or

(6) If there are other unavoidable reasons.

Article 9. (Matters not Provided for Herein)

Matters not provided for herein shall be governed by the Work Rules for Contract Employees.

IN WITNESS WHEREOF, the Company and the Employee shall execute this Agreement in duplicate, affix their names and seal impressions hereto, and retain one copy each.

MM/DD/YY

The Company   Address:

                     Name: (seal)

The Employee   Address:

                     Name: (seal)

誓約書（入社時）

●●株式会社
代表取締役社長　　　　殿

　私は，この度貴社に採用され入社するに当たり，下記の事項を遵守することを誓約いたします。

記

1. 貴社の就業規則，諸規程，その他の規則及び指示命令等を守り誠実に勤務いたします。

2. 所属長，上司の指示命令及び指揮監督に従い忠実に業務を遂行いたします。

3. 貴社の業務に専念し，社内外を問わず貴社の信用及び名誉の保持に努め，企業秩序を乱すような行為はいたしません。

4. 別途提出する秘密保持誓約書に定める事項を遵守し，貴社在職中はもとより貴社を退職した後も，貴社の業務を遂行するに当たり知り得た貴社の秘密情報を，貴社の書面による事前の許可なく，いかなる方法によっても第三者に開示，漏洩又は業務以外の目的で使用しないことを約束いたします。

Pledge Letter
(Upon Joining the Company)

To: ●● K.K.
   Mr. _____, Representative Director/President

I, the undersigned, hereby promise to comply with the following upon my employment with the Company:

1. I will comply with the Work Rules, the Regulations, other rules, instructions and orders of the Company, and work diligently for the Company.

2. I will perform my duties faithfully following the instructions and orders of my supervisors and superiors.

3. I will devote myself to the Company business, maintain the creditworthiness and honor of the Company inside and outside the Company, and will not contravene company orders.

4. I promise to comply with the matters set forth in a confidentiality pledge letter to be separately submitted. During my employment with and after my retirement from the Company, I will not disclose or divulge to any third party the Company's confidential information that I learned while performing the business, nor use that information for any purpose other than for business purposes.

> 在職中の秘密保持義務については，入社時の一般的な誓約書の中で定める例もありますが，本書式では別途誓約書を提出させることとしています。

5. 採用に当たり提出又は提供した私の個人情報は，入社後提出又は提供するものも含め，私の人事，給与，安全衛生その他の業務管理等に利用し，又はこれを出向先，転籍先の関連会社等に提供し，利用することがあることを承知し，これにあらかじめ同意いたします。

6. 貴社から転勤，出向等の人事異動を命じられた場合はこれに従います。

7. 貴社の従業員としての義務に違背し，故意又は重大な過失により貴社に損害を与えた場合には，直ちにその損害を賠償いたします。

8. 貴社の就業規則に定める試用期間中に従業員として不適格であると認められた場合には，本採用を取り消されても異議ございません。

平成　　年　　月　　日

住所：

氏名：　　　　　　　　　　印

> There are some cases where the confidentiality obligation during employment with the company is stipulated in a general pledge letter upon the employee joining the company; however, in this form, it is stipulated that a confidentiality pledge letter shall be submitted separately.

5. I acknowledge and agree that my personal information that I submitted or provided upon my employment (including that to be submitted or provided after joining the Company) might be used for the purpose of business management, including personnel affairs, wages, safety and health, or provided to affiliates to which I am seconded or transferred for their use.

6. If the Company orders an intercompany transfer such as relocation or secondment, I will accept the order.

7. If I breach my obligations as the Company's employee, and cause damage to the Company intentionally or due to gross negligence, I will compensate the Company for the damage immediately.

8. If the Company determines that I am disqualified for employment as set forth in the Work Rules, I will not raise any objection to possible termination of my employment with the Company.

Date:MM/DD/YY

Address:

Name:_____(seal)

秘密保持誓約書

●●株式会社
代表取締役社長　　　　　殿

　私は，貴社の従業員として業務に従事するに当たり，下記の事項を遵守することを誓約いたします。

> 　本誓約書は，入社時において，在職中の秘密保持の対象となる情報の範囲や遵守すべき事項を明確にし，労働者への注意喚起及び自覚を促すことを目的としたものです。入社時に秘密の特定が困難である場合には，異動時や個別プロジェクトへの参加時に，秘密を特定して別途秘密保持誓約書を提出させることも考えられます。また，退職後の秘密保持義務については，退職時に別途誓約書を徴求することが望ましいといえます。もっとも，退職の経緯等によっては退職時に誓約書の提出を拒否される可能性もあるため，第1項では退職後の秘密保持義務も含めて規定し，第4項では退職時の資料等の返還義務を定めています。

Confidentiality Pledge Letter

To:　　●● K.K.
　　　Mr._____, Representative Director/President

I, the undersigned, hereby promise to comply with the following when I engage in the Company's business as an employee.

> This pledge letter aims to clarify the scope of information subject to a confidentiality obligation and the matters to be complied with during employment, thereby bringing such obligation to the attention and awareness of the employee at the time he/she joins the company. Where it is difficult to specify confidential information at the time of his/her joining the company, it is possible to have the employee submit a confidentiality pledge letter when he/she is relocated or participates in individual projects. Regarding any confidentiality obligation after retirement/resignation from the company, it is advisable to request a pledge letter separately at the time of retirement/resignation. However, it is possible that the employee might refuse to submit such pledge letter at the time of retirement/resignation depending on the grounds of his/her resignation; thus, in this form, the provisions of Paragraph 1 include the confidentiality obligation after retirement/resignation, and those of Paragraph 4 stipulate the obligation to return materials, etc. at the time of retirement/resignation.

記

1. 秘密保持義務
(1) 貴社在職中はもとより貴社を退職した後も，貴社の就業規則その他の規則を遵守し，貴社の業務を遂行するに当たり知り得た次に掲げる貴社の秘密情報（以下，「秘密情報」といいます。）について，貴社の書面による事前の許可なく，いかなる方法によっても第三者に開示，漏洩又は業務以外の目的で使用しないことを約束いたします。
① 製造技術，製品の企画開発，知的財産権に関する情報
② 製品販売，顧客に関する情報
③ 財務，経営，人事管理に関する情報
④ 他社との業務提携，技術提携に関する情報
⑤ 貴社の役員，従業員，その他関係者の個人情報
⑥ 子会社，関連会社に関する事項
⑦ 所属長，上司又は秘密情報の管理責任者により秘密情報として指定された情報
⑧ その他貴社が特に秘密保持の対象として指定した情報

> 本書式では，秘密保持義務の対象となる秘密情報を，ある程度一般的に記載していますが，労働者の業務内容や地位に応じて，当該労働者が取り扱う秘密情報をより具体的に記載することも考えられます。

Confidentiality Pledge Letter

1. Confidentiality Obligation

    (1) During my employment with and after my retirement/resignation from the Company, I hereby promise to comply with the Work Rules and other rules of the Company, not to disclose or divulge the Company's confidential information listed below ("Confidential Information") that I learned while performing Company business, nor to use that information in any manner for any purpose other than for a business purpose without the Company's prior written permission:

    (i) Information about production technology, product planning and development, and intellectual property rights;

    (ii) Information about product sales and customers;

    (iii) Information about financial affairs, management and personnel management;

    (iv) Information about business alliances and technology tie-ups with other companies;

    (v) Personal information regarding officers, employees and other related parties of the Company;

    (vi) Matters relating to subsidiaries and affiliates;

    (vii) Information designated as Confidential Information by supervisors, superiors or the person responsible for the management of Confidential Information;

    (viii) Other information that the Company has specifically designated as confidential.

    In this form, confidential information subject to a confidentiality obligation is described generally to some extent, but it is possible to specifically describe confidential information to be handled by the subject employee depending on his/her job or position.

(2) 下記に該当する情報は秘密情報に含まれないものとします。
　① 開示された時において公知であり，又は開示以後私の責めによらず公知となった情報
　② 貴社から開示される以前に貴社での業務とは関係なく，適法かつ正当に保持していた情報
　③ 貴社の秘密情報を使用せず，かつ貴社での業務とは関係なく，私が独自に開発し，又は将来開発する情報
　④ 貴社に対して秘密保持義務を負わない第三者から，秘密保持義務を負うことなく正当に入手する情報

2．秘密情報の報告及び帰属
　秘密情報の創出又は得喪に関わった場合には，直ちに貴社に報告いたします。私が秘密情報の創出に関わった場合であっても，当該秘密情報は貴社の業務上創出されたものであることに同意し，当該秘密情報の帰属が貴社にあることを確認いたします。

3．第三者の秘密
(1) 報告義務
　第三者との間で秘密保持義務を負担している場合には，本誓約書提出後30日以内に，秘密侵害にわたらない限度において，当該第三者及び負担する義務の内容について報告いたします。
(2) 遵守義務
　第三者との間で秘密保持義務を負担している場合には，貴社の業務執行にあたって，自らの責任において，その義務に違反しないように行動いたします。義務違反・抵触のおそれがある場合には，事前に貴社に報告し，貴社の指示を仰ぎます。

(2) Information listed below shall not constitute Confidential Information:
   (i) Information that was in the public domain at the time of disclosure or that became part of the public domain after disclosure for reasons not attributable to me;
   (ii) Information that I lawfully and duly possessed without regard to performing Company business before being disclosed to me by the Company;
   (iii) Information that I have developed or will develop independently without using the Company's Confidential Information and without regard to performing Company business; and
   (iv) Information that I duly obtain from a third party who does not owe a confidentiality obligation to the Company without assuming a confidentiality obligation.

2. Reporting and Attribution of Confidential Information

Where I am involved in the creation, acquisition or loss of Confidential Information, I will immediately report it to the Company. Even when I am involved in the creation of Confidential Information, I agree that the Confidential Information has been created while performing the Company's business, and confirm that the Confidential Information belongs to the Company.

3. Third Parties' Secrets
   (1) Reporting Obligation
   Where I assume a confidentiality obligation toward a third party, I will report the name of the third party and content of the obligation to the extent that it does not jeopardize the third party's secret within thirty (30) days after submission of this pledge letter.
   (2) Compliance Obligation
   Where I assume a confidentiality obligation toward a third party, I will perform the Company's business in such a manner so as not to breach the confidentiality obligation at my own responsibility. If there is any possible breach or violation of

(3) 協力義務

　第三者から，貴社に対して，私が負担する秘密保持義務の違反・侵害に関する問合わせ・請求・訴訟提起等がなされた場合には，貴社に損害・不利益等を生じないよう，防御に必要な行動・協力をいたします。また，私の故意又は過失により貴社が損害を被った場合には，自らの責任において解決し，貴社には一切の迷惑をかけないことを約束いたします。

4．書類等の保管及び返還等

　秘密情報に関連して入手した書類，電子情報，記録媒体，サンプル等一切の資料は，在職中は秘密として大切に保管し，貴社の許可なく社外に持ち出さないことを約束いたします。また，貴社を退職する場合又は貴社の指示があった場合には，私が管理又は所持する秘密情報及びこれに関連する一切の資料を，直ちに貴社の指示に従って返還，消去又は破棄することを約束いたします。

5．誓約書提出義務

　貴社の指示があった場合には，直ちに貴社の指示に従って誓約書を追加提出することを約束いたします。また，誓約書の追加提出に応じることが，私の貴社における昇進・異動・プロジェクト参加のための必須条件とされる場合があることをあらかじめ承諾いたします。

6．在職中のメールモニタリングの同意

　貴社の情報システム及び情報資産の一切が貴社に帰属していることを理解し，貴社が情報システム及び情報資産の保護のために必要であると認める場合には，私の職務上利用する電子メール，パソコンその他の貴社に帰

that obligation, I will report it in advance to the Company so that the Company may issue instructions.

(3) Cooperation Obligation

If the third party makes an inquiry about any breach or violation of the confidentiality obligation that I assume, makes a claim, or institutes a lawsuit against the Company, I will take action and provide the cooperation necessary to defend the lawsuit, etc. and will not cause any loss or disadvantage to the Company. If the Company suffers damage due to my intentional act or negligence, I promise to remedy that damage at my own responsibility and not to cause any trouble to the Company.

4. Storage and Return of Documents

I hereby promise to safeguard documents, electronic data, recording media, samples and other materials that I obtained in relation to Confidential Information as confidential during my employment with the Company, and not to take it away from the Company without the Company's permission. Also, upon my retirement/resignation from the Company or if the Company so instructs, I promise to immediately return, delete or destroy Confidential Information and any materials that I have managed or possessed in accordance with the Company's instructions.

5. Obligation to Submit a Pledge Letter

If the Company so instructs, I promise to immediately submit an additional pledge letter according to that instruction. I agree in advance that acceptance of the instruction to submit an additional pledge letter may become a precondition for my promotion, relocation or participation in projects in the Company.

6. Consent to Monitoring of E-mails during my Employment

I hereby understand that the information system and information assets of the Company all belong to the Company; where the Company deems it necessary to protect the information system and information assets, I understand and agree that the Company

属する機器の利用状況等を私に断りなくモニタリングすることがあることを承知し，これに同意いたします。

7. 損害賠償等

　本誓約書に違反して貴社の秘密情報を開示，漏洩又は使用した場合は，貴社が私に対して懲戒解雇を含む懲戒処分，損害賠償請求，刑事告訴等の法的処分を採り得ることを十分に理解しており，またこれにより貴社が被った一切の損害を賠償することを約束いたします。

平成　　年　　月　　日

住所：

氏名：　　　　　　　印

might monitor my e-mail activity or use of personal computers or other Company equipment that I use for business purposes without notifying me.

7. Compensation for Damage, etc.

I fully understand that the Company may take disciplinary action including disciplinary dismissal, demand compensation for damage, or take legal action such as lodging a criminal complaint against me if I disclose, divulge or use the Company's Confidential Information in breach of this pledge letter. I promise to compensate the Company for any damage incurred by the Company due to that breach.

Date:MM/DD/YY

Address:

Name:_____(seal)

誓約書(退社時)

●●株式会社
代表取締役社長　　　　殿

　私は,貴社を退職するに当たり,下記の事項を遵守することを誓約いたします。

記

1. 退職後の秘密保持義務
　(1) 貴社を退職するに当たり,次に掲げる貴社の秘密情報(以下,「秘密情報」といいます。)について,貴社の書面による事前の許可なく,いかなる方法によっても,私自身のため又は第三者のために,開示,漏洩又は使用しないことを約束いたします。
　　① 製造技術,製品の企画開発,知的財産権に関する情報
　　② 製品販売,顧客に関する情報
　　③ 財務,経営,人事管理に関する情報
　　④ 他社との業務提携,技術提携に関する情報
　　⑤ 貴社の役員,従業員,その他関係者の個人情報
　　⑥ 子会社,関連会社に関する事項
　　⑦ 所属長,上司又は秘密情報の管理責任者により秘密情報として指定された情報
　　⑧ その他貴社が特に秘密保持の対象として指定した情報

Pledge Letter
(Upon Retirement/Resignation from the Company)

To: ●● K.K.
　　　Mr._____, Representative Director/President

I, the undersigned, hereby promise to comply with the following upon my retirement/resignation from the Company.

1. Confidentiality Obligation after Retirement
   (1) Upon my retirement/resignation from the Company, I hereby promise not to disclose, divulge or use the Company's confidential information listed below ("Confidential Information") for my benefit or for any third party's benefit in any manner without the Company's prior written permission:
      (i) Information about production technology, product planning and development, and intellectual property rights;
      (ii) Information about product sales and customers;
      (iii) Information about financial affairs, management and personnel management;
      (iv) Information about business alliances and technology tie-ups with other companies;
      (v) Personal information regarding officers, employees and other related parties of the Company;
      (vi) Matters relating to subsidiaries and affiliates;
      (vii) Information designated as Confidential Information by supervisors, superiors or the person responsible for the management of Confidential Information;
      (viii) Other information that the Company has specifically designated as confidential.

> 秘密情報に接する機会の多かった労働者については，秘密保持の対象となる情報をできるだけ具体的に特定することが望ましいといえます。上記では，入社時の秘密保持誓約書と同じ定義を用いていますが，在職中のプロジェクト参加時等に，別途秘密保持の誓約書を取得していた場合には，当該誓約書で秘密として指定された情報も追加して具体的に記載しておくとよいでしょう。

(2) 下記に該当する情報は秘密情報に含まれないものとします。
  ① 開示された時において公知であり，又は開示以後私の責めによらず公知となった情報
  ② 貴社から開示される以前に貴社での業務とは関係なく，適法かつ正当に保持していた情報
  ③ 貴社の秘密情報を使用せず，かつ貴社での業務とは関係なく，私が独自に開発し，又は将来開発する情報
  ④ 貴社に対して秘密保持義務を負わない第三者から，秘密保持義務を負うことなく正当に入手する情報

> Regarding employees who have a lot of opportunity to access confidential information, it is advisable to specify the information subject to the confidentiality obligation as specifically as possible. In the first sentence of this paragraph, the definition of Confidential Information is the same as that which is in a confidentiality pledge letter upon joining the company; however, if the company obtains a confidentiality pledge letter when the subject employee participated in a project during his/her employment with the company, it is advisable to include the information designated as confidential in that pledge letter in the definition of Confidential Information herein.

(2) Information listed below shall not constitute Confidential Information:

(i) Information that was in the public domain at the time of disclosure or that became part of the public domain after disclosure for reasons not attributable to me;

(ii) Information that I lawfully and duly possessed without regard to performing Company business before being disclosed to me by the Company;

(iii) Information that I have developed or will develop independently without using the Company's Confidential Information and without regard to performing Company business; and

(iv) Information that I duly obtain from a third party who does not owe a confidentiality obligation to the Company without assuming a confidentiality obligation.

2. 資料の返還等
　　私が管理又は所持していた貴社の秘密情報及びこれに関連する書類，電子情報，記録媒体，サンプル等一切の資料を，貴社退職日までに貴社の指示に従って返還，消去又は破棄し，退職後は何ら保有しないことを誓約いたします。

3. 秘密情報の帰属
　　私が貴社在職中に創出に関わった秘密情報は，貴社の業務上創出されたものであり，貴社に帰属することを確認いたします。

4. 競業避止義務
　　私は，第1項の秘密保持義務を遵守するため，貴社退職後［6ヶ月］は，次の行為を行わないことを約束いたします。
 (1) 貴社と競合関係に立つ事業者又はその提携先企業に，就職し又は役員に就任すること
 (2) 貴社と競合関係に立つ事業を自ら開業，設立し，又はその他の方法により支配すること

> 労働者の職業選択の自由や営業の自由を過度に制限しないよう，業種によっては，競業を禁止する期間や対象事業，場所的範囲を限定して規定することも考えられます。

 (3) 貴社の役員又は従業員に対して，退職の勧奨，引抜き行為等を行うこと

5. 名誉毀損等の禁止
　　私は，貴社退職後，貴社を誹謗・中傷すること，その他貴社の名誉及び信用を傷つけるおそれのある一切の行為をしないことを約束いたします。

2. Return of Materials

I hereby promise that I will return, delete or destroy the Company's Confidential Information, and documents, electronic data, recording media, samples and other materials that I have kept or possessed by the retirement/resignation date in accordance with the Company's instructions, and will not be in possession of any Confidential Information after my retirement/resignation.

3. Attribution of Confidential Information

I hereby confirm that Confidential Information the creation of which I was involved in has been created while performing the Company's business and thus belongs to the Company.

4. Non-Competition Obligation

In order to comply with the confidentiality obligation set forth in Paragraph 1, I hereby promise not to conduct any of the following acts [for six (6) months] after my retirement/resignation from the Company:

(1) Join, or assume the office of officer in, any business operator or allied company competing with the Company;

(2) Inaugurate, establish or otherwise control a business competing with the Company; or

It is possible to limit the period, the business or geographical area for which competition is prohibited depending on the type of business so that an employees' freedom to choose an occupation or freedom to engage in business is not excessively restricted.

(3) Induce officers or employees of the Company to resign from the Company or recruit them away from the Company.

5. No Defamation

I hereby promise not to defame or abuse the Company, nor conduct any act that is likely to degrade the Company's honor and creditworthiness after my retirement/resignation from

6. 秘密補償手当

　私は，本誓約書各条項の遵守のため，貴社から，給与及び退職金の外，秘密補償手当として●円の交付を受けることを確認いたします。

> 競業避止義務等を課す代償として一定の金銭を支払うときは，競業禁止特約の効力が争われた場合に，当該金銭が競業禁止の代償措置であることを立証できるよう，明確に規定しておくことが望ましいといえます。

　　　　　　　　　　　　　　　平成　　年　　月　　日

　　　　　　　　　　　　　　　住所：

　　　　　　　　　　　　　　　氏名：　　　　　　　印

the Company.

6. Allowance for Confidentiality Obligation

I hereby confirm that I will receive a payment of ● yen as allowance for the confidentiality obligation (*himitsu hosho teate*) from the Company in order to comply with each provision of this Pledge Letter, in addition to wages and retirement allowances.

> **Where the company pays a certain amount of money in consideration for imposing a non-competition obligation, it is advisable to clearly stipulate herein the payment so as to prove that the payment is a compensating measure for non-competition in the event that the special clause for non-competition is disputed.**

Date:MM/DD/YY

Address:

Name:_____(seal)

解雇通知書

●年●月●日

● 部
● 殿

株式会社 ●●
代表取締役 ●

解雇通知書

　当社は，貴殿の下記行為が就業規則第21条第1項第●号に該当するため，貴殿を●年●月●日をもって解雇いたします。なお，法定の予告期間に満たない日数である●日分の解雇予告手当は，貴殿の給与振込口座に送金いたします。

> 労働者を解雇する場合，解雇の30日以上前に解雇予告をするか，平均賃金の30日分以上の解雇予告手当を支払う必要があります。本書式は，解雇予告期間が30日に満たない場合の通知例です。

記

［解雇理由を記載］

以上

> # Dismissal Notice

[MM/DD/YY]
To:　● Department
　　　Mr./Ms. ●

●● K.K.
●, Representative Director

DISMISSAL NOTICE

　This is to inform you that the Company will dismiss you as of MM/DD/YY because your acts mentioned below fall under Article 21, paragraph 1, item ● of the Work Rules. The Company will pay a dismissal notice allowance for　● days, which are the days which fall short of the statutory advance notice period, by remittance to your bank account.

> 　In order to dismiss an employee, the employer must provide at least 30 days advance notice of dismissal, or pay a dismissal notice allowance that corresponds to the employee's average wage for 30 days or more.　This form is a sample notice where the advance notice period for dismissal is less than 30 days.

[Reasons for the dismissal to be stated here]

End

懲戒解雇通知書

●年●月●日

● 部
● 殿

株式会社　●●
代表取締役　●

懲戒解雇通知書

当社は，貴殿の下記行為が就業規則第77条第●号に該当するため，貴殿を本日付をもって懲戒解雇とします。解雇予告手当は，貴殿の給与振込口座に送金いたします。

> 懲戒解雇の場合も，原則として労働基準法20条の解雇予告手当の規定が適用され，30日前の予告か予告手当の支払が必要となります。ただし，労働者の責めに帰すべき事由に基づく解雇の場合は，労働基準監督署長の認定を受けると解雇予告義務が免除されます。実務上，懲戒解雇の場合は即時解雇とすることが一般的ですが，解雇予告手当の支払を免れるためにはあらかじめ労働基準監督署長の認定を受ける必要がありますので留意が必要です。

記

［懲戒解雇理由を記載］

以上

Disciplinary Dismissal Notice

[MM/DD/YY]
To: ● Department
     Mr./Ms. ●

●● K.K.
●, Representative Director

DISCIPLINARY DISMISSAL NOTICE

This is to inform you that the Company will subject you to disciplinary dismissal as of today because your acts mentioned below fall under Article 77, Item ● of the Work Rules. The Company will pay a dismissal notice allowance by remittance to your bank account..

> As a general rule, provisions regarding dismissal notice allowance (i.e., under Article 20 of the Labor Standards Act) will apply even in the case of disciplinary dismissal. Therefore, a 30-day advance notice or a notice payment must be provided. However, if the dismissal is for reasons attributable to the employee, the employer is exempted from the obligation to provide an advance notice of dismissal if the chief of the labor standards supervision office approves. In practice, dismissal with immediate effect is common in the case of disciplinary dismissal; however, please note that in order to avoid payment of a dismissal notice allowance, the employer must obtain the approval of the chief of the labor standards supervision office in advance.

[Reasons for the dismissal to be stated here]

End

解雇理由証明書

_____殿

　当社が，____年____月____日付けで貴殿に予告した解雇については，以下の理由によるものであることを証明します。

　　　　　　　　　　　　　　　　　　　　　　　年　　　月　　　日

　　　　　　　　事業主氏名又は名称
　　　　　　　　使 用 者 職 氏 名

〔解雇理由〕
1.　就業規則第21条第1項第3号に定める「勤務態度が不良で注意しても改善しないとき」による解雇

　　　・貴殿は，●年頃から退職日までの間，遅刻は延べ●回，無断欠勤は●日以上に及び，業務時間中も度々長時間離席するなど，勤務態度が著しく不良であり，当社は●年●月●日以降，●回に亘り口頭及び書面での注意警告を行ったが，全く改善が見られなかった。

2.　就業規則第21条第1項第7号に定める「その他会社の社員として適格性がないと認められたとき」による解雇

　　　・貴殿は，●年●月頃，転居したにもかかわらず，転居届の提出を怠り，通勤実態がないにもかかわらず，通勤手当差額分合計●円を不正に受給した。

> 解雇された労働者又は解雇を予告された労働者が，使用者に対して，当該解雇の理由について証明書を請求した場合，使用者は遅滞なく理由を記載した証明書を労働者に交付しなければなりません（労働基準法22条1項及び2項）。就業規則の一定の条項に該当することを理由として解雇する場合には，就業規則の当該条項の内容及び当該条項に該当するに至った事実関係を記載する必要があります。解雇理由証明書においては，解雇の効力が争われた場合を想定して，解雇の理由となった事実関係を可能な限り網羅的かつ具体的に記載することが望ましいといえます。

Certificate for Reasons for Dismissal

Mr./Ms. _____

I hereby certify that the reasons for the dismissal which the Company notified you of in advance as of <u>MM/DD/YY</u> are as follows:

[MM/DD/YY]

Name of Employer:
Title of Employer:

[Reasons for Dismissal]
1. Dismissal for the reason provided in Article 21, paragraph 1, item 3 of the Work Rules: "If his/her attitude towards work is unsatisfactory, and does not improve despite warnings"

    • Starting from around [YY] until your last date of work, you were late ● times and absent from work without notice for ● days or more in total, and often left your desk for a long time during business hours; in this way, your attitude towards work has been substantially unsatisfactory. The Company has provided oral and written notices and warnings since [MM/DD/YY], but your attitude has not improved in any way whatsoever.

2. Dismissal for the reason provided in Article 21, paragraph 1, item 7 of the Work Rules: "If an Employee is considered unqualified for employment for any other reason"

    • Despite the fact that you moved around MM/YY, you failed to submit a notification of change of address to the Company and unlawfully received the difference in commute allowance of ● yen in total without actual commuting from such location.

> If an employee who was dismissed or received an advance notice of dismissal requests a Certificate for Reasons for Dismissal from the employer, the employer must deliver the certificate stating the reasons for the dismissal without delay (Article 22, paragraphs 1 and 2 of the Labor Standards Act). When the employer intends to dismiss the employee for reasons falling under certain provisions of the Work Rules, the employer must state the details of such provisions and the facts that fall under such provisions. It is advisable to state in a Certificate for Reasons for Dismissal the facts regarding dismissal as exhaustively and specifically as possible, in case the validity of the dismissal is disputed.

退職合意書1

退職金規程に基づく退職金のみを支払うシンプルな形の退職合意書です。

退 職 合 意 書

●●株式会社（以下「甲」という。）と●●（以下「乙」という。）は、乙の甲における雇用の契約の終了に関し、以下のとおり合意する（以下、本書を「本合意書」という。）。

1．（雇用契約の終了）
　甲及び乙は、乙の甲における雇用が●年●月●日付（以下「退職日」という。）で終了することについて、ここに合意する。

2．（退職金の支払等）
　甲は、乙に対し、退職金規程に基づき、退職金として●円（税引前）を、同金額から源泉税その他法令上要求される金額を差し引いた上、平成●年●月●日までに、乙の給与振込口座に振り込むことにより支払う。乙は、本合意書記載以外の金員の支払を甲に請求又は要請しないことをここに同意する。

Termination Agreement 1

This is a simple version of a Termination Agreement whereby the Company shall pay a retirement allowance only pursuant to the Retirement Allowance Regulations.

TERMINATION AGREEMENT

This Agreement (this "Agreement") is entered into between ●● K.K. (the "Company") and ●● (the "Employee") with respect to the termination of the Employee's employment with the Company as follows.

1. (Termination of the Employment Agreement)
The Company and the Employee hereby agree that the Employment Agreement between the Company and the Employee will terminate as of [MM/DD/YY] (the "Termination Date").

2. (Payment of Retirement Allowance)
The Company shall pay to the Employee a retirement allowance of ● yen (before tax) in accordance with the Retirement Allowance Regulations by remitting to the Employee's bank account the amount after deducting withholding tax and other amounts required by law no later than [MM/DD/YY]. The Employee shall not claim or demand any other payments from the Company.

> 日本法において，使用者には退職金の支払義務はありませんが，就業規則等で退職金の定めがある場合は，これに従って退職金を支払う必要があります。

3．（資料の返還等）
　乙は，退職日までに，備品（書籍，鍵，セキュリティ・カード，名刺，パソコン及び携帯電話を含むがこれらに限らない。）を甲に返却し，乙が管理又は所持していた甲の秘密情報及びこれに関連する書類，電子情報，記録媒体，サンプル等一切の資料を，甲の指示に従って返還，消去又は破棄する。

4．（秘密保持）
　乙は，別途甲に提出する誓約書に定める秘密保持義務等が，退職日後も引き続き有効であることを確認し，これらの義務を遵守する。

> ここでは退職に際して別途秘密保持義務等を定めた誓約書を提出する形としています。本条で具体的な秘密保持義務を定めることも可能です。

5．（誠実協力）
　乙は，退職日後に，乙の在職中の行為によって第三者の甲に対する苦情及び損害賠償の申し立て等が発生した場合は，甲の要請に従って速やかに行動し，問題解決に全面的に協力する。

6．（名誉毀損等の禁止）
　乙は，退職日後においても，甲及び甲の役職員の名誉及び信頼を損なう言動を行わないことを確約する。

> Under the laws of Japan, employers are not obligated to pay a retirement allowance; however, if the work rules, and the like, contain a provision about retirement allowance, the employer must pay the allowance in accordance with such rules.

3. (Return of Materials)

The Employee shall return all equipment (including, but not limited to, books, keys, security cards, visiting cards, personal computer, and mobile phone) to the Company by the Termination Date, and return, delete or destroy the Company's confidential information and related documents, electronic data, recording media, samples, and other materials in its control or possession in accordance with the Company's instructions.

4. (Confidentiality)

The Employee confirms that the confidentiality obligation set forth in a pledge letter to be separately submitted to the Company shall remain effective after the Termination Date, and the Employee shall comply with such obligation.

> This paragraph provides that a pledge letter providing for a confidentiality obligation shall be separately submitted upon termination of the employment. It is possible to stipulate a specific confidentiality obligation in this paragraph.

5. (Good-faith Cooperation)

In the event that any complaint or any petition for damages is filed after the Termination Date by a third party against the Company due to the Employee's acts during his/her employment, the Employee shall take prompt action upon the Company's request and fully cooperate with the Company in resolving such problems.

6. (No Defamation)

The Employee shall commit to not conducting any act that would damage the reputation and creditworthiness of the Company or the Company's officers and employees after the Termination Date.

7．（本合意書の違反）

　乙が第2項乃至前項までの規定に違反し，これによって甲に損害を与えたときは，甲に生じた損害について一切の賠償の責めを負う。

8．（債権債務）

　甲及び乙は，別途書面による合意が無い限り，甲の乙に対する債務が一切存在しないことを相互に確認する。

9．（管　　轄）

　甲及び乙は，本合意書に関連して生じる一切の法律上の争訟については，東京地方裁判所を第一審の専属的合意管轄裁判所とすることに合意する。

　本合意書の成立を証すため本書を2通作成し，甲，乙各1通を保有するものとする。

●年●月●日

甲　　住所

　　　氏名　　　　　　　　　　　　　　　　　　　　㊞

乙　　住所

　　　氏名　　　　　　　　　　　　　　　　　　　　㊞

7. (Violation of this Agreement)

If the Employee violates any provision in paragraphs 2 to 6, thereby causing any damage to the Company, the Employee shall be liable for the damage incurred by the Company.

8. (Claims and Obligations)

The Company and the Employee mutually confirm that the Company owes no obligations with regard to the Employee, unless otherwise agreed in writing.

9. (Jurisdiction)

The Company and the Employee shall submit any legal disputes arising in relation to this Agreement to the exclusive jurisdiction of the Tokyo District Court as the court of first instance.

IN WITNESS WHEREOF, the Company and the Employee shall execute this Agreement in duplicate, and retain one copy each.

MM/DD/YY

    The Company   Address:

                              Name: (seal)

    The Employee   Address:

                              Name: (seal)

退職合意書2

　退職勧奨等により一定の条件で退職合意に至った場合を想定した退職合意書です。なお、退職条件は会社と退職者との交渉により決まるもので、必ずしも下記の条件によらなければならないものではありません。

退 職 合 意 書

　●●株式会社（以下「甲」という。）及び●●（以下「乙」という。）は、乙の甲における雇用の終了に関し、以下のとおり合意する（以下、本書を「本合意書」という。）。

1.　（雇用契約の終了）
　(1)　甲及び乙は、甲と乙との間の雇用が●年●月●日（以下「退職日」という。）付で終了することについて合意する。
　(2)　乙の最終出社日は●年●月●日（以下「最終出社日」という。）とする。ただし、最終出社日より後退職日以前において、業務の引継ぎ等のため、甲が乙に指示をした場合には、乙は出社し、業務の引継ぎ等を行うものとする。

Termination Agreement 2

This is a Termination Agreement prepared assuming that the termination is agreed on certain conditions after encouraging the Employee to retire, and so on. The termination conditions will be determined upon negotiation between the Company and the Employee, and do not necessarily include the following conditions.

TERMINATION AGREEMENT

This Agreement (the "Agreement") is entered into between ●● K.K. (the "Company") and ●● (the "Employee") with respect to the termination of the Employee's employment with the Company as follows.

1. (Termination of the Employment Agreement)
   (1) The Company and the Employee hereby agree that the Employment Agreement between the Company and the Employee will terminate as of [MM/DD/YY] (the "Termination Date").
   (2) The Employee's last working day shall be [MM/DD/YY] (the "Last Working Day"). However, upon the Company's instructions, in order to handover his/her business, the Employee shall come to the office and conduct a handover of his/her business, even after the Last Working Day and before the Termination Date.

> 退職日よりも前に最終出社日を設けて，再就職のための準備期間等として一定期間出社させないことも，実務上しばしば見られる対応です。この場合，業務の引継ぎ等の必要がある場合には会社の指示により出社させることができるよう，その旨明記しておくことが望ましいといえます。

2．（退職金等の支払等）
　(1)　甲は，乙に対し，退職金規程に基づく退職金として●円（税引前）を支払う。
　(2)　甲は，乙に対し，乙が本合意書の各条項及び就業規則（その附属規程を含む。以下同じ。）を遵守することを条件として，特別加算金として●円（税引前）を支払う。なお，甲及び乙は，特別加算金は，第7項に定める乙の競業避止義務に対する補償としての性質も有するものであることをここに確認する。
　(3)　甲は，前2号に定める金額から源泉税その他法令上要求される金額を差し引いた上，●年●月●日までに，乙の給与振込口座に振り込む。

> 退職金規程に基づく退職金に加えて，一定の特別加算金を支払うことを条件に合意退職する場合を想定しています。特別加算金の金額に退職後の競業避止義務に対する代償としての性質が含まれている場合には，その旨明確に規定しておくことが望ましいといえます。

3．（有給休暇）
　本退職日時点で未消化の有給休暇がある場合，甲が1日当たり金●円で買い上げるものとし，前項第2号に定める特別加算金の額に加算して支給する。

In practice, it is often the case that the Company sets the Last Working Day before the Termination Date and absolves the Employee from working for a certain period as a preparatory period for re-employment. In such cases, it is advisable to clearly stipulate that the Company may demand that the Employee come to the office to conduct a handover of his/her business, whenever necessary.

2. (Payment of Retirement Allowance)

  (1) The Company shall pay to the Employee a retirement allowance of ● yen (before tax) in accordance with the Retirement Allowance Regulations.

  (2) Subject to the Employee's compliance with each provision of the Agreement and the work rules (including the supplementary regulations; hereinafter the same), the Company shall pay to the Employee an early termination payment of ● yen (before tax). The Company and the Employee hereby confirm that such payment serves as compensation for the non-competition obligation of the Employee set forth in paragraph 7.

  (3) The Company shall remit to the Employee's bank account the amount set forth in the preceding two items after deducting withholding tax and other amounts required by law no later than [MM/DD/YY].

This is the case assuming that the Employee will terminate his/her employment based on agreement, on condition that a certain amount of early termination payment will be paid in addition to the retirement allowance under the Retirement Allowance Regulations. Where the payment serves as compensation for the non-competition obligation after the termination, it is advisable to clearly stipulate to that effect.

3. (Paid Leave)

The Company shall purchase back unused paid leave as of the Termination Date, if any, at a price of ● yen per day, and pay the amount to the Employee in addition to the early termination payment set forth in item 2 of the preceding paragraph.

> 日本法において，使用者には未消化の有給休暇の買取義務はありませんが，会社が特別に買取制度を設けている場合や，退職者との交渉により有給休暇の買取を退職の条件とした場合を想定した条項です。

4．（退職日の前倒し）
　乙は，第１項の規定にかかわらず，乙が退職日前に退職を希望する場合，甲に対し退職を希望する日の１ヵ月前までに申し出を行うことにより，甲を退職することができるものとし，退職日までの月例給●●円（税引前）を，第２項第２号に定める特別加算金の額に加算して支給する。

5．（再就職支援サービス等）
　甲は，乙に対し，乙の再就職を支援するため，乙が本合意書の各条項を遵守することを条件として，甲が指定する再就職支援サービス機関による再就職支援サービスを，甲の費用にて●か月間提供するものとする。再就職支援サービスの内容及び条件は，甲の指定した再就職支援サービス機関の定めるところによるものとする。

> 退職勧奨においては，実務上，退職条件として再就職支援サービスの提供を提示することもあります。

6．（秘密保持）
　乙は，別途甲に提出する誓約書に定める秘密保持義務等が，退職日後も引き続き有効であることを確認し，これらの義務を遵守する。

7．（競業避止）
　乙は，別途甲に提出する誓約書に定めるところにより，退職日後６か月の間，甲と競合関係に立つ事業者及びその提携先企業に就職し又は役員に就任し，あ

> Under the laws of Japan, employees are not obligated to purchase back unused paid leave. This provision is for when the Company specifically establishes a paid-leave purchase system, or the purchase of paid leave is a condition for the termination based on the negotiation with the Employee.

4. (Acceleration of Termination Date)

Notwithstanding paragraph 1, where the Employee desires to terminate the employment prior to the Termination Date, he/she may do so by giving notice one month prior to the desired termination date. The Company shall pay to the Employee the monthly salary of ●● yen (before tax) till the Termination Date, in addition to the early termination payment set forth in paragraph 2, item 2.

5. (Outplacement Service)

In order to support re-employment of the Employee, the Company shall, at its cost, provide an outplacement service via the outplacement consulting firm designated by the Company for ● months, subject to the Employee's compliance with each provision hereof. The details and conditions of the outplacement service shall be those specified by the outplacement consulting firm designated by the Company.

> Where an Employee's retirement was encouraged, there are instances where an outplacement service is offered as a condition for termination, in practice.

6. (Confidentiality)

The Employee confirms that the confidentiality obligation provided in the pledge letter to be separately submitted to the Company will remain effective after the Termination Date, and the Employee shall comply with such obligation.

7. (Non-Competition)

In accordance with the provisions of the pledge letter to be separately submitted to the Company, for six months after the Termination Date the Employee shall neither obtain

るいは，甲と競合関係に立つ事業を自ら開業，設立し，又はその他の方法により支配してはならない。

> 競業避止義務については第1部第1章8-1-2を参照してください。

8．（資料の返還等）
　乙は，最終出社日までに，備品（書籍，鍵，セキュリティ・カード，名刺，パソコン及び携帯電話を含むがこれらに限らない。）を甲に返却し，乙が管理又は所持していた甲の秘密情報及びこれに関連する書類，電子情報，記録媒体，サンプル等一切の資料を，甲の指示に従って返還，消去又は破棄する。

9．（名誉毀損等の禁止）
　乙は，退職日後においても，甲及び甲の役職員の名誉及び信頼を損なう言動を行わないことを確約する。

10．（本合意書等の違反）
　乙は，本合意書の各条項又は就業規則に定める乙の義務に違反した場合，甲に対し，甲の請求次第直ちに，第2項第2号に基づいて受領した特別加算金の全てを返還するものとし，これを上回る損害が甲に生じた場合には，その損害を賠償するものとする。

11．（債権債務）
　甲及び乙は，本合意書に規定されるもの以外，両当事者間に債権債務が存在しないことを確認する。

employment nor assume the office of an officer in a business operator or its affiliated companies which is a competitor to the Company, nor open, establish, or otherwise control a business that is a competitor to the Company.

> **For a non-competition obligation, please refer to Section 8-1-2, Chapter 1 of Part I.**

8. (Return of Materials)

The Employee shall return all equipment (including books, keys, security cards, visiting cards, personal computer, and mobile phone) to the Company by the Last Working Day, and return, delete or destroy the Company's confidential information and related documents, electronic data, recording media, samples, and other materials in its control or possession in accordance with the Company's instructions.

9. (No Defamation)

The Employee shall commit to not conducting any act that would damage the reputation and creditworthiness of the Company or the Company's officers and employees after the Termination Date.

10. (Violation of the Agreement)

If the Employee violates any provision of the Agreement or its obligations provided in the work rules, the Employee shall return all early termination payments received pursuant to paragraph 2, item 2, immediately upon the Company's request. Where the Company incurs damage exceeding such amount, the Employee shall compensate the Company for such damage.

11. (Claims and Obligations)

The Company and the Employee mutually confirm that there are no claims and obligations between them other than those stipulated herein.

12. （管　　轄）

　甲及び乙は，本合意書に関連して生じる一切の法律上の争訟については，東京地方裁判所を第一審の専属的合意管轄裁判所とすることに合意する。

　本合意書の成立を証すため本書を２通作成し，甲，乙各１通を保有するものとする。

　●年●月●日

　甲　　住所

　　　　氏名　　　　　　　　　　　　　　　　　　㊞

　乙　　住所

　　　　氏名

　　　　　　　　　　　　　　　　　　　　　　　　㊞

12. (Jurisdiction)

The Company and the Employee agree to submit any legal disputes arising in relation to the Agreement to the exclusive jurisdiction of the Tokyo District Court as the court of first instance.

IN WITNESS WHEREOF, the Company and the Employee shall execute this Agreement in duplicate, and retain one copy each.

MM/DD/YY

The Company   Address:

                      Name: (seal)

The Employee   Address:

                      Name: (seal)

三六協定

時間外労働
休日労働　　に関する協定届

様式第9号の2（第16条第1項関係）

事業の種類	事業の名称
機械製造販売業	●●株式会社

		時間外労働をさせる必要のある具体的事由	業務の種類	労働者数（満18歳以上の者）
時間外労働	① 下記②に該当しない労働者	急な顧客との打合せのため	営業	10人
		納期切迫，集中受注，臨時受注のため	製造	30人
	② 1年単位の変形労働時間制により労働する労働者			

	休日労働をさせる必要のある具体的事由	業務の種類	労働者数（満18歳以上の者）
休日労働	急な顧客との打合せのため	営業	10人
	納期切迫，集中受注，臨時の受注のため	製造	30人

上記で定める時間数にかかわらず，時間外労働及び休日労働を合算した時間数は，1箇月について100時間未満でなければならず，かつ2箇月から6箇月までを平均して80時間を超過しないこと。

労働保険番号	□□□□□□□□□□□□□□
法人番号	□□□□□□□□□□□□□

事業の所在地（電話番号）					協定の有効期間	
（〒100-●●●●） 東京都千代田区大手町●-●-● （電話番号：03-●●●●-●●●●）					●●年●●月●●日から ●●年●●月●●日まで	
所定労働時間 (1日) (任意)	延長することができる時間					
	1日		1箇月 (①については45時間まで，②については42時間まで)		1年 (①については360時間まで，②については320時間まで)	
					起算日 (年月日)	●●年 ●●月●●日
	法定労働時間を超える時間数	所定労働時間を超える時間数 (任意)	法定労働時間を超える時間数	所定労働時間を超える時間数 (任意)	法定労働時間を超える時間数	所定労働時間を超える時間数 (任意)
7.5時間	3時間	3.5時間	30時間	40時間	250時間	370時間
7.5時間	2時間	2.5時間	15時間	25時間	150時間	270時間
所定休日 (任意)			労働させることができる 法定休日の日数		労働させることができる 法定休日における 始業及び終業の時刻	
土，日，祝日			1か月に1日		8：30～17：30	
土，日，祝日			1か月に1日		8：30～17：30	
☑ （チェックボックスに要チェック）						

様式第9号の2（第16条第1項関係）

時間外労働
休日労働　に関する協定届（特別条項）

臨時的に限度時間を超えて労働させることができる場合	業務の種類	労働者数（満18歳以上の者）	1日（任意) 延長することができる時間数	
			法定労働時間を超える時間数	所定労働時間を超える時間数（任意）
集中受注，臨時受注のため	製造	30人	6時間	6.5時間

限度時間を超えて労働させる場合における手続	協議
限度時間を超えて労働させる労働者に対する健康及び福祉を確保するための措置	(該当する番号)　(具体的内容) ①　産業医による面談

上記で定める時間数にかかわらず，時間外労働及び休日労働を合算した時間数は，1箇月について100時間未満でなければならず，かつ2箇月から6箇月までを平均して80時間を超過しないこと。

協定の成立年月日　　　　　●●年●月●日

協定の当事者である労働組合の名称（事業場の労働者の過半数で組織する労働組合）又は労働者の過半数を代表する者の協定の当事者（労働者の過半数を代表する者の場合）の選出方法（**投票による選挙**）

●●年●●月●●日
労働基準監督署長殿

1箇月 (時間外労働及び休日労働を合算した時間数。 100時間未満に限る。)				1年 (時間外労働のみの時間数。 720時間以内に限る。)			
				起算日 (年月日)	●●年●●月●●日		
限度時間を超えて労働させることができる回数(6回以内に限る。)	延長することができる時間及び休日労働の時間		限度時間を超えた労働に係る割増賃金率	延長することができる時間		限度時間を超えた労働に係る割増賃金率
	法定労働時間数を超える時間数と休日労働の時間数を合算した時間数	所定労働時間を超える時間数と休日労働の時間数を合算した時間数 (任意)		法定労働時間を超える時間数	所定労働時間を超える時間数 (任意)	
6回	90時間	100時間	35%	700時間	820時間	35%

☑
(チェックボックスに要チェック)

　　　　　　職名
　　　　　　氏名　●●●●
使用者　　職名　●●●●
　　　　　　氏名　●●●●　　　㊞

Labor-Management Agreement regarding Overtime Work and Work on Holidays

Labor-Management Agreement Regarding Overtime
Work and Work on Holidays

Form No. 9-2 (related to Article 16, Paragraph 1)

Type of business			Name of the enterprise	
Machinery manufacturing and sales business			●●K.K.	
Overtime work		Specific reasons for requiring Overtime Work	Type of services	Number of employees (aged 18 or over)
	(i) Employees who do not fall under category (ii)	Urgent client meeting	Sales	10
		Facing a deadline, rush of orders, and occasional orders	Manufacturing	30
	(ii) Employees who work under the Modified Annual Working Hours			
Work on holidays	Specific reasons for requiring Work on Holidays		Type of services	Number of employees (aged 18 or over)
	Urgent client meeting		Sales	10
	Facing a deadline, rush of orders, and occasional orders		Manufacturing	30
Irrespective of the number of hours set forth above, the total number of hours of Overtime Work and hours of Work on Holidays is less than 100 hours for a single month and not more than 80 hours per month on average over a two- to six-month period including the current month.				

Labor-Management Agreement regarding Overtime Work and Work on Holidays

| | | Labor insurance number | □□□□□□□□□□□□□□□□ |
| | | Corporation number | □□□□□□□□□□□□□ |

Location of the enterprise (Telephone number)	Effective period of the agreement
●-●-●, Otemachi, Chiyoda-ku, Tokyo 100-●●●● (Telephone number: 03-●●●●-●●●●)	From MM/DD/YY to MM/DD/YY

Designated working hours (per day) (optional)	Number of hours by which working hours can be extended						
	Number of hours by which working hours can be extended within a day		One month (up to 45 hours for category (i) and up to 42 hours for category (ii))		One year (up to 360 hours for category (i) and up to 320 hours for category (ii))		
					Initial date	MM/DD/YY	
	Number of hours exceeding statutory working hours	Number of hours exceeding designated working hours (optional)	Number of hours exceeding statutory working hours	Number of hours exceeding designated working hours (optional)	Number of hours exceeding statutory working hours	Number of hours exceeding designated working hours (optional)
7.5	3	3.5	30	40	250	370
7.5	2	2.5	15	25	150	270

Designated holidays (optional)	Number of statutory holidays on which the employer can require employees to work	Starting and finishing times on statutory holidays on which the employer can require employees to work
Saturdays, Sundays, national holidays	one day per month	8:30-17:30
Saturdays, Sundays, national holidays	one day per month	8:30-17:30

☑
(required to check the check box)

Labor-Management Agreement Regarding Overtime
Work and Work on Holidays (Special Provision)

Form No. 9-2 (related to Article 16, Paragraph 1)

Case where the employer can temporarily require employees to work in excess of maximum working hours	Type of service	Number of employees (aged 18 or over)	Number of hours by which working hours can be extended		
				One day (optional)	
				Number of hours exceeding statutory working hours	Number of hours exceeding designated working hours (optional)
Rush of orders and occasional orders	Manufacturing	30	6		6.5
Procedures to apply where the employer requires employees to work in excess of maximum working hours	Consultation				
Measures to secure the health and welfare of employees who the employer requires to work in excess of the maximum working hours	(Relevant number) (i)	(Specific measure) Interview with industrial physician			
Irrespective of the number of hours set forth above, the total number of hours of Overtime Work and hours of Work on Holidays is less than 100 hours for a single month and not more than 80 hours per month on average over a two- to six-month period including the current month.					

Execution date of this agreement MM/DD/YY

Name of the labor union (organized by a majority of the employees at the workplace) or title of the person representing a majority of the employees, who is a party to this agreement

Selection process of the parties to this agreement (in the case of the person representing a majority of the employees) **(Election by voting)**

MM/DD/YY

To the Chief of the Labor Standards Supervision Office

Labor-Management Agreement regarding Overtime Work and Work on Holidays

One month (total number of hours of Overtime Work and hours of Work on Holidays; limited to less than 100 hours)					One year (number of hours only of Overtime Work; limited to not more than 720 hours)		
					Initial date (MM/DD/YY)	MM/DD/YY	
Number of occasions that the employer can require employees to work in excess of maximum working hours (limited to not more than six occasions)	Number of hours by which working hours can be extended and number of hours of Work on Holidays		Extra wage rate for work exceeding maximum working hours	Working hours by which working hours can be extended		Extra wage rate for work exceeding maximum working hours
	Total number of hours exceeding statutory working hours and hours of Work on Holidays	Total number of hours exceeding designated working hours and hours of Work on Holidays (optional)		Number of hours exceeding statutory working hours	Number of hours exceeding designated working hours (optional)	
6	90	100	35%	700	820	35%

☑
(required to check the check box)

        Title   [Title]
        Name [Name of employee]
Employer Title   [Title]
        Name [Name of employer (Seal)]

第4部
FAQ

Part IV
FAQ

＜就業規則の作成・変更手続＞

1. 正社員以外の社員（パートタイマー，アルバイト，定年後の高年齢者継続雇用の嘱託社員等）について，正社員と別途に就業規則を作成する必要がありますか。作成する場合，過半数代表者からの意見聴取を含む手続はどのようにすればよいですか。

　正社員，パートタイマー，アルバイト，嘱託社員等の従業員の区分によって労働条件や福利厚生を異なるものとする場合は，それぞれの区分に応じた就業規則を作成する必要があります。
　作成手続としては，従業員区分を問わず，当該事業場の全従業員の過半数で組織する労働組合又は全従業員の過半数代表者からの意見聴取を行い，就業規則とあわせて意見書を労働基準監督署に提出することが必要です。また，あわせて，それぞれの従業員区分ごとの半数代表者の意見を聴くことが望ましいとされています。

2. 就業規則が英語の場合，労働基準監督署への届出も英語で行うことでよいですか。日本語訳を添付する必要はありませんか。

　就業規則の適用を受ける従業員全員が英語の就業規則を理解できる場合，英文のみの届出で足りることもありますが，労働基準監督署からは日本語訳の添付を求められることが通例のようです。また，英語の理解に疑義がある従業員がいる場合には，和文の作成及び届出が必要となります。
　なお，労働基準監督署から就業規則に関する質問がなされた場合には日本語での回答が必要であり，届出の際の必要書類（就業規則届，従業員代表の意見書等）は日本語での作成が求められます。

<Procedures for Providing and Changing Work Rules>

1. **Is it necessary to provide work rules applicable to non-regular employees (such as part-time employees, casual employees (*arubaito*), or short-term contract employees (*shokutaku shain*; ordinarily elderly workers who are working as regular employees after retirement)) separately from regular employees? If so, what kind of procedures should be taken, including soliciting opinions of a person representing a majority of the employees at the workplace?**

If an employer intends to set different employment conditions or welfare benefits for employees of different categories, such as full-time employees, part-time employees, casual employees (*arubaito*), or short-term contract employees (*shokutaku shain*), the employer must provide work rules applicable to each category of employees.

With respect to procedures, irrespective of the employee category, the employer must first solicit opinions from a labor union organized by a majority of the employees at the workplace, or a person representing a majority of the employees at the workplace; thereafter, the employer must submit the opinions together with the work rules to the labor standards supervision office. It is also advisable to solicit opinions from a person representing a majority of the employees for each employee category.

2. **If work rules are provided in English, is it sufficient to submit such work rules in English to the labor standards supervision office? Is it necessary to attach a Japanese translation?**

If all employees, who are covered by the work rules, understand the work rules in English, it may be sufficient to submit only the English version. The labor standards supervision office, however, customarily requires the Japanese translation to be attached. If there are employees, whose understanding of English is questionable, an employer must provide work rules in Japanese and submit them to the labor standards supervision office.

3. 和文・英文の就業規則が作成されており、どちらが正文か定められておらず、和文・英文の解釈に争いが生じた場合、どちらが優先されるのですか。

就業規則に和文と英文がある場合には、どちらを正文とするかあらかじめ定めておくことが重要ですが、仮に定められていなかった場合には、社内での適用慣行や従業員の認識等の実態に即して判断され、最終的には司法判断によることとなります。

＜採用＞

4. 従業員の雇用時に必要となる手続にはどのようなものがありますか。

従業員を雇用するに当たっては、主に、以下のような手続が必要となります。
(1) 雇用契約書の締結
(2) 労働条件通知書の交付（賃金・賞与、労働時間、契約期間、就業場所等の労働条件を書面に明記して交付）
(3) 労働保険（雇用保険、労災保険）、社会保険（厚生年金、健康保険）への加入
(4) 外国人を雇用する場合、外国人雇用報告をハローワークに届出
(5) 健康診断の実施
(6) （必要に応じて）秘密保持義務、競業避止義務、個人情報取扱等に関する覚書の締結、誓約書の提出要請

If the labor standards supervision office asks questions about the work rules, the employer must respond to them in Japanese, and provide requisite documents in Japanese (e.g., a written notification for work rules, opinions from the person representing a majority of employees, etc.) when submitting the work rules.

3. **If the work rules are provided both in Japanese and English without designating which version is the authentic text, and there is a dispute concerning the interpretation between the Japanese and the English version, which version should prevail?**

It is important to designate either the Japanese version or the English version of the work rules as the authentic text. If there is no such designation, the authentic text will be determined based on the customary application by the company or recognition by employees, and ultimately by judicial rulings.

<Recruitment>

4. **What types of procedures must an employer take when employing an employee?**

   When employing an employee, the following procedures are generally necessary:
   (1) Execute an employment agreement;
   (2) Deliver written employment conditions (deliver a written document specifying employment conditions such as wages, bonus, working hours, employment term, workplace, etc.);
   (3) Carry labor insurance (employment insurance and employee's compensation insurance), and social insurance (employee's pension insurance and health insurance);
   (4) Submit a foreigner employment report to Hello Work (public employment security office), if employing a foreign national;
   (5) Conduct a medical examination; and

5. 雇用契約書において定めた条項と法令や就業規則・労働協約の規定はどちらが優先されますか。

　雇用契約の内容は原則として雇用契約（使用者と従業員の合意）によりますが，強行法規に反する合意は無効となります。例えば，法定最低賃金を下回る給与額を合意しても，会社には法定最低賃金額以上の支払義務があり，会社が任意に解雇できると規定しても，客観的に合理的な理由を欠き，社会通念上相当であると認められない場合には解雇は無効となります。
　また，就業規則・労働協約を下回る労働条件を定める雇用契約は，その部分について無効となり，就業規則・労働協約の基準まで労働条件が引き上げられます。

6. 委任や請負の形式で契約すれば，雇用に関する労働関連法令は適用されないのでしょうか。また，委任や請負と雇用の違いは何ですか。

　会社の指揮命令に基づき労務を提供している実態がある場合は契約の形式を問わず「雇用」と判断されるため，形式的には委任や請負の名目で契約しても，労働関連法令が適用されます。
　委任と認められるには，受任者（取締役等）の広い裁量権が前提となり，また，請負は，労務提供ではなく「仕事の完成」が目的である必要があります。

(6) Execute a memorandum of understanding on confidentiality obligations, non-competition obligations, or handling of personal information, etc., and/or requesting submission of a pledge letter (as necessary).

5. **Which provisions will prevail? Provisions of the employment agreement, laws, work rules, or collective labor agreements?**

As a rule, details of an employment agreement are based on an agreement on employment (an agreement between the employer and the employee). Any agreement, however, that is against compulsory provisions are deemed invalid. For example, even if there is an agreement on a wage that is below the legal minimum wage, the company is obligated to pay wages equal to or more than the legal minimum wage. In addition, even if it is stipulated that the company may dismiss an employee at its discretion, such a dismissal will be invalid if it is not based on objectively reasonable grounds or is not socially acceptable.

Furthermore, if an employment agreement provides employment conditions less favorable than the work rules or collective labor agreements, such conditions that are less favorable will be invalid, and the remaining employment conditions will be raised to the standard of work rules or collective labor agreements.

6. **If an agreement is executed in the form of an entrustment (*Inin*) or a contract for work (*Ukeoi*), are work-related laws regarding employment inapplicable? What are the differences between an entrustment or contract for work and employment?**

Where an employee provides labor based on the company's direction or order, it is determined to be an "employment," regardless of the form of agreement. Therefore, work-related laws will apply even where an agreement is executed in the form of an entrustment or a contract for work.

In order for an agreement to be considered an entrustment, a trustee (e.g., a director,

＜競業避止義務＞

7. 退職する従業員が競合他社に就職しないよう，就業規則や雇用契約で制限を加えることができますか。

　　退職後の従業員には，憲法上の権利として職業選択の自由が認められているため，裁判例では，競業避止義務を課すことができる範囲を厳しく制限する傾向にあります。競業避止義務に関する制限が有効と認められるためには，制限の対象職種・期間・地域が最小限であり，また，代償措置が講じられている等，競業避止義務の内容が合理的なものでなければなりません。

＜労働者派遣＞

8. 労働者派遣法における派遣期間の制限について教えて下さい。

　　労働者派遣法においては，第1部第1章9-2の解説のとおり，派遣先の同一事業所において3年を超えて労働者派遣を受け入れてはならないという事業所単位の期間制限が存在しますが，当該制限との関係では，派遣先の事業所の過半数労働組合等の意見聴取手続を経ることにより3年を上限に期間を延長することができ，その後も同様の手続を経ることにより更に延長することが可能です。また，同法において，同一の派遣労働者を派遣先の事業所における同一の組織単位で3年を超えて就業させてはならないという個人単位の期間制限が存在し，当該制限との関係では，期間を延長し，同一の派遣労働者を同一の組織単位で就業させることはできないも

etc.) must have considerable discretionary power. To constitute a contract for work, the purpose must be for the "completion of work," not provision of labor.

<Non-Competition Obligation>

7. In the work rules or an employment agreement, is it possible to enforce a non-competition obligation on an employee after the termination of an employment relationship?

An employee is free to choose the place of employment after terminating the employment relationship, guaranteed under the Constitution. As such, judicial precedents tend to strictly limit the permissible scope of imposing a non-competition obligation. In order for the non-competition obligation restrictions to be considered valid, the details of such non-competition obligation must be reasonable—in that, the business line, period, or geographical area are minimally restricted, or compensatory measures are taken.

<Worker Dispatching>

8. Please inform us of restrictions on the length of time for dispatch arrangements under the Worker Dispatching Act.

The Worker Dispatching Act, as stated in the commentary in 9-2 of Chapter I. of Part I, sets forth a restriction on the length of time for dispatch arrangements with respect to the place of business, under which Clients may not accept any dispatched worker for a period exceeding 3 years at one particular place of business of the Client; however, in relation to that restriction, the length of time may be extended for up to 3 years by holding an opinion hearing procedure with a labor union organized by a majority of the employees at that Client's place of business, etc., and may be further extended by following a similar procedure thereafter. In addition, the Worker

のの、派遣労働者を事業所のある組織単位で3年間受け入れた後に、当該派遣労働者を別の組織単位で更に就業させることは可能です。この「組織」とは、課、グループ等の業務としての類似性や関連性のある組織で、かつ、その組織の長が業務の配分や労務管理上の指揮命令監督権限を有するものであって、派遣先における組織の最小単位よりも一般に大きな単位が想定されており（労働者派遣事業関係業務取扱要領第6の2(1)イ(ハ)②)、派遣先の実態を踏まえて判断する必要がありますが、派遣先の課やグループ等が異なれば、別の組織であると考えることができます。

さらに、いずれの期間制限についても、労働者派遣を受け入れていない期間が3ヶ月を超えて存在していれば、直前に受け入れていた労働者派遣の期間は通算されないため（派遣先が指針第2の14(3)及び(4))、その後、新たに労働者派遣を受け入れることが可能になります。

＜出向＞

9. 海外の親会社から日本国内の子会社へ出向させている場合、どのようにすれば当該出向者を解雇することができますか。また、どの国の法律が適用されますか。

Dispatching Act sets forth a restriction on the length of time for dispatch arrangements with respect to the individuals, under which the same dispatched worker may not be engaged in dispatch work for a period exceeding 3 years within the same organizational unit at the Client's place of business. In relation to that restriction, it is prohibited to extend the length of time and to cause the same dispatched worker to engage in dispatch work within the same organizational unit; however, after accepting a dispatched worker for 3 years within a certain organizational unit of a place of business, it is possible for Clients to have the dispatched worker further engage in dispatch work within another organizational unit of the same place of business. Such an "organizational unit" means any organizational unit whose tasks are similar or relevant to another, such as a section or group, etc., and whose head has the authority to assign tasks and to instruct, order, and supervise personnel administration; and this organizational unit is assumed to be generally larger than the Client's minimum organizational unit (No. 6-2(1)a(c)(ii) of the Administrative Instructions for Handling Worker Dispatching Business and Related Service). While we need to consider the Client's actual situation, a different section or group, etc. of the Client can be considered a separate organizational unit. Furthermore, for either restriction on the length of time for dispatch arrangements, if the period for which a Client has not accepted any dispatched worker exceeds 3 months, the length of time for the immediately preceding dispatch arrangement during which any dispatched worker has been accepted will not be included in the total length of time of accepting a dispatched worker (No. 2-14(3) and (4) of the Client Guidelines); therefore, the Client will thereafter be able to newly accept a dispatched worker.

<Secondment>

9. **If an employee is seconded from an overseas parent company to its Japanese subsidiary, how can the employer terminate such secondee's employment? Which country's laws are applicable to this termination?**

出向の場合，雇用契約関係は出向元と従業員の間に存続しており，出向者を解雇する権限は，出向先でなく出向元に属します。そのため，出向者を解雇するには，出向を解き，出向者を海外の親会社（出向元）に復帰させた上で，海外の親会社（出向元）が当該出向者を解雇することが必要です。この場合，解雇には海外の親会社（出向元）の本国法が適用されます。

＜労働時間＞

10. 年俸制の従業員にも，時間外労働に対する割増賃金を支払う必要はありますか。

　　年俸制であっても，基本的には，月給制の場合と同様，時間外労働に対する割増賃金を支払う必要があります。
　　なお，①手当として通常の賃金と区別され，②対象時間数と支給額が明示されており，③対象時間数を超過する時間外労働があった場合に精算されることが明確であるときには，見込まれる一定時間数の時間外労働に対して固定額の手当を設けることが可能であり，実務上，当該手当の対象時間内で時間外労働が収まるようにコントロールする運用も行われています。

11. 出張の際の移動時間は労働時間に含まれますか。

　　業務時間中に，会社の業務命令により会社と出張先との間を移動する場合には，労働時間と扱うことが妥当と思われます。一方，出張先への直行直帰については，移動時間を自由に利用できる場合には労働時間に含まれないとされることもあり得ますが，移動時間中も運搬商品の管理等を会

In the case of a secondment, an employee maintains an employment agreement with the company that seconded the employee. Furthermore, the right to terminate the secondee's employment belongs to the company that seconded the employee, not the company to which the employee is seconded to. As such, in order to terminate the secondee's employment, it is necessary to lift the secondment order, revert the secondee to the overseas parent company (the originating company), and then, the overseas parent company (the originating company) should terminate the secondee's employment. In such cases, the laws of the country where the overseas parent company (the originating company) is located will apply.

<Working Hours>

10. Is it necessary to pay extra wages for overtime work to employees working under an annual wage system?

An employer must pay extra wages for overtime work to employees working under an annual wage system, similar to employees working under a monthly wage system. It is possible to establish a fixed-amount allowance for estimated overtime work within certain hours where: (i) the amount is distinguished from regular wages as an allowance, (ii) the subject hours and payment amount are specified, and (iii) it is obvious that any overtime work exceeding the subject hours should be settled. Practically, the employer controls overtime work that is within the subject hours of the allowance.

11. During a business trip, is travel time included as working hours?

When an employee travels between the company and the business trip destination during business hours pursuant to the company's instruction, it is reasonable to consider this time as working hours. In the meantime, when the employee goes directly to or returns home directly from the business trip destination and freely uses

社の指示に基づいて行っている場合には，労働時間に含まれます。

12. テレワークを行う従業員の労働時間管理に関して，会社はどのような点に留意すべきですか。

　　テレワークとは，労働者として会社に雇用されている従業員が情報通信技術を利用して行う事業場外勤務のことをいい，業務を行う場所に応じて，①労働者の自宅で業務を行う在宅勤務，②労働者の属するメインのオフィス以外に設けられたオフィスを利用するサテライトオフィス勤務，③ノートパソコンや携帯電話等を活用して臨機応変に選択した場所で業務を行うモバイル勤務に分類されています。

　　テレワークは，従来の会社等での勤務に比して，従業員が働く時間や場所を柔軟に活用することを可能とし，ワークライフバランスの実現等にとってのメリットがある一方で，使用者により労働時間について適切に管理する必要があるものの，管理には一定の困難が伴うといったデメリットが指摘されています。特に，従業員のニーズに応じて，一定程度従業員が業務から離れる時間（いわゆる中抜け時間）を設ける場合には，中抜け時間の管理が難しいため，タイムシート等を用いて報告させる等の対応が望まれるところです。

　　なお，テレワークにより，労働者が使用者の事業場の外で業務に従事した場合において，以下の要件をいずれも満たす場合には，労働時間を算定し難いとして，事業場外労働に関するみなし労働時間制を適用することが可能となります（情報通信技術を利用した事業場外勤務の適切な導入及び実施のためのガイドライン）。

①　情報通信機器が，使用者の指示により常時通信可能な状態におくこととされていないこと（すなわち，情報通信機器を通じた使用者の指示に即応する義務がない状態であること）

②　随時使用者の具体的な指示に基づいて業務を行っていないこと

travel time, such time may be deemed to be not included in the working hours. If the employee, however, manages goods on transport during travel time pursuant to the company's instruction, it should be included in the working hours.

12. **Regarding working hours management of employees engaging in telework, what should an employer keep in mind?**

Telework means work conducted outside of the employees' usual workplace by persons who are employed by a company, using information and communication devices, and, depending on the place the work is conducted, there are the following categorizations of work: (i) Work-At-Home for work conducted at the employee's own house; (ii) Satellite Office Work for work using offices other than the main office to which an employee belongs; and (iii) Mobile Work for work conducted at places selected according to the circumstances by utilizing laptop computers and mobile phones, etc.

While telework enables the flexible utilization of hours and places in which employees work, in comparison to conventional work at a company, etc., and there are merits in terms of promoting "work-life balance," etc., there are indications of demerits such as certain difficulties in management, such that it is necessary to appropriately manage working hours by the employer. Particularly, in case of setting a certain number of hours in which employees are removed from work (so-called temporary leave hours) depending on the needs of employees, as there is a difficulty in managing temporary leave hours, it is desirable to formulate a response, such as by requiring employees who engage in telework to report using timesheets, etc.

Further, if an employee works outside of his or her usual workplace due to engaging in telework and fulfills all of the following requirements, it will be possible to apply a deemed-working-hours (minashi rodo jikan) policy regarding work conducted outside his or her usual workplace as there is a difficulty in calculating working hours (Guidelines for Appropriate Introduction and Implementation of Work Outside Workplace Using Information and Communication Technology).

13. 通常の労働時間規制の例外として、どのような制度があるのですか。

(1) フレックスタイム制

　フレックスタイム制は、労働時間、休憩、休日及び深夜労働に関する規定がすべて適用されるものの、労働者が各日の始業・終業時刻を自ら決定して労働することにより、業務と個人生活の調和を図る制度です（労働基準法32条の3）。

　具体的には、一定の清算期間内の労働時間を平均して法定労働時間内に収まっていれば、特定の1日又は1週の所定労働時間が法定労働時間を超過していても、法定時間外労働として取り扱わなくてよいとするものです。ただし、当該清算期間における労働時間の合計が清算期間における法定労働時間の枠を超えていれば、時間外割増賃金を支払う必要があり（労働基準法36条1項）、休憩（同法34条）、休日（同法35条）、休日・深夜の割増賃金（同法37条1項・3項）も適用されます。

　フレックスタイム制については、第2部第3章の解説もご参照ください。

(2) 裁量労働制

　裁量労働制は、労働時間、休憩、休日及び深夜労働に関する規定がすべて適用されるものの、実際の労働時間数に関係なく、一定の時間を労働時間とみなす制度です。したがって、みなし労働時間が法定労働時間を超えていれば時間外割増賃金を支払う必要があり、また、休憩、休日、休日・深夜の割増賃金も適用されます。

　裁量労働制は、実労働時間ではなく、労使であらかじめ定めた時間を

(i) Information and communication devices are not constantly available for communication, instructed by the employer (i.e., there is no obligation to immediately conform to the direction of the employer through information and communication devices); and

(ii) Work is not conducted under the specific direction of the employer at any time.

13. **What systems are there as exceptions to the ordinary working hour policies?**

(1) Flexible Working Hours

Flexible working hours allow an employee to determine the starting time and finishing time of each day on his/her own and to balance work and private life, subject to the application of all rules for the working hours, breaks, holidays and late hour work (Article 32-3 of the Labor Standards Act).

Specifically, if the average working hours in a specified settlement period are within the statutory working hours, any excess of the designated working hours on or in a given day or week over the statutory working hours is exempted from being treated as statutory overtime work. However, if the total working hours during the relevant settlement period exceed the limit on the statutory working hours for that settlement period, the employer must pay extra wages for overtime work (Article 36, Paragraph 1 of the Labor Standards Act); and the rules for breaks (Article 34 thereof), holidays (Article 35 thereof), and extra wages for work on holidays and late hour work (Article 37, Paragraphs 1 and 3 thereof) will also apply.

For details of the flexible working hours, please also refer to the commentary in Chapter III. of Part II.

(2) Discretionary Working System

The discretionary working system is a policy where working hours should be calculated by a specified hours ("deemed working hours"), irrespective of the

働いたものとみなすという点で，例外的な取扱いであるものの，使用者の一定の労働時間管理の下で労働者が働き，労働時間に応じた賃金が支払われるという大枠は維持されています。

裁量労働制については，第2部第3章の解説もご参照ください。

(3) 管理監督者

労働条件の決定その他労務管理について経営者と一体の立場にある管理監督者については，その権限や待遇等の特殊性から，法定労働時間，休憩及び休日に関する規制が適用除外とされています（労働基準法41条2号）。したがって，管理監督者に該当する者が法定時間外労働や法定休日労働を行っても，時間外割増賃金や休日割増賃金を支払う必要はありませんが，深夜労働に関する規定は適用されることから，深夜労働を行った場合の割増賃金は支払う必要があります。

本項で挙げる他の制度と異なり，ある労働者を管理監督者として労働時間規制の適用除外とするために必要な手続は法令に定められていませんが，裁判例や通達により管理監督者の要件が制限されており，その要件を満たすかどうかについて紛争が生じやすいため，運用には留意が必要です。

管理監督者については，第2部第3章第35条の解説もご参照ください。

(4) 高度プロフェッショナル制度

高度プロフェッショナル制度は，高度に専門的な業務に従事する労働者を対象として，労働者本人の同意を得ることや一定の健康管理等を行うことを条件として，労働時間，休憩，休日及び深夜の割増賃金に関する規定の全てを適用除外とする制度です。自己の裁量で自律的に働く労働者について，労働基準法の労働時間規制を完全に外し，労働時間ではなく成果や能力に応じて賃金が支払われることとする，新しい働き方といえます。

高度プロフェッショナル制度については，第2部第3章の解説もご参照ください。

actual number of working hours, subject to the application of all rules for the working hours, breaks, holidays and late hour work. Accordingly, if the deemed working hours exceed the statutory working hours, the employer must pay extra wages for overtime work. The rules for breaks, holidays, and extra wages for work on holidays and late hour work will also apply.

The discretionary working system is an exceptional treatment in that an employee is deemed to have worked for the hours provided in the labor-management agreement, instead of the actual working hours. However, it maintains the general framework where an employee works under the employer managing the working hours and receives wages according to the working hours.

For details of the discretionary working system, please also refer to the commentary in Chapter III. of Part II.

(3) Managers and Supervisors

Managers and supervisors who, together with the management of the Company, engage in administration such as determining employment conditions of the other employees, are exempted from the regulations for statutory working hours, breaks and holidays, due to the special nature of their authority, treatment and other factors (Article 41, Item 2 of the Labor Standards Act). Accordingly, if an employee who is a manager or supervisor engages in statutory overtime work or works on a statutory holiday, there is no need to pay extra wages for overtime work or work on holidays; but extra wages for late hour work, if engaged in, must be paid as the rules for late hour work will apply.

Unlike other systems discussed in this Section, no laws or regulations provide procedures required to exempt an employee from working hour policies on account of being a manager or supervisor. However, it is necessary to take note in operating the system as court precedents and governmental notices strictly regulate the requirements for an employee to be a manager or supervisor, and whether an employee satisfies the requirements is prone to develop into a

<有給休暇＞

14. 未消化分の有給休暇を買い取る義務がありますか。

　　使用者に未消化分の有給休暇を買い取る法令上の義務はありません。もっとも，労働協約，就業規則又は雇用契約において未消化分の有給休暇の買取制度を定めた場合には，使用者に未消化分の有給休暇を買い取る契約上の義務が生じます。

15. 有給休暇は1年間のうちに消化しなければ失効することとしてよいですか。

　　有給休暇を取得する請求権は，付与日から2年間の消滅時効に服すると一般に解されており，当該年度内に有給休暇が全部消化されなかった場合，残日数は翌年度まで繰り越されます。したがって，有給休暇を1年間

dispute.

For details of managers and supervisors, please also see the commentary on Article 35 in Chapter III. of Part II.

(4) Advanced Professionals System

The advanced professionals system is a policy where an employee engaged in highly skilled work is exempted from all rules on working hours, breaks, and extra wages for work on holidays and late hour work, subject to conditions including the employee's consent and providing specified health management. It is a new working rule where employees working autonomously at their discretion are completely exempted from the working hours regulations under the Labor Standards Act, and where they receive wages according to their work performance and capabilities, instead of their working hours.

For details of the advanced professionals system, please also see the commentary in Chapter III of Part II.

<Paid Leave>

14. Is an employer obligated to purchase back unused paid leave?

An employer is not legally obligated to purchase back unused paid leave. If the employer, however, specifically establishes a paid-leave purchase system in collective labor agreements, work rules or an employment agreement, the employer is obligated to purchase back unused paid leave.

15. Is it acceptable to stipulate that a paid-leave claim that has not been used within a one-year period will expire?

The general interpretation is that a claim for paid leave is subject to an extinctive prescription of 2 years from the day it is granted. If any paid leave is not used during the applicable year, then this leave may be carried forward to the following year.

のうちに消化しなければ失効するとすることはできません。

＜賃金＞

16. 給与・賞与の支給に当たって株式を交付することはできますか。

　「賃金」は，原則として，全額を通貨で支払う必要があり（通貨払の原則，全額払の原則），給与及び支給条件が明示されている賞与は「賃金」に該当するため，その一部又は全部を株式で支払うことはできません。
　なお，ストック・オプションの付与は，従業員に権利行使の有無や時期の決定権があり，利益の発生時期・額が従業員の判断に任されていることから，労働の対償ではなく，賃金に当たらないとされています。もっとも，賃金の支払に代えてストック・オプションを付与することは，通貨払の原則に反し違法となります。

17. 年俸制の場合は，自由に賞与を設定することができますか。

　賞与の支払額・年俸額に占める割合・支払時期・支払回数等は，自由に設定することができます。また，就業規則等に規定すれば，能力や業績に連動してその都度賞与額を決定することも可能です。
　ただし，年俸制の場合でも，各月の給与の支払は必要であり，当該給与の額は法定最低賃金以上とする必要があります。

18. 年俸制の場合，年俸の支払回数は自由に決定してよいですか。

Therefore, it is not possible to stipulate that the claim for paid leave will expire after one year.

\<Wages\>

16. Is it possible to distribute stock instead of paying a salary or a bonus?

As a principle, "wages" must be paid in full in currency (the principle of paying in currency; the principle of paying in full). Compensation and bonus for which payment conditions are stipulated constitutes "wages," and it is not possible to pay part or all of them in stock.

In the case of a stock option grant, an employee has the right to decide whether and when he/she will exercise the option, and it is within the employee's discretion to decide the timing and profit amount. Thus, a stock option grant is not construed to constitute compensation for labor. Therefore, it is not a wage. Please note that a stock option grant instead of a wage payment violates the principle of paying in currency, and is therefore, illegal.

17. Is it possible to freely fix the bonus amount under the annual wage system?

An employer may freely fix the bonus payment amount, percentage against the annual wage, payment timing or frequency. By stipulating it in the work rules, it is possible to fix the bonus amount each time in tandem with the employee's ability or performance.

Under the annual wage system, however, it is necessary to pay compensation each month, and the amount should be no less than the legal minimum wage.

18. Is it possible to freely set the number of annual wage payments under the annual wage system?

賃金は，毎月1回以上，一定の期日を定めて支払わなければならないため（毎月1回以上一定期日払の原則），年俸制であっても，分割して毎月1回以上の特定の日に支払う必要があります。なお，具体的な支払日や月1回を超える支払回数については，雇用契約等で自由に決めることができます。

19. 従業員の能力が低い場合や業績が悪い場合に，給与額を減額することは可能でしょうか。年俸制と月給制で違いはありますか。

月給制の場合，①能力・業績に連動して賃金額が増額又は減額することが就業規則等において定められており，かつ，②公平性（複数評価による恣意性の排除等）及び透明性（客観的評価基準の設定等）が担保された能力・業績の評価が行われる場合には，就業規則等に則って給与を減額することも可能です。

年俸制の場合は，契約で毎年金額を改めて定めることとされている場合が多いですが，年俸額決定のための成果・業績評価基準，年俸額決定手続，減額の限界等が制度化されて雇用契約や就業規則に明示されており，かつ，その内容が公正な場合には，会社に評価決定権が認められ，減額を含む年俸額の見直しが可能となります。

＜服務規律＞

20. 社内調査等のため，会社支給のパソコンで送受信された従業員のメー

Since an employer must pay wages at least once a month on a definite date (the principle of paying wages more than once a month on definite dates), it must also pay annual wages in installments at least once a month on a definite date under the annual wage system. The employer may stipulate freely a specific payment date or the payment frequency of more than once a month in an employment agreement.

19. **Is it possible to decrease the compensation amount of an employee if the employee's ability is low or performance is poor? Are there any differences between an annual wage system and a monthly payment system?**

In the case of a monthly payment system, if it is stipulated in the work rules that (i) the amount of wages may be increased or decreased in tandem with an employee's ability or performance, and (ii) the employee's ability and performance are fairly assessed (avoiding arbitrariness through multiple assessments, etc.) and the assessment procedure is transparent (setting objective assessment criteria, etc.), it is possible to decrease the compensation amount in accordance with the provisions of the work rules.

In the case of an annual wage system, the amount of annual wages is generally arranged to be decided each year. If there are fair and transparent measures to determine the amount of annual wages, such as: an evaluation criteria for the employee's accomplishments and performance; a procedure on how to decide the annual wage amount; and a limitation on reducing the amount etc., and these measures are stipulated in the work rules or the contract, it is possible for an employer to decrease the amount of annual wages according to an evaluation by the employer at the time of annual revision.

<Work Discipline>

20. **What things should an employer keep in mind when inspecting employee's**

ルを閲覧する際，どのような事項に留意するべきですか。

　調査の合理的必要性があり，手段方法が相当である場合には，会社の設備・備品を用いたメールのやり取りを閲覧することは可能です。ただし，あらかじめ，メールの利用規程等において，調査・閲覧権限について明示・周知しておくことが望ましいと考えられます。
　また，パソコンを閲覧した際に，個人情報を取得することとなるときには，使用者は，個人情報保護法に基づき，調査により取得する情報の利用目的（営業秘密の漏洩防止等）を特定し，公表又は通知する必要があり，従業員の同意を得ずに，取得した情報を当該目的外のために利用したり，第三者に提供したりしてはならないことに留意しなければなりません。

＜労働契約の終了＞

21.　有期労働契約の締結時に，期間満了時の紛争を回避するため，どのような対応を行っておく必要がありますか。

　手続面では，契約締結時に，書面で，有期契約である旨及び更新予定の有無を明示し，更新時は，契約書の再度の締結を行うべきです。
　また，漫然と契約更新を続けた場合には，①通算5年を超えて有期労働契約を継続している従業員には無期労働契約への転換申込権が生じるほか，②通算期間が5年未満であっても，更新への合理的な期待がある場合や無期契約と実質的に同様の状況がある場合には，契約更新拒絶が「解雇」と同様に扱われ，客観的に合理的な理由を欠き，社会通念上相当であると認められない場合は，従業員が希望すれば，会社は，従前の有期労働契

e-mails that were sent/received using the company's PC during an internal investigation?

If an investigation is reasonably necessary and is conducted in an appropriate manner, an employer can view employee's e-mail exchanges using the company's equipment or property. It is, however, advisable to specify and notify beforehand in e-mail usage regulations regarding the ban on personal use and the employer's authority to investigate and view e-mails.

When viewing employee's emails, the employer will be in a position of dealing with the employee's personal information. As such, the employer should keep in mind that it must identify, publicize, or notify the purpose of using the information that may be acquired through an investigation (such as the prevention of business information leakage) pursuant to the Act on the Protection of Personal Information. Furthermore, it must neither use the acquired information for any purposes other than the above-mentioned purpose, nor provide it to any third party without obtaining the employee's consent.

<Termination of an Employment Agreement>

21. When entering into a Fixed Term Employment Agreement, what measures, if any, should be taken in order to avoid disputes upon the expiration of the term?

With respect to procedures, an employer should provide in writing at the time of entering into the agreement, that the agreement is on a fixed term and whether it plans to renew the agreement. Furthermore, upon renewal, the company executes the agreement in writing again.

If the employer continues to renew the agreement without much contemplation, (i) an employee with a Fixed Term Employment Agreement that has continued for more than 5 years has a right to propose a conversion to a Non-Fixed Term Employment Agreement, and (ii) even for employees whose aggregate employment period is less

約と同一の条件で契約を締結したものとみなされる可能性があります。したがって，会社としては，有期雇用の従業員であっても，その能力及び適性を早期に適切に評価するように努め，長期的に必要な人材でないと判断される場合は，早期に契約関係を終了させるといった運用が有効です。

22. 従業員を解雇する際，どのような名目の金員をいくら支払わなければなりませんか。

　解雇に当たっては，原則として，30日以上前に従業員に解雇予告をするか，予告手当として30日分以上の平均賃金を支払わなければなりません。また，雇用契約や就業規則に規定されている退職金等の支払も必要となります。
　さらに，解雇を行った場合は，客観的に合理的な理由を欠き，社会通念上相当であると認められない場合は無効とされる可能性があり，また，この解雇の有効性は裁判において厳しく判断されることから，実務上は，合意退職が多く行われており，その場合，合意を取り付けるためのインセンティブとして上乗せの退職金が支払われることがあります。この上乗せの退職金の額等の条件は，基準があるものではなく，従業員との交渉によって定められることとなります。

23. うつ病等のメンタル疾病で休職している従業員を解雇するには，どの

than 5 years, if there is reasonable expectation for renewal, or the reality is substantially similar to a Non-Fixed Term Employment Agreement, the employer's refusal to renew the agreement will be treated similarly as a "dismissal." If this refusal is not based on objectively reasonable grounds or is not socially acceptable, it is possible to consider that the employer has executed a new agreement on similar conditions to that of the previous Fixed Term Employment Agreement, if the employee desires to do so. Therefore, it is effective to proceed as follows: the company will try to evaluate the ability and aptitude of an employee under a Fixed Term Employment agreement at an early stage; thereafter, if the company determines that the employee would not be required in the long run, it will terminate his or her employment at an early stage.

22. **When terminating the employment of an employee, what type and amount of remuneration must an employer pay?**

As a rule, in order to dismiss an employee, the employer must provide a 30-day advance notice of dismissal, or pay a dismissal notice allowance that corresponds to his or her average wages for 30 days or more. The employer must also pay a severance payment as stipulated in the employment agreement or the work rules.

In addition, if the dismissal is not based on objectively reasonable grounds or is not socially acceptable, the dismissal is likely to be deemed void, and the validity of the dismissal is strictly determined at a trial. Therefore, practically, a termination by mutual agreement is common; in such cases, an extra severance payment may be paid as an incentive to reach such an agreement. There are no standard conditions for this extra severance payment, and the conditions will be determined upon negotiation with the employee.

23. **How can an employer terminate the employment of an employee who has been**

ようにすればよいですか。

　業務外の傷病による休職期間満了後，会社が，傷病が治癒しておらず職務に堪えられないため復帰が相当ではないと判断した場合には，当該休職期間の満了をもって解雇する又は当然に退職とする旨の規定を，就業規則に置くことが有効です。もっとも，治癒したかどうかについては争いになりやすいため，復職に当たっては，会社の指定する医師の診断書を提出させる等の手続をあらかじめ就業規則に規定しておくことが望ましいです。
　うつ病等の疾病が業務に起因するものである場合には，療養期間及びその後30日間は解雇することができず，通常，労災保険が適用されて保険から給付が行われることとなります。療養開始後３年間を経過した時点で労災保険から傷病補償年金の支給を受けている場合，又は，会社が打切補償（平均賃金の1200日分）を支払った場合には，解雇制限が解除され，解雇が可能となります。

＜その他＞

24.　社内で働く女性について，雇用管理上どのような点に配慮すべきでしょうか。

　女性労働者については，男女雇用機会均等法が，募集・採用，配置・昇進・降格・教育訓練，一定範囲の福利厚生，職種・雇用形態の変更，退職勧奨・定年・解雇・労働契約の更新についての，性別を理由とする差別の禁止（同法５条，６条），間接的な差別の禁止（同法７条），婚姻，妊娠・出産等を理由とする不利益取扱いの禁止（同法９条），事業主に対するセクシュアル・ハラスメント及び妊娠・出産等に関するハラスメント対

placed on a leave of absence due to mental illness, such as clinical depression?

It is effective to stipulate in the work rules that an employee will be dismissed or that the employment will be automatically terminated when an employer determines that an employee is unable to perform his/her duties due to a non-work related mental or physical disorder after the expiration of the leave-of-absence period. It is disputable, however, whether the employee is completely cured. Therefore, it is advisable to stipulate in the work rules the procedures for returning to work, such as the submission of a medical certificate from the doctor designated by the company.

If the source of clinical depression is work-related and attributable to the company's business, the company cannot dismiss the employee during the medical treatment period and for the subsequent 30 days, during which period the Industrial Accident Compensation Insurance Act will apply to this employee and he/she will usually receive insurance benefits. If the employee is still receiving illness and injury compensation pension after 3 years from the date of commencement of medical treatment, or compensation for discontinuance (equivalent to average wages for 1,200 days), restrictions on dismissal will be lifted, and the company may dismiss the employee.

<Other>

24. **Regarding female employees working in the company, what should an employer keep in mind in terms of employment management?**

Regarding female employees, Act on Securing, Etc. of Equal Opportunity and Treatment between Men and Women in Employment (the Equal Employment Opportunity Act) prescribes prohibition of discrimination on the basis of sex of employees in recruitment and employment, assignment, promotion, demotion, and training, a certain scope of welfare benefits, change in job type and employment status, encouragement of resignation, mandatory retirement age, dismissal, and

策の義務付け(同法11条,11条の2)等を定めています。

　この他,女性の職業生活における活躍推進については,平成28年4月に女性の職業生活における活躍の推進に関する法律(女性活躍推進法)が施行されており,301人以上の労働者を雇用する事業主は,女性の職業生活における活躍推進に関する取組みの内容等を記載した行動計画を定め,都道府県労働局へ届け出ることが必要とされています(同法8条1項)。

　また,現時点では,企業に対し,役員・管理職に占める女性の割合を一定以上とするような法的義務は課せられていませんが,男女雇用機会均等法においては,労働者の募集,採用,配置,昇進,教育訓練,職種の変更及び雇用形態の変更において女性労働者を男性労働者に比べて有利に取り扱う措置(ポジティブ・アクション,アファーマティブ・アクション)が上記の性別を理由とする差別及び間接的な差別に該当しないことが定められています(同法8条)。もっとも,このような有利な取扱いが認められるのは,一定の区分・職務・役職において女性労働者が男性労働者と比較して相当程度少ない(女性の割合が4割を下回っている)等の場合に限られる点には留意が必要です(事業主が適切に対処するための指針(平成18年厚生労働省告示第614号)第2,14(1),改正雇用の分野における男女の均等な機会及び待遇の確保等に関する法律の施行について(平成18年10月11日雇児発第1011002号,最終改正平成28年8月2日雇児発0802第1号)第2,3(6))。

renewal of the labor contract (Articles 5 and 6 of the Equal Employment Opportunity Act), prohibition of indirect discrimination (Article 7 of the Equal Employment Opportunity Act), prohibition of disadvantageous treatment by reason of marriage, pregnancy, childbirth, etc. (Article 9 of the Equal Employment Opportunity Act), and obligating employers to take preventive measures against sexual harassment and harassment regarding pregnancy and childbirth, etc. (Articles 11 and 11-2 of the Equal Employment Opportunity Act).

In addition, regarding promotion of women's participation and advancement in the workplace, the Act on Promotion of Women's Participation and Advancement in the Workplace (Women's Participation and Advancement Promotion Act) was implemented in April 2016; and employers who employ 301 or more employees are required to prescribe action plans stating the contents of the initiatives for the promotion of women's participation and advancement in the workplace, etc. and to notify prefectural labor offices (Articles 8 Paragraph 1 of the Woman's Participation and Advancement Promotion Act).

Also, at present, even though companies are not legally obligated to ensure that the ratio of women in officer and management roles is a certain level or above, under the Equal Employment Opportunity Act, measures to treat female employees favorably in comparison to male employees for recruitment and employment, assignment, promotion, and training, change in job type and employment status (positive action, affirmative action) are prescribed not to fall under discrimination on the basis of sex or indirect discrimination above (Article 8 of the Equal Employment Opportunity Act). However, it is necessary to note that such favorable treatment is approved only in cases where female employees are considerably fewer than male employees concerning certain categories, duties, and titles (ratio of women is 40% or below), etc. (Guidelines on Ways for Employers to Take Appropriate Measures (Public Notice of the Ministry of Health, Labour and Welfare No. 614 of 2006) II, 14(1), On Implementation of the Amendment to the Act on Securing, Etc. of Equal Opportunity and Treatment between Men and Women in Employment (Circular Notice, Kojihatsu No. 1011002, October 11, 2006, last amendment Circular Notice, Kojihatsu 0802 No.

25. LGBTに当たる社員に対し，会社としてどのような配慮をすればよいでしょうか。

　LGBTとは，女性の同性愛者（Lesbian: レズビアン），男性の同性愛者（Gay: ゲイ），両性愛者（Bisexual: バイセクシャル），こころの性とからだの性の不一致（Transgender: トランスジェンダー）を総称した概念です。近年公表された厚生労働省の通達により，LGBTに対してもセクシュアル・ハラスメントは成立することが確認されており，会社は，LGBTに対する嫌がらせを含めたセクシュアル・ハラスメントにより，労働者の就業環境が害されたりすることのないよう，雇用管理上必要な措置を講じる必要があります。

　現時点では，以上より更に進んで，LGBTに対して特別に配慮する法的義務が会社に課されているわけではありませんが，あらゆる人材を組織に迎え入れて活用するという観点からは，LGBTであることにより不利益を被らないような職場環境を整備することが望ましいといえます。この場合，例えば，トイレ・更衣室などの社内設備や健康診断実施時における配慮，あるいは同性婚カップルの福利厚生制度上の取扱いが検討の対象となりえます。

　また，LGBTに該当することや，自己の性自認及び性的指向等は，個人のプライバシーにわたる事項ですので，会社としては，かかる事項を公表するか否かに関して，社員の自己決定権を十分に尊重する必要があります。会社が社員にこれらの事項を公表するよう強要した場合はもちろん，他の社員がこれらの事項を暴露したことを，会社として十分認識しつつ放置した場合には，会社自身に対して訴訟が提起されるリスクもありますので注意が必要です。

1, August 2, 2016) II, 3(6)).

25. **Regarding employees who fall under the category of LGBT, what should an employer keep in mind as a company?**

LGBT is a collective concept for female homosexual (Lesbian), male homosexual (Gay), bisexual (Bisexual), and people who have a mental gender identity or a gender expression that differs from their physical or assigned sex (Transgender). Based on the recent circular of the Ministry of Health, Labour and Welfare, it was confirmed that sexual harassment also applies toward LGBT; furthermore, it is mandatory for companies to implement the statutorily required measures in terms of employment management so that employees' working environments will not be affected by sexual harassment, including harassment towards LGBT.

Currently, even though companies are not legally obligated to particularly consider LGBT further than the foregoing, from the viewpoint of utilizing various personnel by welcoming them into organizations, it is considered desirable to develop a working environment in which employees will not be disadvantaged just because they are LGBT. For example, consideration regarding internal facilities such as bathrooms and dressing rooms, consideration regarding medical examinations, and the handling of same-sex marriage couples in a welfare benefits system should be discussed.

Also, as LGBT applicability and one's own gender identity and sexual orientation, etc. are matters relating to individual privacy, companies are required to adequately respect an employee's right of self-determination regarding the question of whether to come-out. It is necessary to note that the company owes the risk of lawsuits being filed in cases where the company forces its employees to come-out, and where the company does not take any action and leaves the situation as it is when other employees are divulging or "outing" the LGBT employees, and the company is fully aware of such situations.

<民法改正>

26. 平成32年（2020年）4月1日施行の改正民法により，雇用に関する規律に変更は生じますか。

　平成32年（2020年）4月1日施行の改正民法において，雇用に関する規律に変更が生じる主要な点としては，以下の，①履行の割合に応じた報酬に関する規定の新設，及び②期間の定めのない雇用における解約の申入れに関する規律の改正があります。

①履行の割合に応じた報酬に関する規定の新設について

　現行民法に明文の規定は存在しないものの，労働者は，たとえ自らの責めに帰すべき事由によって中途で労働に従事することができなくなった場合であっても，既に労働に従事した部分についてはその履行の割合に応じて報酬を請求することができると解釈されていたところ，これを明確化するために，改正民法において，労働者は，(1)使用者の責めに帰することができない事由によって労働に従事することができなくなった場合，又は(2)雇用が履行の中途で終了した場合，既にした履行の割合に応じて報酬を請求することができる旨が明文化されました（改正民法624条の2）。

　なお，労働者は，使用者の責めに帰すべき事由によって労働に従事することができなくなった場合においては，報酬の全額を請求できます（民法536条2項）。

②期間の定めのない雇用における解約の申入れに関する規律の改正について

　現行民法において，労働者が期間の定めのない雇用の解約の申入れをするに当たり，(1)当事者が6か月未満の期間によって報酬を定めた場合には当期の前半に次期以後の解約の申入れをすることが必要であり，(2)当事者が6か月以上の期間によって報酬を定めた場合には3か月前に解約の申入れをすることが必要であるものとされていました（現行民法627条2項3項）。しかし，これでは労働者の辞職の自由が過度に制約されていると

\<Amendment to the Civil Code\>

26. Will there be any changes to the employment-related discipline due to the amended Civil Code to be enforced on April 1, 2020?

The main points regarding future changes to the employment-related discipline due to the amended Civil Code to be enforced on April 1, 2020 are (i) the newly established provision regarding remuneration in proportion to work performed, and (ii) the amendment to the provisions regarding the request to terminate employment with an indefinite term, as stated below.

(i) Newly Established Provision Regarding Remuneration in Proportion to Work Performed

Although the current Civil Code has no express provisions, it has been construed that even if an employee ceases to be able to engage in work due to reasons attributable to the employee, the employee may demand remuneration in proportion to the work already performed. In order to clarify this, the amended Civil Code provides that (1) if an employee ceases to be able to engage in work due to reasons not attributable to the employer, or (2) if employment terminates while performing work, the employee may demand remuneration in proportion to the work already performed (Article 624-2 of the amended Civil Code).

Further, if an employee ceases to be able to engage in work due to reasons attributable to the employer, the employee may demand remuneration in full (Article 536, Paragraph 2 of the Civil Code).

(ii) Amendment to the Provisions Regarding the Request to Terminate Employment with Indefinite Term

Under the current Civil Code, when an employee requests to terminate employment with an indefinite term, (1) if the parties specified remuneration with reference to a period of less than 6 months, the employee is required to request to terminate

して，改正民法においては，当事者が期間によって報酬を定めたか否かを問わず，労働者は，いつでも解約の申入れをすることができ，雇用は，解約の申入れの日から2週間を経過することによって終了するものとされました（改正民法627条）。

なお，改正民法においては，「月又はこれより短い時期によって定めた使用人の給料に係る債権」を1年の消滅時効とする規定を含め，職業別の短期消滅時効が廃止され，一般債権の消滅時効期間は，権利行使できることを知った時から5年間，権利行使できる時から10年間に統一されました（改正民法166条1項）。労働基準法115条は，民法の消滅時効に関する規定の特例として，労働基準法の規定による賃金，災害補償その他の請求権の消滅時効期間を2年間（退職手当については5年間）と定めており，改正民法施行後も当該特例は維持されますが，民法改正を踏まえて，厚生労働省において今後の賃金等請求権の消滅時効の在り方について検討が進められています。

employment with respect to the following period of time onward in the first half of the current period, and (2) if the parties specified remuneration with reference to a period of 6 months or more, the employee is required to request to terminate employment 3 months before the termination (Article 627, Paragraphs 2 and 3 of the current Civil Code). However, it has been argued that this provision excessively limits employees' freedom to resign; therefore, the amended Civil Code provides that regardless of whether the parties specified remuneration with reference to a period, an employee may request to terminate employment at any time, and employment shall terminate on the expiration of 2 weeks from the day of the request to terminate (Article 627 of the amended Civil Code).

The amended Civil Code will abolish the system of short-term extinctive prescription that varies according to occupation, including the provision that "a claim pertaining to the salary of an employee which is fixed by 1 month or any shorter period" shall be extinguished by prescription if not exercised for 1 year. Furthermore, it will establish a uniform provision that a general claim shall be extinguished by prescription if not exercised for 5 years from the time when the creditor is aware that it can exercise the right, or if not exercised for 10 years from the time when the creditor is able to exercise the right (Article 166, Paragraph 1 of the amended Civil Code). As an exception to the provisions relating to extinctive prescription under the Civil Code, Article 115 of the Labor Standards Act provides that claims for wages, accident compensation, and other claims under the Labor Standards Act shall be extinguished by prescription if not exercised for 2 years (claims for retirement allowances shall be extinguished by prescription if not exercised for 5 years). This exception will be maintained after the amended Civil Code comes into effect. However, in light of the amendment to the Civil Code, the Ministry of Health, Labour and Welfare has advanced discussions on future ideal approaches to this exception.

■〈初版〉編著者紹介

森　倫洋

杉原　えり

上村　文

池田　崇

木島　彩

■〈第2版〉編著者紹介

森　倫洋

池田　崇

木島　彩

木野　博徳

高山　陽太郎

松井　博昭

由良　知也

金子　正紀

下向　智子

村田　智美

黒田　はるひ

鈴木　正靖

中村　崇志

大石　真帆

塚本　健夫

料屋　恵美

■〈第3版〉編著者紹介

森　倫洋（もり　みちひろ）

1993年	東京大学法学部卒業
1995年	司法修習修了（47期），判事補任官（東京地方裁判所判事補（民事部・民事執行部勤務），その後，最高裁判所事務総局民事局付，福岡地方裁判所判事補（労働部勤務）を歴任（～2005年まで））
1999年	ハーバード大学ロースクール卒業（LL. M.）
2005年	弁護士登録，西村あさひ法律事務所入所
現　在	西村あさひ法律事務所パートナー

〈著作〉

『アジア進出・撤退の労務』（編著，中央経済社，2017年），『現代型契約と倒産法』（共著，商事法務，2015年），『会社裁判にかかる理論の到達点』（共著，商事法務，2014年），『詳説　倒産と労働』（編著，商事法務，2013年），『現代民事法の実務と理論』（共著，金融財政事情研究会，2013年），『概説　倒産と労働』（編著，商事法務，2012年），『ビジネスパーソンのための企業法務の教科書』（共著，文藝春秋，2012年），『アメリカ事業再生の実務―連邦倒産法Chapter11とワークアウトを中心に』（共著，金融財政事情研究会，2011年）ほか著作・論文多数

松井　博昭（まつい　ひろあき）

2006年	早稲田大学法学部卒業
2008年	早稲田大学法科大学院修了
2009年	弁護士登録，西村あさひ法律事務所入所
2017-2018年	ペンシルベニア大学アジア法学誌編集委員
2018年	ペンシルベニア大学ロースクール卒業（LL. M.）
2018-2019年8月（予定）	Okada Law Firm（香港）（西村あさひ法律事務所の香港プラクティスにおける連絡先事務所）出向

現　在　　西村あさひ法律事務所アソシエイト（Okada Law Firm（香港）出向中）

〈著作〉

『働き方改革とこれからの時代の労働法』（共著，商事法務，2018年），『アジア進出・撤退の労務』（編著，中央経済社，2017年），『2015年 派遣法改正と実務対応』（共著，第二東京弁護士会，2016年），『日本企業のためのシンガポール進出戦略ガイドQ&A』（共著，中央経済社，2014年）ほか著作・論文多数

木島　彩（きじま　あや）

2006年　　東京大学法学部卒業
2008年　　東京大学法科大学院修了
2009年　　弁護士登録，西村あさひ法律事務所入所
現　在　　西村あさひ法律事務所アソシエイト

〈著作〉

『働き方改革とこれからの時代の労働法』（共著，商事法務，2018年）

塚本　健夫（つかもと　たけお）

2005年　　慶應義塾大学法学部卒業
2005年　　東海旅客鉄道株式会社（〜2008年）
2011年　　東京大学法科大学院修了
2012年　　弁護士登録，西村あさひ法律事務所入所
現　在　　西村あさひ法律事務所アソシエイト

〈著作〉

『働き方改革とこれからの時代の労働法』（共著，商事法務，2018年），『フリーランス＆"複"業で働く！完全ガイド』（共同監修，日本経済新聞出版社，2018年），『労働事件ハンドブック2018年』（共著，労働開発研究会，2018年），『危機管理法大全』（共著，商事法務，2016年）ほか著作・論文多数

中川　佳宣（なかがわ　よしのぶ）

2005年　　中央大学法学部中退
　　　　　（中央大学法科大学院へ飛び入学）
2008年　　中央大学法科大学院修了
2009年　　弁護士登録，西村あさひ法律事務所入所
現　在　　西村あさひ法律事務所　アソシエイト

大村　慧（おおむら　さとし）

2010年　　慶應義塾大学法学部卒業
2013年　　早稲田大学法科大学院修了
2014年　　弁護士登録，西村あさひ法律事務所入所
現　在　　西村あさひ法律事務所アソシエイト

松本　周（まつもと　いたる）

2011年　　京都大学法学部卒業
2013年　　京都大学法科大学院修了
2014年　　弁護士登録，西村あさひ法律事務所入所
現　在　　西村あさひ法律事務所アソシエイト

益田　美佳（ますだ　みか）

2011年　　京都大学法学部卒業
2013年　　京都大学法科大学院修了
2014年　　弁護士登録，西村あさひ法律事務所入所
現　在　　西村あさひ法律事務所アソシエイト
〈著作〉
　『会社法実務相談』（共著，商事法務，2016年）

東條　桜子（とうじょう　さくらこ）

- 2012年　　慶應義塾大学法学部卒業
- 2014年　　慶應義塾大学法科大学院修了
- 2015年　　弁護士登録
- 2016年　　西村あさひ法律事務所入所
- 現　在　　西村あさひ法律事務所アソシエイト

杉浦　起大（すぎうら　ゆきひろ）

- 2014年　　東京大学法学部卒業
- 2015年　　弁護士登録
- 2016年　　西村あさひ法律事務所入所
- 現　在　　西村あさひ法律事務所アソシエイト

〈著作〉

『働き方改革とこれからの時代の労働法』（共著，商事法務，2018年），『新株予約権ハンドブック［第4版］』（共著，商事法務，2018年）

江口　響子（えぐち　きょうこ）

- 2013年　　千葉大学法経学部卒業
- 2015年　　一橋大学法科大学院修了
- 2016年　　弁護士登録，西村あさひ法律事務所入所
- 現　在　　西村あさひ法律事務所アソシエイト

〈著作〉

『働き方改革とこれからの時代の労働法』（共著，商事法務，2018年）

大日方　史野（おびなた　ふみや）

- 2013年　　早稲田大学法学部卒業

2015年　　早稲田大学法科大学院修了
2016年　　弁護士登録，西村あさひ法律事務所入所
現　在　　西村あさひ法律事務所アソシエイト
〈著作〉
『働き方改革とこれからの時代の労働法』（共著，商事法務，2018年）

■ **Editors and Authors of the First Edition**

Michihiro Mori

Eri Sugihara

Aya Kamimura

Takashi Ikeda

Aya Kijima

■ Editors and Authors of the Second Edition

Michihiro Mori

Takashi Ikeda

Aya Kijima

Hironori Kino

Yotaro Takayama

Hiroaki Matsui

Tomoya Yura

Masanori Kaneko

Tomoko Shimomukai

Tomomi Murata

Haruhi Kuroda

Masayasu Suzuki

Takashi Nakamura

Maho Oishi

Takeo Tsukamoto

Megumi Ryoya

■ **Editors and Authors of the Third Edition**

Michihiro Mori

2005-Present	Partner, Attorney at Law, Nishimura & Asahi Law Office
2005	Certified to Practice Law in Japan
1999	Harvard Law School (LL.M.)
1995-2005	Judge of Tokyo District Court (Civil Affairs, Civil Execution); Staff Attorney, Civil Affairs Bureau, General Secretariat of the Supreme Court; Judge of Fukuoka District Court (Labor)
1993	The University of Tokyo, Faculty of Law (LL.B.)

<Publications>
Titles:
- Labor Matters at the Time of Advance into or Withdraw from Asian Market: Chuokeizai Co., Ltd., 2017. Print.
- Modern Type of Contracts and Insolvency, Co-author: Shojihomu Co., Ltd., 2015. Print.
- Terminus of Theory on Commercial Litigation, Co-author: Shojihomu Co., Ltd., 2014. Print.
- Exposition on Insolvency and Labor Law: Shojihomu Co., Ltd., 2013. Print. Theory and Practice of Current Civil Laws, Co-author: Kinzai Institute for Financial Affairs, Inc., 2013. Print.
- Outline of Insolvency and Labor Law: Shojihomu Co., Ltd., 2012. Print.
- Textbook on Corporate Law for Business persons, Co-author: Bungeishunju Ltd., 2012. Print.
- Practice of Restructuring in the United State-with a Focus on Chapter 11 of the Bankruptcy Code and Workout, Co-author: Kinzai Institute for Financial Affairs, Inc., 2011. Print.
And more.

Hiroaki Matsui

2009-Present   Associate, Attorney at Law, Nishimura & Asahi Law Office
(currently seconded to Okada Law Firm (Hong Kong))
2018-August, 2019 (estimated)   Seconded to Okada Law Firm (Hong Kong) (Affiliate office of Nishimura & Asahi for Hong Kong practice.)
2018   University of Pennsylvania, Law School (LL.M.)
2017-2018   University of Pennsylvania, Asian Law Review, Associate Editor
2009   Certified to Practice Law in Japan
2008   Waseda Law School (J.D.)
2006   Waseda University (LL.B.)

<Publications>
Titles:
· Work Style Reform and Employment Law in the Coming Future, Co-author: Shojihomu Co., Ltd., 2018.
· Labor Matters at the Time of Advance into or Withdraw from Asian Market: Chuokeizai Co., Ltd., 2017. Print.
· Amendment and Practice to Worker Dispatching Act 2015, Co-author: Daini Tokyo Bar Association, 2016. Print.
· Singapore Entry Strategy Guide Q&A for Japanese Companies, Co-author: Chuokeizai Co., Ltd., 2014. Print.
And more.

Aya Kijima

2009-Present   Associate, Attorney at Law, Nishimura & Asahi Law Office
2009   Certified to Practice Law in Japan
2008   The University of Tokyo, School of Law (J.D.)
2006   The University of Tokyo, Faculty of Law (LL.B.)

<Publications>
Titles:
· Work Style Reform and Employment Law in the Coming Future, Co-author: Shojihomu Co., Ltd., 2018.

Takeo Tsukamoto

2012-Present	Associate, Attorney at Law, Nishimura & Asahi Law Office
2012	Certified to Practice Law in Japan
2011	The University of Tokyo, School of Law (J.D.)
2005-2008	Central Japan Railway Company
2005	Keio University (LL.B.)

<Publications>
Titles:
· Work Style Reform and Employment Law in the Coming Future, Co-author: Shojihomu Co., Ltd., 2018.
· Working as Freelance & "Multi-skilled" worker, Co-editor: Nikkei Publishing Inc., 2018. Print.
· Labor and Employment Case Handbook 2018, Co-author: Roudou Kaihatsu Kenkyukai Co., Ltd., 2018. Print.
· Corpus Juris Crisis Management, Co-author : Shojihomu Co., Ltd., 2016. Print. And more.

Yoshinobu Nakagawa

2009-Present	Associate, Attorney at Law, Nishimura & Asahi Law Office
2009	Certified to Practice Law in Japan
2008	Chuo Law School (J.D.)
2005	Chuo University (completing three years of Bachelor degree program; early enrollmet to Chuo Law School under the law

school's program to admit highly qualified candidates)

Satoshi Omura

2014-Present	Associate, Attorney at Law, Nishimura & Asahi Law Office
2014	Certified to Practice Law in Japan
2013	Waseda Law School (J.D.)
2010	Keio University (LL.B.)

Itaru Matsumoto

2014-Present	Associate, Attorney at Law, Nishimura & Asahi Law Office
2014	Certified to Practice Law in Japan
2013	Kyoto University Law School (J.D.)
2011	Kyoto University (LL.B.)

Mika Masuda

2014-Present	Associate, Attorney at Law, Nishimura & Asahi Law Office
2014	Certified to Practice Law in Japan
2013	Kyoto University Law School (J.D.)
2011	Kyoto University (LL.B.)

<Publications>
Titles:
· Practical Guide to the Companies Act of Japan, Co-author: Shojihomu Co., Ltd., 2016. Print.

Sakurako Tojo

2016-Present	Associate, Attorney at Law, Nishimura & Asahi Law Office

2015	Certified to Practice Law in Japan
2014	Keio University Law School (J.D.)
2012	Keio University (LL.B.)

Yukihiro Sugiura

2016-Present	Associate, Attorney at Law, Nishimura & Asahi Law Office
2015	Certified to Practice Law in Japan
2014	The University of Tokyo, Faculty of Law (LL.B.)

<Publications>

Titles:

· Work Style Reform and Employment Law in the Coming Future, Co-author: Shojihomu Co., Ltd., 2018.

· Handbook on Share Options (Fourth Edition), Co-author: Shojihomu Co., Ltd., 2018. Print.

Kyoko Eguchi

2016-Present	Associate, Attorney at Law, Nishimura & Asahi Law Office
2016	Certified to Practice Law in Japan
2015	Hitotsubashi University Law School (J.D.)
2013	Chiba University (LL.B.)

<Publications>

Titles:

· Work Style Reform and Employment Law in the Coming Future, Co-author: Shojihomu Co., Ltd., 2018.

Fumiya Obinata

| 2016-Present | Associate, Attorney at Law, Nishimura & Asahi Law Office |

2016 Certified to Practice Law in Japan
2015 Waseda Law School (J.D.)
2013 Waseda University (LL.B.)

<Publications>

Titles:

· Work Style Reform and Employment Law in the Coming Future, Co-author: Shojihomu Co., Ltd., 2018.

和文・英文対照　モデル就業規則〔第3版〕
Japanese-English Model Work Rules〔Third edition〕

2012年2月20日	第1版第1刷発行
2014年4月30日	第2版第1刷発行
2019年2月1日	第3版第1刷発行

編集代表	森　　倫　　洋
編　者	松　井　博　昭
	木　島　　　彩
	塚　本　健　夫
著　者	西村あさひ法律事務所労働法グループ
発行者	山　本　　　継
発行所	㈱中央経済社
発売元	㈱中央経済グループパブリッシング

〒101-0051　東京都千代田区神田神保町1-31-2
電話　03（3293）3371（編集代表）
　　　03（3293）3381（営業代表）
http://www.chuokeizai.co.jp/
印刷／文唱堂印刷㈱
製本／誠　製　本㈱

©2019
Printed in Japan

＊頁の「欠落」や「順序違い」などがありましたらお取り替えいたしますので発売元までご送付ください。（送料小社負担）
ISBN978-4-502-29261-3　C3032

JCOPY〈出版者著作権管理機構委託出版物〉本書を無断で複写複製（コピー）することは，著作権法上の例外を除き，禁じられています。本書をコピーされる場合は事前に出版者著作権管理機構（JCOPY）の許諾を受けてください。
JCOPY〈http://www.jcopy.or.jp　eメール：info@jcopy.or.jp　電話：03-3513-6969〉

会社法・法務省令大改正を収録!

「会社法」法令集 第十一版

中央経済社 編　A5判・688頁　定価3,024円(税込)

◆新規収録改正の概要
◆重要条文ミニ解説　付き
◆改正中間試案ミニ解説

会社法制定以来初めての大改正となった、26年改正会社法と27年改正法務省令を織り込んだ待望の最新版。変更箇所が一目でわかるよう表示。

本書の特徴

◆会社法関連法規を完全収録
☞ 本書は、平成17年7月に公布された「会社法」から同18年2月に公布された3本の法務省令等、会社法に関連するすべての重要な法令を完全収録したものです。

◆好評の「ミニ解説」さらに充実!
☞ 重要条文のポイントを簡潔にまとめたミニ解説。平成26年改正会社法と平成27年改正法務省令を踏まえ大幅な加筆と見直しを行い、ますます充実!

◆引用条文の見出しを表示
☞ 会社法条文中、引用されている条文番号の下に、その条文の見出し(ない場合は適宜工夫)を色刷りで明記。条文の相互関係がすぐにわかり、理解を助けます。

◆政省令探しは簡単!条文中に番号を明記
☞ 法律条文の該当箇所に、政省令(略称=目次参照)の条文番号を色刷りで表記。意外に手間取る政省令探しもこれでラクラク。

◆改正箇所が一目瞭然!
☞ 平成26年改正会社法、平成27年改正法務省令による条文の変更箇所に色付けをし、どの条文がどう変わったのか、追加や削除された条文は何かなどが一目でわかる!

中央経済社